The Lottocratic Mentality

The Lottocratic Mentality

Defending Democracy against Lottocracy

Cristina Lafont
Nadia Urbinati

OXFORD
UNIVERSITY PRESS

Great Clarendon Street, Oxford OX2 6DP,
United Kingdom

Oxford University Press is a department of the University of Oxford.
It furthers the University's objective of excellence in research, scholarship,
and education by publishing worldwide. Oxford is a registered trade mark of
Oxford University Press in the UK and in certain other countries

© Cristina Lafont and Nadia Urbinati 2024

The moral rights of the authors have been asserted

All rights reserved. No part of this publication may be reproduced, stored in a retrieval system, transmitted, used for text and data mining, or used for training artificial intelligence, in any form or by any means, without the prior permission in writing of Oxford University Press, or as expressly permitted by law, by license or under terms agreed with the appropriate reprographics rights organization. Enquiries concerning reproduction outside the scope of the above should be sent to the Rights Department, Oxford University Press, at the address above

You must not circulate this work in any other form
and you must impose this same condition on any acquirer

Published in the United States of America by Oxford University Press
198 Madison Avenue, New York, NY 10016, United States of America

British Library Cataloguing in Publication Data

Data available

Library of Congress Control Number: 2024949884

ISBN 9780192890627

DOI: 10.1093/9780191982903.001.0001

Printed and bound by
CPI Group (UK) Ltd, Croydon, CR0 4YY

Links to third party websites are provided by Oxford in good faith and
for information only. Oxford disclaims any responsibility for the materials
contained in any third party website referenced in this work.

The manufacturer's authorised representative in the EU for product safety is Oxford University Press España S.A. of el Parque Empresarial San Fernando de Henares, Avenida de Castilla, 2 – 28830 Madrid (www.oup.es/en).

Contents

Acknowledgments	vii
Introduction	1

I. THE RISE OF THE LOTTOCRATIC MENTALITY

1. The Lottery Revival	**17**
1.1 Precursors to the Revival of Lotteries in Democratic Theory	19
1.2 The Historical Paradigm	54
1.3 Conclusion	80
2. Deliberative Democracy's Turn to Lottery-Based Institutions	**82**
2.1 The Deliberative Turn in Democratic Theory	83
2.2 The Microdeliberative Turn within Deliberative Democracy	87
2.3 Deliberative Democracy and the Lottocratic Mentality	90
3. The Clash Between Electoral Democracy and Lottocracy: Three Options	**95**
3.1 Substitution Proposals	96
3.2 Complementarity Proposals	102
3.3 Auxiliary Proposals	115
3.4 Conclusion	121
4. The Targets of Lottocracy Revisited	**123**
4.1 Voting Power and Elections	123
4.2 Political Mandate Representation and Accountability	138
4.3 Political Parties and the Partisan Divisions among Citizens	151
4.4 Conclusion	169

II. WHAT'S WRONG WITH THE LOTTOCRATIC MENTALITY?

5. Disempowering The People: The Lottocratic Reinterpretation Of Political Equality	**173**
5.1 Levelling Down for the Sake of Equality?	174
5.2 Equalizing Asymmetric Power Relations	176
5.3 Would Lottocracies Generate Fewer Political Inequalities Than Electoral Democracies?	189

vi Contents

6. **A Sample Embodying Everyone: A New Populist Conception of Representation** — **194**
   6.1 Traditional Populism: The Leader as an Embodiment of the People — 199
   6.2 Lottocratic Populism: Citizens' Assemblies as an Embodiment of the People — 206
   6.3 What's Wrong with Lottocratic Representation? — 215

7. **The Technocratic Conception Of Politics** — **219**
   7.1 Lottocratic Epistocracy: Technical Problem-Solving vs. Political Freedom — 221
   7.2 The Tensions within Lottocratic Technopopulism — 228

III.   LOTTERY WITHOUT THE LOTTOCRATIC MENTALITY

8. **The Democratic Alternative: Institutionalizing Minipublics to Empower the Citizenry** — **233**
   8.1 Deliberative Minipublics as Auxiliary Institutions: Two Approaches — 233
   8.2 Minipublics' Potential Contribution to Improving Public Debates — 238
   8.3 An Alternative to Usurpation: From Being *Like Us* to Speaking *to Us* — 242
   8.4 Minipublics' Contribution to Empowering the Citizenry: A Few Examples — 244

Conclusion — **248**

References — 252
Index — 268

Acknowledgments

The story of this book deserves to be briefly told to explain the character of this four-handed work and, more importantly, to thank all those who participated in it, inspiring and enriching it along the way. The story begins during the lockdown due to the COVID-19 pandemic when all our work engagements were conducted online. It was during a panel held at the 2021 APSA annual meeting that, without any foresight and almost spontaneously, we found ourselves sharing similar thoughts and concerns about the allure of sortition as a strategy to solve the crisis of democracy. We thus found ourselves rediscussing the foundations of democratic sovereignty and the limits it poses on any institutional imagination, whereby not everything that shines is of equal value or works according to the democratic principles. These conversations ignited our interest in writing this book together. Along the way, we were fortunate to discuss our work on two very important occasions, a workshop at Columbia University in April 2023 and a workshop at the University of Mainz the following June. The generosity, expertise of the participants, and pleasantness of the dialogues have been invaluable for giving the manuscript the structure and form in which it is published. Colleagues and friends to thank are therefore many, and to all of them we owe a debt of gratitude that these acknowledgments can only partially offset. The thanks follow the manuscript's processing stages and start with the positive feedback we received from the anonymous reviewers of the draft that we sent to Oxford University Press in the spring of 2021. During the workshop at Columbia University, we benefited from the contribution of Palle Bech-Pedersen, Hubertus Buchstein, Jean L. Cohen, James Fishkin, Carlo Invernizzi Accetti, Dimitri Landa, Matthew Landauer, Jane Mansbridge, Ryan Pevnick, Yves Sintomer, and also of Turkuler Isiksel, Clara Maier, Karuna Mantena, and the graduate students of the Department of Political Science, in particular Nicole Peisajovich who in addition managed the organization of the workshop impeccably. During the workshop at the University of Mainz, we received very enriching comments and suggestions from Svenja Ahlhaus, Maike Albertzart, André Bächtiger, Palle Bech-Pedersen, Julian Frinken, Samuel Hayat, Julia Jakobi, Manuel Kautz, Eva Krick, Annabelle Lever, Katharina Liesenberg, Peter Niesen, Aril Ohren, Claudia Ritzi, Victor Sanchez-Mazas, Pierre-Etienne Vandamme, and Claudia Landwehr and Armin Schäfer who in addition to their insightful contributions organized an extraordinarily fruitful workshop. Other colleagues with whom we had proficuous conversations about different aspects of the book are Mirko Canevaro, Giulia Oskian, Dino Piovan, David Ragazzoni, Matthew Simonton, and Alexander Guerrero to whom we are especially grateful for his willingness to share with us the unpublished manuscript of his book *Lottocracy: Democracy Without Elections* that we engage at length in the book. Special and final thanks we owe to Max Cherem for his invaluable help in editing the manuscript, and to Les Harris and the team at

viii Acknowledgments

Oxford University Press for their excellent professional support. We are especially grateful to Dominic Byatt for his encouragement to take upon the completion of the project.

Needless to say, we are solely responsible for the shortcomings of the published text, but we are also very aware of how much the final product has benefited from the contributions and support of this wonderful community of colleagues and friends who have made our research and exchange of ideas enjoyable and humanly rich on countless occasions. We are deeply grateful to all of them.

The material we present in this book is new. However, in two chapters we draw on specific publications and we are grateful to have permission from the publishers to do so. In Chapter 6, we drew upon Lafont, C. *Democracy without Shortcuts: A Participatory Conception of Deliberative Democracy*. Oxford: Oxford University Press, 2020. This was used with the permission of Oxford University Press. In Chapter 8, we drew upon Lafont C. "A Democracy, If We Can Keep It. Remarks on J. Habermas' The New Structural Transformation of the Public Sphere." *Constellations* 30, no. 1 (2023): 77–83. We thank Wiley-Blackwell for permission to do so.

Introduction

The institutions of representative democracy are under siege. The problems plaguing these institutions fuel the impression that democracy is not delivering on its promises.[1] These problems range from the decline and dysfunction of political parties to the sharp inequality of opportunities that citizens have to influence political decisions, make their voices heard, and participate on an equal footing. In short, citizens no longer feel that they have even remotely equal opportunities to exercise political power. Elections select the people who serve in institutions like representative assemblies. Yet, contrary to what nearly all constitutions promise, large segments of the population now feel that such assemblies do not truly enable popular sovereignty. For many, democracy that is mediated in this way seems to have produced a self-referential political class that exists at a significant remove from the lives of ordinary citizens (though not from the phones of their more well-heeled constituents) and that, in any case, is not as competent or honest as it was made out to be. The most striking symptoms of this "crisis of democracy" are the growth of populism and an increasingly low voter turnout.

Political scholars read this decline as regression, a backslide of our political systems into less democratic forms of opinion and will formation.[2] This dawning realization is also reflected in the growing literature on alternative methods of political selection, the digital transformation of political parties, and the negative effects of social media and artificial intelligence on the political public sphere. There is no question that the changes taking place in almost all democratic countries affect both the content of politics and the methods or styles of political expression. These changes are intertwined with phenomena that are not directly political but which can no longer be ignored, e.g., the enormous growth of economic inequality and poverty or the shift from unemployment to the normalization of precarious labor relations.[3] All of this generates the sense that there is a broad "crisis of democracy," a legitimacy crisis that is not merely political. Yet, the solutions that many scholars offer are often limited to political institutions and procedures and are even inconsistent with the

---

[1] See, e.g., the Pew Research Center's International Survey on "Global Public Opinion in an Era of Democratic Anxiety": https://www.pewresearch.org/global/2021/12/07/global-public-opinion-in-an-era-of-democratic-anxiety/.

[2] Heinrich Geiselberger, Arjun Appadurai, and Zygmunt Bauman, *The Great Regression* (Cambridge: Polity, 2017); Steven Levitski and Daniel Ziblatt, *How Democracies Die* (New York: Crown, 2018).

[3] See, among others, Thomas Piketty, *Capital in the Twenty-First Century* (Cambridge, MA: Harvard University Press, 2017); Wolfgang Streeck and Armin Shäfer, eds., *Politics in the Age of Austerity* (New York: Polity, 2013); Angus Deaton, *The Great Escape: Health, Wealth, and the Origins of Inequality* (Princeton, NJ: Princeton University Press, 2013); Stanford M. Jacoby, *Labor in the Age of Finance* (Princeton, NJ: Princeton University Press, 2021).

The Lottocratic Mentality. Cristina Lafont and Nadia Urbinati, Oxford University Press. © Cristina Lafont and Nadia Urbinati (2024). DOI: 10.1093/9780191982903.003.0001

2 The Lottocratic Mentality

basic promise that democracy should be improved with *more* (not less) democracy and that any reforms should be consistent with the democratic principles of political equality and freedom.

To save democracy, some scholars have proposed a radical institutional cure: replacing suffrage with sortition and elected bodies with lottocratic assemblies. If current electoral democracies are essentially something akin to de facto oligarchies, then why not simply get rid of them? In several democratic countries, important experiments—for instance, with citizens' assemblies or other lottery-based institutions—have attracted a growing constituency around the democratic potential of such a radical "cure." Supporters of random selection claim that the transition from our old (electoral) democracy to a new (lottocratic) democracy is simply a matter of time. For them, the future *will be* lottocratic. Indeed, several books have recently been published that explicitly put suffrage and electoral representation on trial.[4]

Our book takes root in the soil of this "lottocratic turn"—a trend that has understandably grown out of the broader worry that democracy itself is under siege and in decline. We worry that the remedies that are supposed to nurse democracy back to health actually contain the seeds of further destruction. Lottocracy promises to improve democracy. In reality, it would create a threatening new regime if it were ever actualized. Like colorful mushrooms that one finds in the woods, lottocracy is attractive until one eats it. Our book is motivated by both a concern for the decline of representative democracy and the realization that the "lottocratic turn" is not simply an academic fad. The appeal of lottocracy is catching on in public debates and inspiring citizens' assemblies around the globe. It is attracting democratic and nondemocratic regimes in the vision of a unified global order based on allotted assemblies that are set up to "solve problems" and that are free from electoral competition. The increasing interest in lottery-based institutions is leading to the spread of a "lottocratic mentality," not only among academics and democratic theorists but also among politicians, social movements, and the citizenry at large.

As we show in the book, despite appearances to the contrary, this mentality is inimical to democracy. It justifies conferring legislative power on allotted assemblies and, in so doing, legitimizes the antidemocratic idea that the many should be "ruled" by "the few" chosen by chance. We think lottery-based institutions such as citizens' assemblies and other deliberative minipublics have a lot of potential for democratization. Indeed, at the end of the book, we propose several ways that these institutions could be used to empower the citizenry. However, we worry the broader lottocratic mentality that guides most thinking about how to design and organize lottery-based institutions harbors antidemocratic features that would erode democratic commitments in society more generally. Its negative ripple effects extend well

---

[4] For example, Hélène Landemore, *Open Democracy: Reinventing Popular Rule for the Twenty-First Century* (Princeton, NJ: Princeton University Press, 2020); David Van Reybrouck, *Against Elections: The Case for Democracy*, trans. Liz Waters (London: Bodley Head, 2016); Alexander Guerrero, "Against Elections: The Lottocratic Alternative," *Philosophy & Public Affairs* 42, no. 2 (2014): 135–78, and Guerrero, *Lottocracy: Democracy Without Elections* (forthcoming, Oxford University Press).

beyond the narrow context of discussions about the future of these institutions. Thus, the main task of this book is to identify the core of the lottocratic mentality and to reveal its antidemocratic implications. We organize the many existing proposals for using lottery-based institutions into three different types, depending on how they envision the relationship between elections and sortition. The most radical option is to *substitute* electoral democracy with lottocracy. Advocates propose to dismantle electoral assemblies of elected officials and to instead confer all legislative power to assemblies of randomly selected citizens. Less radical proposals envision *complementing* electoral institutions with lottery-based institutions that would share (some) legislative power. The least radical proposals envision using lottery-based institutions as *auxiliary* tools for supplementing and enhancing the democratic functions of current electoral institutions *without conferring legislative power on them.* To mark this *fundamental* difference between auxiliary proposals and the other two types, throughout the book we use the term "lottocrat" to refer to anyone who appeals to the core elements of the lottocratic mentality to justify conferring legislative authority on allotted assemblies. Defenders of *lottocracy* are simply the most radical of these theorists in that they follow the lottocratic mentality to its ultimate conclusion and propose to confer, not just *some*, but *all* legislative authority on lottery-based institutions.

While auxiliary proposals are currently the most widely endorsed, complementarity proposals are becoming increasingly popular. By contrast, the most radical substitution proposals currently have low levels of support. Nevertheless, we think the most radical lottocratic proposals also give the clearest and most consistent articulation of the lottocratic mentality. Thus, analyzing the criticisms of electoral democracy and the justifications for lottocracy that stem from these theorists can be helpful in identifying the antidemocratic core of the lottocratic mentality. As we will show, there are three features at the core of this mentality: first, a reinterpretation of political equality that drastically weakens the democratic commitment to both substantive political equality and toward effective inclusion of the citizenry in political decision-making; second, a reinterpretation of political representation in terms of a populist conception of representation as embodiment; and third, a technocratic conception of politics. The lottocratic mentality gives rise to a peculiar form of *technopopulism* that profoundly transforms our democratic understanding of politics, the relationship between citizens and their representatives, the value of elections and political parties, and much more. This transformation has many worrisome implications for democratic aspirations: from legitimizing the unilateral exercise of political power by "the few" and the attendant expectation of blind deference by the citizenry to downplaying the democratic significance of elections, political parties, and accountability as mechanisms through which the citizenry can exercise their political freedom collectively as equals. The lottocratic mentality undermines collective political agency in favor of an individualistic and passive vision of citizens. While we do not think that a lottocratic regime is going to be established anytime soon, we fear the lottocratic mentality is beginning to pervade thinking about democracy and that it can negatively impact our understanding of the roots of democratic deficits

4 The Lottocratic Mentality

as well as the best paths toward institutional reform. Our criticism of the lottocratic mentality seeks to redirect current thinking about institutional reform of electoral democracies in a genuinely democratic direction.

While we think electoral institutions are democratically superior to lottocratic institutions, we neither defend the status quo nor conceal or deny the grave dysfunctions and oligarchic tendencies within current representative democracies. Moreover, when understood as an auxiliary supplement to representative institutions, we actually endorse the use of "lotted" citizen assemblies in certain specific ways and circumstances. However, we think that any proposal for improving democracy should be consistent with its tenets of political equality and democratic control through accountable institutions—that is to say, with equal political freedom for all citizens. Lottocracy directly conflicts with both the tenets of democracy (as a form of government) and the nature of the law (as an expression of power) itself. It does not deliver a more radical form of democracy but rather something else: a technocratic system that does not have any space for accountability to the citizenry. By reducing politics to technical problem-solving and conflating political deliberation with cognitive diversity, lottocrats lose sight of the fact that societies qualify as "democratic" not in virtue of their cognitive diversity but rather in virtue of their pluralism, dissent, and political freedom. The task of democracy is not simply solving problems but, above all, governing dissent by transforming a raucous collective of dissenting views, values, and projects into an opportunity for making collective decisions under conditions of political equality and democratic control by all those who will be subject to those decisions. Lottocrats entirely ignore this process. Given that they do so in the name of improving democracy, it is important to critically analyze both lottocratic theory and lottocratic proposals for reform.

Paradoxically, lottocratic proposals promise to give power to the people while depriving the citizenry of any venue for exercising such power. Citizens must wait for their turn and, in the meantime, simply obey all the decisions that are handed down, with no one to blame but chance. Lottocrats achieve this conjurer's trick through a populist sleight of hand. In using stratified random sampling as a selection mechanism to mirror the population according to statistical (and thus supposedly) objective criteria, lottocrats claim that the randomly selected few embody the "real people" (instead of the "political elite") and that they can therefore legitimately rule in their name. Ironically, this reproduces the same vice as populism but without its traditional features of mobilization, collective action, and electoral engagement. In a sense, lottocracy is actually *further* from democracy than populism. However, it replaces democracy with a technopopulist system of decision-making that promises to fix the problems of representative democracy by getting rid of politics altogether. Squarely identifying the antidemocratic features of the lottocratic mentality helps shed light on the genuinely democratic significance of commitments to political equality, inclusion, and democratic control under representative democracy. Indeed, if the future is going to be democratic, then any proposals for improvement need to stick to these core democratic commitments and fend off lottocratic reinterpretations. To justify this claim, we build our argument in the following steps.

Introduction **5**

In Chapter 1, we discuss lottocrats' most popular and reiterated claim, namely that ancient democracy proves that only selection by lottery is consistent with democratic equality. We dismantle the binary logic of lottery/election and question the implicit assumption (which is also often framed as a conclusion) that democracy is identical with lotteries and inherently opposed to elections. We introduce this chapter by first going back to the ideas of three key seminal political theorists, Robert A. Dahl, Jon Elster, and Bernard Manin. Each of these theorists drew attention to the lottery well before it became popular. They investigated the difference between lotteries and elections and thought about the possible role for lotteries in terms of facilitating participation, combating corruption/partisanship, and strengthening representation. None of these theorists is a lottocrat. In fact, taken against the backdrop of the current lottocratic resurgence, we can see that their reflections addressed the issue of lotteries with a depth of analysis that has largely been lost.

These theorists examined the possible advantages and pitfalls of lotteries more carefully than most subsequent scholars, and they remain fundamental to examining and even questioning the most popular lottocratic assumptions. However, each author suggested a parallel between contemporary and ancient democracies that opened the door to a historical reinterpretation that has now become popular among lottocrats. This reinterpretation heavily relies on the analysis of the institutional order of democracy in Aristotle's *Politics* and, to a lesser degree, on the early modern Italian experiences of republican government. Lottocrats are not and do not claim to be historians; they use history for theoretical and political purposes. We do not question this "use" of history. Knowledge of political history is often a useful foil for understanding the political issues of our own time. The problem is that when the past is used in a ritualized fashion, the function of historical knowledge itself easily falls by the wayside when history happens to cut against an author's theoretical aims. This is precisely what has happened with the foundational generalization that lottocrats routinely deploy against representative democracy: the identification of democracy with lottery and of aristocracy (or oligarchy) with elections. In order to challenge this oft-repeated claim, we combine an account of the institutions of ancient democracy with a conceptual analysis of the principles that animated them. There is no complete agreement among specialists on the tasks and scope of the allotted institutions in legislation. We take this scholarly disagreement into account to question the granitic certainty behind lottocrats' statements about the Athenian constitution. In addition, we call attention to the fact that, in affirming a contrast between lottery (democracy) and elections (aristocracy/oligarchy), contemporary lottocrats gloss over the fact that in ancient and early modern societies lotteries were certainly *not* an exclusively democratic tool. Indeed, aristocrats often used lotteries. Lottocrats also ignore the fact that lotteries were used to choose administrative and judicial personnel but *not* to select members of the legislature.[5] Finally, lottocrats also routinely disregard

---

[5] There was an allotted council of judges selected to check on legislation (to guarantee consistency of the new laws with the existing ones), but this does not mean, as lottocrats suggest, that the sovereign power was in the allocated council and not in the Assembly. This is incorrect for two reasons: first, because the

6   The Lottocratic Mentality

the fact that the ancients did not use the lottery *instead* of elections but rather used *both* in different contexts. In the end, the false election/lottery dichotomy alters the meaning of democracy itself. When seen through the distorted historical lens used by many lottocrats, "democracy" morphs from a regime characterized by mass participation among adult citizens in the popular assembly into one in which the many are "ruled" by "the few" who are chosen by chance.

In Chapter 2, we turn to deliberative democracy in order to identify the motivations and concerns that, over the past several decades, have led many theorists in this tradition to increasingly focus on lottery-based institutions. Given the prominent role that deliberative democrats currently play in developing these institutions, it is important to analyze their specific motivations, interests, and concerns since they are quite different from those animating the lottery revival (e.g., antioligarchy, anticorruption, and so on) that we analyzed in the first chapter. Indeed, examining why deliberative democrats increasingly left the focus on the institutions of mass democracy behind and instead started to focus on deliberative minipublics provides us with essential cues for understanding the rise of the lottocratic mentality. As we shall illustrate, the normative commitments at the core of deliberative democracy are ultimately incompatible with key elements of the "lottocratic mentality." However, we also show that the deliberative paradigm of democratic theory is capacious and ambiguous enough to enable and even foster the development of that mentality. Highlighting the tensions between the core normative assumptions of deliberative democracy and key elements of the lottocratic mentality is also essential for our argument in the last chapter of the book. There we show that lottery-based institutions *could* serve genuinely democratic aims but only if scholars and practitioners decisively reject the lottocratic mentality.

In Chapter 3, we evaluate three different types of proposals for using lottery-based institutions. We organize these proposals according to whether they conceptualize lotteries as *replacing, complementing,* or *supplementing* electoral institutions. While the first two models are guided by the lottocratic mentality, the last is perfectly consistent with the ideal institutional forms of democracy. Proposals within this last model are designed to supplement and enhance the democratic functions of existing electoral institutions without undermining their legislative power or the voting power of citizens. In its ancient and recent history, democracy has shown an extraordinarily creative ability to respond to the problems of governing society with institutions and procedures that were always consistent with the principle of self-government through the exercise of equal political freedom. This is also true of the new forms of deliberation among the citizenry that certain types of lottery-based institutions can activate. By contrast, the first two models are based on the lottocratic mentality that

---

nomothetai were sorted from within the assembly (interestingly, Mill took from Athens the inspiration of "parliamentary commissions"); second, because they exercised a juridical function (judging on what was proposed by citizens and decided in the Assembly) but did not originate laws. Indeed, it is empirically proved that the numerical proportion between *nomothetai* decisions and decrees was incommensurable— of the fourth-century Athenian acts preserved in stone, about 600 are decrees of the Assembly and only about 10 *nomoi* were approved by the *nomothetes.*

is bound up with an idea of government that is indirect but yet *not* based (or only partly based) on suffrage and elections. We highlight how, for lottocrats themselves, less radical, "hybrid" proposals to *complement* elections with lotteries in legislative assemblies or, more generally, within decision-making institutions, are anything but a viable solution. As they plausibly argue, this mix of institutional forms will exacerbate rather than contain the dominant role of parties and political competition in the electoral system. From this point of view, the only alternatives are either electoral-representative democracy or its radical overcoming in a fully lottocratic system. In short, once the lottocratic mentality is embraced, lottocracy cannot be moderated. This dilemma indicates that only if lottery-based institutions serve as auxiliaries to electoral institutions it is possible for both types of institutions to coexist and thus preserve the sovereignty of the citizenry and their power to vote on both issues and representatives. This point coincides with Dahl's primary insight that the proper role of lotteries would be to merely assist the deliberative process in all levels of representative institutions. We agree that current efforts to design and organize lottery-based institutions such as citizens' assemblies, deliberative polls, etc., should be guided by an auxiliary model where lotteries merely supplement electoral-representative institutions. In this vein, we analyze some interesting and ambitious proposals in Chapter 8.

In order to bolster our case against lottocratic proposals that would dismantle electoral democracy in Chapter 4, we turn to the core institutions that the lottocratic mentality deems responsible for the crisis of democracy: elections, voting, representation, and political parties. According to lottocrats, these institutions cannot be reformed because they are inherently incompatible with political equality and foster corruption, partisan divisions, and the need for compromise. Consequently, a lottocratic polis would require the elimination of political parties and professional politicians, as well as the elimination of elections as an occasion for the citizenry to review policy, select their representatives, and hold them accountable. To make this drastic transformation palatable, lottocrats downplay the value of elections, representation, and political parties to such an extent that *their fundamental contributions to democracy* fall entirely by the wayside. This is an essential move. For once we accept that elections, representation, and parties produce little to no value, then it seems like there is little cost to give them up. In order to counter this move, we offer an alternative analysis of elections, representation, and political parties that highlights and vindicates their fundamental democratic value.

We start our analysis with elections and voting. We note that when citizens vote on both issues and candidates, they exercise their political power and their political freedom collectively as equals. By choosing some political programs and parties over others, they shape the political and ideological public space within which the elected representatives must operate until the next election. Yet, this rather obvious insight does not fit within the lottocratic characterization of elections. Indeed, the role elections play in enabling political choice and freedom is simply absent from their account. As we show throughout the book, political freedom is the main casualty of the lottocratic mentality. This is also apparent in the lottocratic understanding

8 The Lottocratic Mentality

of representation. Lottocrats interpret representation as a matter of sociological likeness that transcends all volitional choice and aims at empirical sameness. Against this view, we show that through elections representation acquires a form of *mandate* that is not legal (as in the principal/agent relation) but rather genuinely political; it aims at a form of *representativeness* that is not sociological but instead constructed by all the protagonists involved. Such representativeness creates an expectation of *advocacy* and generates *responsibility* as the "acting for" process that elections activate. Political representation defines the nature of democratic representation and its complex *accountability*. From this perspective, we then turn to political parties to show that they do not simply play a functional role in electoral democracy. While parties do play such a role, they are, above all, the expression of political freedom in action. Parties grow as soon as citizens are free to openly express themselves. Presumably, they would emerge even under a lottocratic regime. The problem is that once parties are disconnected from electoral forms of accountability, they would create the following dilemma throughout the polis: they would either constitute an arbitrary system of political influence or activate a censorious and repressive system of government. Thus, while they are often woefully suboptimal in practice, the institutions of representative democracy do not merely possess a functional, output-oriented value. Elections, representation, and political parties are forms of political freedom. Fundamental democratic goods would therefore be lost if the lottocratic mentality were to take hold of our democratic imagination.

Even if the democratic value of electoral institutions is much different and much higher than lottocrats believe, the defects of these institutions are also undeniable. Thus, lottocrats could still be right when they claim that we could realize more democratic benefits if we were to move in a lottocratic direction than if we were to try to improve existing electoral institutions. In order to show why this is not so, the second part of the book analyzes the core antidemocratic features of the lottocratic mentality.

In Chapter 5, we focus on the lottocratic interpretation of political equality. It is widely assumed that one of the main attractions of lottery-based institutions is that they promote political equality better than electoral institutions. As shown in Chapter 4, the argument is that in electoral democracies only the political elite can truly exercise political power while the rest of the citizenry is effectively excluded. By contrast, selection by lottery would better reflect the ideal of political equality since any citizen could exercise political power and everyone would have equal chances of being a candidate. Unfortunately, as we show, the lottocratic interpretation of political equality has two worrisome features: (1) it severely weakens the political rights and power that citizens in electoral democracies regularly and collectively exercise as equals (under the "one person, one vote" principle) and (2) it makes this sacrifice for the sake of equalizing *asymmetric relationships of power* among citizens—which are objectionable from the perspective of democratic equality. Against this lottocratic reinterpretation, we argue that the democratic ideal of political equality and inclusion in decision-making requires not that we *equalize the chances of "ruling"* (i.e., of exercising unilateral power over others) but rather that we *equalize citizens' effective opportunities to collectively make important political decisions as equals.* To be politically equal, citizens must be able to exercise political power *omnilaterally* (to adopt the Kantian term) rather than letting a few citizens unilaterally impose their political decisions on the rest of the citizenry.

To understand why lottocrats do not see a problem with establishing a lottocratic "rule of the few" and why they even claim that this is a radical form of democracy, in Chapter 6 we turn to conceptions of representation as a "mirror" and as an "embodiment." These conceptions of representation are another core feature of the lottocratic mentality. Through a concise historical analysis, we show how the process of democratization developed alongside both the decline of the idea of an assembly that reflected and embodied the estates and the ascent of the idea of a political mandate, whereby the representative was meant to serve as an intermediary actor. With the emergence of the idea of a political mandate, a new kind of constructed but non-pictorial "similarity" was needed so that the assembly could perform its tasks and accrue legitimacy—not because it mirrored society but rather because it acted in the name and the interests of its citizens. The sociological mirroring conception that the lottocrats want to resurrect assumes that society is made up of fixed ascriptive identities that seek recognition. Since selection by lot does not represent through an authorization process that includes each of the represented but instead represents through a miniaturized patchwork of society, any legitimacy it would manage to produce would simply reside in the idea of representatives being *like* those represented. Political history reveals that ideas of representation as both an embodiment and as a mirror marched alongside one another and that the expansion of universal suffrage never fully defeated either; these conceptions of representation are bound to reemerge whenever political representation begins to neglect its function of "advocacy." The resurgence of representation as social "mirroring" or "embodiment" signals a strong dissatisfaction with electoral democracy but does not in and of itself offer any viable solutions. We can understand the contemporary crisis of mandate representation through the lens of the main challenges it faces which are equally rooted in ideas of embodiment and descriptive representation—populism and lottocracy. We analyze the similarities and differences between populism and lottocracy as direct challenges to political mandate representation. While both movements rely on a conception of representation as mirror or embodiment, lottocracy differs from traditional populism in that it advances an entirely new form of embodiment that results from randomly selecting members of statistically defined pools whereas in populism it is the leader who claims to embody the "ordinary people" because he or she is one of them and therefore just *like* them. In short, while mirror and embodiment representation have made their comeback as reactions to crises within electoral democracy and party intermediation, they have done so in two very different ways. Embodiment representation has resurfaced either in the populist guise of a plebiscitary kind of leadership or in the lottocratic guise of antileadership sociological/descriptive kind of representation; the first is marked by a bombastic mobilizing rhetoric and the second by a will to bypass both politics and rhetoric in order to replace political choice with probability.

10 The Lottocratic Mentality

Through a detailed analysis of both models, we show that there are worrisome similarities between them. By using a conception of representation as embodiment, populists and lottocrats aim to achieve two major goals: (1) unifying the represented with the representative(s), thereby avoiding the formation of a political elite; and (2) neutralizing any accountability of the rulers toward those who are subject to their decisions. Indeed, both goals are two sides of the same populist coin. To the extent that the representatives do not *stand for* the represented but are actually *like* them, there is neither room nor need for the latter to hold the former to account. After analyzing some differences between populist and lottocratic varieties of "embodied representation," we highlight the features that both share which are inimical to democracy: exclusionary majoritarianism and the assumption of a homogeneous citizenry. As we show, these are not just contingent features of the embodiment conception of representation, but also inherent within it. For only if the citizenry is politically homogeneous—only if the interests, values, and policy objectives of the random sample coincide with those of the citizenry at large—does it then make sense to assume that the former will make the *same decisions* as the latter because they are *like* them. This is why citizens supposedly do not lose democratic control by blindly deferring to the lottocratic assembly's decisions. Under a troubling assumption of homogeneity, lottocrats want to take us back to a time of embodiment and ascriptive groups. Instead of citizens choosing their representatives based on the political programs or agendas that they favor, they should let themselves be represented by a random sample of individuals who are supposed to share their interests, values, and policy objectives simply in virtue of their ascriptive characteristics (such as gender, profession, geographical location, etc.).

As we argue, the fundamental problem with the assumption of homogeneity at the core of the lottocratic mentality is that it obliterates political freedom. Indeed, if citizens are free to shape their social world in genuinely different and mutually incompatible ways, regardless of their ascriptive characteristics, then it is to be expected that, under conditions of freedom, they will develop different and mutually incompatible ideas, interests, values, and policy objectives. Yet, if that is so, then how can lottocracy be democratic if the few members of the lottocratic assembly are the only ones setting the political agenda and the rest of the citizenry has no say? The assumed homogeneity among citizens' interests, values, and policy objectives offers the answer. Against the backdrop of assuming that the citizenry shares a homogeneous and singular "common good," it is sufficient if a few randomly selected people do the thinking, deliberating, and deciding for the rest of the citizenry who do not need to form their own political opinions and wills. Reaching political goals does not require citizens to resolve political conflicts among themselves, convince one another, or change one another's hearts and minds. All they need is the disposition and epistemic resources to figure out the best political decisions. Consequently, any random sample of the citizenry can get the job done equally well. The flip side of the apolitical conception of representation as embodiment is a depoliticized conception of politics. This key feature of the lottocratic mentality is then the focus of the next chapter.

In Chapter 7, we analyze the technocratic conception of politics that is at the core of the lottocratic mentality. This conception is most explicitly articulated by radical lottocrats who would replace elections with lotteries. However, since this conception of politics fits the conception of representation as embodiment, its influence can also be seen (albeit in a more ambiguous form), among less radical proposals that would complement electoral institutions with lottery-based institutions that would also have a share of legislative authority. Indeed, if citizens are homogeneous and basically agree on what they collectively want, then the only question left is how best to get there: knowing what the world is like and, on that basis, finding out the right solutions to the problems that everyone allegedly agrees we face. The task of politics simply becomes one of technical problem-solving. If political questions are ultimately a matter of *knowledge* (of knowing what the world is like and, on that basis, finding out the right solutions to objectively existing problems), then what matters for determining who ought to have decision-making authority is simply who the most likely person or body is that can make the right decisions. Anyone among those able to identify the right solutions would be as good as any other.

What the technocratic view of politics entirely misses is that political questions are always *also* a matter of *freedom*: the freedom to decide which political direction a community would like to go; which values and goals it aims to prioritize; which risks it is willing to take; which trade-offs, compromises, and sacrifices it is willing to make; and so on. Political decision-making is never merely a matter of exercising the technical "competence" to identify the best solutions to objective problems—a competence that could be achieved through training and deliberation and which, as lottocrats assume, could therefore be exercised equally well by any random subset of the community. Instead, the fact that citizens are free to choose among different political programs, goals, and policy objectives means that they cannot defer to others. No one can exercise *their* political freedom for them. Once we recognize that citizens are politically free, there are only two options: either *all* citizens make fundamental political decisions collectively as equals (e.g., through regular elections) or *only some* individuals set the political agenda as they see fit, and the rest of the citizenry simply blindly defers to their decisions. Electoral democracy is the first option, and lottocratic proposals represent the second.

This analysis shows that the core of the lottocratic mentality is a peculiar form of *technopopulism*. Indeed, our analysis shows that the populist conception of representation as embodiment and the technocratic conception of politics *reinforce one another*. They are the two sides of the lottocratic coin. However, in the last section of this chapter, we turn to the question of whether the populist and the technocratic strands of the lottocratic mentality are actually compatible. After showing the internal tensions between both strands, we argue that, if justificatory push comes to shove, lottocrats would have to choose between the populist and the technocratic justifications of their proposals. Yet, no matter which option they choose, both are equally antidemocratic in that (albeit for very different reasons) they would exclude the bulk of the citizenry from decision-making and require them to blindly defer to the randomly selected few.

12 The Lottocratic Mentality

Regardless of how lottery-based institutions fare in the foreseeable future, the spread of the lottocratic mentality is a worrisome development in its own right. Endorsing the populist conception of representation as "embodiment" challenges the priority of political over descriptive representation and thereby undermines citizens' political agency and freedom. Indeed, it normalizes the antidemocratic idea that it is fine to let others make political decisions for us so long as they share some ascriptive characteristics with us (e.g., profession, gender, and geographical location). This same point is true of technocracy. Endorsing a technocratic view of politics questions citizens' rights to make political decisions and thereby undermines citizens' political agency and freedom. It dusts off the distinctly antidemocratic idea that we should let others make political decisions for us so long as they have been properly informed and deliberated about the issues. Whether it arises in populist or technocratic guises, if the lottocratic mentality takes hold in our societies it will weaken the commitment to democratic self-government. This is true irrespective of whether lottery-based institutions are ever established in one form or another. This conclusion opens up an important question, namely, is it possible to design and organize lottery-based institutions without endorsing the lottocratic mentality? We turn to this question in the last chapter of the book.

In Chapter 8, we focus on current proposals for institutionalizing deliberative minipublics such as citizens' assemblies or deliberative polls. These sorts of proposals are so abundant that it would be impossible to try to provide an overview of all of them. Our task is more limited. We focus on proposals for institutionalizing minipublics as auxiliaries or supplements to representative institutions in order to show that they can be crafted and justified without embracing the lottocratic mentality. We argue that there are two fundamentally different ways of thinking about the ultimate goal of institutionalizing minipublics. Minipublics can be used either to *empower their (few) participants* to do the thinking, deliberating, and deciding for the rest of the citizenry or to *empower the citizenry* to have greater influence over the political process. Thus, proposals for institutionalizing minipublics can follow two different approaches: (1) the *lottocratic* approach that aims to give minipublics advisory or even decision-making authority while bypassing deliberation and decision-making by the citizenry, and (2) the *participatory* approach that aims to empower the citizenry to initiate public debate, influence policy making, set the political agenda, influence the decision-making process, and/or have the final say on certain political decisions. Following the participatory approach, we show that minipublics could contribute to improving political deliberation in the public sphere and act as intermediaries between legislative institutions and the citizenry without usurping their sovereignty. In the last section, we discuss several proposals for institutionalizing minipublics that follow the participatory approach we support while providing different levels of citizens' empowerment: citizen-initiated citizens' assemblies and deliberative agenda setting for ballot propositions. There are many more possibilities than those that we discuss. The point of our analysis is only to show that precisely because these proposals do not embrace the lottocratic mentality they could have important and ambitious *democratic effects*.

Lottery-based institutions are not a panacea for overcoming the grave democratic deficits of our democracies. But precisely considering the current crisis, it would be a shame to squander whichever democratic contribution these institutions could make toward empowering the citizenry by letting them become yet another shortcut for bypassing the citizenry and further cementing the rule of the few.

I

THE RISE OF THE LOTTOCRATIC MENTALITY

Chapter 1
The Lottery Revival

The lottocratic mentality is nourished by several key assumptions and a very specific interpretation of history. In a nutshell, the assumptions suppose that selection by lottery is the only institutional mechanism of selection that is consistent with democratic equality and, relatedly, that institutionalizing lotteries within government will produce epistemically better and more procedurally ideal deliberation (e.g., noncorrupt and nonpartisan). To illustrate these interlocking assumptions, we shall primarily focus on the ideas of three seminal political theorists: Robert A. Dahl, Jon Elster, and Bernard Manin. These theorists drew attention to lotteries well before their current rise in popularity. Each theorist explicitly highlighted how lotteries differ from elections, and each also emphasized the possible positive role that lotteries could play in combatting corruption and partisanship and fostering participation and representation. None of these theorists identifies as a lottocrat. Indeed, each of them addressed the normativity of lotteries with a deep analysis that has fallen out of fashion amid the recent lottocratic resurgence. As such, their accounts of lotteries remain fundamental to assessing and challenging some of the assumptions that compose the lottocratic mentality.

The specific interpretation of history that lottocrats endorse deploys a paradigm of democracy drawn from the institutional order of fourth-century Athenian democracy and, secondarily, from the early-modern Italian experiences of republican government—particularly as it existed in Florence and Venice. Lottocrats take Aristotle as their main inspiration since "he focused on the difference between sorting and electing, calling the former democratic and the latter not."[1] Lottocrats neither are nor claim to be historians; they use history for theoretical and political purposes. We certainly do not question this "use" of history. Within both the study of politics and the justification of political decisions, making the past into a theoretical political tool is a long-standing practice. The tradition of constitutionalism has benefited from this method at least as far back as Polybius and has consistently continued to do so through figures like Machiavelli and the Founding Fathers and beyond. The comparative and selective use of history within debates about the nature of democracy is part of this tradition. Such uses of history are important, and they often shed light on contemporary political issues. We do not dispute any of this.

However, problems crop up when these ways of using the past become "ritualized," and certain versions of history get uncritically repeated as mantras. In that

---

[1] Van Reybrouck, *Against Elections*, 45–6.

The Lottocratic Mentality. Cristina Lafont and Nadia Urbinati, Oxford University Press. © Cristina Lafont and Nadia Urbinati (2024). DOI: 10.1093/9780191982903.003.0002

18 The Lottocratic Mentality

context, whenever history happens to cut against an author's theoretical aims, the function of historical knowledge itself is easily sacrificed. For instance, in stressing the polarization between lottery (democracy) and elections (oligarchy), lottocrats repeatedly gloss over the fact that, within ancient and early-modern republics, lotteries were never an exclusively democratic tool—oligarchs and aristocrats also used them. Lottocrats also overlook the fact that, in Athens, lotteries were used to choose administrative and judicial organs but were *not* used to choose lawmakers (as we shall see "the *nomothetai* were none other than a special session of the Assembly").[2] Similarly, lottocrats are insufficiently clear about the fact that lotteries did not actually apply to *all* citizens but rather were often employed with important limitations upon their scope. Finally, lottocrats fail to appreciate the implications of the fact that even within their historical paradigms of democracy lotteries were not used *instead* of elections but rather *both* mechanisms were used at the same time but in different contexts.

Against the backdrop of this sort of selective historical narrative, the very meaning of democracy itself is altered and somehow de-democratized. Democracy is transformed from a political regime founded upon the participation of adult (male) citizens in the lawmaking assembly to one in which the many are "ruled" by "the few"—who are chosen by chance.[3] As discussed in this chapter, a very specific and contested interpretation of Athenian democracy has been tacitly passed off as an uncontested historical fact upon which the lottocratic mentality is based. We, therefore, end this chapter with a critical analysis of lottocrats' interpretation of history. We question how lottocrats exclusively identify democracy with lotteries and elections with oligarchy. We agree with Hubertus Buchstein that "[c]ontrary to the current dominant narrative about ancient political thought, sortition was not seen as exclusively linked to democracy."[4] In conclusion, regarding the lottocratic mentality, we will show that the lottocratic logic is highly misleading in relation to democracy. Equalization of opportunities to exercise asymmetric power is not a form of horizontal equality. True horizontal equality consists of exercising power collectively as equals, as in the Athenian assembly and elections![5]

---

[2] See below. The quotation is from Mirko Canevaro and Alberto Esu, "Extreme Democracy and Mixed Constitution in Theory and Practice: *Nomophylakia* and Fourth-Century *Nomothesia* in the Aristotelian *Athenaion Politeia*," in *Athenaion Politeiai tra storia, politica e sociologia: Aristotele e Pseudo-Senofonte*, ed. C. Bearzot, M. Canevaro, T. Gargiulo, and E. Poddighe (Milan: LED, 2018).

[3] "To proponents of the democracy thesis [of lot versus election], quotes from Aristotle serve as nothing less than statements by a crown witness. By contrast, most ancient historians exercise significantly more restraint regarding Aristotle's writings when it comes to researching the democracy that actually existed in ancient Greece." Hubertus Buchstein, "Countering the 'Democracy Thesis'—Sortition in Ancient Greek Political Theory," *Redescriptions* 18, no. 2 (2015): 140.

[4] "The democracy thesis of political lotteries, which serves such differing political needs, is incorrect—not only with respect to the actual use of lotteries in ancient Greece, which has already been demonstrated by classical studies research, but also with respect to those who theorized about this issue at that time" (ibid., 128).

[5] The relationship between ancient Athens and the humanist Italian republics proves our argument. Scholars have recently stressed the egalitarian mindset of ancient Greeks who saw each other as equals in a horizontal way. Which means that lottery cannot be deemed an uncontested expression of that mindset since the use of lots served among the elites to avoid strife in the Italian republics, as we shall see in this chapter. In fine, the Athenian Assembly was the true reflection of horizontal equality and not the drawing of lots. Irad Malkin and Josine Blok, *Drawing Lots: From Egalitarianism to Democracy in*

1.1 Precursors to the Revival of Lotteries in Democratic Theory

1.1.1 Robert A. Dahl

In the 1970s, "citizen juries" began to bring selection by lot back into politics in both Germany and the United States "almost simultaneously."[6] In the United States, Yves Sintomer claims that this revival took place within the broader context of long-running debates about the selection procedure for trial juries, which had started to denounce the underrepresentation of minorities. From at least as far back as the 1880 case *Virginia v. Rives*, US courts began to acknowledge that excluding African American citizens from juries created normative problems. In the intervening period leading up to the civil rights movement, this issue acquired increasing importance, which was then catalyzed by the mobilization against segregationist policies in the South.[7]

Within this same broad arc of US history, there was also simmering interest in using lotteries for the legislature—even before the mass democratic engagement of the 1960s. Hanna Fenichel Pitkin notes that, as far back as the 1930s, concepts such as representativeness and proportionality were understood by some scholars to be a "condensation" or a "miniature" of the body politic. This general line of thought led Harold J. Laski and Marie Collins Swabey to conceptualize an ideal legislature as one made up of "an average sample of ordinary men." Notably, in 1939, Swabey proposed using a lottery to make the US Congress "fully representative."[8] The idea that representation could be fruitfully thought of as a "sampling" of a "smaller group, selected impartially or at random" figured prominently within the organicist theory of the state pioneered by theorists such as Otto von Gierke and Karl Löwenstein. This theoretical frame impacted debates throughout the 1930s about the "crisis of democracy."

In the early 1950s, Swabey's idea of selecting "samples" of representatives showed up within the work of two leading theorists of democratization, Robert A. Dahl and

---

Ancient Greece (Oxford University Press, 2024) in particular the introduction; and Daniel Hutton Ferris, "Lottocracy or Psephocracy? Democracy, Elections, and Random Selection," *European Journal of Political Theory*. First published online December 17, 2023, 1-24. https://doi-org.ezproxy.cul.columbia.edu/10.1177/14748851231220555,

[6] Yves Sintomer, "Sortition and Politics: From Radical to Deliberative Democracy—and Back?," in *Brill's Companion to the Reception of Athenian Democracy*, ed. Dino Piovan and Giovanni Giorgini (Leiden: Brill, 2021), 502.

[7] "The Supreme Court started admitting statistical arguments in 1935, and in 1940 in a case involving race, it invoked for the first time the requirement that the jury should be 'really representative of the community'. . . . In 1968, the US Congress passed a law requiring the random selection of jurors from extensive lists (electoral registers, for example) for all federal trials." Yves Sintomer, *The Government of Chance: Sortition and Democracy from Athens to the Present* (Cambridge: Cambridge University Press, 2023), 192. See also Ned Crosby, "Citizens Juries: One Solution for Difficult Environmental Questions," in *Fairness and Competence in Citizen Participation, Technology, Risk, and Society* 10, ed. Jeryl Mumpower, Ortwin Renn, and Peter Wiedemann (Springer: Dordrecht, 1995), 157–74.

[8] Marie Collins Swabey, *Theory of the Democratic State* (Cambridge, MA: Harvard University Press, 1937), particularly chap. 1; Harold J. Laski, *Democracy in Crisis* (Chapel Hill: University of North Carolina Press, 1933), 80. Today Swabey is almost totally forgotten, yet she was a pioneer of lottocracy.

20 The Lottocratic Mentality

Charles Lindblom.[9] In the 1960s and 1970s, interest in lotteries resurfaced within a burgeoning literature that focused on how to redefine democracy to guard against the elitist tendencies of electoral representation. This redefinition pursued two different goals: restricting the social function of the state and promoting participatory democracy. It was proposed that these goals could be realized by both depoliticizing representation as much as possible and expanding the number of citizens involved in public debate. When these goals were formulated in this way, they could be equally well received by neoliberals and radical leftists. Both rejected the traditional role of party politics, though for precisely the opposite reasons: neoliberals did not want party politics to expand the social function of the state, whereas radical leftists did not want party politics to impose homogenizing discipline and centralization over disparate social movements. Both ends of the political spectrum found a viable solution in lotteries.

In his book *Law, Legislation and Liberty* (1973–1979), Friedrich August von Hayek coined the term "demarchy" to denote a radical institutional reform of existing democracies that sought to restrict the function of both politics and the state; "demarchy" was envisioned as an alternative to liberal democracy based on party competition. Hayek postulated that the centrality of an elected legislature and the principle of majoritarianism were combined to make liberal democracy inherently corrupt and totalitarian in nature.[10] According to Hayek, throughout all areas of life (e.g., economics, intellectual progress, and morality), the best "solutions" were produced not by the centralized knowledge of a subject (be it an individual, a class, or a party) but rather from a spontaneous process of experimentation within society that was based on individual freedom and an awareness of the limits of reason. Demarchy is the name of a political system based on a decentralized diffusion of decision-making groups who are selected by lot so as to deal with specific governmental functions in a given area. According to the core argument in Hayek's 1945 article "The Use of Knowledge in Society," the central economic problem is "how to secure the best use of resources known to any of the members of society, for ends whose relative importance only these individuals know."[11] Parties and the democratic centrality of the legislature were cast as invidious forces that worked together so as to block the process of uncovering and utilizing this knowledge and also increase the role of governmental agencies.[12] Hayek proposed demarchy as an alternative to

---

[9] Hanna Fenichel Pitkin, *The Concept of Representation* (Berkeley, CA: University of California Press, 1967), 73–5 and 265.

[10] Friedrich A. von Hayek, *Law, Legislation and Liberty*, vol. 3, *The Political Order of a Free People* (Chicago: University of Chicago Press, 1981) and "The Law of Legislation," chap. 6 in *Law, Legislation and Liberty*, vol. 1, *Rules and Order* (Chicago: University of Chicago Press, 1978); see Regina Queiroz, "Jeopardizing Liberal Democracy: The Trouble with Demarchy," *Critical Political Studies*, published online October 16, 2023, https://www.tandfonline.com/doi/full/10.1080/19460171.2023.2267631?src=.

[11] Friedrich A. von Hayek, "The Use of Knowledge in Society," *American Economic Review* 35, no. 4 (1945): 519.

[12] It is interesting to note the link between these Hayekian ideas and anxieties about administrative bureaucracy that have recently emerged in (far-right) US political culture. For an academic gloss on such anxieties, see Philip Hamburger, *Is Administrative Law Unlawful?* (Chicago: University of Chicago Press, 2014) and Adrian Vermeule's critique, "No," review of Philip Hamburger, *Is Administrative Law Unlawful?*,

the centrality of elections in representative democracy. Even today, this same basic ideal underlies Alexander Guerrero's proposal of disseminating allotted assemblies throughout the country so as to replace the national congress or parliament.[13]

The idea of demarchy would later resurface in a 1985 book by John Burnheim, a former Catholic priest from Australia. His book, *Is Democracy Possible? The Alternative to Electoral Politics*, cast itself as a blueprint for a political order wherein many small allotted "citizen's juries" would deliberate and make decisions about public policies. For Burnheim, demarchy was a kind of democracy where citizens directly communicated through minipublics. Each minipublic would be devoted to specific problems according to the motto: "*from the hands of political parties to the hands of those most strongly affected by particular problems*."[14] In this same vein, in 1984 Benjamin Barber noted the participatory potential involved in sortition, arguing that "election by lot on a limited basis might act to save representation from itself."[15]

At roughly the same time but on the leftist side of the theoretical spectrum, Allin Cottrell and Paul Cockshott proposed numerous "organs of public authority" to "be controlled by citizens' committees chosen by lot." Their proposal was formulated to block the formation of a new elite in a postcapitalist society. In their 1993 book *Toward a New Socialism*, they revived the lottery model from Athenian democracy and, as part of their ideal of a socialist democracy, pitched it as a strategy to avoid the formation of homogenizing political parties. Cottrell and Cockshott made loose use of Aristotle in order to stress the aristocratic/oligarchic character of elections, thereby anticipating a reading that Bernard Manin would soon popularize; from there they concluded with a call to fully restore lottocratic practices as the only way to fill the gap between rulers and ruled, and to prevent the formation of an elected caste.[16] Many of these rhetorical tropes are now part of the vocabulary on democracy by lot.

All the theorists noted so far wrote about the role for lotteries in democracies. But, within democratic theory, Dahl's *After the Revolution?* (1970) was the first book to consider whether lotteries in a representative democracy might also serve an auxiliary role beyond the expansion of knowledge or participation among the citizenry. Unlike either neoliberal or radical leftist critics of representative democracy, Dahl neither challenged the social role of the state nor proposed a new scheme of decision-making via citizens' assemblies so as to solve the problem of size. Nevertheless, Dahl's

---

Texas Law Review 93 (2015), available at https://ssrn.com/abstract=2488724. I thank Max G. Cherem for this suggestion.

[13] Guerrero, *Lottocracy*.

[14] John Burnheim, *Is Democracy Possible? The Alternative to Electoral Politics* (Sydney: Sydney University Press, 1985; new ed., 2006), particularly chap. 5.

[15] Benjamin Barber, *Strong Democracy: Participatory Politics for a New Age* (Berkeley, CA: University of California Press, 1984), 291. Barber reiterated Robert Michel's dilemma of the oligarchic iron law inherent within the problem of scale and electoral politics. On the implications that Barber's study of the local forms of administrations had upon the use of subsidiary panels selected by lot, see Antonio Floridia, *From Participation to Deliberation: A Critical Genealogy of Deliberative Democracy* (Colchester: ECPR Press, 2017), 47–9.

[16] Allin Cottrell and Paul Cockshott, *Toward a New Socialism* (Nottingham: Spokesman, 1993). Along the same lines, see also Hayek, *Law, Legislation and Liberty*, 3: 38–40.

22 The Lottocratic Mentality

theoretical work would come together with James Fishkin's experiments involving "deliberative minipublics" to propel lottocracy to lofty heights.

Starting with *Democracy and Deliberation* (1991), Fishkin used minipublics in his Deliberative Poll experiments. He sought to reconcile the democratic principle of political equality with the role deliberation played in the development of collective choices—holding up deliberative minipublics as an alternative to prior metrics that supposedly "measured" (but in reality distorted) opinions. In subsequent years, he articulated a forceful rebuke of the technology of the persuasion industry that "has made it possible for elites to shape opinion and then invoke those opinions in the name of democracy."[17] Lottery allowed samples of the population to gather in spaces where the quality of deliberation could be improved—albeit among a small number of citizens and for consultative purposes only rather than lawmaking.

1.1.1.1 Diffuse Advisory Assemblies or Participation by Lot

The central question of Dahl's *After the Revolution?* is this: if collective self-government is ideally thought of as "rule by the people" ("primary democracy") then who exactly should we consider "the people" to be? Dahl included his reflections on "lottery" within a chapter about potential improvements that could bring representative government closer to "primary democracy." He proposed "participation by lot" after explaining that the main weakness of polyarchy was its exclusion of the vast majority of citizens from the people that rule (participation in institutions), and that this was a weakness that could never be completely overcome. For Dahl, lottery was a way to partly correct polyarchy by bringing authority closer to the citizens without doing away with the electoral system. Later, in *Democracy and Its Critics*, he built on his early thought and argued that an advanced democracy should create opportunities for engendering an "attentive public" that is both informed and thoughtful, as well as "representative of the broader public." This dual goal brought him to the idea of "minipopuli," groups of citizens "randomly selected out of the entire demos" that would set an agenda of issues and also deal with specific major issues. These assemblies drawn by lot would "hold hearings, commission research, and engage in debate and discussion."[18] As in his earlier book, Dahl suggested that lottery might play an auxiliary role to decision-making institutions: the "minipopuli" would *supplement* rather than replace or even interact on an equal footing with legislative bodies. For both Dahl and his student Fishkin, random selection would help reconcile representation with participation by propagating the country with innumerable deliberative minipublics—whether they existed in the domain of justice (popular juries) or as consultative bodies with respect to the sorts of issues that most interested citizens. The seminal contribution of *After the Revolution?* was that we could use minipublics

---

[17] James S. Fishkin, *When the People Speak: Deliberative Democracy and Public Consultation* (Oxford: Oxford University Press, 2009), 6.

[18] Robert A. Dahl, *Democracy and Its Critics* (New Haven, CT: Yale University Press, 1989), 340; and *Controlling Nuclear Weapons: Democracy versus Guardianship* (Syracuse, NY: Syracuse University Press, 1985), 101.

to make "good citizens" who were more informed and capable of dealing with others in a climate of respect and openness.

Dahl thought of random selection from a pragmatic perspective. He believed that polyarchy was the best imperfect form of democracy and that it could be improved to make politics—rather than economics—the central operative force in society. For him, the main cause of dissatisfaction with representative government was not the state per se but its large size. This problem could never be completely solved unless nation-states were radically reduced. In Dahl's time, the large size of the polity and the unifying function of state authority formed the crux of a dilemma that pit political equality and the principle of interests against one another. "The smaller an association, the more fully it can adhere to the principle of political equality," and there are subsequently fewer problems in equalizing political resources to foster participation and attention toward the many different issues that interest citizens. Democratic theorists must not ignore the deplorable fact of polyarchy: "the number of people involved alone places severe limits on effective participation in 'democratic' decisions."[19] Representative democracy is based on the recognition that all citizens never enjoy *full* authority over decisions, and it seeks to resolve this problem in ways that approximate "primary democracy." The key question that guided Dahl's interest in lotteries was this: How can we *intensify and expand participation without returning to direct democracy*? "Several hundred constituencies chosen in the same way and used to ensure randomness in modern sample surveys" can bring a wide range of issues that elections and the party system invariably simplify, filter, and even neglect back into the political arena. Random selection can improve party politics and ameliorate certain dynamics of representative democracy by, for instance, "selecting advisory councils of every elected official of the gigantic polyarchy: big city mayors, state governors, members of the US House and Senate, and even the president."[20] *The tension between parties and assemblies drawn by lot is key in Dahl's argument.*

Parties also exist to collect information. Yet, as voluntary associations, they are exposed to partiality and partisan loyalty. These dynamics hinder competent deliberation. Parties have their own internal rules and procedures, which can be changed whenever key members decide. This should not be the case with allotted assemblies that have a consultative function for elected branches of government: their modalities, times, and the formats in which they gather, meet, and discuss should be governed by rules that are valid for and applicable to all.[21] While they are not intended to replace elected bodies and parties, citizens' assemblies should ideally combine the formality of selection and deliberation procedures with the informality of an auxiliary function—this hybrid form of authority and informality makes them distinct from both parties and the formal decision-making bodies of the state.

---

[19] Robert A. Dahl, *After the Revolution? Authority in a Good Society* (New Haven, CT: Yale University Press, 1970), 118.

[20] Ibid., 123. Dahl reframed those proposals some years later in his "Sketches for a Democratic Utopia," *Scandinavian Political Studies* 10, no. 3 (1987): 195–206.

[21] Dahl argued that the regulation of the advisory councils selected by lot makes all the difference: as with popular juries, randomly selected citizens must be placed in a condition of "service obligation" (and they must be paid and obliged to serve).

Unlike parties, the *nonvoluntary* character of such assemblies would make them open to a variety of ordinary citizens and animated by a genuine process of free deliberation. Voluntariness makes an association partisan, keeps discussion among affiliates within predefined assumptions, and limits free speech. On the contrary, in the case of "advisory councils" selected at random, the criterion of chance makes them open and assures that debates are not entered into with a "primed" adversarial mentality. But, *unlike* the formal decision-making bodies of the state, these councils have no formal authority. Elected officials can simply decide not to listen to them—though it would be hard for them to completely ignore their suggestions once the state initiates a selection procedure to gather their input in the first place.

Dahl's proposals contain the latent kernels of at least *four arguments* that would subsequently become pivotal in lottocratic thinking.

The first argument concerns the *definition*. Dahl introduced the lottery as an alternative to elections. Although he did not propose that lotteries replace electoral procedures, he did point to two opposing methods for selecting political officials, one more "open" than the other. Then, he invited his readers to ask why elections had become so hegemonic. This juxtaposition gave the impression of a historical conflict between these two systems and their supporters. "Selecting representatives by election has completely displaced selecting by lot in modern democracies."[22] While Dahl characterized a proposal to introduce the lottery into modern democracy as "bizarre," he nevertheless unintentionally suggested an interpretation of political history that lottocrats make extensive use of today to "disprove" the democratic pedigree of representative government.

The second argument concerns the *auxiliary role of the lottery. Dahl compared modern and ancient democracies not to counter electoral representation directly but to stress the different senses of participation. Since Dahl never questioned elections, his call for participation was different from* that made by theorists of participatory democracy in the 1960s and 1970s. What Dahl questioned was the *exclusive use* of elections. In comparing the two selection methods, he wanted to convey how the lottery could aid elected officials.

The third argument concerns *limitations* on the functions fulfilled by allotted assemblies and casts doubt on the desirability of lotteries playing a direct decision-making role. Dahl explicitly thought that replacing elections with a lottery would damage democratic legitimacy: "I cannot think of a better way to discredit the idea [of lottery] and democracy itself."[23] Instead, he thought lotteries could correct the "most unfortunate fact of polyarchy": the few people involved and the small variety of issues that parties and interest groups brought to deliberation. Given his highly participatory perspective and his conviction that large-scale groups limited modern democracy, lottery aided the basic electoral-representative setup.

The fourth argument concerns the *ameliorative character* of polyarchy. It shows that Dahl had a specific hope for lotteries: they could limit the exclusionary function

---

[22] Dahl, *After the Revolution?*, 122.
[23] Ibid., 125.

of elections by containing the role of elites and parties. Dahl conceptualized random selection by lottery as potentially structuring and organizing polyarchy in such a way as to come as close as possible to the democratic ideal of making participation technically accessible to all. In short, Dahl prefigured a polyarchy enriched with *numerous advisory councils* (each consisting of several hundred selected citizens). This would allow many more interests and opinions to emerge and give those citizens selected by the lot the opportunity to refine their knowledge and enrich the quality of their participation.

By inaugurating a renaissance of the role lotteries could play in democracy, Dahl established a direct relationship between elections and parties as well as between elections and lotteries. These connections spoke in favor of a lottocratic turn, although not a turn toward the lottocratic mentality. He approached the issue of elections from the perspective of the two main problems that he thought plagued polyarchy: factionalism (partisan divisions and/or polarization) and leadership (forming a political class). He thought lotteries could partly address both flaws, as they did not simply extend participation but also promoted a *type* of participation that could constrain partisanship within deliberation.

Why was he so skeptical of *voluntary* political participation? Dahl seemed to think that parties aggravate the dilemma between "the principle of political equality" and "the principle of affected interests" because they select issues from a partial point of view that sows divisions; he also thought parties were willing to co-opt the process of filling important governmental positions and offices to reward their affiliates— people who they preferred above all others since they had more control over them. In short, for Dahl, democratic participation mediated by parties is prejudicial and discriminatory from beginning to end. Thus, his idea of advisory councils drawn by lot seems to have *parties* as its real target. However, as we have seen, Dahl conceives of the relationship between lotteries and elections in an auxiliary or supplemental fashion rather than along the lines of substitution or complementarity models. Indeed, whereas elections rely on the criteria of "choice" or "individual responsibility" to satisfy the criterion of accountability, lotteries can satisfy the criterion of disinterested participation precisely because they exclude personal choice from the selection process. Integrating polyarchy with allotted advisory councils would be a pragmatic way to expand the range of political issues beyond partisan priorities and actually to contain partisanship.

1.1.1.2 Contrasting Conclusions

Dahl's reflections can lead reasonable people to contrasting conclusions since they are rather broad-ranging and concern how lottocratic institutions might take shape in the *future*. Yet, his reflections raise doubts about the specifically democratic credentials of any such developments. Let's clarify this important point.

First, Dahl aptly demonstrates the inherent tension between party politics and genuine deliberation, yet also clarifies that parties are inexorably intertwined with elections. By insisting upon the validity of polyarchy, Dahl acknowledged that, despite any tensions or invidious dynamics, elections and parties were here to stay.

26 The Lottocratic Mentality

But he thought we could mitigate the negative effects of both elections and parties, bringing polyarchy as close as possible to "primary democracy." This suggests that neither elections nor parties were at the core of "primary democracy." Dahl wanted to expand opportunities for citizens to gather in small assemblies and discuss key issues with an open mind. These assemblies were intended to become the main source of information for representatives who wanted to know the thoughts and desires of the general populace.[24] Yet, Dahl also made arguments that opposed extending lottery to decision-making. He based his theory of polyarchy on two intertwined criteria: "competence" and "personal choice." Let's start with the latter, which is his main argumentative strategy for challenging lottery-based political authority.

Dahl pointed out the "undemocratic" implications of lottery when it was applied to the legislative process.[25] Personal choice (suffrage) was at the core of democratic legitimacy, the condition that authorizes citizens to hold elected officials accountable to not only the legal order itself but also to the citizenry more generally. In other words, with no personal choice comes no political accountability. Dahl was also keen to remind his readers that in ancient democracies the antipode to elections was not lottery but rather direct lawmaking by the citizens in the Popular Assembly. He was adamant about the priority of "choosing" over "being drawn": "In Athens, after all, the officials chosen by lot were subject to the Assembly. In the absence of elections, to whom would a legislature chosen by lot be subject?"[26] This is a good question. Substituting the criterion of choice with that of chance would have dramatic implications for a democracy since all citizens must in some way be authorizing the decisions—either by voting for representatives (like the moderns) or by voting upon issues (like the ancients and, at times, the moderns). But in a lottocratic regime, a randomly selected assembly would decide for all the citizens without asking them for any authorization whatsoever. Removing suffrage (the criterion of "personal choice") would subvert democracy. For, although it is true that a sample of the sovereign body can be made to mirror the population in statistical proportion, "occasionally we might find ourselves with a highly unrepresentative legislature subject to no authority except the next lottery."[27] Thus, while Dahl advocated "reinstating" the use of lottery to "select the advisory councils of every elected official of the giant polyarchy," he was also very clear that the basic criterion of democratic legitimacy pulls in the opposite direction as chance. The lottery works well for advisory bodies, not for legislative bodies.

Dahl's insight cuts against the lottocratic mentality of some contemporary lottocrats, who question whether democratic legitimacy truly resides in the principle of "one person, one vote." Without the expression of political freedom that flows from this principle, the hallmark of a randomly selected assembly's legitimacy would simply be acceptance by citizens outside the assembly—what Cristina Lafont calls

---

[24] Ibid., 123.
[25] Ibid., 122.
[26] Ibid., 125.
[27] Ibid.

"blind deference."[28] In this same vein, Dahl cautioned that replacing the traditional criterion of personal choice with one of chance or probability would drain politics out of democracy: "Finally, the Criterion of Personal Choice argues against choosing all or most policy-making officials by lot in a polyarchy. . . . In the absence of elections, to whom would a legislature chosen by lot be subject? . . . I cannot think of a better way to discredit the idea [of representation] and democracy itself."[29]

A strongly lottocratic revision of democracy would not only lack accountability but it would also generate the *paradox of a ballooning bureaucracy* that, ironically, would be created in the name of citizens' participation. As discussed below, Elster fleshed out the nature of this problem several years after Dahl initially noted it. Dahl argued that, apart from the damage that would come from replacing the criterion of personal choice, lotteries would also damage what he called the criterion of "competence." He thought that the short-term period of service under lotteries would undercut the consolidation of institutional experience and knowledge. The obvious solution to this problem would be to require longer terms of service—but this then creates tension with the countervailing goal of expanding participation and preventing elitism. Since short-term service fatally hinders the stabilization of knowledge and the transmission of experience within institutions, we might seek to address this problem with more bureaucracy. However, this strategy creates problems, as it ends up undercutting the goal of using lotteries to improve the knowledge and competence of the citizenry.

1.1.2 Jon Elster

The interest in the lotteries is not only driven by the aspiration to expand participation. Honesty and transparency are also important motivations. Jon Elster was one of the first theorists to link lotteries to realizing these goals and think that lotteries would thus be preferable to elections. He also acknowledged the bureaucratic paradox and the inability of lotteries to generate accountability. He, therefore, largely did not speak about the precise role and institutional place of lotteries within democratic decision-making in representative government or at least refrained from doing so in the detailed way that is common among lottocrats today.

1.1.2.1 From Voters to Candidates

The use and meaning of lotteries that interest us are discussed in a single chapter of Elster's *Solomonic Judgments* (1989). The main task of that book was the reconciliation of "honesty with self-interest." He sought to achieve such reconciliation by deflating and even overcoming the competition for power.[30] He looked to lotteries as a solution to these problems and as an alternative to elections, which he thought

---

[28] Ibid., 123; Cristina Lafont, *Democracy without Shortcuts: A Participatory Conception of Deliberative Democracy* (Oxford: Oxford University Press, 2020), *passim*.

[29] Dahl, *After the Revolution?*, 125.

[30] Jon Elster, *Solomonic Judgments: Studies in the Limitations of Rationality* (Cambridge: Cambridge University Press, 1989), 87.

rightly instigated a power competition among candidates and electors alike. Elster was one of the first theorists to compare elections and lotteries in order to prove the moral and functional superiority of the latter. He was also among the first to bring the lottery into lawmaking: "This proposal would appear strange, to say the least, yet surprisingly, there are a large number of arguments to be made for it."[31] He thought that the success of elections in modern society flowed from the way that they played into the general desire for individual direct agency: lotteries had ceased to be attractive because modern citizens had come to identify political freedom with the equal opportunity to *choose* someone to do a job rather than identifying it with the equality *to be selected* for that job. Elster did not advance a philosophical interpretation of this paradigm change, but his argument dovetails with the liberal interpretation of the difference between the liberty of the ancients and that of the moderns—an interpretive distinction that harkens back to at least Benjamin Constant. But, if we take the liberty of the moderns as a given, then we might begin to wonder: Why should we upend modern citizens' preferences in order to revive lotteries? Elster's answer is a moral one: We should do this in order to combat corruption. Elster singles out corruption as the central driver or catalyst of the dynamics of competition for power. As such, he proposes to extend lotteries not only to the realms of justice and administration but also to political representation itself: "Today, lotteries have virtually no role in the public process beyond that of occasionally being used as tiebreakers. In the past, however, they were widely used to select members of legislative or executive assemblies."[32] While Dahl's goal was to expand participation, Elster's was to liberate representation from partisan competition. Yet, both theorists thought that partisan dynamics distorted the country's "true preferences."[33]

Echoing Joseph A. Schumpeter's dualism between perfectionist and minimalist conceptions of democracy, Elster was adamant that the problem of dishonesty did not require changing the actors in power but instead required adopting procedures that could ex ante neutralize the self-interested disposition of human beings (citizens and political actors as well). The fact that lotteries are antithetical to accumulating power means that they could potentially free politics from power struggles without pushing democracy toward perfectionistic or illiberal remedies. From this perspective, elections were a procedural failure. Fortunately, history offered an alternative mechanism that combined individual and collective rationality (self-interest and the general interest). Interestingly, Elster's core historical example was not Athens but rather the Italian republics of early modernity. While the system in Athens was conceived to secure the participation of the largest possible number of citizens (e.g., it gave everyone the chance to serve in office at least once in their life), the Republic

---

[31] Ibid.

[32] Ibid., 79–80. Elster's generalization concerning the "past" would have an undeniably evocative force among political theorists, making some of them conclude that in ancient Athens lottery was applied to the three (legislative, executive, and judicial) powers; See Van Reybrouck, *Against Elections*, 45–6; Terrill Bouricious, "Democracy through Multi-body Sortition: Athenian Lessons for the Modern Day," *Journal of Public Deliberation* 9, no. 1 (2013); Filimon Peonidis, "On Two Anti-democratic Uses of Sortition," *Democratic Theory* 3, no. 2 (2016): 29.

[33] Elster, *Solomonic Judgments*, 87.

of Florence had to solve problems of domestic strife and social instability. In short, in Florence, the challenge was selecting lawmakers in a society that was modern in *many* (e.g., economic and social) respects but certainly not all respects. Elster was intensely interested in why Florence failed to stabilize itself into a lottocratic republic because he thought this precise historical failure ushered in the subsequent success of elections—a historical argument later developed by both Manin and Sintomer.

Elster did not elaborate on the distinction between ancient democracy and early-modern republics. However, he prioritized early-modern republics because of a key historical fact that has largely been forgotten: Athens managed lawmaking through the People's Assembly rather than through lottery. Athens used a combination of "random choice of officials and simple majority voting in the assembly." Elster agreed with Staveley that it is a "mistake" to suppose "that it was basically sortition which kept the [Athenian] democracy in being." Instead, it was "the principle of rotation—the rule applied in all but a few cases, that no citizen should hold any one office for more than once in his lifetime."[34] However, only with the Republic of Florence lotteries were applied to the "choice of laws" in combination with elections. This historical fact made the Florentine Republic an interesting foil for contemporary democracies. Florence was not a democracy; it was a republic partly ruled by a powerful oligarchy and partly based upon a social structure of guilds that could not countenance a system of elections based on individual suffrage. Moreover, Florence was a turbulent community that tried vainly to use lotteries to make pluralism a condition of stability and civil peace.

The history of Florence showed that, at least with respect to the values of *order and concord*, elections won out against lotteries.[35] According to Elster, that victory was the price that the values of "transparency" and "loyalty to the city" (i.e., the general good) paid to secure social stability and competence. Historically, this either/or compromise solution was voiced by the chancellor of the Florentine Republic, Leonardo Bruni, who claimed in the early fifteenth century that the practice of extraction by lot "extinguishes any motivation for prudent conduct, since, if men were forced to compete in direct elections and openly put their reputations on the line, they would be much more circumspect" in their public and private behavior.[36] Elster took Bruni's comment to mean that there is a trade-off between reconciling pluralism with unity on the one hand and reconciling self-interest with honesty on the other. At the time, historical memories of civil war and instability induced Florence to accept competition as a practice that gave centrality to the citizens' performance: lotteries were useful "in eliminating the struggles that so frequently erupted among the citizens competing for elections" but were "harmful" in that "many unworthy persons are placed in the magistracy."[37]

---

[34] Ibid., 72.
[35] We will return to this theme in Chapter 4 when we canvass arguments against political partisanship.
[36] Ibid., 85.
[37] Leonardo Bruni cited in ibid.

30 The Lottocratic Mentality

According to the account given in Elster's chapter, lotteries failed in Florence not because of some inherent flaw but rather for external and contingent reasons—namely, early-modern republics had not yet developed techniques of power limitation: a written constitution, a legal system of individual rights, the separation of powers, etc. But this explanation only goes so far because history tells us that the transition to elections was *also* a failure: elections did not stabilize Florence. Indeed, the equal rights and rights to political participation that would have been good for lotteries would also have been good for elections. The real question should be: in the eighteenth century, when those conditions had finally come about, why did republics opt for elections rather than reactivate lotteries?

Answering this question became a puzzle for Manin, who would approach elections from the perspective of their historical victory over lottery. For Manin, expunging lotteries from lawmaking looked like a premeditated move by social elites, who succeeded in duping their fellow citizens into believing that lotteries produced inefficiency and incompetence. This extended interpretation of Elster's original thoughts turned out to be one of the largest impacts that Elster's *Solomonic Judgments* had upon theorists of representation and lotteries. Elster's other large impact upon this literature came in the form of an important methodological innovation: using political history as "evidence" to prove the legitimacy or burnish the credentials of political procedures. Elster compared Athens, Florence, and Venice and then concluded that the combination of randomly chosen officials with simple majority voting in the people's assembly "was potentially so unstable that no society adopting it could survive without some quasi-constitutional restrictions."[38] But, naturally, this invites a question: what if a society had such "constitutional restrictions"?

For Elster, history showed that democracy could prevent the formation of an elite through lotteries, but it had failed to provide "constitutional restrictions" that sensibly limited the principle of equality. Historical examples inspired Elster's two central observations: that "one might deny . . . that elections are democratic,"[39] and that lotteries were used by democratic and nondemocratic republics alike (Venice used lotteries in its governing oligarchy for centuries). The main lesson that Elster seemed to take away from comparing lotteries and elections was that selection by lot prevents the formation of an elite since it simply expunges traditional dynamics of competition. Secondarily, he seemed to think that the inherent shortcoming of lotteries came from the way in which they realized *radical* equality: while they were taken to be fairer than elections, they could also fetishize the "democratic passion for equality." Elster noted that, "Democracy creates preferences for undiscriminating allocation of procedures—equality, even-chance lotteries, queuing, rotation—that minimize the need for discretionary and potentially controversial comparisons among people. The basic axiom of political democracy is that people have to be *treated as equal in wisdom even when they do not* tend to carry over to other arenas and forces institutions

---

[38] Ibid., 80.
[39] Ibid., 104.

to treat people as equal in need or merit when in fact, they are not."[40] If we assume that democracy is a potentially extreme regime of equality, then certain external strategies of containment—e.g., a constitution, the division of power, the rule of law—could open up space for lotteries to be sensibly used even if, to quote Bruni, they might occasionally put manifestly "unworthy persons" in governmental power. For Elster, democracy is a system of decision-making that should be judged by the ability of its procedures to combat corruption and foster transparency—qualities that could be achieved more easily if politics was not exclusively controlled by elites. Within this evaluative context, lotteries were to be preferred to elections; the problem was how to situate them in a constitutional system that limited power and to do so within a society that was composed of thoroughly modern individuals: people who are unenthusiastic about the demands of persistent participation and whose primary focus is their own personal interests rather than the common good.

1.1.2.2 Lottery Voting: A Question of Anticorruption and Fair Representation

Turning to contemporary democracy, Elster proposed combining lotteries with elections to prevent inequalities of influence upon government. His main question was how to avoid the systematic advantage that some privileged segments of society can develop. He thought that a unique institutional form called "lottery voting" could satisfy this goal in a way that elections could not. Elster analyzed past uses of the lottery before detailing his own proposal. His analysis of the past paid particular attention to the Florentine Republic, whose government had adopted lotteries in order to include the largest possible number of citizens and to prevent "many [of them] from rocking the boat." The thought was that the high probability of being chosen to serve would legitimize and stabilize the republic (but, as we shall see, in practice lotteries were never how these functions were achieved). In contrast to many contemporary discussions of lotteries, Elster put the *candidates* front and center rather than the voters: "Modern discussions of random elections emphasize, as I said, the voter rather than the candidate as the unit of selection. [But] an election should [instead] be decided by choosing a 'random dictator' from the electorate." With his proposal of "lottery voting," Elster wanted to explore the viability of emphasizing candidates or officials who would serve in various offices as the normatively salient unit of selection. He saw four advantages and two disadvantages with lottery voting. Let us begin with the *advantages.*[41]

The first advantage is *fairness toward the candidates*: the concept of "lottery voting" showed that democracy could fulfill its promise of equality better if it avoided traditional elections. The aim of Elster's book was to make a case for political justice and equality rather than democracy as such: he thought that the traditional selection of candidates through a combination of elections and majority rule was unjust because it predictably violated equality insofar as members of the minority would

[40] Ibid., 115–6.
[41] Ibid., 86–7.

be "excluded from influence." This exclusion would produce dynamics of social and political domination where one part of society subjects another to its will. If democracy basically means that each voter has an equal chance of being the actor who gets to make a decisive choice, then voting by lottery honors democracy better since it both fosters equal influence and reconciles "honesty with self-interest" without attempting to change people's imperfect nature.[42]

As Ben Saunders has recently noted in his revival of the concept: "Lottery voting" is "an alternative procedure ... that satisfies the conditions of democracy and political equality" better than majority rule. Even before Elster examined the concept in 1989, it was defended by Akhil Reed Amar: in a 1984 *Yale Law Journal* article he argued that lottery "would create a legislature of rotating citizen-legislators instead of a group of lifetime lawmakers."[43] Lottery voting would combine elections and lotteries in order to comport with the principle of majority.[44] In lottery voting, all citizens initially vote like they normally do in a first round, but the "winner" is then selected by lottery from among a group of those who received the most votes. The criteria of choice and chance work sequentially. This combination of principles causes majority rule to give up its traditional primacy. In the end, relatively few people might have voted for the winner. Indeed, the winner might reflect the views of a minority rather than a majority. *What matters here is the switch from a principle of majoritarianism to that of "probability."*[45]

Elster's proposal endorses lottery in a way that deprioritizes the majority principle because of an assumption that an overreliance on the will of the majority is unjust since it "excludes" the members of the numerical minority from "influence," thereby causing some to rule over others. While this sounds plausible, it is unclear how the alternative of a sorted assembly that decides for the nonsorted people does not broadly produce the same type of undesirable inequality of influence in that the few rule over the rest. Elster did not consider other forms of influence that citizens can exercise—for instance, through social movements, parties, or the press. Instead, he adopted a strictly procedural approach that focused on the rules that aggregated individual votes and then rendered decisions on that basis. Moreover, he conceptualized majority rule from within the paradigm of an electoral system based on single-member plurality voting. He, therefore did not consider proportional representation—a system that is *also* based on fairness toward the candidates but which enshrines the possibility that those who lose at the ballot will still be able to exercise their influence within the deliberation process of parliament. Instead, Elster simply neglected proportional representation entirely and instead proposed lottery voting as the only way to obtain fairness toward the candidates and to neutralize both the hegemony of majority and bad decisions: "the only voting procedure which

[42] Ben Saunders, "Democracy, Political Equality, and Majority Rule," *Ethics* 121 (2010): 159.
[43] Respectively, Saunders, "Democracy," 151 and Akhil Reed Amar, "Choosing Representatives by Lottery Voting," *Yale Law Journal* 6, no. 7 (1984): 1298.
[44] This would essentially be a weak application of the complex combination that was used in the Republic of Venice.
[45] As discussed later, Manin developed Elster's idea of "probability" in his interpretation of the kind of equality that belonged to democracy and that justified the use of lottery in ancient Athens.

is Pareto-optimal, nondictatorial and strategy-proof is 'random voting,' the simplest case of which exists when the probability of an option being chosen is equal to the proportion of individuals who rank it as their first choice."[46] On this view, fairness toward the candidates is obtained by blocking "misreported" preferences (i.e., partisanship in nominating candidates) and then putting all viable candidates and their preferences on equal footing. To Elster, the advantage of lotteries was not that they eliminate opportunistic interests, but rather that they neutralize their effects when it comes to selecting and aggregating impulses. In the sort of system Elster endorses, since all interests would count in a literally equal fashion, they would have the exact same probability of being expressed and therefore influencing decisions. In a way, it would seem that mixing equal suffrage (voting for a candidate) with equal candidacy (the equal chances of all those elected in the first round, who will then be chosen from by lot in the second round) would limit the desire for power that competition unleashes and also make deliberation capable of producing "good decisions."

Lottery impacts politics ex ante by using equality in the sense of *probability* to induce fairness toward all candidates enjoying a certain threshold of support. Does it also impact ex post deliberation—for instance, by preventing organized plans and parties from emerging? Should the takeaway from Elster be that a lottery-drawn assembly avoids corruption and the formation of factions because these dynamics do not dominate the selection process? Why discount the possibility that interest groups and partisanship outside the allotted assembly might lobby specific assembly members? Granted, such lobbying would target some members more than others, but it seems like even this could be enough to taint the impartial atmosphere and corrupt the process. After all, citizens who are chosen by a stroke of luck are just as subject to human "vices" as those who are chosen in elections.

Indeed, Elster repeatedly emphasizes that procedures should work with people *as they are* instead of trying to change them. He believed that "in the long run, respecting procedural values leads to better substantive outcomes."[47] Procedures may be judged on the ground that they train agents to consistently act toward a designated goal and, in this sense, they are capable of containing or exalting the passion for power. Yet, even people who happen to be selected in a competition-free manner do not necessarily lack a desire for power, money, or reputation, nor are they immune from the will to realize their ideas and interests. Lotteries do not have any special way to protect deliberation in the assembly against partisan citizens who vigorously advocate for their own interests. So, while it is clear how selection by lottery can neutralize some dynamics of partisan manipulation, it is unclear how a lottery-drawn assembly would escape political corruption. Indeed, we know that it was not unusual for citizens to "sell" their sorted posts in ancient Athens.[48] As discussed in the following

---

[46] Elster, *Solomonic Judgments*, 87. The issue of the limits of vote aggregation in deliberation became the core of Elster's theory after this book, and in particular in the decade he devoted to deliberative theory of politics.

[47] Ibid., 118.

[48] Mogens H. Hansen, *The Athenian Democracy in the Age of Demosthenes* (London: Bristol Classical, 1991), 104.

34   The Lottocratic Mentality

chapters, new risks crop up with the randomness of the selection procedure and the fact that individuals who are drawn from the citizenry are completely independent. Namely, there may be a shrewd "independent" person who is drawn by lot and can now pursue their selfish plans without any accountability, or there may be shrewd citizens outside the assembly who can successfully lobby assembly members so as to manipulate the deliberative process. To preempt these new risks, there would need to be a rigid code of deliberation and some sort of trustee system that oversaw the process. For, unlike an elected assembly, an allotted assembly can hardly be expected to be a self-governing body that forms its own internal regulations for the deliberative process: external guidance would be needed.

But in order to obtain honesty and competence, there are some additional decisions beyond those concerning the selection of assembly members. For example, if the lottery is to create a collective decision-making body that avoids manipulation and corruption, it is important that *the pool of people from which the assembly is drawn is large enough and also that the assembly which is ultimately selected is as large as possible.* This is why the popular juries of ancient Athens were made up of several hundred people—the underlying idea was that no rich citizen could single-handedly buy a verdict (a majority) at trial. The duration of the mandate was also crucial. Hence, rotation in public offices, short tenure, and lottery *together— not lottery alone*—were the combined suite of anti-oligarchic strategies adopted by the Athenian demos. As we shall see shortly, it is important to bear in mind that Athens kept processes of lawmaking within the Assembly itself and adopted lottery and elections in different contexts and for different functions.[49] Those various strategies were used together to contain corruption and the dominance of an elite. In essence, the pressure of vested interests upon lawmaking could only be fully prevented by robust intervention in the social order that realized a perfect economic and social equality among the citizens. Indeed, in *The Republic,* Plato explained that *the goodness of a decision-making process depends on the fact that those citizens who make decisions are truly independent of* material and social needs. Thus, at least concerning the supposed advantage of lotteries, Elster's question—"Could one not design a system in which it is never in people's interest to misrepresent their preferences?"[50]— remained unanswered. A lottery could *help* people realize their interests without misrepresentation, but it would have to rely on something beyond a procedure.

Elster's system of lottery voting was supposed to ameliorate dynamics within electoral and direct democracy. His broad approach suggested that if an assembly included diverse views—such as those excluded by majority rule—there would be a better chance of good deliberation. Elster was interested in promoting cognitive diversity, which he considered a condition for good deliberation. He saw this as part

---

[49] As discussed in the second part of this chapter, the anti-oligarchic value of lottery was achieved not merely by practicing it but by a special technology of selection by lot. This involved complex "machines" (*klērōtēria*) along with multiple rounds of selection and random allocation to separate courts. So, the point was not just lottery per se, but rather the "technological" advantage of lottery in making sure that no rich Athenian could possibly foresee (and therefore bribe or influence) who would sit in a given law court; this "technology" made all the difference in the anti-oligarchic use and function of lottery in democracy.

[50] Elster, *Solomonic Judgments*, 87.

of an epistemic endeavor that neither elections nor a people's assembly would fully satisfy. While democracy required some form of selection, he thought the processes that selected members of deliberative organs should replace choice with chance. Elster disregarded the political relationship of a mandate traditionally created by elections and instead argued that lotteries could produce a different and preferable form of representation. He was the first theorist to advance the idea that a type of representation could be attained by lottery.

The second advantage of Elster's "lottery voting" would be the *reduction of wasted votes*. This dynamic plagues elections, particularly in first-past-the-post systems or, as Elster calls it, a "deterministic voting system."[51] He invites us to notice how electoral systems can disincentive voter participation both in instances when a candidate is predicted to win or when nobody expects the preferred candidate will be elected.[52] While it is true that electoral systems based on proportional representation tend to promote more voter turnout, Elster did not consider such systems. This is an unfortunate omission. Since the nineteenth century, these systems have been a key way that defenders of electoral democracy have responded to the critiques of wasted votes and a majoritarian bias. But, whether by accident or design, Elster limited his reflections to a first-past-the-post electoral system combined with a lottery. In that conceptual landscape of possibilities, it is clear that the problem of wasted votes "would be solved by lottery voting, which ensures that each vote counts equally, that is, increases by the same amount the likelihood of the candidate's being elected."[53]

Moreover, Elster conceptualized votes as numerical probabilities (e.g., he compared them to the probability of being sorted). He, therefore disregarded other features of electoral democracies that are not immediately quantifiable but which are still quite important—for instance, the role played by diffuse processes of opinion formation or dynamics of "moral authority" and "respectability" in the political public sphere. While they are not easily amenable to quantification, these are nevertheless important factors in voting and electoral processes. Indeed, Elster recognized that a candidate competing for a seat in parliament might seek to secure more than a simple arithmetical majority "so as to give him [the candidate] the moral authority or mandate needed to carry out major reforms."[54] He then quickly backpedals from this insight, noting that such electoral dynamics "are secondary considerations." But, it is worth considering whether these dynamics might indeed be primary considerations. Elections that choose representatives bring issues to the forefront that

---

[51] Ibid.

[52] In ancient Athens, Elster alludes to the fact that this solution was not achieved with lottery but rather by combining formal majority voting with institutions that were designed to uphold deliberative standards and foster consensus as far as possible; the last issue relates to the method of solving disagreements and avoiding conflicts, and we will return to it in the second part of this chapter and in Chapter 4. On this general topic see Mirko Canevaro, "Majority Rule versus Consensus: The Practice of Democratic Deliberation in the Greek *Poleis*," in *Ancient Greek History and Contemporary Social Science*, ed. Mirko Canevaro, Andrew Erskine, Benjamin Gray, and Josiah Ober (Edinburgh: Edinburgh University Press, 2018), 101–56.

[53] Elster, *Solomonic Judgments*, 88.

[54] Ibid.

36   The Lottocratic Mentality

have an impact beyond the numerical tally of votes—even though it is undoubtedly true that votes count identically and must be counted correctly. Elster's prejudicial stance against elections is connected to the fact that elections generate various "secondary considerations"—such as partisan identities and ideological narratives—and the legitimacy of these considerations is not simply a quantifiable or formal matter but also a function of the way that citizens participate in selecting candidates and forming parties' agendas.

The third advantage of Elster's "lottery voting" would be *justice toward minorities*, which is a corollary of justice toward candidates. Elster supposes that under a system of lottery-drawn lawmaking assemblies, "there will be no permanent unrepresented minorities."[55] In nearly all democratic countries, the representation of minorities has been and currently is a much-debated issue—particularly in instances where ethnic, cultural, linguistic, or religious minorities are dispersed throughout vast territory. Different democracies have adopted various strategies to ensure sufficient "weight" or representation for minorities within national parliaments. For instance, there are various ways to achieve this through proportional representation or even quotas that predetermine a set number of parliamentary seats reserved for specific minorities. Elster does not engage with these proposals. Instead, he tasks lotteries with securing proportionality in minority representation. This suggests that he thinks lotteries can be employed to represent the diversity of the citizenry more fairly than elections. Elster only introduced this representative claim in relation to cultural minorities who are dispersed throughout a nation's vast territory. Nevertheless, his claim has played a central role in the arguments of contemporary lottocrats, who argue that sortition generates a more inclusive representation.

The fourth and final advantage of lottery voting is *the elimination of professional politicians.* As mentioned earlier, Dahl had already touched on this issue although he did not go so far as to introduce lotteries into lawmaking. Elster endorsed Amar's proposal to use lotteries to close the gap between an election's promise to count all votes equally and the reality of "legislatures that fail to represent the whole community." Amar had advanced "a thought experiment inviting the reader to consider seriously an alternative method of selecting representatives to legislatures that combines features of four traditional egalitarian systems: voting, lottery, quota, and rotation." He had positioned himself in contrast to prior attempts by Bruce Ackerman and Robert Paul Wolff to include lotteries in modern democracy. Ackerman and Wolff had discussed lotteries as a way of deciding issues and a method for selecting representatives. Amar thought that neither Wolff nor Ackerman offered "extensive discussion or analysis of the implications of lottery voting" and therefore invited others to do so.[56] Elster took this invitation seriously.

---

[55] Ibid.

[56] Bruce Ackerman, *Social Justice in the Liberal States* (New Haven, CT: Yale University Press, 1980), 285–9; Robert Paul Wolff, *In Defense of Anarchism* (Berkeley, CA: University of California Press, 1970), 44–8.

1.1.2.3 Disadvantages and Problems

Apart from the advantages of lotteries, Elster also carefully analyzed what he took to be their intrinsic and ineliminable *disadvantages* in order to show why the mechanism of lotteries "has never been adopted" in electoral democracies and to "suggest that it never will be."[57] He stressed two intertwined disadvantages: the *lack of continuity* between successive cohorts of representatives and also their *lack of accountability* toward the people. Both disadvantages flow from a central feature of lotteries: the fact that they block the formation of a "group of lifetime lawmakers."[58] This core function is often characterized and lauded as democratic. Yet, this characterization is somewhat inapt since lotteries fail to replicate precisely what electoral representation achieves and what the state requires: constructing and preserving a legislative institutional memory by linking each assembly to subsequent assemblies.

Elster sees elected legislatures as simply one common type of democratic institution. It turns out that lotteries are better than elections regarding picking issues or magistrates. At the same time, lotteries are radically individualistic, even atomistic, and this means that any assemblies they are used to create would be characterized by a "lack of continuity among the representatives." Thus, while lotteries prevent the formation of a political class, they interrupt the connections between one assembly and its successor, generating two problems that lottery cannot solve: an increasingly powerful bureaucracy and a lack of accountability.

Elster makes this point by way of quoting Horace Greely: random selection "denies the citizen's demand for participation in and accountability for the method of allocation," depletes political participation, and "cut[s] down on social interaction," thereby producing alienation and apathy.[59] Furthermore, selection by lot would make it more difficult for "representatives" to learn from experience. After all, each assembly seat would be filled by individuals who were fully "independent" because they possessed neither a political mandate nor a link to the past or future. Each assembly is a sort of free-floating and "absolute" issuer of decrees, much like its members. In the tradition of Alexis de Tocqueville, Elster characterized the lottery as being consistent with radical democracy or anomic individualism.

> Against all the advantages, lottery has several disadvantages that explain why it has never been adopted and suggest that it never be. Most obviously, the lack of continuity among the representatives counts against the proposal. Lottery voting would make it more difficult for representatives to learn from experience. What Tocqueville identified as a major problem of democracies, that 'each generation is a new people' and that 'after one brief moment of power, officials are lost again amid the everchanging crowd', would be exacerbated under a system of lottery voting. Disproportionate power would accrue to the bureaucracy.[60]

---

[57] Elster, *Solomonic Judgments*, 89.
[58] Ibid., 104.
[59] Horace Greely, "The Equality of Allocation by Lot," *Harvard Civil Rights-Civil Liberties Law Review* 12 (1977): 122–3; Elster, *Solomonic Judgments*, 118.
[60] Cited in Elster, *Solomonic Judgments*, 89.

38 The Lottocratic Mentality

Elster's conclusion was that the self-contained sovereignty of each subsequent assembly would engender an intractable problem: a system designed to have high turnover in political personnel would require some sort of stable, functional structure in the background, and it seems like this could only take the form of a pervasive and powerful bureaucracy. So, the lottery is both *the* preferred selection method in a democracy and the main threat to democracy. Clearly, this is an inherently unstable and untenable position, and it appears to show that truly "pure" (lottocratic) democracy is not a good form of government after all. For, as Elster correctly notes, the permanent flux of magistrates and political personnel that would be "coming and going" under such a system would ultimately serve democracy quite "badly." Thus, lottery seems to be a democratic Trojan horse insofar as it cannot live up to its principle of "equality of probability": although it avoids producing permanent minorities and a permanent political class, it cannot effectively realize public goals for the simple reason that it cannot produce a functional and coherent group that governs. Ultimately, elections are required as a correction to such a disjointed dynamic since they make accountability possible. This severe disadvantage of lottery requires additional thought that Elster's analysis only vaguely gestures toward.

In order to evaluate the role that lotteries play in decision-making systems we must, in Elster's words, be attentive to criteria of both "context" and "function"—that is, we must make a distinction between the "formation" of a lawmaking assembly and the subsequent "organization" and "functioning" of that assembly over its term. With respect to this latter day-to-day organization and functioning, "the drawing of lots can be an instrument for integrating the mechanisms of mandate representation." For instance, drawn lots could be used to regulate either the formation of parliamentary committees (or other working groups) or agenda-setting itself—which could be randomly set by lot rather than by majority vote or a compromise among lawmakers)[61]. However, when it comes to the "formation" of any given cohort of assembly members, democracy does not require us to use a lottery. This is precisely because of the nonintentional or nonvolitional nature of lotteries: while they do ensure that all citizens have an equal probability to serve, they do not afford the citizenry political control over the sorted few. As discussed in the following chapters, lottery does not allow for relations of accountability and this is a necessary condition of political freedom. In a lottocratic scenario like ancient Athens, control over the magistrates comes from the law itself. Lottery is secured from corrupt manipulation if punishment for corruption is backed by authority (legal sanctions) rather than being secured by reliance on the electorate's judgment (horizontal accountability); clearly, this same dynamic imposes a specifically legalized system of censorship on society.

Elster concluded his analysis by emphasizing an unsolvable contradiction: a perfect democratic method of selection (lottery) fails when it comes to accountability *because* it does not make room for the formation of a political class that can govern. Within an electoral system, the mechanism of reelection is "not simply a source of vulnerability to special-interest groups." Instead, Elster acknowledged that reelection

---

[61] Ibid., 90.

is a condition of political accountability such that, without it, "the temptation to plunder the spoils of incumbency might be overwhelming."[62] He therefore suggested that lotteries and short-term rotations in the legislature should be confined to the day-to-day working processes that are used within parliament and its committees—for instance, in order to decide upon the order of issues to be discussed; or by using lot to assign members to various key congressional committees so as to neutralize the corrupting power of lobby groups and special interests.

As with Dahl, for Elster the most promising use of a lottery within democracy ends up being an auxiliary role with respect to the outcomes of elections rather than a replacement for or complement to elections. Elster concluded that "on balance" and in certain key domains, it would be less problematic to side with values such as continuity of political personnel, institutional memory, and accountability even if by doing so we created potential setbacks for values like honesty and transparency.[63] In Elster's book, he makes a persuasive case that redistricting is the specific domain related to lawmaking where randomness would have positive democratic side effects. Especially in the United States, this is a plausible argument, as redistricting ideally seeks to adjust the number of representatives so as to keep pace with demographic changes, but the American reality is that it has become irrevocably tainted by incentives to gerrymander.

We can conclude by paraphrasing Jane Mansbridge: once we find that institutions and procedures comport with democratic principles, "contingency" is an important criterion to use when evaluating their impact. This insight seems particularly true for lotteries, as their beneficial qualities might be lost if they were applied in the wrong contexts. While Elster tried to make a case for bringing lotteries into the lawmaking process, in the end he concluded that the disadvantages outweigh the advantages: a parliament chosen by lot would generate such intractable problems that the effectiveness and legitimacy of the democratic decision-making system itself would be jeopardized.

1.1.3 Bernard Manin

While Elster's analysis failed to show that a democratic government based entirely on the lottery was feasible and desirable, it nevertheless launched a broad theoretical inquiry about the meaning of elections and representation. Bernard Manin's *The Principles of Representative Government* (1997) followed this lead. This is a seminal book that tries to uncover systematic and conceptual links between democracy and lottery, on the one hand, and between elections and "aristocracy" or oligarchy, on the other. Manin's work became an indispensable source of inspiration for the lottocratic mentality that would follow.[64] Manin did not advocate lottocracy.

---

[62] Ibid., 89.

[63] Ibid.

[64] In France, this book also helped lottery to become the symbol of a citizen-based movement against the approval of the Constitutional Treaty of Europe in the referendum of 2005; Samuel Hayat, "La carrière

40   The Lottocratic Mentality

Indeed, he explicitly tried to defend the democratic credentials of representative government. But, in retrospect, we can identify two main strains of his thought that lottocrats used to establish "a link between democracy and the drawing of lots, both in political theory and in the activist world":[65] first, an interpretative revision of the traditional distinction between "direct" and "indirect" democracy; and second, the thought that elections are inherently "aristocratic" (or oligarchic) even if they can be made to work passably well in contexts of "impure" representative democracies.

1.1.3.1 On the Meaning of Direct Democracy

Aristotle's assertion that elections were inherently oligarchic (thus undemocratic) had a ripple effect throughout subsequent political history and theory. This claim was picked up and repeated by James W. Headlam in the late nineteenth century. In 1951, Gaetano De Sanctis repeated the same claim: in the context of writing about the Athenian oligarchy of 411, he noted that the "boulé of the Five Hundred drawn by lot was the palladium of democracy." George Sabine then popularized this claim among political scientists in 1959 when he claimed that "elections are according to Greek ideas an aristocratic method."[66] Maurice Pope reiterated similar claims in a manuscript that was written and circulated in the 1980s and posthumously published in 2023 as *The Keys to Democracy: Sortition as a New Model for Citizen Power.*[67]

Obviously, these associations have been around for quite some time. However, Manin's unique contribution was that his argument in defense of a democratic lottery and against the supposedly aristocratic or oligarchic nature of elections is itself set within a revisionist interpretation of the traditional distinction between "direct" and "indirect" democracy.[68] His revision relies on two basic ideas: first, within the context of our representative governments "elections treat citizens unequally as candidates," but in the context of ancient Athens lotteries gave every citizen an equal chance of being chosen; thus, the idea that our contemporary form of democracy "empowers

---

militante de la référence à Bernard Manin dans les mouvements français pour le tirage au sort," *Participations*, hors série (2019): 440, https://www.cairn.info/revue-participations-2019-HS-page-437.html (accessed April 30, 2023). Hayat also explains that the "rediscovery" of lottery in France occurred in the 1990s, the same decade in which Manin worked and published his book.

[65] Ibid., 437.

[66] James Wycliffe Headlam, *Election by Lot at Athens* (Cambridge: Cambridge University Press, 1891); Gaetano De Sanctis, *Studi di storia della storiografia greca* (Florence: La Nuova Italia, 1951); George Sabine, *History of Political Theory* (New York: Holt, 1959), 82. For an outline of the modern interpretations of the ancient usages of lottery and election, see Buchstein, "Countering," 127–9.

[67] Maurice Pope, *The Keys to Democracy: Sortition as a New Model for Citizen Power*, with a foreword by Hélène Landemore and a preface by Paul Cartledge (Exeter: Imprint Academic, 2023).

[68] On using the terms "aristocratic" and "oligarchic" interchangeably (a posture that finds inspiration in Aristotle) there is a rich debate among ancient historians, who have almost entirely abandoned the label of "aristocrats" in favor of "elites," which then brings the term closer to an oligarchy. The argument concerns the absence, even in the archaic period, of blood nobility, or even of elites stable enough to constitute aristocracies—there was great fluidity at all times, and much upward and downward social mobility; see Nick R. Fisher and Hans van Wees, eds., 'Aristocracy' in Antiquity: Redefining Greek and Roman Elites (Swansea: Classical Press of Wales, 2015) and Matthew Simonton, *Classical Greek Oligarchy: A Political History* (Princeton, NJ: Princeton University Press, 2017), 8n, 22.

us as individuals" is inaccurate since it in fact "empowers groups" or parties insofar as we risk powerlessness if we do not affiliate ourselves with a certain voting block[69]; and second, a close study of democracy in ancient Athens helps us to see it is "a mistake" to think that it was "entirely" *direct* (if we use "direct" to characterize the lawmaking power of the Assembly and the absence of electoral representation) since it hosted "a myriad of representative institutions that engaged the energies of citizens outside the Assembly" through random selection by lot.[70] We can find some version of these ideas in nearly all contemporary writings that suppose lottocracy is the best form of democracy. While Manin's book was not a defense of lottocracy as a system, it nevertheless launched the "democracy thesis of the lottery" by setting up a direct comparison between ancient and contemporary democracies that was based in their selection methods rather than a comparison based in how citizens participated in lawmaking.[71]

Manin took up Elster's suggestions and directly compared lotteries with elections in order to answer three questions. First, what makes representative government different from direct government? Second, does democracy have its own internally appropriate method for selecting political personnel? Third, why did elections ultimately come to replace lotteries even though lotteries were widely used in both ancient democracy and early-modern republics? Manin's interrelated answers to these questions also form the central thesis of his book: the unique feature that characterizes democracy is *not* so much the direct presence of the citizens in the Assembly but rather selection by lot. Lottery solves the main problem of direct self-government: citizens cannot do everything together simultaneously, so there must be a division between doers and nondoers that does *not* violate democratic equality. Like Elster before him, Manin thinks that equality is the principle of democracy and moreover that it consists in an "equality of probability" of being selected to fulfill public functions and offices. Lottery creates a division between rulers and ruled without opening a gap between them and without producing an elite. Manin primarily relies on Aristotle for this claim—returning repeatedly to several passages from Aristotle's *Politics*. Aristotle was one of several theorists who criticized the Periclean model of democracy as too extreme. He explained that, in Athens, citizens ruled and were ruled "in turn" through a combination of rotation and lottery—the citizen is the one who participates in governing (*archein*) and is governed (*archesthai*) in turn. Hence, "political freedom" (*eleutheria*) meant obeying not only oneself but "to someone on whose place one would be tomorrow."[72]

In direct democracy, the central problem is how we can justify indirect forms of participation in government. Clearly, in the context of ancient direct democracy, lotteries can help us resolve this problem while the Assembly cannot. Yet, Manin's

---

[69] Jason Brennan and Hélène Landemore, *Debating Democracy: Do We Need More or Less?* (Oxford: Oxford University Press, 2022), 3 and 5–6.

[70] Fishkin, *Voice of the People*, 18.

[71] For the "democratic thesis of the lottery" see Buchstein, "Countering."

[72] Bernard Manin, *The Principles of Representative Government* (Cambridge: Cambridge University Press, 1997), 28.

42 The Lottocratic Mentality

examination of lotteries and his analysis of Aristotle are situated within an intellectual current formed in response to and that at least partially challenges contemporary institutions of representative government. This perspective is quite far from Aristotle's context, and it drew its main inspiration from figures such as Francesco Guicciardini, Montesquieu, and Carl Schmitt.

In Guicciardini's *Dialogo* (1511–1513), we find a stark dualism set up between elections (which are associated with an oligarchy or the *ottimati*) and "selection by lot" (which would not "exclude the rest of us forever" from public offices);[73] in Montesquieu's *The Spirit of the Laws* (1748), we find that drawing by lot is the cornerstone of democracy and should be of interest to those who study democratic institutions;[74] Montesquieu's dualism came to be rephrased almost verbatim by Schmitt in his *Constitutional Theory* (1928).[75] The intellectual current that these theorists formed is the main plotline of Manin's book, where "oligarchy" is also used as "aristocracy."[76] Manin's narrative profoundly changed contemporary theorists' understanding of the relationship between direct and indirect democracy. At the same time, his work lent unwittingly strong support to lottocrats' claim that elections are out of step with democracy. Indeed, when Manin asks, "But then what, in this case, does 'direct democracy' mean?" he answers that it must mean horizontal selection or selection by lot rather than "being identical to or identified with the people."[77]

Manin was incredibly innovative in that he reoriented democratic theory *away* from "directness" and also revived interest in the value and meaning of representation. We can truly appreciate just how radical these interventions were if we take stock of the political–theoretical context in which he wrote. When Manin published his book, most scholars of democracy still regarded representation as an ancillary topic and representative government as a betrayal of genuinely democratic participation. While a few pioneering scholars such as David Plotke and George Kateb defended representation as a form of participation and opinion formation that was crucial to democracy, throughout the democratic theory of that time these authors were the exception that proved the general rule.[78]

---

[73] Francesco Guicciardini, *Dialogo del reggimento di Firenze*, ed. Gian Mario Anselmi and Carlo Varotti (Turin: Bollati Boringhieri, 1994), 41–2; Montesquieu, *The Spirit of the Laws* (1748), trans. Anne M. Cohler, Basia Carolyn Miller, and Harold Samuel Stone (Cambridge: Cambridge University Press, 1989), 13 (bk. 2, chap. 2). The French text has "suffrage" not "voting," so we amended the translation adopted by Cambridge Press. Carl Schmitt, *Constitutional Theory* (1928), trans. and ed. Jeffrey Seitzer, foreword by Ellen Kennedy (Durham, NC: Duke University Press, 2008), 284.

[74] Montesquieu notes, "suffrage by *lot* is in the nature of democracy; suffrage by *choice* is the nature of aristocracy." However, here he drops the term "oligarchy" (which was also used by Aristotle in his *Politics*) for the more praiseworthy term of "aristocracy." This change would fit well with the Federalists' belief that elections serve to select virtuous and "enlightened" "statesmen."

[75] Schmitt, *Constitutional Theory*, § 19.

[76] In talking of Aristotle, Manin writes that "lot is described as the democratic selection method, while election is seen as more oligarchic or aristocratic" (Manin, *The Principles*, 27). See in this chapter footnote 68. The term "aristocracy" proves more malleable to the qualities of the individual candidates that modern voters evaluate and choose.

[77] Ibid., 25.

[78] "The opposite of representation is not participation. The opposite of representation is exclusion. And the opposite of participation is abstention. . . . Representation is not an unfortunate compromise

Generally speaking, both proponents and critics of direct democracy modeled their views on Rousseau, who, in *The Social Contract* (1762), wrote that citizens who vote for representatives are sovereign only on election day. Even avowed liberals like Benjamin Constant shared this view: he compared popular sovereignty in election-based governments to a comet that vanishes the moment it materializes. Up until the late twentieth century, political theorists of all stripes shared this eighteenth-century view that identified sovereignty with "the will" (of the sovereign) and which then concluded that "the people" *cannot* delegate its will and remain sovereign at the same time. This set up a taken-for-granted dualism between true (participatory and direct) democracy and indirect (representative and electoral) democracy that remained unquestioned until Manin's book. Manin followed the general framework of Guicciardini, Montesquieu, and Schmitt in that he constructed a comparative political history that used systems of selection as its core conceptual pivot;[79] this allowed him to rescue representative government from the charge of being undemocratic by changing the central terms of comparison. Manin went back to Athens but depicted it anew: now the Assembly receded into the background, and selection by lottery was conceptually foregrounded.

This move raises the natural question: *Which* Athens? Manin did not utilize a generic historical notion of Athenian democracy. For example, instead of looking to the age of Pericles, he chose to focus his comparative lens on fourth-century Athenian democracy, which Aristotle had characterized as a more moderate form of democracy. Historically speaking, this was the last form democracy took before Philip of Macedonia conquered the city and installed an oligarchic regime in 332. Thus, 181 years after Solon's constitution, both the autonomy of the Athenian city–state and its democratic government came to an end.[80]

According to Manin, in the final decades of its existence (the so-called "age of Demosthenes"), Athens embodied a mixed model of government that nicely illustrated his thesis. After two coups and several reforms, Athenian democracy took on a final institutional form that relegated the Assembly to the minimal role of ratifying proposals that came from a Council of 500 hundred allotted citizens (*boulē*) ("half of them voted on by the Assembly [so as to] seem in fact to have been ratifications"). The Assembly also voted on decisions that were then forwarded on to separate councils of jurors (chosen by lot) for consideration, and these councils were responsible for compiling or enacting legislation (*nomothetai*). The councils were responsible for examining any proposed changes to the laws that were passed by

---

between an ideal of direct democracy and messy modern realities. Representation is crucial in constituting democratic practices." David Plotke, "Representation Is Democracy," *Constellations* 4, no. 1 (1997): 19.

[79] This was also dear to Rousseau of course who followed Jean Bodin and characterized representative government as an aristocratic form of power; see Nadia Urbinati, "Continuity and Rupture: The Power of Judgment in Democratic Representation," *Constellations* 12 (2005): 194–222. Yet, when he had to design the institutions of the republic, Rousseau embraced elections rather than lottery or rotation (which he characterized as democratic), and in order to amend the aristocratic character of elections, he changed the statute of representation from trusteeship to delegation with an imperative mandate.

[80] The regime continued unaltered after the battle of Chaeronea in 338 and was only overturned (and transformed into a short-lived oligarchy) by Antipater in 322—after the death of Alexander and the ensuing revolt against the Macedonians (the so-called "Lamian War").

44 The Lottocratic Mentality

the Assembly and ensuring that they were consistent with the existing body of law (*graphē paranomōn* was the name of the legal action). Thus, on Manin's telling, while the Assembly played a part in the overall legislative process, the councils made the final decisions: in the fourth century, "legislative activity invariably took the form of revision, with the Assembly retaining the initiative, but the final decision being taken by the *nomothetai*, following adversarial proceedings. . . . So, in the fourth century, legislative decisions as such were in the hands of an organ distinct from the Assembly and appointed by lot."[81]

Manin's account here makes two important claims: that the *nomothetai* were external to the Assembly and that, in the fourth century, the Assembly did not carry out any real legislative activity. These claims are controversial. As we detail in the second part of the chapter, recent research suggests that these characterizations are inaccurate. First, the *nomothetai* were an incarnation of the Assembly itself rather than an external body. Second, the role of *nomothetein* was narrower than the modern sense of lawmaking because it was limited to *nomoi* (general permanent rules) but did not extend to decrees (the closest equivalent to ordinary lawmaking). Thus, much of what we take to be a modern legislature's "legislative activity" was indeed undertaken by the Athenian Assembly. Manin also makes the claim that, on the whole, selection by lot had more of a determinate impact than direct participation in the Assembly. The fact that Manin framed selection by lot as opening up space for a "moderate" version of democratic lawmaking has caused a persistent misunderstanding among contemporary lottocrats: they rely on Manin's account to back their claim that the penultimate form of Athenian democracy primarily used the lottery to make laws instead of the Assembly.

Manin's reading relied on an influential book written by the Danish historian of antiquity Mogens H. Hansen: *The Athenian Democracy in the Age of Demosthenes* (translated into English in 1991). By undertaking a detailed reconstruction of Athenian procedures and institutions, Hansen showed that late Athenian democracy selected governmental personnel for functions that rotated annually. This meant that everyone could serve the public at least twice in their adult lives if they wished—each citizen could stand for selection by lot according to the principle of *ho boulomenos* ("whoever wishes"). Much like Aristotle's *Politics* had claimed: the sign of a true democracy was taken to be governing and being governed in turn rather than governing all at once. Thus, this particular system of government was predicated on selection by lot and the division of political labor.

Manin's book built on these historical insights to suggest that the so-called "direct democracy" in Athens was actually indirect in several ways. According to Manin, it was, in certain respects, much more like our representative democracy than one might have assumed; the main *difference consisted in the mode of selection*. Manin repeatedly invites readers to compare our representative democracy with a government ruled by magistrates chosen by lot rather than to compare it with a system of direct democratic self-government: "So if we wish to throw light on one of the major

---

[81] Manin, *The Principles*, 23.

The Lottery Revival   **45**

differences between representative government and 'direct' democracy, we need to compare the effects of election with those of lot."[82]

As we noted, Manin's goal was to defend representative government against critiques that were common at the time. The main critics he had in mind were essentially the heirs of Antifederalist thought from the eighteenth century: those American founders and their disciples who, in arguing about the proper way to institutionalize representative government, had adamantly maintained that self-government was incompatible with elections. They held this view because they thought that elections made representation the construction of candidate-led constituencies rather than, as John Adams would later put it, an "exact portrait, in miniature, of the people at large."[83] This is clearly along the lines of the "mirroring" conception of representation. While the Antifederalists did not have the idea of random statistical selection from among the population in mind, and they certainly did not refer to lotteries, they nevertheless advanced a vision of representation that was based on small constituencies and not achieved through elections. This framework would inspire the citizen assembly movements that began in the last decades of the twentieth century.

In order to counter this trend, Manin revived ideas from the eighteenth-century Federalists. The Federalists had sought to distance representative government from democracy (which they deemed a poor form of government) and had argued that a main virtue of their proposed regime was that it assigned no institutional role to the assembled people: in the *Federalist Papers* elections are often approvingly described as functioning to exclude the many (or as undemocratic) and to instead wisely select the competent and virtuous few who can then be entrusted with advancing proposals that best serve the nation's interest. In the eighteenth century, the same basic idea was also explicitly put forward by Montesquieu and Sieyes; ironically, this same idea was later deployed by scholars who wished to *criticize* representative democracy.[84]

In short, when we place Manin's interpretive reading in the context of the intellectual milieu in which it was written, we can see that it was directed against the intellectual heirs of Antifederalism: those who thought that the idea of self-government was opposed to elections and who endorsed a "mirroring" conception of representation over a political-mandate conception of representation. Yet, by placing his gloss of late Athenian democracy and its use of lotteries against the backdrop of these contrasts, he also tacitly contrasted elections with lotteries. His argument easily lent itself to a conclusion that he did not advocate but which lottocrats were only too happy to make: if it is true that the touchstone of democracy is *not* the presence of citizens in the Assembly *but* rather (as the Antifederalists maintained)

---

[82] Ibid., 10.

[83] John Adams, "Letter to John Penn," in *The Works of John Adams*, vol. 4 (Boston, MA: Little and Brown, 1851), 205. The French revolutionary Honoré Gabriel Mirabeau coined the image of the "representative body" as a "map" of the nation, "in part or in whole the copy must always have the same proportions as the original" (which looks like an anticipation of the lottocrats' idea of a miniaturized sample); see Pitkin, *The Concept of Representation*, 62.

[84] Notably by Schmitt, whose work (as mentioned) exerted an important influence on Manin's argument.

46   The Lottocratic Mentality

a random system of selection that sociologically reproduces the nation in miniature, then representation can be operationalized not only by elections but also by
lotteries—indeed, lotteries might even be the best way to reconcile representation
with democracy.[85] Thus, ironically, in building his argument against the Antifederalists, Manin inadvertently offered subsequent lottocrats a readymade scheme of
argumentation: we could reconstruct the genealogy of the main institutions of representative government, principally elections, in order to reveal their antidemocratic
core. The basic logic of elections had remained constant throughout the centuries,
even as suffrage had expanded, political parties had grown, and a panoply of intermediary agencies had arisen in order to construct the representative system. Thus,
if one could genealogically reveal the central conceptual problem of elections, then
this would have radically revisionist implications for our understanding of how we
should operationalize genuine democracy.

Manin's use of history to address theoretical questions about the conceptual core
of democracy (be it direct or indirect) also led him to investigate the factors that
caused the moderns to largely abandon lotteries.[86] As mentioned earlier, Dahl and
Elster had already surveyed why lotteries had declined among the moderns. Manin
returned to this topic and gave a two-pronged answer that fits with elections rather
than lottery: he emphasized how modern political subjects placed increasing importance on the competence of political leaders; and he emphasized the role of consent
in the choice of candidates. These two factors explain why the moderns gave a hegemonic role to elections even though the ancients used both elections and lotteries.
This shift occurred despite the fact that the moderns clearly thought elections were
undemocratic, albeit for far different reasons than those we find convincing today.
Manin's descriptions of Athens and the Italian republics, refracted through the lenses
of Aristotle and Guicciardini, attract contemporary lottocrats. These historical narratives appear to give an authoritative argument that counters the idea that elections
can be democratic and which also suggests lotteries as a natural alternative. Such
narratives also suggest lotteries have several attractive features in that they satisfy an
epistemic goal (good deliberation and respect for the general interest), safeguard the
quality of deliberation (by avoiding elitism and parties), respect democratic equality,
and realize justice as impartiality (by avoiding corruption and the unfair treatment
of candidates).

Manin's work inspired a new generation of democratic theorists who grew up after
the golden age of participatory democracy, when the rediscovery of representation
and, specifically, *deliberative* theories of democracy worked together to reemphasize
the importance of mediated forms of participation and decision-making. But while
his goal was to defend the representative government against critiques that came from
participatory theories of democracy, he unwittingly opened the door for a conception

---

[85] On the link between lottery, pictorial representation, and sampling, see Philip Pettit, "Meritocratic Representation," in *The East Asian Challenge for Democracy: Political Meritocracy in Comparative
Perspective*, ed. D. A. Bell and C. Li (Cambridge: Cambridge University Press, 2013), 138–60.

[86] His investigation strayed from the actual views of American or French revolutionaries, whose
polemical target was direct government rather than lottery itself.

The Lottery Revival   47

of democracy that put elections on trial in the name of representation by lotteries. Ironically, an advocate of the realist theory of representative government like Manin handed the new critics of elections their most formidable argument.

1.1.3.2 Voluntary Decision and Equality of Probability

Manin's analysis shows that, ultimately, direct democracy and representative government are not necessarily in opposition to one another. For, even in the purest case of classical direct democracy, the Assembly was under the authority of the *nomothetai*. But Manin's clarificatory analysis poses another question: What does "direct" democracy mean? In his view, the core of direct democracy stems not so much from the right of adult male citizens to sit in the *ekklēsia* and vote on the laws but rather from the power to volunteer for administrative functions. This reading changes the way we interpret representative government. The electoral foundation of representative government has traditionally been identified with anti-absolutism.[87] This ideological current hit its peak with the English Revolution, when the election of members of parliament became a symbol of the struggle of "commoners" against the hereditary functions traditionally held by both the nobility and the absolute monarch. Over time, elections became a bastion of legitimacy because they gave primacy to those who were bound by the laws. This primacy slowly accrued in virtue of a transformation of the nature of politics that ascribed natural rights to individual persons—a transformation that, when institutionally realized, would justify the right of free and voluntary voting as well as the majority principle. "This belief that consent constitutes the sole source of legitimate authority and forms the basis of political obligation was shared by all Natural Law theorists from Grotius to Rousseau, including Hobbes, Pufendorf, and Locke."[88] In both lottery and elections, equality and voluntary participation were shared bedrock values. But, this was a superficial similarity since the lottery relied on a different *kind* of equality—it is *this distinction* that differentiates the two modes of selection.[89]

Manin's argument amends the traditional reading of representative government by way of interpreting equality in a fashion that not only involves but also changes the meaning of voluntariness. First, he problematizes the traditional opposition between elected and hereditary government in order to bring out an aspect of representative government that "remains hidden so long as the hereditary system constitutes the sole point of contrast."[90] This hidden aspect is, of course, the mechanism of lottery, which embodies a different kind of equality.

As we noted above, Manin's argument derives from *The Spirit of the Laws*, where Montesquieu explicitly claims that regimes have to be studied in relation to their systems of selection: "Just as the division of those having the right to vote is a

---

[87] On the elected parliament as anti-absolutism revolution, see Schmitt's *Constitutional Theory*, a text that is extremely important for Manin's argument.

[88] Manin, *The Principles*, 84.

[89] Manin mentions Schmitt's commenting on lot as "the method that best guarantees an identity between rulers and ruled" (*The Principles*, 100 n80).

[90] Ibid., 11.

48 The Lottocratic Mentality

fundamental law in the republic, the way of casting a vote is another fundamental law. Voting by *lot* is the nature of democracy; voting by *choice* is the nature of aristocracy." Lottery protects equality in power, and elections protect the liberty to compete. Moreover, lottery is "a way of electing that distresses no one; it leaves to each citizen a reasonable expectation of serving his country." Lotteries do not discriminate because they do not entail competition and give everyone a realistic hope of serving the republic, sooner or later.[91] Rousseau came to the same basic conclusion even more explicitly: "Elections by lot would have few disadvantages in a true democracy where all things being equal both in mores and talents as well as in maxims and fortunes, the choice would become almost indifferent."[92] Manin follows this Montesquieu–Rousseau path, but it is worth mentioning that it is quite different from the account given by Aristotle, who analyzed and evaluated selection procedures not in the abstract but as part of a variety of constitutions and with reference to the "parts" (*merē* or *moirai* of the *polis*) or the socioeconomic classes within society that had varying degrees of access to power.[93] Thus, Manin essentially deploys Aristotle in a non-Aristotelian manner: he isolates the procedures of selection from the socioeconomic powers that, according to Aristotle, defines political regimes. We will return to this issue later. At present, we need to focus on the two normative principles that regulate methods of selection: the principle of equality and the voluntariness of citizens' decision to serve in public office. Recall that in Athens, neither lotteries nor elections drew from a generalized pool of "all citizens." Instead, each drew on only those over the age of 30 years who also "offered themselves as candidates." The self-selection of more prominent citizens as candidates helped provide some reassurance concerning performing one's duties effectively and the requisite responsibility to serve in important civic positions. The real point of contrast between the two selection procedures was *equality*. To appreciate the originality of Manin's theoretical move here, his treatment of lottery must be compared with Hansen's.

Hansen approached equality through the lens of a well-known distinction between "negative" and "positive" freedom. To paraphrase Constant: this distinction is often cast as the difference between the liberty of the moderns and the liberty of the ancients. Hansen's aim was to resist the dominant trend in the literature that contrasted the two liberties and thereby associated the moderns with legal or formal equality ("equality of opportunity") and the ancients with substantive equality ("equal in everything"). In opposition to this framework, Hansen sought to vindicate the "liberal" nature of ancient political freedom. "Selection by lot," Hansen writes, "was believed to be a more 'democratic' method of appointment than election. Modern historians often connected the democratic preference for sortition with the democratic belief in equality: but, once again, it is only the critics of democracy who

---

[91] Montesquieu, *The Spirit of the Laws*, 3 (bk. 2, chap. 2).

[92] Rousseau, *The Social Contract*, bk. 4, chap. 3, in *The Basic Political Writings*, trans. Donald A. Cress (Indianapolis, IN: Hackett, 1987), 207–8.

[93] See the illuminating article by Canevaro and Esu, "Extreme Democracy and Mixed Constitution in Theory and Practice."

connected sortition with equality, whereas the democrats themselves seem to have preferred sortition not because of its being the obvious method of selection when all are alike, but because it safeguarded the powers of the people, prevented conflict and counteracted corruption."[94] Hansen was trying to prove that Athenian democracy was never predicated on an attempt to make citizens equal in every respect: "equality before the law" was "a matter of normative, not natural, noun" such that citizens "may differ in wealth, power, social status, cleverness or eloquence," but they "all ought to be equally treated by the law."[95]

In short, to Hansen the narrative that liberal thinkers from Constant until Isaiah Berlin had maintained is unwarranted. While liberal thinkers had often characterized the liberty of the ancients as something close to the Jacobin project, ancient liberty (certainly that of the Athenian republic) was, in fact, perfectly compatible with the liberal tradition. Hansen wanted to distance lottery from radical democracy, at least in part as an indirect response to both the supporters and critics of direct democracy. He was particularly keen to respond to critics who called lottery (and thereby democracy) into question based on the lack of competence and accountability that it was supposed to generate. Hansen argued that while critics of direct democracy linked "lottery to equality," ancient Athenians apparently preferred lottery *not* because it was an "obvious method of selection when all are equal, but because it safeguarded the powers of the people, prevented conflict and counteracted corruption." For Hansen, lottery was primarily connected to *equality before the law and stability* (antifactionalism) rather than any more radical notion of equality. He questioned the liberal shibboleth that democracy sacrificed liberty on the altar of equality and indirectly raised the question of the *type of equality* at the heart of lottery. This was a question that Manin would pick up and develop, although only after he made an important conceptual move.

Manin reinterpreted equality in a way that allowed him to contrast lotteries with elections: neither "equality of opportunity" nor "radical equality" were the basis of lottery. These two types of equality were consistent with the conceptions that had been developed by modern societies: liberal equality of opportunity and radical substantive equality realized through participatory democracy. Unlike Hansen, Manin claimed that the Athenians themselves were not conceptually aware of the distinct two forms of equality that Hansen had ascribed to them (thereby implying that they were also unaware of the attendant distinction among liberties: liberty as enjoying equal opportunity to develop individual "talents" versus liberty of all citizens to rule contemporarily).[96] First, the voluntary choice to serve the Athenian polis did not reflect some underlying idea of natural-formal rights or equal opportunity to compete. Second, equal rights to participate did not stem from a substantive model of equality but instead grew out of the internal logic of rotation. Let's unpack these points.

---

[94] Hansen, *The Athenian Democracy*, 84.
[95] Ibid.
[96] Ibid., 85.

50 The Lottocratic Mentality

Like Hansen, Manin utilized the twofold conception of "arithmetical" and "geometrical" equality that we find in both Plato's *Laws* and Aristotle's *Politics*. Arithmetical equality belonged to radical democracy, which held that citizens who were equal as freeborn must be equal in all respects. Oligarchs subscribed to geometrical equality, which held that only those who were equal in merit or wealth should be treated equally and that, accordingly, only *they* should be entrusted with public functions. The basic logic of the two types of equality—treating the equals equally—was the same; what changed was the "basket" of who the equals were.[97]

Plato and Aristotle criticized these two versions of equality when they were practiced as "simple" types. They thus criticized both pure democracy and pure oligarchy.[98] For them, a good government mixed the two "pure" opposites and thereby also combined equality of opportunity with substantive equality. Unlike Hansen, Manin thought fourth-century Athenian democracy provided precisely this type of mixed equality and, just as Elster had anticipated, that it yielded a *third form of equality* (*equality of probability*) which supported the use of lotteries: "The equality achieved by the use of lot was certainly not equality of opportunity as we understand it today, since it did not distribute offices in accordance with talent and effort. Neither was it the same as what we call equality of outcome: it did not give everyone equal share. However, this double difference does not prove that lot had nothing to do with equality, because equality may also assume the third form, which modern theories of justice overlook, namely the equal probability of obtaining a thing."[99]

Manin calls this third form "democratic" equality. He conceptualized it as belonging to a democracy where the core institutions were sorted bodies *rather than* an Assembly. His reading challenges the idea that democratic equality rules out the use of selective criteria and that all citizens must do in a democracy is simultaneously "rule" in some fashion. When taken in isolation, the Athenian Assembly was based on a nonselective model of self-government (radical democracy) that realized arithmetical equality. Lotteries then were the distinctive mechanism that enabled the realization of mixed equality, especially when, as in Athens, they were based on an age threshold and citizens' voluntary choice to serve. Lottery was the only selection mechanism that was consistent with "democratic equality" because it guaranteed "anyone *who so desired*—the 'first comer'—the chance to play a prominent part in politics." The voluntary dimension (the free choice to join the government) and the equality of probability (to nominate oneself to serve the public) were the twin

---

[97] Aristotle explains that both the equality of democrats and that of oligarchs are understood and conceptualized as geometric (i.e., *kat'axian*, according to value, according to merit), and since the value criterion favored by the democrats is free birth, for them all who are free deserve equal consideration, so to speak, so that when viewed from the outside their equality looks arithmetical. I thank Mirko Canevaro for inviting me to see the overlap between arithmetical and geometrical equality (we will come back to this in the second part of this chapter). Manin recognizes that Aristotle acknowledges that "this" (i.e., democratic) definition "constitutes a particular version of the true concept of justice" and that the merit of the equal birth is the source of the wrong because this makes all "equal in every respect"—this predisposes democracy toward selection by lot as the only consistent selection method (*The Principles*, 37).

[98] Aristocracy, while good in theory, risks becoming a bad regime, an oligarchic regime, if it rules alone or as "pure" form.

[99] Manin, *The Principles*, 40.

pillars of lotteries. Lottery was the only *genuinely democratic method of selection.*[100] On such a reading, the distance between lottery and election could not have been greater. Lottery alone was consistent with "democratic equality" because it did not distribute power "exactly" but rather distributed "the (mathematical) probability of achieving power"; in contrast, elections stressed freedom by granting every citizen the opportunity to choose.[101]

Manin does not deny that elections secure equality among candidates. He argues that with elections, "everyone shares the same starting line" but that the final distribution is "determined solely by individual merit." If a candidate is chosen, then this entails that they have met voters' wishes and were preferred over other candidates. This overall logic is completely foreign within a lottery, where a failure to be chosen does not depend upon another's will.[102] Elections were ruled by a logic that fits within the aristocratic paradigm of being qualified for a position based upon merit or other personal qualities. Thus, it is correct to say that equality is at the core of both lottery and elections. But the type of equality is different and the one that fits democracy is associated with the probability of being selected. As for freedom (which Aristotle's *Politics* claims has a central role in a democracy), it is relegated to peripheral importance—essentially, one should obey now in the hope of ruling tomorrow.

In sum, while equality of outcomes entails a "radical" democracy that is directly participatory and equality of opportunity entails that candidates share the same "starting line" and no predetermined result (elections), democratic equality entails "the equal probability of obtaining something" and is based upon an utterly unique condition: that *individual choice lies only in the decision to voluntarily nominate oneself* (those who so desire) *for either the process of selection or direct participation in the assembly.* In neither case does competition take place. In sum, elections were an eccentric institutional outlier vis-à-vis the most characteristic and distinctive form of democratic equality since, in contradiction to democracy, they were primed to form a political class or a system of leadership. At the same time, it is important to see that the type of equality that lotteries realized was also *not* radical equality in all respects of the sort aimed at by proposals for all citizens to participate in all functions of self-government.

According to Manin, any comparison between direct and representative government must, therefore, focus *not on the form of presence* in the place where laws are decided but rather, as Montesquieu clarified, on "the way of casting the vote" or *the method of selection* used to choose political personnel. Choosing a procedure or method of selection for key governmental positions is something that no democracy can avoid and which every democracy must make compatible with its underlying egalitarian principle. Elections have nothing to do with either direct self-government (radical democracy) or equality of probability (moderate democracy). Rather, elections rely on dynamics of competition that end up categorically excluding

---

[100] Ibid., 38 and 34.
[101] Ibid., 39.
[102] Ibid., 34.

and disenfranchising some portion of the population. In this sense, elections are not democratic. From this conclusion it is not hard to see how one might make the further implication that lotteries do not exclude because they are not based, as Dahl put it, on the "criterion of choice."

Summing up, according to Manin, Athens had a sophisticated system of indirect self-government. The Assembly was an arena in which rhetoric aroused agonism and exalted individual personalities; its decisions consisted of decrees. However, lotteries ultimately "constituted truly political authority" in the polis. They governed the selection of the people's court and the legislative oversight councils that, in determining the admissibility of proposals and whether decrees were consistent with the existing ones, ultimately rendered "final decisions" on the work of the Assembly. Selection by lot excluded all forms of distinction, competition, and discrimination. Lotteries made it impossible for rhetorically skillful citizens to influence decisions (this was not entirely successful at the margins, so to speak, as Athens often used ostracism to expel powerful citizens deemed "too dangerous" for democracy). Ultimately, on Manin's telling, direct self-government played a minor role and was under the control of a select few. Yet the equality on which democracy is based is associated to the right-power to contribute, directly or indirectly, to the making of collective decisions, not to the equal probability, in a statistical sense, of being drawn to office. We believe that in his defense of the democratic nature of the lottery, Manin overlooks this crucial distinction.[103] In the last section of this chapter, we will return to this argument. It has become a mainstay of the lottocratic mentality which holds that elections are undemocratic and should be supplemented or even replaced by the lottery.

1.1.3.3 Lottery beyond Democracy

Manin put forward two fundamental arguments about using selection by lottery, one historical and the other theoretical. In the *historical or interpretive argument*, Manin backed the idea of a rupture within the republican tradition that was on full display in the eighteenth century. On this telling of political history, for centuries, selection by lottery was a familiar institution that functioned alongside elections—for instance, both in Venice and the late Republic of Florence, as well as in England's age of Revolution.[104] It was in Florence that political leaders (Leonardo Bruni) and scholars (Francesco Guicciardini) first began to think of elections as an *alternative* to lotteries. Manin's reading advanced an interpretation of the political history suggesting that the founders of representative government had made a deliberate choice to replace lottery. Supposedly, the lesson that eighteenth-century Republican leaders learned from the decline of the Florentine Republic was that lotteries could not guarantee social stability or trust in the magistrates. Thus, they took elections to

---

[103] See Valentina Pazé, *I non rappresentati: Esclusi, arrabbiati, disillusi* (Turin: Gruppo Abele, 2024), 23.

[104] Kishlansky demonstrated that before the civil law in England, the main concern of the electorate was to avoid divisions and achieve consensus; one reason for discontent was that local gentry might be voted against and this would put honor and respectability in jeopardy—hence, the recourse to lottery. Mark A. Kishlansky, *Parliamentary Selection: Social and Political Choice in Early Modern England* (Cambridge: Cambridge University Press, 1986), 16–7, 68, 81.

be an institutional answer that secured the republic. These leaders did not have Athens in mind, but rather the Italian early-modern republics. The memories of those republics were closer at hand, and the problem there had not been how to operationalize direct self-government but rather how an effective method of selection could be found that would neutralize violence and instability. Manin suggested that the American and French founders' choice of representative government was the result of a considered decision between lotteries and elections rather than the result of a decision between direct and electoral democracy. The undemocratic or even antidemocratic intentions that drove this choice altered the long-standing relationship between lotteries and elections: while Athenian democracy and the Florentine Republic (albeit less successfully) allowed for a conjunction of elections and lotteries, the eighteenth-century US republic was designed so as to specifically preclude any possible conjunction of these mechanisms. As Yves Sintomer observed, within modern republics, the institutional foundations for selecting government personnel unanimously sided with elections as opposed to lotteries.[105] After Manin's book, this historical argument became pivotal to the lottocratic mentality.

In his *theoretical argument*, Manin claimed that the specific conception of democratic equality that justified the use of lotteries in Athens was displaced by another conception of equality arising from the natural rights and the contractual theory of legitimacy based on consent. These newer foundations underpinned a society based on individualism and entrepreneurial creativity. This combination brought another equality to the forefront—an equality of opportunities for individuals to compete in both social and political life as well as to seek consent through a system of voting. Hence, while lotteries made all citizens candidates, elections made all citizens into selectors and potential agents. With the rise of elections, the role of individual judgment became preeminent evaluating the qualities of competing candidates. Thus, the issue at stake for the moderns was not the probability of rotation in public office, but instead, consent and the formation of judgments about the candidates that were then elected—a system of information, public surveillance, and accountability became an essential component of selection through elections.

However, Manin also raised a crucial point that not all lottocrats pause to consider fully: lotteries can also be deployed by nondemocratic regimes, whereas competitive elections cannot. Elster had already argued that lotteries are not exclusive to democracy, as they can be applied whenever there are several candidates "who are equally and maximally good." Manin took this point from Elster and gave an account of the plurality of reasons why politics and government in Athens, Florence, and Venice had adopted the use of lotteries. In particular, Venice and Florence each had different reasons for using lotteries: in Venice, their use grew out of a need to distribute magistrate seats amid a narrow oligarchic class with mixed government, whereas in Florence, lotteries were used because the scope of the relevant "citizenry" who could vote was *not* delimited by a system of individual and equal rights but rather

---

[105] Yet Sintomer moderates the drastic lottery/election dualism even in relation to the modern political order; see *The Government of Chance*, 7–9.

by membership in guilds or social groups (Florence). Manin advanced three conclusions: first, that it was possible to combine elections with lotteries before elections became hegemonic; second, once elections took over, their prior combination with lotteries faded away; and third, that lotteries can be used in nondemocratic societies or aristocratic/oligarchic republics.

Elster and Manin both consulted ancient and early-modern political history in order to analyze how lotteries have been (and could continue to be) justified according to different frameworks with different goals: *equality* in democratic Athens, *impartiality and social stability* in the pre-Medici republic of Florence, *unity* of the ruling class in the republic of Venice. However, irrespective of these different historical applications and functions, lotteries have always been and will always be based on some notion of equality. Historically, this was true *both* when all male citizens were included in the decision-making power (Athens) *and* when only some of them were (as in Florence and Venice). Lotteries do not question the criteria of inclusion (or any extension or restriction of it) within the sovereign power. As discussed below, this means that the application of lotteries is not inherently incompatible with oligarchic or undemocratic regimes. This makes the identification of lotteries with democracy highly problematic and quite conceptually fraught rather than being direct and simple. Yet, Manin's important insight on this score disappeared within the lottocratic mentality.

1.2 The Historical Paradigm

In the second and final part of this chapter, we retrace the lineage drawn up by Elster and Manin back to ancient Athens and early-modern Florence. This historical story has become inseparable from the lottocratic mentality. The main target of our critical analysis is the simplistic identification of democracy with lotteries and of oligarchy or aristocracy with elections. This generalization is often attractive to critics of representative democracy, particularly lottocrats. However, the selectively reimagined history behind this generalization is a "simplistic contrast [that] misconstrues the real concerns and practices" of ancient republics.[106] We will develop our argument by trying to bring together an account of the institutions of ancient democracy and a conceptual analysis of the principles that animated them.

1.2.1 Oligarchs, Democrats, and the Polis

1.2.1.1 Lottery and Elections: Democratic and Oligarchic?

"Deep disunity prevails amongst historians as to when the Athenians first began to select their magistrates by lot."[107] It is an interpretative "confusion" to primarily

---

[106] Melissa Lane, *The Birth of Politics: Eight Greek and Roman Political Ideas and Why They Matter* (Princeton, NJ: Princeton University Press, 2014), 119.

[107] Hansen, *The Athenian Democracy*, 29.

understand selection by lot as a mechanism of democratic government because in Athens, lotteries were used before democracy and then persisted even when tyrants ruled the city. Indeed, Isocrates (436–338 BCE) praises elections as "an element" of "'original' democracy." He writes that elections were already present in Solon's constitution (seventh century BCE) and then reintroduced by Cleisthenes in the first truly democratic constitution (508/7) that followed the coup by Pisistratus (600–527 BCE).[108] Aristotle's *Constitution of Athens* asserts that both lottery and elections were present before democracy started; they existed in Solon's moderate constitution, which retained elements of the previous order.[109] According to Aristotle, it was Draco (seventh century BCE) who set up the *boulē* of 400 (the Council of government whose function was to elaborate the proposals to be discussed and voted on by the Assembly) "chosen by lot from those possessing full rights of citizenship" and "other magistracies" also "chosen by lot from those citizens who were more than thirty years old" (an age limit that democracy retained).[110] The tyrant Pisistratus, who seized power in the years after Solon departed from Athens (560s), "administered the state in a moderate fashion" without subverting previous institutions but restricting the criteria of citizenship. Decades later, after the disastrous expedition to Sicily (415/13), democracy was overturned by a bloody oligarchic coup in 411. In that short convulsion, a Council of 400 was instituted and a new constitution was proposed that restricted participation in political decisions and divided a narrow subset of citizens into four equal groups selected by lot to rule in turn.[111]

Ancient thinkers also gave different interpretations of selection by lot. The author variously called the "Old Oligarch" or "Pseudo-Xenophon" was the most radical critic of democracy. In emphasizing the differences between the "government of the many" and the "government of the better" he did not focus on the distinction between sorting by lot and electing; rather, he simply argued that in a democracy, ordinary citizens are allowed to hold all public offices but he "does not view the lot as the only typically democratic form of appointment to office." Moreover, "he characterizes elections as nothing less than a perfidious method of the democrats to push their interests through at the expense of the rich."[112] Not even undemocratic thinkers such as Plato or Xenophon set up an elections-versus-lotteries-type contrast. Instead, when they want to criticize democracy, they express disdain for chance just as much as they do for voting in the Assembly, and then go on to emphasize that only

---

[108] Ibid., 51.

[109] "Sortition, albeit from among a very restricted group of citizens who were registered in the first property class, was of pre-Solonian origin." E. S. Staveley, *Greek and Roman Voting and Elections* (London: Thames and Hudson, 1972), 48.

[110] Greg Anderson, however, warns against assuming Aristotle's chronology, first because his *Constitution of Athens* was largely a composition by his students, and second because the narrative on the Athenian history of political reforms was often used to retro-date later innovations so as to stress the legitimacy of these practices. Greg Anderson, *The Athenian Experiment: Building an Imagined Political Community in Ancient Attica, 508–490 b.c.* (Ann Arbor, MI: University of Michigan Press, 2003), 206–7.

[111] Aristotle, *Constitution of Athens* 4.3; 14–6; 30.2; Thucydides, *The Peloponnesian War* 8.69 and 93. "In some form or other the lot had always been used in the selection of the archons, though the method of application doubtless varied" (Headlam, *Election by Lot at Athens*, 85).

[112] Buchstein, "Countering," 132.

competence should guide the choice of rulers.[113] In contrast to the Athenian aristocrats, Plato, or Xenophon, Aristotle adopts a class-based framework as the proper lens through which constitutions should be evaluated. As a non-Athenian proto-*bourgeois* figure, Aristotle sees institutions as tools in the conflict between the rich and poor. For instance, in book 4 of his *Politics*, "the constitutional nature of a given city is determined" not by the procedures of selection but "by what socioeconomic 'part of the city' is dominant, and variations in constitutional forms are determined by what socioeconomic group is in charge of specific bodies and functions, namely political decision-making, the administration of justice, and the magistracies."[114] Yet, it is true that when he criticized the democratic constitution under Pericles (which he saw as radical because it allowed for public service payments to increase participation), he proposed that elections could be a moderating element, since they allow the upper class to come forward as candidates for key administrative posts.[115]

The general interpretive gloss in Aristotle's *Politics* lent unearned credence to "the view that the principle of the lot was itself the very cornerstone of radical democracy and embraced by the Athenians on purely doctrinaire grounds."[116] According to Stavely, "this is a misleading doctrine. . . . What the Athenian people, or at least their leaders, were intent on preserving was the overriding supremacy of the popular Assembly."[117] Even one of the early radical champions of the lottery-versus-election dichotomy, James Wycliffe Headlam, conceded that "the lot might be used in other states with other results. . . . The system is really the extension of oligarchic principles to the whole body of citizens . . . at Athens, of which we alone have knowledge, it was only one (though an essential) part of the democratic system."[118] Indeed, as confirmation of this speculative thought we can turn to contemporary ancient historian Matthew Simonton, who cites a fourth-century text, the *Rhetoric of Alexander*, which recommends that in oligarchy, "the majority of political offices should be assigned by lot."[119]

In reality, the *important change* that democracy introduced (decisively with Cleisthenes) was *the inclusion* of all the adult male Athenians in the process of

---

[113] Buchstein writes that they thought the decisive factor was not elite members based on social distinctions but the elite's contribution to the community in terms of patrimonial cohesiveness domestically and military vigor toward external enemies (ibid., 140).

[114] Mirko Canevaro, "Institutions and Variations in Greek Democracy." In *The Cambridge History of Democracy*, vol. 1, edited by Valentina Arena and Eric Robinson (Cambridge: Cambridge University) 2023 (Accepted/In press).

[115] For the comparison between these ancient theorists, see Karen Piepenbrink, "Zur Relation von politischen und sozialen Ordnungsmustern und Handlungsfeldern in der attischen Demokratie des vierten Jahrhunderts v. Chr.," *Göttinger Forum für Altertumswissenschaft*, no. 22 (2019): 117–39, https://journals.ub.uni-heidelberg.de/index.php/gfa/issue/view/5184 (accessed March 10, 2023).

[116] Staveley, *Greek and Roman Voting*, 54.

[117] Ibid., 55. In contrast to his *Politics*, when Aristotle schematizes the forms of government in *The Art of Rhetoric*, he links lottery to democracy but does not suggest that aristocracy and oligarchy use elections: "Democracy is a constitution in which offices are distributed by lot and oligarchy one in which this is done on the basis of owning property, and aristocracy one in which it is based on education (*paideia*)" (1365b30). See Buchstein, "Countering," 140.

[118] Headlam, *Election by Lot at Athens*, 88.

[119] Simonton, *Classical Greek Oligarchy*, 88, in which we also read that when oligarchs had to distribute important offices among them, they used lottery and "the secret ballot accompanied by oaths." The *Rhetoric to Alexander*, though attributed to Aristotle in antiquity, was "probably written by the sophist Anaximenes of Lampsacus" (ibid.).

decision-making. This specific scope of inclusion began with the Assembly and other magistrate seats and then continued to be used throughout the processes of lottery, rotation, and elections. Therefore, it seems like the constitutive principle of Athenian democracy lies *not* in the lottery or any other procedure of selection per se but rather in the fact that all the adult male citizens (ideally with no exceptions) can decide whether they want to participate in the political and selection process (*ho boulomenos*—"whoever wishes").[120] While the drawing of lots for magistrate positions dated back to the aristocratic age, the specific thing that changed with democratization was that selection by lot was gradually deployed with respect to a sizable body of citizens in order to choose all magistrate seats and, in particular, the highest position (the archonship). As for the rotation of appointments (which functioned to block the monopolization of power), Aristotle recommended that it be used within his constitutional government (*politeia*) and Plato applied this mechanism to his aristocratic republic, where he envisioned the same few good men would rotate and hold offices in turn.

Thus, while it is true that the core logic of lottery is an equality of probability, only once the empowered community (the relevant citizenry) has been defined and delimited can this equality hold for democrats and oligarchs alike. In *The Art of Rhetoric*, Aristotle explains that the method of selecting public officials must be consistent with the interests of each form of government and the purposes to be achieved by it. Lottery can be used by either a democracy or an oligarchy—it is simply that, in the first case, all (adult male) citizens are candidates whereas, in the second case, the shortlist of selectees is made according to the criteria of wealth (oligarchy) and merit (aristocracy).[121] Similarly, in the *Laws*, Plato states that lotteries can be used by either democrats and aristocrats: in the former case, the names of all the citizens in the free polity are put into the selection box; in the latter case, the names of those previously elected are drawn from.[122] But, historically speaking, if both advocates of "rule by the few" as well as committed democrats have always made use of lotteries, then what is the nature of the equality that lotteries express?

1.2.1.2 Which Equality?

We observed above that in order to stress the democratic character of lotteries, Manin connects it to "equality of probability." This type of equality is less radical than equality in every material respect and more radical than equality of opportunity.[123] However, equality of probability was an eighteenth-century achievement

---

[120] See Cynthia Farrar, "Taking our Chances with the Ancient Athenians," in *Démocratie athénienne— démocratie moderne: Tradition et influences*, ed. Mogens Herman Hansen (Geneva: Édition Fondation Hardt, 2009), 167–217; Daniela Cammack, "The Democratic Significance of the Classical Athenian Courts" (unpublished manuscript), https://www.danielacammack.com/_files/ugd/3c6e57_fd36c60f058948cc812f10f6250bddeb.pdf, 8.

[121] Aristotle, *The Art of Rhetoric* 1.8.

[122] Milena Bontempi, "Il misto della 'politeia' in Platone," *Filosofia politica* 19, no. 1 (2005): 21.

[123] As noted earlier, Manin intended to correct Hansen, who tried to oppose identifying democracy with radical equality (the right to share in everything equally). Hansen pointed out that only critics of democracy, yet never democrats themselves, identified democracy with the idea of sharing everything equally. Hansen, *Athenian Democracy*, 81–4.

58   The Lottocratic Mentality

that explained the logic of lotteries but did not make them democratic: this kind of equality can be used with respect to *any* predefined group of equals. Since the main characteristic feature of this type of equality is avoiding competition and discrimination among peers, aristocrats and oligarchs predictably found it very attractive. Equality of probability can be applied within contexts where equality entails *sameness or likeness* and within contexts where it entails *equality under the law (isonomia)* and the inclusion of all in the political process. As noted above, in Athens antidemocratic reforms were used to alter the criteria for citizenship but not to abolish selection by lot.

What was unique about democracy was that it included the largest number of male citizens based on what was an undisputed criterion: *autocthony* (being "born from the earth").[124] Solon claimed freedom of the poor from debt-slavery on the basis of being ethnically rooted in the Athenian people.[125] The city began its democratic journey when, in the name of belonging to the same city (under the protection of the same goddess, Pallas Athena), the commoners gave themselves the equality that the aristocrats had previously claimed belonged exclusively to them.[126] The idea of equal value of the poor and the powerful was already present in Homeric society: Hesiod (between 750 and 650 BCE) harshly criticized the arrogance of the aristocrats who "dragged off" Dike (the goddess of justice) and gave "crocked verdicts."[127] The Athenians inaugurated their democracy when they formalized ancestral equality and safeguarded it against arguments from competence and virtue. *In that specific context, democratic lotteries clashed with oligarchic lotteries.*

The clash between democratic and oligarchic lotteries does *not* take place in the space of equality of probability, but rather within the space defined by basic equality secured under and through law, and within the more specific institutional contexts of an equal power to sit on the Assembly, to compete for positions (elections), and to volunteer to serve in offices filled by lot. For the Athenians, lottery was part of their democratic efforts to enact and preserve their citizenship.[128] The unbridgeable difference between oligarchic lotteries and democratic lotteries thus laid outside the shared premise of equality of probability. Sparta was also composed of equals;

---

[124] In Thucydides's telling, Pericles spoke of the "whole people." Nicole Loraux, "L'autochtonie: Une topique athénienne. Le mythe dans l'espace civique," *Annales: Économies, Sociétés, Civilisations* 34, no. 1 (1979): 1–26. The attribution of citizenship remained strongly indigenous, associated with birth to an Athenian mother and then also to an Athenian father. Vincent J. Rosivach, "Autochthony and the Athenians," *Classical Quarterly* 37, no. 2 (1987): 294–306.

[125] Plato, *Menexenus* 239a, in *The Dialogues of Plato*, trans. B. Jowett, 4 vols. (Boston: Jefferson Press, n.d.), 4:569. The idea of humans being equal by nature (*isogonía*), which is the ideal foundation of democracy, can be seen as an extension of that old vision of coming from the same mother earth.

[126] In Solon's poem one reads, "I set up a strong shield around both parties [the rich and the poor] by not allowing either to defeat the other unjustly.... But we and our citizens are brethren, the children all of one mother, and we do not claim to be one another's masters or servants; but the natural equality of birth compels us to seek for legal equality, and to recognize no superiority except in the reputation of virtue and wisdom." In *Early Greek Political Thought from Homer to the Sophists*, ed. Michael Gagarin and Paul Woodruff (Cambridge: Cambridge University Press, 1995), 26.

[127] Hesiod, *Works and Days*, in *Greek Lyric Poetry*, ed. and trans. M. L. West (Oxford: Oxford University Press, 1993), 213.

[128] Josiah Ober, *Mass and Elite in Democratic Athens: Rhetoric, Ideology, and the Power of the People* (Princeton, NJ: Princeton University Press, 1989), 6 and 259–61.

they were *homoioi* ("alike" or "similar"). While critics of democracy, such as Plato, idealized the Spartan model because it instituted equality among the best, Sparta was never a democracy. The Spartan *homoioi* (full citizens) enjoyed freedom at the expense of the *helotes* (slaves who were also Greeks); they had privileges and values that were typically associated with the oligarchy in Greece. When it comes to Sparta, we find absolutely no mention of the individual freedom (*eleuthereia*) that characterized classical democracies, along with the freedom to speak in the Assembly (*isēgoria*).[129]

Indeed, Herodotus linked democracy to equal political freedom or *isonomia*. How would aristocrats accommodate *this* type of equality? They would accommodate it by *moderating the identification of democracy* with *isonomia*. Thus, Paul Cartledge proposes that sameness tempered *isonomia*—that social equality tempered political equality: since they were "exactly equal, identical, and the same" as citizens, Athenian democrats did not need to be the same (*homoi*) in the sense of aristocrats.[130] This distinction corresponds to the difference Aristotle posited between arithmetical and geometrical equality. Whereas arithmetical equality was associated with democracy, geometrical equality was associated with oligarchy.

Democratic equality is normative or artificial in nature; the purpose of *isonomia* was to moderate and hopefully neutralize the preeminence that had accrued to qualities that by their very nature could not be extended to and acquired by all—a social dynamic that had meant that only some Athenians could be taken to be equal. In whatever form democracy is realized, the basis of counting individual votes identically with one another descends from this use of *isonomia* and takes the form of arithmetical equality. Both Plato and Aristotle identified this equality with democracy and proposed to amend it with aristocratic (proportional) equality. In such a combination, it was assumed that elections would attract aristocrats (who were dedicated to learning rhetoric) and that lotteries would interest *everyone* since they required nothing but a willingness to run for office. Democracy applied lotteries in the context of political equality so as to protect ordinary citizens against oligarchic preeminence in public life. Indeed, with the democratization of the archonship after the reforms of Cleisthenes (508–507 BCE), *isēgoria* became the primary attraction for elites; they intensively cultivated the art of rhetoric and tried to control the Assembly.[131] Later, after the overthrow of the Thirty Tyrants in 403 BCE, regulating the work of the Assembly became the primary concern of democrats. Democrats "enforced a stark distinction between laws as general permanent rules and decrees as executive or administrative order of the Assembly or the Council; they enforced a

---

[129] Kurt A. Raaflaub and Robert W. Wallace, "'People's Power' and Egalitarian Trends in Ancient Greece," in *Origins of Democracy in Ancient Greece*, ed. Kurt A. Raaflaub, Josiah Ober, Robert W. Wallace (Berkeley, CA: University of California Press, 2007), 41.

[130] Paul Cartledge, "Comparatively Equal," in *Dēmokratia: A Conversation on Democracies, Ancient and Modern*, ed. Josiah Ober and Charles Hedrick (Princeton, NJ: Princeton University Press, 1996), 179–80.

[131] "But since by now most officers were certainly filled by lot, the politically ambitious elite might not be able to secure an official position that would give him the right to speak to the Assembly. The result was a conviction in elite circles that a greater freedom of political debate was a good idea." Ober, *Mass and Elite*, 79.

60 The Lottocratic Mentality

complex procedure for enacting new laws (*nomothesia*) whose aim was to secure the lawfulness of the new laws."[132] We will come back to this issue below.

To conclude, democracy meant giving and protecting the equal "access to political participation and office," the equal right to speak in public with the "property qualification for offices only rarely" used, and making sure that no citizen should hold office more than once in his lifetime and that no magistracy was monopolized by a single group of citizens.[133] As Baruch Spinoza wrote in his *Political Treatise* (1676), "we can conceive different kinds of democracy," but all of them have in common the following basic conditions: that all the citizens "have the right to vote . . . and undertake offices of the state."[134]

1.2.1.3 Let the Gods Decide

Various interpretations of the role and meaning of both lotteries and elections inevitably reflect the overall aims of interpreters. When Manin articulated a link between lotteries and probabilistic logic—a link that was made explicitly in the eighteenth century—this was meant to counter a religious reading dating back to Fustel de Coulanges, which aimed to paint lotteries as aristocratic and elections as democratic.[135] Political history suggests that the ideal aristocratic form of selection is by lot, since when properly administered, it admits of no human intervention or discrimination among peers. In England, in the early days of representative government based on elections, the nobility simply could not tolerate competition for votes among peers with an attendant risk of losing the final ballot count: "To be rejected by fortune was less dishonorable than to be rejected by the community."[136] Across time and place, all types of nobles and oligarchs thought that lotteries would protect their "equioptimality" (to use a word employed by Elster). As for elections, Hansen shows that Athenian citizens did "not regard . . . [it] as antidemocratic provided that all citizens could vote and any citizen could in principle be elected."[137] On the other hand, electoral competition was not necessarily favored by the Athenian elites, as they claimed distinction and sought to compete in the broader arena but, among themselves, would have probably disliked using elections as a final and quantitatively demonstrable criterion of victory. Indeed, in the *Iliad* (bk. 7) when the Achaean kings gather to choose who would fight against Hector, they selected by lot. This was taken to be the only means of selection acceptable to equals as the lot leaves the choice to fate:

---

[132] Canevaro and Esu, "Extreme Democracy and Mixed Constitution," 108.

[133] Kurt A. Raaflaub, "Equalities and Inequalities in Athenian Democracy," in Ober and Hedrick, *Dēmokratia*, 140.

[134] Baruch Spinoza, *Political Treatise*, trans. Samuel Shirley, with introduction and notes by Steven Barbone and Lee Rice (Indianapolis, IN: Hackett, 2000), 136 (XI, 3).

[135] "It is surprising that modern historians represent the drawing of lots as an invention of the Athenian democracy. It was, on the contrary, in full rigor under the rule of the aristocracy. . . . For them the lot was not chance; it was the revelation of the divine will." Numa Denis Fustel de Coulanges, *The Ancient City: A Study on the Religion, Laws, and Institutions of Greece and Rome* (Garden City, NY: Doubleday Anchor Books, 1956), 182–3. Manin counters Coulanges's reading in *The Principles*, 25.

[136] Elster, *Solomonic Judgments*, 107; Kishlansky, *Parliamentary Selection*, 14–6.

[137] Hansen, *Athenian Democracy*, 233, referring to Aristotle's *Politics*.

> Lest thirst of glory your brave souls divide,
> What chief shall combat, let the gods decide.
> Whom heaven shall choose, be his the chance to raise
> His country's fame, his own immortal praise
> The lots produced, each hero signs his own.

Scholars connect that archaic practice with the myth of divination; among equals, the "luck of the draw" was similar to the relation of *moirai* (fate) that awaited each person. Religious justification (particularly vivid in ancient Rome) was consistent *to preserve concord in the city* since it made hard choices acceptable and thus reduced conflicts between peers. As we can see in Plato's *Laws*, it is the nonhuman or religious dimension that makes lotteries legitimate and accepted. There we see lotteries linked to the will of the gods, who know the value of each person and thus distribute honors and sacrifices justly: "the equality of the lot, [is used] in order to avoid the discontent of the people" because that which is not in the hands of men cannot be subject to arbitrariness.[138] If concord among elites (averting factions) and the acceptance of one's fate (the drawing of lots by justice) were already quite important in the archaic age, then scholars speculate that the random selection of political offices in the so-called "democratic age" was born out of a slow secularization of politics—a process indicated by the fact that Athens invented a mechanical device (*klērōtērion*) which allowed the many to witness the procedure of selection and thereby ensure the process was quick and safe from manipulation. This technology revealed the city's rational control over random selection and its greater efficacy at limiting the power of the few when compared to the traditional method of drawing lots.

1.2.1.4 Lottery to Obtain What?

To sum up, the elites used sortition to preserve their unity and concord as a group. The senatorial nobility of the Roman Republic pursued this goal even more explicitly, as they used lottery to distribute functions among themselves to control rivalries.[139] What then was the goal of democrats? Democracy also sought to preserve the unity and concord (*homonoia* and *philia*) of the city, and this meant protecting the institutional conditions that kept politics free, inclusive and peaceful—"preventing *stasis* or internal fragmentation." Lottery served these goals by precluding the wealthy few

---

[138] Plato, *Laws* VI, 757 (ed. Jowett, 4: 274). Interestingly, the dualism between political principle (choice or election) and impolitic principle (chance or fate or the will of God) played a central role in the transition from the Roman Empire to the Christian Empire. Beginning with Augustus (who deified the figure of the *princeps*), the *imperator*'s selection problem arose, whether by election by the military or senatorial oligarchy or instead by chance of birth or heredity. The method that relied on divine discretion as the basis of the sovereign's legitimacy (influenced by Neoplatonism and the victory of religious monotheism) prevailed over the political one. The criterion of natural lottery (hereditary monarchy) was the solution that projected the Christian Roman empire out of the ancient political orbit with a transcendent or unpolitic solution to the problem of succession of power; see among other, Giovanni Brizzi, *Imperium. Il potere a Roma* (Laterza 2024), 244-48.

[139] In the Roman Republic, the main political functions distributed among the members of the senatorial class were adjudicated through lottery, a procedure "that clearly sought to control aristocratic rivalry and to save aristocratic pride." Andrew Lintott, *The Constitution of the Roman Republic* (Oxford: Oxford University Press, 2004), 101.

62　The Lottocratic Mentality

from acquiring preeminence in the processes of political decision, selecting magistrates, or judicial personnel.[140] As scholars have argued, "the initial motive for Athenians to introduce the lottery was to counter intra-elite strife and allow the prevalence of a unified elite, although at the end it produced the adverse effect of disempowering the elite."[141]

Thus, while oligarchy preserves its own delimited scope of power against their own recalcitrant or ambitious peers and against encroachment from the poor or the "worst" elements of society, democracy contains and dilutes the power of the few by stretching the political system of decision-making to all male adult citizens. Both democracy and oligarchy aimed at preserving concord, and lottery served the goals of each insofar as it protected their respective principles of inclusion by either preventing the formation of a superior class (democracy) or by blocking factionalism among themselves (oligarchy). Drawing lots was essential to any society that wanted to put a brake on the struggle for power because it knew how horrific political conflict could be (we will come back to this issue in Chapter 4); this is also why, even though majority-counting took place in both the Athenian Assembly and the Council, the "majority principle" used in contemporary electoral democracies was not employed there.

The Greek city was based on a common ethos—a civic concord conceptualized as *philia* or friendship. To base democracy on the majority principle or legitimate opposition would have been tantamount to validating a principle of disunity that would yield the ruin of the city.[142] Thus, in Athens, two conditions made the application of lotteries democratic: the *large number* of citizens involved in the selection process, and the use of lotteries alongside the *rotation* of offices.[143] According to Staveley, more than lottery per se rotation is what served democracy, and the mark of democracy was the "enforcement of rotation" among the included "many."[144]

---

[140] Oliver Dowlen, *The Political Potential of Sortition: A Study of the Random Selection of Citizens for Public Policy* (Exeter: Imprint Academic, 2008), 49. Hansen writes: "the democrats themselves seem to have preferred sortition . . . because it safeguarded the powers of the People, prevented conflicts and counteracted corruption . . . and obviated factionalism and corruption, not because they believed in the equality of all citizens." Hansen, *The Athenian Democracy*, 84, 341–2. But protection of concord, which was the first good, was achieved with strategies that were internal to the decision-making process in the Assembly, like the exclusion of organized parties and relying not on the principle of majority rule that we have today ("aggregative" system) but rather upon consensus instead. See Canevaro, "Majority Rule versus Consensus."

[141] Anthoula Malkopoulou, "The Paradox of Democratic Selection: Is Sortition Better than Voting?" in *Parliamentarism and Democratic Theory: Historical and Contemporary Perspectives*, ed. Kari Palonen and José María Rosales (Opladen: Verlag Barbara Budrich, 2015), 239. "Holding power for no other reason than the luck of the draw diminishes the impositions that government officials can make on the governed, and so does the frequency of alternating between governing and being governed." George Tridimas, "Constitutional Choice in Ancient Athens: The Rationality of Selection to Office by Lot," *Constitutional Political Economy* 23, no. 1 (2012): 9.

[142] On the strength of unanimity or consensus and the absence of the principle (although not the method) of majority in ancient Athenian democracy, see Francesco Galgano, *La forza del numero e la legge della ragione. Storia del principio di maggioranza* (Bologna: Il Mulino, 2007), chap. 1 and Canevaro, "Majority Rule versus Consensus."

[143] Aristotle calculated almost 1,100 magistrates elected each year; 500 members of the boule and 600 other assorted magistrates. *Constitution of Athens* 43.1, 50–60; Hansen, *Athenian Democracy*, 232.

[144] Staveley, *Greek and Roman Voting*, 55.

In the perfect aristocracy that Plato called *kallipolis*, democracy, and sortition were scourged, but lots were retained. Philosopher-kings would use to engineer sexual selection (a theme repeatedly and abrasively emphasized in Aristophanes's *Ekklesiazousai*). Plato envisioned philosophers (conceptualized as rational planners of the political order) drawing lots to make sure that couples thought of their own sexual pairings as produced by chance and not by preference. This mechanism was presumably designed to prevent the growth of affection and thus the formation of families and private interests that could interfere with the republic's administration. Moreover, because the pairing was the outcome of chance, the practice would be *seamlessly accepted* and remain *uncontested* ("Certain ingenious lots, then, I suppose, must be devised so that the inferior man at each conjugation may blame chance and not the rulers").[145] Guardians must abide by the sexual "lottery" that the republic ingeniously implemented by combing eugenics and merit in the context of a lottery, and this would show that politics was just a matter of technique in the service of harmony.[146] Plato makes it clear that this lottery involves neither inclusion nor democracy: in his ideal republic, this mechanism serves harmony and protects the institution of guardianship. In other words, political inclusion was an altogether separate issue from the use of lotteries. In Plato, the sheer will of the sovereign (or sovereign class) is what determined that lottery would be used as a stratagem to retain power.

We can reasonably say that lotteries can be defined as a democratic mechanism of selection provided that: (a) they do not replace voting in the Assembly or the equal power to vote on laws; (b) they are not applied to select individual leaders; (c) they are not utilized with respect to a basis or scope apart from simple membership in the political community;[147] and (d) they are not used to select personnel for a life term or even a long term, but are instead used in ongoing selections and short-term rotations. This means, by default, that lottery alone does *not* make democracy; what makes democracy is *equal political freedom* (*isonomia* and *eleutheria*) among the citizens and explicit inclusion of the poor or "ordinary" common people in the demos such that they enjoy the power to speak in public and vote in the Assembly (*isēgoria*). This allows them to dissent and also defend their reasons for and against certain decisions in front of their fellow citizens. The nature of a constitution is "determined exclusively by the issue of who has access. . . . If it is only a few, it is an oligarchy; if it is all, it is a democracy, regardless of lottery or election."[148]

In the Greek *poleis* property qualifications for both citizenship and holding office were common. The *absence* of property qualifications was peculiar to Athens's *dēmokratia*: this *absence* is what Aristotle identified with radical democracy. A focus on equality of probability does not help explain the difference between oligarchic and democratic uses of lottery. Manin notes that the Athenian democrats

---

[145] Plato, *Republic* V, 460a (trans. Shorey).
[146] In his utopian *City of the Sun* (1601), Tommaso Campanella mimicked Plato and employed lottery to rule reproduction in order to preserve the stability of the ideal city through generations.
[147] For example, they are not used to create or protect a homogeneous society made up of "perfect men" or invincible warriors as in *kallipolis*, where lotteries were widely used.
[148] Canevaro and Esu, "Extreme Democracy," 118.

"had the intuition" that elections could not guarantee their equality. Yet that "intuition" would not help Athenians create and preserve their democratic order in the absence of equality to sit in the Assembly, vote equally in elections, volunteer for lotteries, enforce rotation, receive compensation for public services rendered, and lotteries that were highly regulated to immunize them from potential malfunctions, arbitrariness, and corruption. The more citizens were included in public functions, the more the oligarchs' factional inclinations would be contained and concord protected. Hence, quite apart from the use of lotteries, the decision to compensate citizens for serving on juries was what was decisive since it extended service to all that had previously been a luxury that only the wealthy could afford to participate in. As Sinclair comments: "It is a mistake, however, to suppose that it was basically sortition which kept the democracy in being and ensured that power remained at least nominally with the popular Assembly."[149]

1.2.1.5 How Was Lottery Implemented in Athens?

In ancient democracy, the most difficult problem was regulating the process that was used to form public administration. Lottocrats do not pay attention to the fact that Athens did not have a bureaucracy with paid staff selected by either the public or through blind examinations based on defined and testable requirements. All public functions were performed by the citizens. As Hansen writes, these citizens "did not distinguish between politics and administration" even though they obviously understood the distinction between "initiation, decision, and execution." This helps explain why when Aristotle speaks of freedom as the principle of democratic government because citizens are "ruled and rule by turns," he "is thinking of rotation of magistrates, not of any sort of rotation in attending the Assembly." For, attending the Assembly was "the real protagonist of the Athenian democracy."[150] This was because "the election of leaders represents only one of the important votes cast" by the citizens who are also "members of the Assembly."[151] The trickier problem was that associated with forming a public administration, and it was twofold: (1) uphold the principle of legal and political equality so as to preserve the voluntariness of participation and make sure that everyone has the opportunity to exercise administrative functions and (2) prevent the consolidation or concentration of power in the hands of a few—predictably, those who had greater social means and more time to participate or who, once selected, would try to hold onto their office for a long time or pass it on among members of their clan or family group. In Athens, these problems were solved by rotation and using lotteries to staff almost all public offices and elections to staff just a few of them. In the fourth century, the institutions of the polis fell into four distinct kinds: the Council or *boulē* (500 members); a large portion of the magistrate positions or public functionaries; the jurors serving on tribunals; and what

---

[149] R. K. Sinclair, *Democracy and Participation in Athens* (Cambridge: Cambridge University Press, 1988), 115.

[150] Hansen, *Athenian Democracy*, 72–3.

[151] Loren J. Samons II, *What's Wrong with Democracy? From Athenian Practice to American Worship* (Berkeley: University of California Press, 2004), 45.

some scholars conceptualize as a true "second chamber" (*nomothetai*) that was in charge of revising the work of the Assembly (at least 6000 citizens when understood collectively).

What made democratic selection by lottery quite unique and "subversive" was the high number of people involved: relying on Aristotle, Hansen calculates around 1,100 citizens were involved each year. Different institutionalizations of lotteries entailed different sorting processes. Hansen details three different goals that various lottery procedures were used to fulfill: (a) the most complex method of selection, the "double draw," was used to choose the archons; (b) lotteries were also used to select other magistrates (to fill the various necessary functions in the city); and (c) lotteries were also used to select council members. All three types of lottery used individual plaques and the *klērōtērion*—a machine where bronze plaques were thrown.[152] Each citizen over the age of thirty who was chosen received a bronze plaque with his or her name inscribed and the official logo (the Gorgon's head). Substitutes were also selected, who would automatically replace those incumbents who were incapacitated. As a general rule both the selectees and substitutes took an oath before serving, and they also underwent an examination at the end of their service. The purpose of the oath and the final examination of the services that they performed was to enable all citizens to have at least one opportunity in their lives to be drawn on and responsibly serve in one of the various public offices. The opportunity was open to all citizens. The only discriminating or limiting factor was the (tested and judged) commitment to perform one's duties honestly.

With the exception of the archons, all the magistrates in the city were selected through a direct method and a single, central procedure. One representative per tribe was generally required and the draw was made either by authorized persons or was *thesmothetai* (self-drawn). Candidates who were rejected from performing a certain function had the option of being chosen for other functions. Even in the case of minor functions, substitutions were always drawn as well. Important *limits* on the exercise of functions explain the large numbers of people involved and the rotation of offices. For example, since it was forbidden for Council members to hold office more than once any drawing of prospective Council members had to account for this fact: while there was nothing to prevent a person who was drawn but who could not serve from being used for another function, before this could happen, they would be subjected to a public accounting of their past performance. This was the sort of after-the-fact checking that Plato thought was needed to distinguish a tyrannical from a legitimate or a "good" drawing of lots.

Plato deemed the Spartan *ephors* "democratic" because they were selected by lot. Yet, at the same time, he also characterized them as "tyrannical" if they were not subjected to a strict legal control. For Plato, *the way* in which a lottery was held made all the difference. He therefore thought the *ephors* could simply be tyrannical if a lottery

---

[152] The machine consisted of a marble or wooden stele, used both in the annual draw of magistrates and in the daily draw of members of the popular jury (it had vertical columns from which descended a tube where black and white balls used in the draw were placed).

66 The Lottocratic Mentality

was employed *without* legal sanctions.[153] "So the Athenians were far from using lottery as if it presupposed that just any citizens could and should be entitled to fill any role."[154] This is likely why Aristotle suggested that rotation is a democratic procedure only if it is combined with certain arrangements.[155] The text of the oath one took before being considered to serve on a jury selected by lot used the first person singular pronoun extensively: "I will cast my vote . . . I will listen impartially." This oath emphasized the importance of each juror's judgment, his independence from any external influence, and his responsibility in front of and in the service of the law. Each citizen was required to think by himself and those selected were prevented from discussing matters with others prior to voting (in some cases, such as in the courts, a secret ballot was required). This emphasis on the independence that selected citizens must exercise contrasts with contemporary attempts to either use lottery as a means "to represent" stratified samplings or to use random selection to produce specific outcomes.[156] It is important to note that *lottery did not seek to secure representativeness*.[157] It was actually deployed to ensure impartiality and fairness, qualities that are essential to the administrative and judicial domains where lotteries were extensively applied. Special attention needs to be given to the *nomothetai*, because this is the function that contemporary lottocrats often cite in order to "prove" that lotteries can be used to make laws and play a representative function in the legislature.

1.2.1.6 The Contested Role of the Nomothetai

Although lottocrats oppose lotteries and elections, their reference to ancient democracy reveals their target is the popular Assembly. They ground their historical argument on the claim that fourth-century Athens was not truly run by the Assembly since the *demos's* "administrative and executive acts . . . were checked for their adherence to the laws by specific procedures, notably *nomothesia* and the *graphe paranomon* and *nomon me epitedeion theinai*."[158] Pasquale Pasquino, therefore, suggests that we should see the *nomothetai* as playing a function that was equivalent to a constitutional

---

[153] "And yet, Stranger, I perceive that I cannot say, without more thought, what I should call the government of Lacedaemon, for it seems to me to be like a tyranny; the power of our ephors is marvelously tyrannical; and sometime it appears to me to be of all citizens the most democratic; and who can deny that it is an aristocracy. . .; and, therefore, when asked on a sudden, I cannot precisely say which form of government the Spartan is" (Plato, *The Laws* IV, 712d–e, trans. Jowett).

[154] Lane, *The Birth of Politics*, 119.

[155] After explaining the two "fundamental" principles of democracy ("participate in liberty" and "each of the citizens ought to have an equal share"), Aristotle lists a series of limitations on the institutions that are "democratic in character" among which he puts "election of officials by all from all" and rotation ("all by each in turn") and "election by lot wither to all magistracies or to all that do not need experience and skip" (*Politics* 1317b28–30). Plato (*Laws* V, 757) proposed a dualism between lottery and election in relation to equality: arithmetical in one case and proportional to one's value in the other (the divine equality that gives each in reason of his nature).

[156] This problem has been raised by Dowlen (*The Political Potential of Sortition*, 53–8) who argues that lottery, as it was used in Athens, gave no guarantee of any diversity of results; see on this also Peter A. Stone, *The Luck of the Draw: The Role of Lotteries in Decision-Making* (New York: Oxford University Press, 2011).

[157] Fairness was achieved thanks to the redrawing of the demes by Cleisthenes (based on residence and numbers of inhabitants) which was particularly important for the selection of jurors; according to Ober, the new demes as sources of sortation were not "constructed as 'local representatives'" (*Mass and Elite*, 73).

[158] Canevaro and Esu, "Extreme Democracy," 127.

check in the contemporary logic of a division of power, as opposed to a function that is akin to ordinary legislation.[159] But lottocrats think otherwise: they stress that it was not necessarily the case that the Assembly was a genuinely sovereign organ since it did not have the final say on laws—that final say was given to an organ chosen by lot. What then was the role and function of the *nomothetai*? Among ancient historians, there is no unequivocal answer to this question.

Some scholars think the *nomothetai* were selected outside of the Assembly, whereas others think that they were instead selected from within the Assembly.[160] Recent historical research does indicate that the committee of the *nomothetai* was chosen from *within* the Assembly, which must have performed this self-controlling function by itself. Nevertheless, the very character and "identity of the *nomothetai* is also a complex issue" owing to "alleged evidence" that they were judges (selected from those who had sworn the Judicial Oath) but at the same time not a panel that was separate from the Assembly. This is inferred from the fact that

> the *nomothetai* voted by show of hands, as an Assembly and unlike a panel of judges.... The *nomothetai* were none other than a special session of the Assembly, summoned *ad hoc* when there were new laws to enact.... The item on the agenda marked as *nomothetai* leads to a vote of the *demos* on the laws, with the *demos* acting as *nomothetai*.... The *nomothetai* were not a special body, but only a special incarnation of the *ekklēsia*, whether *ad hoc* (more likely) or a special incarnation of the demos at a certain point of a meeting. The fact that the *prytaneis* ποιεῖν ἐκκλησίαν [call an assembly], rather than adding this as an item to an existing meeting, makes the first of these two options ... the most likely.[161]

Canevaro and Esu defend this interpretation. They think that Hansen overstated the ultimate sovereignty of the *nomothetai*, assumed they were a separate body, and glossed over the fact that they enacted laws collaboratively with the Council in standard sessions of the Assembly (with the involvement of the courts). Pasquino thus appears to have been right: this institutional set-up was a case of divided power rather than an instance where one body (whatever its composition or mode of selection)

[159] Pasquale Pasquino, "Democracy Ancient and Modern: Divided Power," in Hansen, *Démocratie athénienne*, 1–49.

[160] In the nineteenth century, the *nomothetai* inspired John Stuart Mill to devise the idea of parliamentary committees.

[161] Canevaro and Esu, "Extreme Democracy," 132–5. "For a long time, however, literary texts have led scholars (including myself) to believe that a session of the *nomothetai* should be seen not as a kind of assembly, though one of a specially restricted body of men, but rather as a kind of lawcourt, in which the *nomothetai* functioned as a jury to decide between a proposal to change the laws and the existing body of laws.... In the past we have been too much impressed by the similarity to assemblies. Piérart has for the first time done justice to their similarity to assemblies." P. J. Rhodes, "Sessions of *Nomothetai* in Fourth-Century Athens," *Classical Quarterly* 53, no. 1 (2003): 124 and 129. The reference is to M. Piérart, "Qui étaient les nomothètes à Athènes à l'époque de Démosthène?" in *La codification des lois dans l'antiquité*, ed. E. Lévy (Paris: Diffusion de Boccard, 2000), 229–50. An opposition to this reading comes from Mogens H. Hansen, "The Authenticity of the Law about *Nomothesia* Inserted in Demosthenes *Against Timokrates* 33," *Greek, Roman and Byzantine Studies* 56, no. 4 (2016): 594–610.

68 The Lottocratic Mentality

was sovereign.[162] And while it is true that a decree of the Council and of the Assembly could not override the laws passed by the Assembly acting as *nomothetai*, it is also true that the majority of the daily decisions were taken by decree. Thus, according to Piérart and Canevaro, the *nomothetai* were the Assembly in a different incarnation, and the function of *nomothetein* was narrower than legislating in the modern sense: it was limited to *nomoi* as permanent general rules.[163] Much of what we would call legislative activity today was carried out by the Assembly. Among the fourth-century Athenian acts that were carved in stone and have survived, more than 600 are decrees of the Assembly, and only about ten are *nomoi* approved by the *nomothetes*.[164]

In short, unless we seriously analyze both lotteries and elections then, irrespective of questions of constitutional form or investigations about the relations, functions, and procedures of the Assembly and other institutions, we risk distorting the Athenian process into something that appears not more but less democratic. Moreover, unless we account for the complexities, the different (ancient and recent) interpretations, and the scholarly disagreement about the specific functions of Athenian institutions, we risk making the history of three thousand years ago a partisan construct in the service of an ideological case for the present. The comparative and dichotomous opposition between lottery and election creates "confusion"; it blinds us to the simple fact that the offices Athenians held by lottery were exercised collectively, whereas the offices that they held by election were those of individual leadership. Athens needed and had offices of both types staffed by both selection procedures. Athens neither used sortition to compose the Assembly, nor to select individual public officials, nor to gather a committee outside and above the Assembly to check it (as a newer interpretation argues). Contemporary lottocrats gloss over these distinctions and instead abstractly compare two procedures (election and lottery) that, taken in the context of the functions that they were expected to fulfill, were simply not comparable.[165]

As noted, lottocrats seem to ignore the possibility that Athens simply lacked a separation of powers despite having a tripartite arrangement (Assembly, Council, and magistrates), and, relatedly, they neglect the implications of the fact that it lacked formal state organization and a bureaucracy. As Dahl aptly observed, in essence, the construction of the *state* is what sealed the fate of lotteries in modern and contemporary societies.[166] Lottery seems to have played a minor role in a state system wherein most public functions are filled by competitions among certified and paid professionals or officers. Athens used lotteries to fill the committees that covered the many administrative functions (care of bridges, the harbor, roads, religious rites, theatrical performances, sports competitions, etc.), to staff all

---

[162] Pasquino, "Democracy Ancient and Modern."

[163] Since this was the function of the *nomothetai* (it was another session of the Assembly), in his *Constitution of Athens*, Aristotle does not take them to indicate a constitutional government; Piérart, "Qui étaient les nomothètes?," and Canevaro and Esu, "Extreme Democracy."

[164] Mirko Canevaro, "Politica, diritto e giustizia tra oralità e scrittura," in *Atene, vivere in una città antica*, ed. Marco Bettalli and Maurizio Giangiulio (Rome: Carocci, 2023), 266–7.

[165] Buchstein, "Countering," 133.

[166] Dahl, *After the Revolution?*, 72–3.

manner of (civil and criminal) juries, and also to compose internal oversight bodies for legislative activity. In modern constitutional democracies, the bureaucracy and a judiciary function take the place of the numerous lottery-drawn bodies in the ancient world. These modern state organs serve similar goals to ancient lottery-drawn bodies: preventing the functions of the state from being captured by those in power who then transfer them to relatives or extended clan networks. "One might say that Athenian lotteries were used to staff the equivalent of the civil service more than the functions of high political decision-making. Key political decisions rested in the hands of the elected generals together with the popular votes won by the selected speakers in the assembly, who advised on public policy."[167] We will therefore conclude with a scheme that Buchstein proposes, and which seems to do justice to Aristotle's *Politics* since it complicates the various combinations of appointment procedures with constitutions that one finds there: polity (with lot and/or election); aristocracy (with lot and/or election); oligarchy (with election, lot, co-optation and sale of offices); democracy (with lot and election).[168]

1.2.2 An Issue of Stability (That Lotteries Did Not Solve)

In Herodotus's famous dialogue on the various forms of government, Othanes contrasts democracy with monarchy (which is close to tyranny) and aristocracy (which is not too far from oligarchy). Both monarchy and aristocracy are portrayed as breeding insolence and arbitrariness through the rivalries that take place within the ruling class—they fuel envy, slander, divisions in the city, and violence. Othanes presents democracy as the only form of government that can neutralize these vices because it includes the many in its principle of *isonomia* and public offices are drawn by lots: "Under a government of the people a magistrate is appointed by lot and is held responsible for his conduct in office, and all questions are put up for open debate."[169] Herodotus goes on to associate the "choosing" of the "best men in the country" with instability ("that a number of men are competing for distinction in public service cannot but lead to violent personal feuds") and to associate lottery with concord ("break[ing] up the cliques").[170] At least with respect to lottery, the troubled history of the Florentine Republic seems to have proved Herodotus wrong on this score.

While the fifteenth-century Florentine Republic arose many centuries after the fall of Athens its secretary, Leonardo Bruni, praised it as a "new Athens." The republic of Florence instituted a system of very complex (and frequently altered) sortitions that was supposed to solve a different problem from that faced by the Greek polis.

---

[167] Lane, *The Birth of Politics*, 120.
[168] Buchstein, "Countering," 145.
[169] Herodotus, *The Histories*, trans. Aubrey de Sélincourt (London: Penguin Books, 1972), 187 (3.80). Hubris was considered as a permanent "crime" threatening cohesion but also the self-esteem of the ordinary people (the *mesoi* that Walt Whitman sings in his *Democratic Vistas* as "middling man"): Ian Morris, "The Strong Principle of Equality and the Archaic Origins of Greek Democracy," in Ober and Hedrick, *Dēmokratia*, 21–2.
[170] Herodotus, *Histories*, 188 (3.82).

70   The Lottocratic Mentality

The challenge was not to prevent the formation of a separate political class, but instead to end the radical instability that had been caused by the bloody struggles between factions or alignments of factions that would use the *Signoria* (state) as a tool to expel or even kill enemies while elevating friends.[171] As Giovanni Villani noted around 1340, choosing by lot was seen to be a "neutral" or "external mechanism" that would allow the commune "to function smoothly and peacefully" while ensuring "a good and equitable order."[172] Florence did not possess what Athens had called *isonomia*—the political equality of each citizen in the demos. This was despite the fact that the main goal of the republic was to ensure a certain type of "equality" before the law as well as just treatment and arbitration. Unsurprisingly, while these goals were always pursued they were rarely achieved due to the high level of discord between factions.[173] In the absence of a fully individual political equality and a written constitution that secured the impartial administration of state functions, a citizenry or sphere of civic inclusion that was guild-based primed the failure of both lotteries and elections. The experience showed that, in a popular government, both selection methods depended upon individual political equality as well as a basic rule of law that applied to all regardless of someone's power or reputation.

Florentine citizenship was very unequal—it was basically a status that was enjoyed by a portion of the humble laborers and artisans as well as by *all* the powerful and wealthy artisans, entrepreneurs, and bankers. The unbalanced and differential levels of power reflected the guild to which the citizens belonged. The democratic principle of "one man one vote" that had existed in Athens was decidedly absent from the Tuscan city which, much like with the Roman Republic, deployed lottery not so much in order to achieve an equal distribution of political functions but rather to neutralize the power of the most powerful by controlling their rivalries so as to "save their aristocratic pride."[174] The multiround selection mechanism used in Florence and in other Italian republics was designed to contain the power of the stronger families and their circles—thereby depoliticizing selection through *ad sortem* (chance) designation. It would be a mistake to include Florence among a list of democracies, although for many decades it was certainly a more inclusive republic than aristocratic Venice or oligarchic Genoa (both of which also deployed lotteries). In Florence, the lottery was meant to ward off the power of government factions (within a political culture where "individuals did not exist"). The best way to achieve that goal was by making sure that the selection of councilors "sufficiently accounted for representation from the different groups that composed the city's political society."[175] Lottery applied to

---

[171] One of those struggles cost Dante Alighieri's exile.

[172] Manin, *The Principles*, 53. Villani's words as cited in Lorenzo Tanzini, "The Practices and Rhetoric of Sortition in Medieval Public Life (13th–14th Centuries)," in *Sortition and Democracy: History, Tools, Theories*, ed. Yves Sintomer and Liliane Lopez-Rabatel (Exeter: Imprint Academic, 2020), 202.

[173] Daniel Waley, *The Italian City-Republics* (New York: McGraw-Hill, 1978), 67–73. Indeed, this virulent factionalism explains why the main executive head of the judiciary, the *podestà*, was a citizen from another commune who was trained in the law and who held his office for six months to a year—yet, he was selected through neither sortition nor elections and he did not come from the citizenry.

[174] Lintott, *The Constitution of the Roman Republic*, 101.

[175] Tanzini, "The Practices," 214 and 208.

the few in order to confirm their equal merit, prevent the long-term concentration of power in a narrow clique of families, and make consensus possible among oligarchs who were always ready to foment divisions and factions. In opposition to Athens where instability was caused by the resistance of the few to abide by the decisions made by the Assembly, in Florence instability was caused by an insoluble competition among the elite and a lack of trust between political winners and losers. In *that* context, the goal of lotteries was to make the losing (nonselected) faction accept the defeat—a goal that was admittedly never fully achieved.

Divine will or blind luck seemed to militate in favor of lottery—as if distrust could be overcome by removing the voluntary element in the selection of public offices. In Florence, sortition was meant to placate the fear that elections would be distorted by the powerful, that preferences would not be free, and that candidates would not be treated equally. Elections would require trust in order to make consent credible and trust would require equality. Lotteries were meant to succeed in this respect where elections had failed. But, the generalized lack of trust made lotteries as dysfunctional as elections. In promoting the latter, Bruni and later Guicciardini explained that elections put individual merit, responsibility, and distinction first and sanctioned the pre-eminence of some over the rest.[176] Bruni clarified that lotteries did not deliver a desirable solution because, firstly, they tended to privilege short-sighted priorities ("present concerns are treated with close attention and shrewdness") and gave relevance to "remote, contingent, and dubious matters." Second, lotteries fell short because they inevitably translated into an impoverished political ethics: the lottery "extinguishes zeal for virtue, as men are much more careful in their behavior if there is a contest for votes and their reputation may openly be put in danger." This was the thinking behind Bruni's conclusion that the practice of elections "was much better and more useful to the state" (an argument that American Federalists would reiterate).[177]

Yet neither Bruni nor Guicciardini recognized that both lotteries and elections required equality: whether it was conceptualized as equality before the law, or as equal access to public offices, or as an equal chance to compete for them. Thus, on the one hand, Bruni cast elections as a better system because they pitted "individuals" against each other; but, on the other, his society was made up of relatively closed social groups and guilds, and the individuals who enjoyed or started enjoying more autonomy were merely the affluent. Thus, not surprisingly, the early expansion of elections was "primarily beneficial for the elites."[178] This meant that "elections were not usually conducted from below and there were no public campaigns; moreover,

---

[176] "It is the people, and not chance, that should be the master; the people, and not Fortune, [that] should distribute honors," wrote Guicciardini in his *Dialogo del reggimento di Firenze* (cited by Sintomer) who, according to Sintomer, "expresses a view of popular legitimacy and representation that will later be crucial in the Age of Enlightenment and the French Revolution—and which, to this day, lurks behind many a spontaneous reaction. He also emphasizes a new and quite pejorative notion of chance that is devoid of rationality" (*The Government of Chance*, 97–8).

[177] Leonardo Bruni, *History of the Florentine People*, vol. 2, *Books 5–8*, trans. James Hankins (Cambridge, MA: Harvard University Press, 2004), 73 (5.81).

[178] Tanzini, "The Practices," 214.

72 The Lottocratic Mentality

at that time, parties and factions (*intelligenze*) were prohibited, even though they existed informally."[179]

The Florentine case highlights the connection between elections and parties; it shows that, in contrast to Aristotle's characterization and the way that they used to function in ancient Athens, elections do not merely consist in voting for individual candidates and a competition between individuals. In Florence, election was a competition involving candidates who associated with some but not others, and who asked for votes based precisely on that difference. As Kyshlansky has shown in his analysis of the English revolution, modern elections and political parties were born together; elections interrupted "symbiotic relationships" between candidates and their communities (or guilds) and opened the door to constructed groups formed around ideas or partisan claims—which is to say, modern political parties.[180] The Florentine constitution was not equipped to protect the individual right to vote and a legitimate opposition. These goals would only be slowly achieved in the United States two centuries after the Florentine Republic.

We can therefore say to those who claim that in contemporary representative democracies the revival of interest in lotteries is consistent with a constellation of principles used by the ancients (rotation, impartiality and anti-corruption) that this revival is actually imbued with an entirely new goal that was wholly foreign to the ancients and which, as we shall see in Chapter 4, can be identified with the "antiparty" and antipartisan spirit. For this reason, Florence is closer to us than Athens. The call for lotteries emanating from within our democracies is directed against elections that choose a government that is not direct but rather representative, and where the legislature plays a representative function. Lottocracy today is a direct challenge to collective electoral institutions and to the role of parties as intermediaries or "middlemen" that insert themselves into an electoral process which they then come to dominate. In this sense, lottocrats propose to use sortition in a different way and for different reasons than it was used for in Athens. This brings us to a final point we must critically analyze in this chapter—an evaluation of the polemical target of lotteries: elections.

1.2.3 Elections, Then and Now

As mentioned earlier, for Manin both modern representative government and the government of fourth-century Athens are examples of "mixed government" since, in

---

[179] Yves Sintomer, "Random Selection and Deliberative Democracy: Note for an Historical Comparison," in *Sortition: Theory and Practice*, ed. Gil Delannoi and Oliver Dowlen (Exeter: Imprint Academic, 2010), 37. Nicolai Rubinstein's studies of the Florentine Republic redirected scholars' attention to the theme of constitutionalism. They showed, for instance, that the Medici were able to emerge and dominate the political life of the city, within an electoral system that was already well established and a network of clienteles that was already ingrained in the Republic. Nicolai Rubinstein, "Politics and Constitution in Florence at the End of the Fifteenth Century," in *Italian Renaissance Studies*, ed. Ernest F. Jacob (London: Faber & Faber, 1960).

[180] Kishlansky, *Parliamentary Selection*, 14.

each case, selection methods play a central role and direct democracy is minimized. But, whereas the ancients located the democratic aspect of mixed government *in* the selection mechanism of lottery itself, in modern representative government the democratic aspect exists *outside* of the selection mechanism of elections: in contemporary democratic societies democracy consists in the enjoyment of rights to free speech as well as freedom of association rights that allow for the formation of proposals and preferences and give consent a sanctioning power. The difference between these two forms of government is noteworthy because of the specific character of lotteries and the equality of probability that they secure. Lottery is an impartial standard to make a selection that bypasses any evaluation of options or sense of choice, whereas elections cannot avoid partiality since "voters are not required to use impartial standards to discriminate among candidates."[181] Consequently, a focus on the selection procedure itself is particularly helpful in showing that representative government is not *purely* democratic. For, while representative government equalizes candidates who are ready to compete and also gives voters an equal opportunity to express their preferences, it does *not* secure an equal probability to serve like lotteries do; in electoral government, citizens do not enjoy any meaningful type of equality as candidates for office but instead enjoy an equality of expressing their voting preferences for a given candidate. Elections inject competition into the governmental process that renders a judgment that discriminates among equals. This type of discrimination in judgment is *not* made on the basis of "inborn" or ascriptive traits but instead on the basis of a kind of quality or trait "that only the free decision of all other people can confer."[182] This is Manin's main argument in a nutshell.

By placing lottery at the very core of democracy, Manin pits lottery against elections. This opposition was quickly picked up by lottocrats, who then seem to reason as follows: If competence is crucial, then elections seem desirable; but if democracy depends on assuming an equal competence among citizens, then elections seem to contradict the very premise of democracy. However, as we have mentioned earlier, Athenian democracy in fact used both lotteries and elections. Athens only used elections for governmental functions that relied on individual initiative (e.g., the chief of the army or (what in our time would be) the president of the republic). Yet, lottery was used for functions that involved collective deliberation and which could therefore not be carried out by all citizens simultaneously. Elections were a means to choose *single magistrates* but not to choose a collective organ like a parliament. They were used to select *individual administrators* and naturally relied on citizens' judgment about the qualities that candidates claimed to have which were required by the function they desired to fulfill (something Montesquieu repeatedly emphasized). But, this is *not* how elections function if they are employed to select collegial councils like they were in humanist Florence, or if they are used to select parliaments or congress as they are in contemporary times. In those more modern contexts, the type of individual authority and judgment given to those selected is quite different. Florence presents

---

[181] Manin, *The Principles*, 136.
[182] Ibid., 40.

74 The Lottocratic Mentality

an interesting case because elections failed to stabilize the city, and this particular failure showed that elections primarily foster competition between factions rather than between individuals. Thus, falling back on the ancient dichotomy between lotteries and elections helps explain neither what was at stake in Florence nor what is at stake in modern representative government more generally.

Lottocrats either do not see this anachronism or else do not see it as an issue. Not only do they identify democracy with lottery, but they also seem to judge representative government by a standard defined by the way that elections were conceptualized and practiced in ancient Athens—a context wherein elections were used to choose individuals for specific civil and military functions. However, when elections are used to select parliaments, they are clearly deployed as an alternative to the direct presence in the Assembly, *not* an alternative to lotteries. Elections in representative institutions are very different from the sort of elections that Aristotle wrote about and from the paradigm that today's lottocrats deem "undemocratic." In short, using ancient history as an explanatory model of various institutions and the values they supposedly embodied has had distorting effects when, without alteration or contextualization, this model is then applied as a lens through which modern institutions of representative government are judged. This is especially true in relation to elections. Irrespective of whether they are direct or indirect, elections are not identical across all forms of government. Moreover, elections fulfill quite different functions depending on whether they are applied in an administrative or a lawmaking context, and depending upon whether they are set up to serve either monocratic or collective functions. Electing a president (the equivalent of an *archē*) is very different than electing the members of a parliament or congress (the equivalent of the *ekklēsia*): while in the first case the focus is mainly on an individual (hence the discrimination among individual candidates),[183] and in the second case the focus is on the set of proposals that a candidate presents himself or herself as committed to and she then asks the citizens as groups or voting blocs for their vote (when elections propagated factions in the Florentine Republic it was not just bad luck that things turned out that way). Quite unlike a political representative, the relation of a sorted leader to the people is unmediated.[184] No candidate running for a seat in a representative assembly simply puts herself forward as an individual. Yet, despite this obvious fact, those who criticize elections often analyze them as if they are essentially a matter of cognitive psychology: a relationship between one person (who judges and chooses) and another (who prepares to be judged and chosen). But, elections are not merely an

---

[183] This might also be true for presidential elections, in which "the personal" factor is more prominently at stake: "We do not merely choose a president or decide or a law [when we cast our ballot]. We chose a total world in which everything is settled." Russell Hardin, "Public Choice versus Democracy," in *The Idea of Democracy*, ed. David Copp, Jean Hampton, and John E. Roemer (Cambridge: Cambridge University Press, 1993), 161.

[184] Cornelius Castoriadis clearly picked up on this point when he proposed a parallel between lotteries and acts of delegation with an imperative mandate. He made it clear that, in Athens, lottery and rotation were not meant to produce "representatives." Castoriadis, "The Greek Polis and the Creation of Democracy," in *Philosophy, Politics, Autonomy: Essays in Political Philosophy* (New York: Oxford University Press, 1991), 107.

individualistic or psychological phenomenon because they are enmeshed within an institutional order that structures them and mobilizes *groups of citizens* rather than isolated candidates.

In representative democracy, a vote for Mrs. Smith always entails simultaneously voting for what Mrs. Smith proposes and stands for, and this is inevitably tied to what groups of citizens believe in and stand for. Indeed, citizens can only claim she represents them on such a basis. Elections in a representative democracy sanction and promote both the formation of collectives (political groups/constituencies and parties) that connect or divide electors and elected. Elections in this context facilitate the permanent process of political opinion formation that animates the legislative assembly—which itself can never be independent from us since we are the agent that sets it in motion (independence was a goal that the Athenians sought with their administrative bodies chosen by lot). Elections do not simply consist in the act of voting but, to paraphrase Dahl, are inclusive and composed of two stages: "the election stage and the interelection stage." Elections also consist of three periods: the voting, the prevoting, and the postvoting.[185]

Elections designate a *longue durée* temporality. This is contrary to lotteries, where the dimension of time merely shows up in the moment of picking a name and where there is no expectation (or possibility) of interference from past or future opinions. Selecting candidates as single competitors is simply not an adequate description of what elections are within a representative democracy. If elections were truly a choice between single candidates, then representation would simply vanish because each elected member would stand for herself or himself alone and truly replace the citizens in making her decision. This is more or less what would also happen if a lottery were applied to lawmaking, as citizens who were not drawn would be "ruled" by the allotted few—who only stand for themselves.

It took time for elections to be accepted and to stabilize competition. As we noted, in proto-electoral England when parliamentary posts were distributed among the nobility as marks of honor, lotteries were then used to choose the candidates because it was a neutral system that did not allow for discrimination among peers.[186] As mentioned earlier, the same difficulty existed in humanist Florence where elections could not stabilize the city because they operated in and contributed to a factional environment at a historical juncture when the republic had not yet found the constitutional and procedural means to deal with party pluralism and fierce competition between political groups, nor had it found an adequate way to conceptualize political equality. In the end, neither elections as individual choice nor lottery as pure chance could work. The failure of the Florentine Republic is an interesting example of how a society that adopts elections has to be ready to accept and govern political divisions between *groups*, not merely quarrels among individuals. But for this to happen, such a society must have a system of legal equality and, furthermore, a written constitution that

---

[185] Robert Dahl, *A Preface to Democratic Theory* (Chicago: University of Chicago Press, 1956), 67 and 71.

[186] Kishlansky, *Parliamentary Selection*, 36.

defines and regulates the divisions and limits of various institutional powers, and that also distinguishes between those holding an office and the functions of that office. Florence had none of this.

The conceptual and historical background that sets up a dualistic framework between lotteries and elections relies on authors and institutions that operated long before representative government existed. Manin writes that despite the significant economic, institutional, and cultural changes that representative government has gone through, elections remained the same from the age of Aristotle up through Guicciardini to Montesquieu and into the present era. He takes the present to be characterized by a decline in party-based democracy and a rise in what he terms "audience democracy." With this term, Manin is signaling a return to the original personalist character of elections: "Voters tend increasingly to vote for a person and no longer for a party or a platform."[187] It would thus seem that parties were afterthoughts or a contingent moment in the life and history of representative government; and that the role increasingly played by personalities and plebiscitary leaders today seems to bring us back to a time when elections were, as per Aristotle's characterization, clearly and explicitly a choice between individuals on the basis of their qualities and character. In this same vein, the chancellor of the Republic of Florence, Leonardo Bruni, rendered the struggle between lotteries and elections as one between irresponsibility and responsibility, and incompetence and competence; Montesquieu followed the same train of thought when he claimed that citizens are capable of judging people's moral and ethical qualities even if they are incapable of deciding competently, and that this makes elections a safer institutional bet than lotteries. Bruni and Montesquieu reframed the Aristotelean paradigm that, on the one hand, gave the popular assembly the capacity to amend incompetent decisions made by individual citizens and, on the other, gave elections the power of selecting the more competent to serve in administration. Updating this paradigm for the modern era, Bruni and Montesquieu believed that the core principle underlying democracy was equality not freedom, and that those who loved freedom would not want democracy but rather a type of republic that recognized a balance between popular consent and individual competence—a balance that only elections could strike.

The "ambiguity of election"[188] has pushed lottocrats to embrace the binary logic of either democracy or leadership, either selecting without creating an elite or selecting while creating an elite—in sum, either lottery or elections. For them, lottery is not simply different from elections, but it is decidedly superior since it does not pit candidates against one other but rather selects ordinary citizens in an apparently harmonious manner that, regardless of whether it is deployed for consultation or decision-making purposes, generates results that hold for all. Lot is meant to contribute to the "ethos that public office-holders should be disconnected or independent of any particular external influence."[189] It is noteworthy that in claiming that

---

[187] Manin, *The Principles*, 219.
[188] Ibid., 156.
[189] Dowlen, *The Political Potential of Sortition*, 50.

lottery is supposedly more egalitarian and respectful of independent judgment and cognitive diversity than elections and thereby more consistent with democracy, lottocrats become blinkered democrats. For, while they stress equality in rotation and selection by impartial choice, they are blind to the basic democratic condition: the universal inclusion of the citizens in the primary power of voting as well as their permanent right to interfere with the activities and opinions of the elected.

According to lottocrats, elections are an intrinsically "aristocratic" method of selection because, as Manin argued, they rely on "the principle of distinction" and lead to the selection of representatives whom voters perceive as "superior" or relevantly distinct from themselves. In Chapter 4, we analyze the lottocratic claim that elections unavoidably fail to select candidates who are representative of the broader population because they violate the principle of descriptive representativeness. In what follows, we want to conclude our examination of Manin's arguments about the intrinsically "aristocratic" character of elections in order to see if they truly support lottocrats' claim that elections, by their very nature, threaten representatives' responsiveness to citizen interests.

First, it is important to keep in mind that Manin's argument is concerned with *inequality* and not with *responsiveness*.[190] Manin aims to show that elections do not and cannot provide "equality of opportunity" *to candidates*. This is relevant for assessing whether his overall argument offers any support to lottocrats' contention that, because elections are intrinsically "aristocratic," they lead to the selection of representatives who are not responsive to citizens' interests. In fact, Manin's arguments do not offer such support. Of his four arguments, the first two are based on intrinsic features of elections which bear on inequality (unequal treatment of candidates) but have nothing to do with responsiveness, whereas the final two arguments, which do bear on responsiveness, are not concerned with intrinsic features of elections but rather with circumstances and conditions of elections that can be changed without dismantling the method of election itself. Let's take a look at the four arguments.[191]

Manin's arguments aim to show that elections necessarily (1) treat candidates unequally (i.e., fail to provide equality of opportunity) and (2) produce candidates that are thought to be in some sense superior to those who elect them (i.e., "principle of distinction"). The reasons are as follows. First, elections fail to treat *candidates fairly* since voters are allowed to elect candidates as they see fit. They can *discriminate* against candidates for reasons unrelated to candidates' actions and choices. This is true. Yet, regardless of whether elections are unfair to candidates, it is important to note that this has nothing to do with responsiveness to citizens' interests. If anything, fairness to candidates would *undermine* responsiveness. If all candidates had to be treated fairly, even if citizens dislike their political agenda, then there would be no reason to expect that elected representatives would be responsive to citizens'

---

[190] Manin develops his argument in a section entitled "The aristocratic character of election: a pure theory." As he explains, the aim of the section is to show that "there are certain elements *intrinsic* to the elective method with inegalitarian implications and leading to the elected being in some way superior to the electors" (*The Principles*, 134).

[191] Ibid., 134–49.

78 The Lottocratic Mentality

political preferences. Responsiveness presupposes that citizens have the right to influence political decisions and, therefore, that representatives ought to attend to citizens' political preferences. But this argument, as Manin recognizes, has nothing to do with the "principle of distinction." The next three arguments do.

The second argument is that election is "irreducibly a choice of persons."[192] This is a doubtful claim. It may have been true of representative systems in the eighteenth century, but it does not seem true of contemporary party-based democracies that enable citizens to choose candidates based on publicly articulated political programs. In Party List systems, for instance, citizens often vote for a party without knowing anything about the listed candidates; in some cases, only the parties appear on the ballot. It can hardly be true of such elections that they are "irreducibly a choice of persons." In general elections, a voter has typically only one candidate from each political party to choose from. In those cases, citizens do not have more than one person to choose from who matches their political preferences. To the extent that citizens vote for candidates mainly based on their political preferences, their choice cannot be "irreducibly a choice of persons." The claim may be plausible in the case of primaries or regarding the selection of candidates within political parties when there is more than one person to choose from. Let's look at these cases to see if they offer support for lottocrats' claims.

Selection of candidates within parties may be intrinsically a choice of persons but, even if it is, it is irrelevant to responsiveness. For any candidate from the political party in question endorses the party's political program and can thus be equally expected to be responsive to the political preferences of citizens who identify with the political program in question and vote for that party for that reason. In primaries, there are two possible scenarios. If the choice among candidates is based on differences in political orientation (e.g., choosing between candidates from different ideological wings of a party—say, the more progressive, centrist, or radical wings), then this choice does not have to be and typically is not "intrinsically a choice of persons" but is rather, above all, a choice of political preferences. As such, it has little to do with an assumption that the candidate has any "superior" qualities over those who elect them. Moreover, this type of choice, far from being detrimental, is *essential* for responsiveness. By contrast, if several candidates share the same political orientation within the party (e.g., they belong to the same political wing of the party in question), then this would indeed be "irreducibly a choice of persons," but there is no obvious reason why it would have to have a detrimental effect on the responsiveness to citizens' political preferences. Let's move on to the last two arguments that bear directly on responsiveness.

The third argument concerns "the cognitive advantage conferred by salience in attracting attention."[193] It is true that "salience" helps candidates attract voters' attention. It tends to favor incumbents as well as otherwise famous individuals over less well-known candidates. This is related to the fourth argument, namely, the cost of

---

[192] Ibid., 141–2.
[193] Ibid., 135.

The Lottery Revival   79

disseminating information (participating in elections), which is also likely to favor wealthy and well-connected candidates over others. Both arguments bear on responsiveness. But, how are they connected to the claim about the intrinsically aristocratic nature of elections?

It is important to note that the advantages of name recognition and wealth have nothing to do with any endorsement of the "principle of distinction," i.e., any general acceptance of the idea that candidates "are thought to be superior in some sense *to those who elect them.*" Recognizing that candidates with more (cultural, social, and economic) resources have an advantage in elections is not the same as recognizing that they are "superior" to the elected in any "aristocratic" sense. In fact, citizens tend to be very suspicious of the undue influence that money plays in elections. Far from leading citizens to believe that politicians have "superior" qualities, this recognition usually fuels the view that politicians are out of touch and untrustworthy.

Yet, it is true that these two features are directly connected to the worry about candidates' lack of responsiveness. However, neither is an intrinsic feature of elections (and the underlying principle of choice) or what would make elections inevitably "aristocratic." They are what Manin calls "aristocratic *effects* derived from the circumstances and conditions in which the elective method is employed." Given that these effects, as Manin himself concedes, can be addressed *without dismantling elections,* they simply cannot be intrinsic features of elections. Manin mentions public campaign financing as a way to eliminate these effects. But, of course, there are other ways of improving the descriptive representativeness of party candidates—for example, through proportional representation, quotas (e.g., for women), random selection among candidates to craft party lists, etc.

In sum, lottocrats' claim that elections are intrinsically "aristocratic" and therefore cannot be improved upon and must be replaced by lottery is not supported by Manin's arguments about "the principle of distinction." The idea that citizens must be able to judge one candidate "superior" to another in order to choose among them is trivially true. But, this "superiority" holds between candidates themselves and not between candidates and voters. Moreover, there is nothing "aristocratic" about the fact that citizens take the candidates that match their political preferences to be "superior" to those that defend alternative political programs. Citizens choosing candidates of one political party over those of other parties do not need to base their choice on any "superior" personality traits of the candidates but can instead simply base their decision on what they take to be a "superior" political program. Later on in the text, Manin clarifies the particular concept of "superiority" that is involved in his argument: "Voters do not have to believe that the candidate is better in every respect, they may despise one or even most of his character traits. The foregoing arguments merely show that voters, if they are to elect a candidate, must regard him as superior in the light of the quality or set of qualities that they consider *politically relevant.*"[194]

Now, this clarification is important because if the political agendas of the different candidates (and the parties they belong to) can be the "politically relevant" quality

---

[194] Ibid., 146.

80 The Lottocratic Mentality

that determines voters' choices, then the claim of superiority loses any "aristocratic" connotation whatsoever. Candidates who are aligned with the political preferences of voters will be perceived as "better" rulers, certainly better than those with the wrong political agendas. But, this "political" superiority by no means justifies the 'aristocratic' claim that representatives "are perceived as superior to those who elect them." Again, this may have been true of representative practice in the eighteenth century, but with the emergence of national parties toward the end of the nineteenth century and the development of multiparty democracy in the twentieth century, the claim that elections are "aristocratic" because citizens "perceive candidates as superior" *to them* seems unfounded. The existence of an obvious alternative—namely, that citizens select candidates according to their political preferences and consequently, the most politically relevant quality of candidates (and their parties) is their political agenda—undermines the plausibility of the claim that elections are intrinsically "aristocratic."

In fact, Manin himself seems to agree with this view. In the Epilogue to the German translation of his book *The Principles of Representative Government*, Manin clarifies that his thesis about the transformation of party democracy into audience democracy in no way implies that political parties are obsolete. In that context, he explains: "Despite an increasing personalization, political parties continue to dominate parliamentary elections. Another development would have been conceivable. Elections could have turned into a contest in which mainly public and prominent personalities run for office independently of parties and party affiliation. This has not happened."[195] There may be other ways to justify the claim that elections are inherently "aristocratic." What we hope to have shown, however, is that lottocrats cannot prove this claim simply by relying on Manin's argument. They must make the case themselves by offering substantive arguments whose plausibility can be scrutinized.

1.3 Conclusion

In this chapter, we have attempted to dismantle the binary logic of lotteries-versus-elections and the implicit assumption (which is also a conclusion) that democracy is identical to the former and the opposite to the latter. We have addressed the usual interpretation of history that this idea is grounded in and found that it is based on a simplistic reading of Athenian institutions and political history. We have shown that lotteries did not possess an exclusively democratic pedigree within Athenian democracy (either in the fourth century or earlier) because what distinguished democracy

---

[195] Bernard Manin, *Kritik der repräsentativen Demokratie* (Berlin: Matthes & Seitz, 2007), 331 (our translation). Manin also points out that even independent candidates with no party affiliation have no choice but to position themselves in relation to parties. He explains: "It is remarkable that political parties are the fundamental powers that design electoral alternatives and offer them to voters in parliamentary elections. Although it is not always party candidates who win, the fact that parties are represented at least in most campaigns forces independent candidates to position themselves in relation to the parties. For this reason, in parliamentary elections voters are faced with a cognitive map that is designed mainly by political parties" (332, our translation).

from oligarchy was the inclusion of both rich and poor citizens in the process of elections and lotteries, not the use of elections or lotteries per se. We have also challenged the unquestioned assumption that direct presence in the Assembly was subordinate to the lawmaking power of an institutional organ selected by lot. We have in addition critically examined the idea that elections are an inherently oligarchic selection mechanism and shown that, historically, even many oligarchs preferred lotteries and rejected elections. Conceptually, we have analyzed Manin's arguments in support of the view that elections are inherently "aristocratic" and found them unconvincing, particularly in the context of contemporary party-based democracies. Ultimately, we have shown that ancient history provides a conception and practice of elections that has little to do with how elections work in mass suffrage-based representative democracy, and thus that this ancient framework neither helps us understand the nature and crisis of representative democracies today nor does it provide consistent solutions. Elections for members of an assembly that functions to pass laws, as is the case today, are not the same as elections for individual administrative officials, as was the case in ancient Athens.

We do not criticize efforts to reconstruct and compare the meanings and functioning of institutions in ancient and modern times. That endeavor helps advance our knowledge of politics and various forms of government. But, lottocrats are not historians; they treat elections and lotteries as if they were eternal models applicable in all times and in all political systems; and they use history as a rhetorical strategy to persuade today's citizens to reshape representative democracy by eliminating or disempowering elections—with the goal of ultimately replacing them with lotteries. Their argumentative strategy is shrewd because once elections are defined as nondemocratic, giving them up seems not only not wrong or inappropriate but also laudable and desirable.

Chapter 2
Deliberative Democracy's Turn to Lottery-Based Institutions

Deliberative democrats are at the forefront of developing deliberative minipublics. However, their distinctive motivations and interest in engaging with deliberative minipublics are primarily driven by their endorsement of deliberative democracy and do not necessarily coincide with the motivations and concerns held by other scholars involved in developing lottery-based institutions. As discussed in Chapter 1, the scholars behind the revival of lotteries had many different concerns in mind. This diversity of thought continues to characterize current debates among those interested in the development of lottery-based institutions. Since these thinkers come from very different political traditions, their proposals for crafting and organizing lottery-based institutions are motivated by a wide variety of reasons. Deliberative democrats do not place the same emphasis on or even share all of the motivating reasons that we discussed in Chapter 1 (e.g., antioligarchy, anticorruption, epistocratic concerns, and so on). Yet, given the prominent role of deliberative democrats in the ongoing development of deliberative minipublics, analyzing their specific motivations, concerns, and interests in lottery-based institutions can shed light on why the lottocratic mentality has become so popular.

As will become clear, we think that the normative commitments at the core of the conception of deliberative democracy are ultimately incompatible with key elements of what we call the "lottocratic mentality." However, a brief analysis of the evolution of this line of thought in deliberative democracy helps show that the deliberative paradigm of democratic theory is both capacious and ambiguous enough to enable and even foster this mentality. Highlighting the tensions between the core normative assumptions of deliberative democracy and the key elements of the lottocratic mentality will also set the stage for the last part of the book where it is shown that lottery-based institutions *could* serve genuine democratic aims—but only if the scholars and practitioners behind them decisively reject the lottocratic mentality.

The Lottocratic Mentality. Cristina Lafont and Nadia Urbinati, Oxford University Press. © Cristina Lafont and Nadia Urbinati (2024). DOI: 10.1093/9780191982903.003.0003

2.1 The Deliberative Turn in Democratic Theory

In recent decades, "deliberative democracy" has become the leading paradigm in democratic theory.[1] The articulation of this paradigm is often seen as having passed through several "turns": the institutional turn, the systemic turn, the empirical turn, etc.[2] Some of these developments have led to an increased focus on institutional innovations such as deliberative minipublics. In some contexts, such minipublics have become directly synonymous with deliberative democracy itself. At the core of the idea of a deliberative democracy is a distinctive conception of legitimacy: legitimate lawmaking issues from the public deliberation of citizens.[3] As Gutmann puts it, "the legitimate exercise of political authority requires justification to those people who are bound by it, and decision making by deliberation among free and equal citizens is the most defensible justification anyone has to offer for provisionally settling controversial issues."[4] Thus, inclusive public deliberation contributes to democratic legitimacy to the extent that it enables citizens to accept the laws and policies to which they are subject as at least being reasonable. This lets them avoid being simply coerced into obedience. To the extent that citizens can mutually justify the political coercion they exercise over one another, they can see each other as equal participants in a democratic project of self-government. This is the internal connection between public deliberation and the democratic ideal of self-government.

This public justification criterion of legitimacy is what distinguishes deliberative democracy from both purely aggregative and purely epistemic conceptions of democracy.[5] For purely aggregative conceptions of democracy, it is the fairness of decision procedures such as majority rule—which affords each participant equal chances to

---

[1] For an overview of the deliberative turn in democratic theory, see Floridia, *From Participation to Deliberation* and "The Origins of the Deliberative Turn," in *The Oxford Handbook of Deliberative Democracy*, ed. André Bächtiger, John S. Dryzek, Jane Mansbridge, and Mark E. Warren (Oxford: Oxford University Press, 2018), 35–54. See also John Dryzek, "The Deliberative Turn in Democratic Theory," in *Deliberative Democracy and Beyond* (Oxford: Oxford University Press, 2002). For surveys of the development of deliberative democracy, see James Bohman, "Survey Article: The Coming of Age of Deliberative Democracy," *Journal of Political Philosophy* 6, no. 4 (1998): 400–25; Simone Chambers, "Deliberative Democratic Theory," *Annual Review of Political Science*, 6 (2003): 307–26. For recent collections that include various approaches, see Bächtiger et al., *Oxford Handbook of Deliberative Democracy*; Seyla Benhabib, ed., *Democracy and Difference: Contesting the Boundaries of the Political* (Princeton, NJ: Princeton University Press, 1996); Samantha Besson and José Luis Martí, eds., *Deliberative Democracy and Its Discontents* (Aldershot, UK: Ashgate, 2006); James Bohman and William Rehg, eds., *Deliberative Democracy* (Cambridge, MA: MIT Press, 1999); Jon Elster, ed., *Deliberative Democracy* (Cambridge: Cambridge University Press, 1998); James S. Fishkin and Peter Laslett, eds., *Debating Deliberative Democracy* (Oxford: Blackwell, 2003); John Gastil and Peter Levine, eds., *The Deliberative Democracy Handbook* (San Francisco, CA: Jossey-Bass, 2005); Stephen Macedo, ed., *Deliberative Politics* (Oxford: Oxford University Press, 1999).

[2] For a brief overview, see, e.g., John Dryzek and Simon Niemeyer, "Deliberative Turns," in *Foundations and Frontiers of Deliberative Governance*, ed. John Dryzek (Oxford: Oxford University Press, 2010), 6–9.

[3] See Bohman and Rehg, *Deliberative Democracy*, ix; Dryzek and Niemeyer, *Foundations and Frontiers*, 21, 34.

[4] Amy Gutmann, "Democracy, Philosophy, and Justification," in Benhabib, *Democracy and Difference*, 340–7, our italics.

[5] For an overview of the origins of the public justification criterion of legitimacy and its various interpretations, see Kevin Vallier, "Public Justification," in *Stanford Encyclopedia of Philosophy* (Winter 2022 ed.), ed. Edward N. Zalta and Uri Nodelman, https://plato.stanford.edu/archives/win2022/entries/justification-public/.

84 The Lottocratic Mentality

influence the outcome and thus treats them as equals—that lends legitimacy to the outcomes of democratic decisions. On this view, legitimacy is a function of citizens' equal exercise of power by means of a procedure that treats everyone's views and preferences equally.[6] By contrast, deliberative democrats reject the idea that—regardless of how unjust, misinformed, or manipulated they may be—everyone's views and preferences should be treated equally. For them, legitimacy requires better reasons to have greater influence over outcomes while still upholding equal voting rights. Thus, it is the quality of the justificatory reasons (and not just a higher number of votes) that can lend legitimacy to the outcomes of democratic decisions. Legitimacy is internally linked to the quality of the deliberative process that takes place before collective decisions are made. By adding a deliberative requirement as a condition for democratic legitimacy, the deliberative conception highlights a way in which minorities may be able to prevent political domination by the majority. They can try to contest dominant public opinion by showing that their counterproposals are supported by better reasons and, in so doing, hold out hope that "the unforced force of the better argument" may eventually transform public opinion accordingly so that enough of their fellow citizens come to endorse the proposals that they favor.

The public justification criterion of legitimacy also distinguishes deliberative conceptions from purely epistemic conceptions of democracy. According to the latter, the epistemic quality of public deliberation lends legitimacy to democratic decisions to the extent that it enables participants to figure out the best answers to political questions—or, as it is often put, to "track the truth."[7] By contrast, this is not enough for deliberative democrats. The aim of political deliberation is not simply to figure out the best answers to political questions, according to someone or other. It is to find out the best answers that can be justified *to those who must comply with them* such that they too can accept these policies as reasonable—and thus not simply be coerced into blind obedience. Deliberative democracy is neither *the rule of true opinion*, according to someone or other (like in purely epistemic conceptions), nor *the rule of actual public opinion* (like in purely aggregative conceptions). It is the rule of *considered public opinion*.[8]

Now, the difference between purely epistemic and deliberative conceptions of democracy is subtle because, in both cases, deliberation conceived of as a form of

---

[6] See, e.g., Richard Bellamy, *Political Constitutionalism* (Cambridge: Cambridge University Press, 2007), 163, 176, 192; Jeremy Waldron, *Law and Disagreement* (Oxford: Oxford University Press, 1999), 114; Nicholas Wolterstorff, *Understanding Liberal Democracy: Essays in Political Philosophy*, ed. Terence Cuneo (Oxford: Oxford University Press, 2012), 131.

[7] See, e.g., David Estlund and Hélène Landemore, "The Epistemic Value of Democratic Deliberation," in *Oxford Handbook of Deliberative Democracy*, ed. Bächtiger, et al., 113–31. For purely epistemic defenses of democracy, see, e.g., Carlos Nino, *The Constitution of Deliberative Democracy* (New Haven, CT: Yale University Press, 1998); Hélène Landemore, *Democratic Reason: Politics, Collective Intelligence, and the Rule of the Many* (Princeton, NJ: Princeton University Press, 2013) and "Beyond the Fact of Disagreement? The Epistemic Turn in Deliberative Democracy," *Social Epistemology* 31, no. 3 (2017): 277–95. For an in-depth analysis of different epistemic defenses of deliberative democracy, see José Luis Martí, "The Epistemic Conception of Deliberative Democracy Defended," in *Deliberative Democracy and Its Discontents*, ed. Besson and Martí, 27–56.

[8] For a paradigmatic articulation of this view, see Jürgen Habermas, "Political Communication in Media Society," in *Europe: The Faltering Project* (Cambridge: Polity, 2009), 158–67.

valid reasoning is guided by the epistemic standards of truth, justification, access to information, avoidance of errors, and so on. However, while these are indeed the only standards that matter in pursuing "true opinion," when it comes to "considered public opinion," deliberation must not only be informed and aim to reach the best decisions but must also be sensitive to the interests, values, and ideas of those who will be bound by the decisions in question. Understood in this sense, the considered judgments of citizens are not simply informed judgments that track the relevant facts. Given the collective nature of political decisions, these judgments must also reflect proper sensitivity to, appreciation of, and familiarity with the plural concerns, views, attitudes, interests, and values of other citizens—citizens with different social perspectives and experiences who will nonetheless be subject to the political decisions in question.[9] Although citizens who participate in political deliberation may all aim at true opinion, they are likely to disagree not only with blatantly misinformed or clearly mistaken opinions of other citizens but also with the considered opinions of other citizens, even with those of the majority. We do not need to go too far back in history to find many examples of views that were once defended by very small minorities, but which have recently become the considered judgments of the majority (e.g., views on interracial marriage, sexual harassment, same-sex marriage, transgender rights, etc.). However, for all their disagreements, democratic citizens who participate in political deliberation cannot simply aim at reaching true opinions, according to someone or other. To the extent that they are involved in a collective project of self-government, they must engage each other's views, perspectives, and reasons if their decisions are to be democratically legitimate. Whereas in their search for "true" opinions citizens may choose their deliberative partners based on their epistemic credentials, in order to truly "justify their opinions to others" they must account for the cognitive stances of precisely those "others" who might not be their chosen deliberative partners but who must comply with the decisions in question nevertheless.[10] They owe justifications not only to (whoever they consider) their epistemic peers but also to all those over whom they exercise coercion. Thus, in addition to making up their own mind, citizens' shared aim is transforming actual public opinion by getting as many citizens as possible to endorse their considered judgments so that such judgments can eventually become *considered public opinion*. Thus, "considered public opinion" does not merely have epistemic value. It is not simply an epistemically better opinion than

---

[9] In his account of political deliberation in "The Idea of Public Reason Revisited," Rawls explains the difference by pointing out that "public justification is not simply valid reasoning, but argument addressed to others" (in *Collected Papers*, ed. Samuel Freeman [Cambridge, MA: Harvard University Press, 1999], 594). It is important to keep in mind that in the context of public justification the addressees are not just any random others but those who will be subject to the decisions in question. As Cohen puts it, "Deliberative democracy is about making collective decisions and exercising power in ways that trace in some way to the reasoning of the equals who are subject to the decisions: not only to their preferences, interests, and choices but also to their reasoning" (Joshua Cohen, "Reflections on Deliberative Democracy," in *Philosophy, Politics, Democracy: Selected Essays* [Cambridge, MA: Harvard University Press, 2009], 330, our italics).

[10] In Rawlsian accounts, public justification is typically restricted to reasonable citizens (i.e., those who share democratic commitments). Yet, reasonable citizens endorse different comprehensive doctrines and thus may have good reasons not to consider all their reasonable fellow citizens as epistemic peers.

uninformed opinions. It also has democratic value: it is the properly deliberative and inclusive opinion of the citizenry. It reflects what members of a political community can find reasonably acceptable at a given historical time (based on their background beliefs, information, concerns, interests, values, etc.) and, for that reason, it provides the basis for the legitimate imposition of coercion, even in the eyes of the minority who disagrees that it is the best or the correct opinion on the political issues in question.

Now, in order to fulfill this legitimizing function, public deliberation needs to satisfy stringent standards. Deliberative democrats have different views of those standards, but in general they all agree that public deliberation can only lend legitimacy to its outcomes to the extent that it is sensitive to the quality of the reasons or, to use Habermas's expression, to "the force of the better argument," rather than being sensitive to coercion, deception, or purely self-interested considerations. Moreover, it must be properly inclusive if it is to be sensitive and responsive to the concerns, interests, values, and ideas of all citizens. Unfortunately, political deliberation in the public sphere of democratic societies fails to meet (or even remotely approximate!) the demanding standards of legitimacy that the conception of deliberative democracy requires. Across all relevant dimensions—inclusion, diversity, access to reliable and balanced information, independence, impartiality, orientation toward the public interest, and so on—the deliberative conditions that prevail in most social venues that are available to citizens in current democratic societies are the exact opposite of what we would hope. Political debates in the public sphere tend to be dominated by powerful political actors whose interests often deviate from those of the general public but who nevertheless exercise a disproportional influence on actual public opinion. Since citizens cannot form considered judgments about contested political questions under these dismal conditions, even if democratic institutions are properly responsive to citizens' opinions, they can at best track *actual* rather than considered public opinion. Indeed, citizens themselves often have no way of knowing what their considered judgments on a variety of contested political issues would be if they were properly informed and had the opportunity to freely deliberate with fellow citizens who hold very different concerns, interests, values, and ideas.

But if the processes of opinion and will formation in which citizens participate are so deeply defective both in epistemic and democratic terms, then there is no way for political actors and institutions to track considered public opinion as the conception of deliberative democracy requires. In fact, what opinion polls can track are simply the raw and uninformed opinions that, unfortunately, exercise a tremendous influence upon the behavior of political actors and institutions. This conundrum highlights the distinctive motivation that underpins deliberative democrats' engagement with deliberative minipublics. Indeed, in contrast to regular opinion polls that only reflect the poor quality of actual political debates in the public sphere, the microdeliberative processes that take place within deliberative minipublics offer a fascinating view into what could become considered public opinion in a political community at a given time.

2.2 The Microdeliberative Turn within Deliberative Democracy

Inspired by Dahl's idea of creating a *minipopulus* that was discussed in Chapter 1, in the 1990s James Fishkin began experimenting with a deliberative minipublic of his own design, namely, Deliberative Polls.[11] Although similar experiments had already taken place,[12] Fishkin's work is especially interesting in our context because it exemplifies particularly well the distinctive concerns and normative motivations that drive deliberative democrats' engagement with deliberative minipublics. In fact, his work paved the way for the microdeliberative turn among deliberative democrats.[13] As with all other types of minipublics, the idea behind deliberative polling is to take a relatively small group of randomly selected participants that everyone has an equal chance to be a part of and to provide it with good conditions for deliberating about some political issue over a relatively short period of time. The techniques of stratified random sampling used in deliberative polling offer scientific support for the claim that the ordinary citizens who participate in the deliberative experience are a mirror of the population as a whole; consequently, their views, interests, values, and so on reflect those of the people. Recreating a microcosm of the people can provide very valuable information. Just as the initial judgments of the participants reflect the raw and uninformed public opinion that can be captured by regular polls, their judgments after the deliberative experience can be assumed to reflect *what the people would think if they were informed and had the opportunity to deliberate about the matter*. As Fishkin puts it, "deliberative polling has a strong basis for representing the considered judgments of the people."[14] And it is for this reason that, from a (deliberative) democratic perspective, they have recommending force. He explains:

> A deliberative poll is not meant to describe or predict public opinion. Rather it prescribes. It has a recommending force: these are the conclusions people would come to, were they better informed on the issues and had the opportunity and motivation to examine those issues seriously. It allows a microcosm of the country to make recommendations to us all after it has had the chance to think through the issues.[15]

---

[11] See James S. Fishkin, *Democracy and Deliberation* (New Haven, CT: Yale University Press, 1991). For an overview of his work on Deliberative Polls, see https://deliberation.stanford.edu/what-deliberative-pollingr.

[12] In 1970s, Ned Crosby developed the Citizen Juries process. He founded the Jefferson Center to refine the Citizens Jury and develop similar democratic processes. For an overview, see https://www.cndp.us/. See also Ned Crosby and Doug Nethercut, "Citizen Juries: Creating a Trustworthy Voice of the People," in *The Deliberative Democracy Handbook*, ed. Gastil and Levine, 111–9. Around the same time, Peter Dienel developed a similar model in Germany, the "planning cell." For an overview, see https://www.planungszelle.de/en/home-en/. See also Peter C. Dienel and Ortwin Renn, "Planning Cells: A Gate to 'Fractal' Mediation," in *Fairness and Competence in Citizen Participation: Evaluating Models for Environmental Discourse*, ed. Ortwin Renn, Thomas Webler, and Peter Wiedemann (Dordrecht: Kluwer Academic, 1995), 117–40. For a detailed overview of the different experiments with sortition since the 1970s, see Sintomer, *The Government of Chance*, chap. 4.

[13] See Floridia, *From Participation to Deliberation*, 45–7.

[14] James S. Fishkin, *When the People Speak* (Oxford: Oxford University Press, 2009), 28.

[15] Fishkin, *Democracy and Deliberation*, 81.

88 The Lottocratic Mentality

When seen against the backdrop of the democratic significance of considered public opinion within deliberative conceptions of democracy, it becomes obvious why minipublics are so interesting to deliberative democrats. They seem to precisely offer the combination of a deliberative filter and a democratic mirror that the deliberative conceptions of the democratic ideal of self-government require. Yet, this combination can only be secured in experimental settings that are explicitly designed for these purposes and wherein a few randomly selected citizens have effective opportunities of engaging in well-informed and in-depth face-to-face deliberation. This becomes obvious if one compares the epistemic and democratic qualities of microdeliberative processes within minipublics and macrodeliberative processes in the public sphere. In a nutshell, here are the most relevant differences:

(1) The techniques of stratified random sampling help ensure *inclusion* and *diversity* (especially the inclusion of marginalized social groups in terms of both presence and voice). This gives a higher level of *representativeness* to minipublics than almost any other political forum where the presence and voice of powerful social groups tend to predominate. This is particularly the case regarding political deliberation in the public sphere.

(2) The random selection of participants among ordinary citizens prevents the group from being co-opted by politicians or captured by organized special interest groups. It helps ensure the political *independence* and *impartiality* of participants and increases the chances that their deliberations are *oriented toward the public interest.*

(3) The provision of *information* helps secure balanced briefing materials as well as the inclusion of all relevant social perspectives. The presence of trained moderators facilitates mutual deliberation, helps weigh the pros and cons of different proposals, and prevents collective deliberation from being hijacked. This allows participants to reach *considered judgments* on the political issues in question.

This brief comparison highlights the potential tension between deliberation and mass participation within the deliberative democracy paradigm. It is quite obvious that even the most general conditions for good deliberation are more easily satisfied in small-scale face-to-face deliberation. For only in small groups, it is possible to evaluate all the relevant information, to have opportunities to listen to competing views, and to challenge them if necessary. Indeed, the more people participate in deliberation, the less feasible it is for all of them to have equal opportunities to explain their views, to ask questions and receive answers in return, to jointly weigh views against one another, and so on. Moreover, over and above the general conditions of deliberation, if one adds further considerations that are particularly relevant for political deliberation about collectively binding decisions (such as impartiality, absence of manipulative intentions, etc.), then the quality of that specific kind of deliberation may also be inversely proportional to its publicity. The more deliberation is insulated from pressures that are exogenous to the discourse at hand (sectarian interests, manipulation, coercion, etc.), the more likely it is that participants will be willing and able to follow the force of the better argument to reach a considered judgment on the matter. Since, according to deliberative democrats, the quality of deliberation has a direct impact on the legitimacy of deliberative outcomes, improving the quality of deliberation is a non-negotiable aim for the realization of deliberative democracy. Thus, if it turns out that the quality of deliberation is inversely proportional to the scope of participation, then the only alternatives would seem to be either nonparticipatory deliberation or nondeliberative participation. In that case, deliberative democrats would have no choice but to drop the aim of enhancing participation. If we acknowledge the poor quality of deliberation in the public sphere and the difficulties of devising effective methods for improvement, then from the perspective of deliberative democrats, focusing on microdeliberative processes within deliberative minipublics can seem like the only feasible option.[16] This difficulty—taken together with the very encouraging findings[17] from the many deliberative minipublics that have been organized over the past decades[18]—explains why many deliberative democrats have taken the microdeliberative turn and "abandoned mass democracy."[19]

[16] Many deliberative democrats are driven to the microdeliberative strategy by the difficulties of imagining feasible improvements in the quality of information and communication within the public sphere. In his piece "Minipublics," Archon Fung exemplifies this view when he claims, "effective large-scale public sphere reforms may consist largely in the proliferation of better minipublics rather than improving the one big public." Fung, "Minipublics: Deliberative Designs and Their Consequences," in *Deliberation, Participation and Democracy: Can the People Govern?*, ed. Shawn W. Rosenberg (New York: Palgrave Macmillan, 2007), 159.

[17] For an overview of key findings on minipublics, see Graham Smith and Maija Setälä, "Mini-publics and Deliberative Democracy," in *Oxford Handbook of Deliberative Democracy*, ed. Bächtiger et al., 300–14. See also M. Gerber et al., "Deliberative Abilities and Deliberative Influence in a Transnational Deliberative Poll (EuroPolis)," *British Journal of Political Science* 48, no. 4 (2018): 1093–118; K. M. Esterling, A. Fung, and T. Lee, "When Deliberation Produces Persuasion Rather than Polarization: Measuring and Modeling Small Group Dynamics in a Field Experiment," *British Journal of Political Science* 51, no. 2 (2021): 666–84; James S. Fishkin, *Democracy When the People Are Thinking* (Oxford: Oxford University Press, 2018).

[18] Since the 1990s, Fishkin has organized over 150 Deliberative Polls in over 50 countries. In the 2000s, citizens' assemblies were launched in British Columbia (2004), Ontario (2006), and the Netherlands (2006) to discuss proposals for electoral reform. They offered a model for subsequent assemblies that have been established with broader mandates such as the recent Irish Citizens' Assembly (2016–2018) or the Citizens Convention for Climate (2019 and 2020). On citizens assemblies, see Min Reuchamps, Julien Vrydagh, and Yanina Welp, *De Gruyter Handbook of Citizens' Assemblies* (Berlin: De Gruyter, 2023). Institutions that include both randomly selected citizens and other political actors are an even more recent development. The best-known examples are the Convention on the Constitution in Ireland (2013–2014) and the G1000 Citizens' Summits in Belgium (2011) and in the Netherlands (2014).

[19] Simone Chambers, "Rhetoric and the Public Sphere: Has Deliberative Democracy Abandoned Mass Democracy?," *Political Theory* 37, no. 3 (2009): 323–50. An exception to this trend is the "systemic turn" that has been recently endorsed by many deliberative democrats. This turn is an important attempt to go back to the "big picture" by focusing on the deliberative system as a whole instead of focusing only on face-to-face microdeliberative processes that take place within small groups like deliberative minipublics. This includes paying attention to macrodeliberative processes such as political debates in the public sphere, alongside the many other deliberative processes that take place at different sites and times in the deliberative system. For an overview of the systemic turn within deliberative democracy, see John Parkinson and Jane Mansbridge, eds., *Deliberative Systems: Deliberative Democracy at the Large Scale* (New York: Cambridge University Press, 2012).

2.3 Deliberative Democracy and the Lottocratic Mentality

So far, we have analyzed key conceptual assumptions, motivations, and concerns that explain deliberative democrats' strong interest in lottery-based institutions like deliberative minipublics. But we have not yet discussed their different proposals for plugging these institutions into democratic societies. We do this in the next chapter. But, before turning to that important question, we first want to highlight some ambiguities and tensions among core normative values and assumptions in the paradigm of deliberative democracy that lend support to lottocratic proposals and the development of the lottocratic mentality.

As mentioned in the previous section, within the paradigm of deliberative democracy there is a potential tension between the values of deliberation and mass participation. However, this tension can be interpreted in different ways. One option is to see these values as mutually irreducible but jointly necessary for realizing the ideal of a deliberative democracy. To the extent that mass participation and deliberation are equally indispensable for achieving a deliberative democracy, there is simply no feasible alternative to the project of advancing both values—and this is so irrespective of the fact that this is going to be much more difficult than the alternative of advancing one at the expense of the other. As Joshua Cohen puts it, "participation and deliberation are both important, but different, and they are important for different reasons. Moreover, it is hard to achieve both, but the project of advancing both is coherent, attractive, and worth our attention."[20] This view of the relationship between mass participation and deliberation is incompatible with lottocratic proposals that confer decision authority on minipublics while bypassing the citizenry. Yet, a different view of the tension is also possible: we might think of these values as often in conflict such that advancing one of them may only be possible by sacrificing the other. Thompson offers a clear statement of this view when he argues that it is a mistake

> to treat deliberative democracy as a cohesive set of values that are jointly realized or jointly fail to be realized, for this ignores the possibility that its elements may conflict with one another, that not all the goods it promises can be secured at the same time, and that we have to make hard choices among them. . . . Equal participation may lower the quality of the deliberative reasoning. Publicity may do the same. Public deliberation may also be less conducive to mutual respect than private discussion. Decision-making authority may encourage polarization and positional rather than constructive politics.[21]

In light of these potential conflicts, deliberative democrats "need to face up to the tensions that empirical research exposes among their key values, and refine their theories to help decide the extent to which one value should be sacrificed for

---

[20] Cohen, "Reflections on Deliberative Democracy," 328.
[21] Dennis Thompson, "Deliberative Democratic Theory and Empirical Political Science," *Annual Review of Political Science*, 11 (2008): 511–3.

another" (ibid.). Thus, when deliberation and participation pull in opposite directions, theories of deliberative democracy ought to help determine which value should be advanced to achieve deliberative democracy. Fishkin has defended this view over the years, although in two slightly different ways. In the book *When the People Speak*, he articulated this view in the strongest possible terms, namely, as a genuine trilemma between core democratic values or principles. As he put it, "the fundamental principles of democracy do not add up to . . . a single, coherent ideal to be approached, step by step. . . . Achieving political equality and participation leads to a thin, plebiscitary democracy in which deliberation is undermined. Achieving political equality and deliberation leaves out mass participation. Achieving deliberation and participation can be achieved for those unequally motivated and interested but violates political equality." Therefore, "the three principles—deliberation, political equality, and mass participation—pose a predictable pattern of conflict. Attempts to realize any two will undermine the achievement of the third." Given this predicament, "a democratic theory is all the more useful the less it requires to work on achieving several normative aims at once." In keeping with this view, he defined deliberative democracy as a theory that is explicitly committed to the principles of political equality and deliberation, but which is "agnostic about participation."[22] This interpretation provides a clear answer to Thompson's request for helpful practical guidance. Whenever the aim of enhancing the quality of deliberation turns out to be incompatible with the aim of enhancing mass participation, deliberative democrats may propose ways of advancing the former at the expense of the latter since mass participation, valuable though it may be, is ultimately an optional value when it comes to realizing deliberative democracy.

In his most recent book *Democracy When the People Are Thinking*, he offers a weaker version of the conflict between core democratic values or principles. Although he mentions the trilemma, he emphatically defends the need, desirability, and feasibility (at least in principle) of a deliberative democracy wherein fundamental democratic principles (political equality, deliberation, mass participation, and nontyranny) would be simultaneously secured.[23] However, he still defends a nonparticipatory conception of deliberative democracy as the second-best option for the nonideal conditions of actual democratic societies.[24] As long as the ideal strategy of simultaneously securing all four democratic principles is unattainable, the second-best strategy is to channel energy toward securing political equality and deliberation (e.g., through the institutionalization of deliberative minipublics such as Deliberative Polls) while, if necessary, temporarily abandoning mass participation.

---

[22] Fishkin, *When the People Speak*, 191. It is interesting to note that in his earlier book *Democracy and Deliberation* (1991), where he articulated and defended the idea of deliberative polls as a new form of democracy, there was no mentioning of mass participation as a democratic value or condition. The only democratic conditions that he recognized there were political equality, deliberation, and nontyranny. On the problems inherent in assuming that political equality does not require mass participation, see footnote 30.

[23] See Fishkin, *Democracy When the People Are Thinking*, 7–8.

[24] See ibid., 24, 169.

It is not hard to see how this view of the conflict between deliberation and mass participation lends support to lottocratic proposals that would confer decision-making authority upon deliberative minipublics. If, as Fishkin contends, the recommendations of deliberative minipublics express "the considered judgments of the people"[25] whereas the raw and uninformed voice of the actual people "is not a voice that by itself deserves any special hearing,"[26] then one may rightly wonder what justifies democratic elections which give the strongest possible hearing to that voice by letting the actual people make crucial political decisions with no deliberative filter whatsoever (i.e., per secret ballot). If the voice of the actual people does not deserve any special hearing, then why let people vote at all? Radical lottocrats' proposals to dismantle elections can find fruitful support here. Indeed, why not use deliberative minipublics to make all the political decisions that are currently made by the actual people in democratic societies (e.g., in general elections, referenda, popular initiatives, and the like)? If institutionalizing minipublics for making some political decisions is a net improvement in the deliberative quality of the political system, then it would seem to follow that the political system as a whole would improve if more decisions were made by minipublics and fewer (or none) by the actual people.

Fishkin himself does not follow this path. However, his approach remains ambiguous in that regard. In his arguments and proposals, one can identify both participatory and lottocratic tendencies. In *Democracy When the People Are Thinking*, Fishkin explicitly endorses the importance of macrodeliberation and signals that the process of opinion and will formation in which citizens participate is a crucial source of legitimacy in democratic decision-making. This view, however, seems directly incompatible with proposals to give decision-making authority to minipublics as the second-best option under nonideal conditions. Let's see why.

These proposals only make sense under the assumption that the considered judgments of minipublics' participants are an improvement over the actual opinions of the citizenry, otherwise there would be no point in organizing deliberative polls rather than simply relying on regular polls (or referenda, etc.). What is special about the outcomes of deliberative minipublics is that they offer a glimpse into what could become considered public opinion in a political community at a given time. At their best, such recommendations reflect the extent to which the majority of citizens could realistically be expected to change their hearts and minds given where they are now in terms of their interests, values, attitudes, and so on. But, deliberative minipublics do not offer a path to get us from here to there. If, as deliberative democrats contend, the legitimate exercise of political authority requires political decisions to be justified to all those who are bound by them so that they can come to see them as at least reasonable rather than being simply coerced into obedience, then *justifying political decisions as reasonable to only a few members of the minipublics is clearly not enough.* Unless and until the minipublics' considered judgments actually become

---

[25] Fishkin, *When the People Speak*, 28.
[26] James S. Fishkin, "Deliberation by the People Themselves: Entry Points for the Public Voice," *Election Law Journal* 12, no. 4 (2013): 504.

Deliberative Democracy's Turn to Lottery-Based Institutions   93

"considered *public opinion*" (i.e., the considered judgments of the actual people), they cannot accrue any legitimacy under that criterion. To reach that point, citizens must first transform each other's actual judgments through political struggles, contestation, and learning processes.[27] This is why the paradigm of deliberative democracy is ultimately incompatible with lottocratic proposals and the lottocratic mentality that animates them.

In fact, as we discuss in Chapter 8, many of Fishkin's proposals for inserting minipublics (such as deliberative polls) into the political system tend to follow the participatory and not the lottocratic approach. Fishkin is no radical lottocrat. Dismantling elections and transferring power to a lottocratic assembly is not something he endorses. He even rejects the less radical lottocratic proposals endorsed by many deliberative democrats that seek to create a bicameral parliamentary system in which one Chamber is selected by elections and the other (generally the Senate or the lower Chamber) by lotteries.[28] Yet, even though he does not back the creation of a permanent second legislative chamber selected by lot, he still endorses a proposal that would confer "final decision to a minipublic for any law that does not pass by two-thirds in the parliament. If there is merely a majority but not a supermajority, then the people, convened in microcosm, have the final say."[29] He does not provide an explanation of why it would be legitimate to let a vanishingly small number of minipublic participants have the final say over legislation.[30] But his claim that this proposal is a way of "empowering the people" suggests that the answer lies in his claim that minipublic participants are a "mirror" of the people. In other words, minipublic participants can legitimately represent the people because they are *like* them. As we discuss in Chapter 6, this conception of representation as "embodiment" is a problematic element of the lottocratic mentality that Fishkin's claims and arguments tacitly support. This element adds to the tensions and ambiguities within Fiskin's arguments between a participatory and a lottocratic interpretation of deliberative democracy that we have been exploring in this chapter. These tensions and ambiguities reverberate throughout his work and ultimately remain unresolved. But precisely

---

[27] For a more detailed articulation of this argument, see Cristina Lafont, "Deliberation, Participation and Democratic Legitimacy: Should Deliberative Minipublics Shape Public Policy?," *Journal of Political Philosophy* 23, no. 1 (2015): 40–63 and Lafont, *Democracy without Shortcuts*.

[28] See Fishkin, *Democracy When the People Are Thinking*, 85–9.

[29] Ibid., 97.

[30] It is also not clear why this proposal does not violate political equality. Fishkin is ambiguously ecumenical in his interpretation of political equality. He often suggests that political equality can be equally well realized either in the standard democratic form that requires everyone to have equal rights of inclusion and participation in decision-making or in the weak lottocratic form that does not require everyone's effective inclusion and participation but only equal chances to be included and participate. For example, in the book *When the People Speak*, he claims: "Deliberative Polling . . . achieves inclusion through political equality, through an equal counting of those randomly sampled—effectively *offering each person in the population sampled a theoretically equal chance* of being the decisive voter. But political equality is not the only form of inclusion. Another method of inclusion is mass participation" (28). Contrary to Fishkin's ecumenism regarding political equality, in Chapter 5 we argue that the lottocratic reinterpretation of political equality at the core of the lottocratic mentality transforms the democratic requirement of having equal access to the exercise of political power into the remarkably weaker requirement of "having equal chances to be selected" to exercise political power and, in so doing, it *severely weakens* the political rights that citizens collectively exercise as equals in electoral democracies regularly.

to the extent that these tensions and ambiguities are unresolved, we can also use Fishkin's work to support and defend our claim that lottery-based institutions could serve genuine democratic aims *if* scholars and practitioners decisively rejected the lottocratic mentality. Indeed, as discussed in Chapter 8, we wholeheartedly endorse Fishkin's proposal for enhancing the agenda-setting capacity of the citizenry since it exemplifies the use of lottery-based institutions that is directly opposed to the lottocratic aims and mentality.

Chapter 3
The Clash Between Electoral Democracy and Lottocracy
Three Options

Ted Wachtel, a member of the conservative "Building a New Reality" initiative, introduces one of his most recent pamphlets by claiming that it is a mistake to think that "voting is democracy": He cautions that "the American Civil Liberties Union and the United Nations refer to voting as the 'cornerstone of our liberty' and the 'crux of democracy.' But they are mistaken. The original democracy in ancient Athens, Greece, chose only ten percent of its public officials by election, selecting the rest by sortition."[1] Wachtel's project of "Building a New Reality" has hardly any support in democratic societies. Indeed, democracies currently face many dangers, but the threat that lotteries may replace suffrage is not one of them. Nevertheless, the overall lottocratic *mentality* is expanding its influence. This mentality is attracting scholars, political leaders, activists, and think tanks from across the political spectrum. This growing popularity is *despite* the fact that lottocratic proposals for institutional reform are often not all that radical, generally not all that feasible, and not even all that popular among the public. We focus on proposals from the more radical end of the lottocratic spectrum, as this reveals core trends within the lottocratic mentality that are often shared by more moderate lottocrats who labor under the mistaken belief that such trends deepen democracy.

To recap what we discussed in Chapter 1, the lottocratic mentality maintains that selection by lot is inherently democratic and that electoral representation is inherently oligarchic or aristocratic. Supposedly, decisions made by an allotted legislature would be able to reconcile equality and selection without falling into the twin traps of either discriminating among equal citizens (and thereby creating a permanent political class) or returning to direct democracy. Our critical interest is in this general mindset and not simply in the more radical proposals. Indeed, even some of the more modest lottocratic proposals reflect a belief that shrinking the role of political representation and citizens' right to vote is the best way to solve the crisis of democracy. A constitutive element of this mentality is the view laid out in Chapter 1, which holds that the electoral transformation of popular governments in the modern era reflects "a deliberate choice" taken against selection by lot. This path was taken in order to

---

[1] Ted Wachtel, *True Representation: How Citizens' Assemblies and Sortition Will Save Democracy* (Pipersville, PA: Piper's, 2020), 19.

The Lottocratic Mentality. Cristina Lafont and Nadia Urbinati, Oxford University Press. © Cristina Lafont and Nadia Urbinati (2024). DOI: 10.1093/9780191982903.003.0004

96 The Lottocratic Mentality

expel the "unrefined" claims and partial interests of ordinary citizens from political institutions.[2] On this telling of history, in the eighteenth century, the founders of representative government thought elections would solve "the problem of size" and of large populations. However, these days, technology can address these problems and it has also made large-scale random sampling feasible. This all means that elections are now not only less necessary but also less justifiable. Representative democracy is poised to do away with elections—indeed, it is becoming increasingly clear that elections in large part persist since the elected few want to retain their power. In short, while elections have become an undemocratic anachronism, lotteries are the way of the future and the way back to true democracy.

The lottocratic mentality stems from an indirect conception of democracy that does not involve elections. This mentality suggests two institutional designs: one wants to *substitute* lotteries for elections and the other wants lotteries to *complement* elections in a way that equally shares sovereignty. These two designs should be sharply differentiated from yet another set of proposals that envision lotteries serving in what we call an *auxiliary* role (whose ancient root and meaning are succinctly explained in the conclusion of this book). An auxiliary view of sortition challenges neither the sovereignty of citizens as a collective nor their individual right to vote on both issues and representatives. In Chapter 1, we revisited Dahl's important and pioneering work, which argued that lotteries should be used in precisely this auxiliary fashion to *assist* in the process of deliberation in congress/parliament and also to gather opinions from society at large. We endorse this auxiliary approach. Our goal is to redirect current efforts to design and implement representative institutions such as citizens' assemblies, deliberative polls, etc., toward achieving genuinely democratic goals. Our goal is to challenge proposals stemming from the lottocratic mentality.

3.1 Substitution Proposals

Many people are convinced that electoral representation is one of the main causes of the entrenchment of a political oligarchy or a cast ("la casta" as we use to call it in Italy). Electoral representation has fueled an increase "in inequality of wealth and income, [an] inability to regulate the most powerful entities in our world, continued injustice and stratification along racial and ethnic and national lines, [thereby] deepening and intensifying social division, and other serious consequences." If this is true, then why not move beyond suffrage? Alexander Guerrero asks this provocative question in the introduction of his new book, *Lottocracy: Democracy Without Elections*. Guerrero's general diagnosis crops up in popular opinion and even in some scholarly work. The overall thesis is that social inequality is essentially driven by political (e.g., procedural and institutional) factors rather than by economics or unequal social norms. Furthermore, the core driver of inequality and the citizenry's loss of power are the mechanism of *elections themselves* and not the influence that

---

[2] Landemore, *Open Democracy*, 21.

global financial capitalism has over sovereign states nor the fact that oligarchies have retreated from a commitment to democratic citizenship. Lottocrats invite us "to reimagine political institutions, to consider what might work better, to consider whether lottocracy might be an attractive direction, and, if so, how we might get there from here. This is our responsibility, but I also see this as one of the oldest roles for philosophers. Who else has the role of questioning foundational assumptions about the world around us?"[3]

The most attractive aspect of the lottocratic mentality is the idealism that inspires proposals for institutional renewal. These proposals see sortition as a tool in the fight against inequality and corruption because it would free institutions from partisanship and partisan deliberation.[4] Moreover, replacing elections with lotteries would radically change the way people think about and experience politics because it entails adopting an impartial way of gathering data, processing information, defining issues of public concern, and then holding deliberations and making decisions. Politics would undergo a radical change and recover the nonpartisan character of "making things get done together" that democracy seems to have had since its Greek origins.

The lottocratic mentality promises that lotteries can give us "enough legitimacy to claim the title of most legitimate democratic representative."[5] Here, we want to recall an exemplary proposal for replacing elections with lotteries in contemporary democracy, which was put forward by a lottocratic movement at the start of the Italian Republic in 1946–1947. After the collapse of fascism but before political parties were in full control of the nascent democracy, various political groups and movements sent their representatives to the Constituent Assembly elected in the first democratic elections (Italian women obtained the right to vote in 1945). However, one movement proposed a real lottocratic democracy rather than a parliamentary democracy. The movement's leader, Guglielmo Giannini, argued that once democracy was established political representation could not be overcome through democratic means. This is because elections generate parties and parties tend to occupy the state in order to persist. As such, any attempt to eradicate or break apart parties would yield a tyrannical solution. It was therefore necessary to seize the constituent opportunity and make Italian democracy into a lottocracy.[6]

Since at least the 2008 financial crisis, there has been a "crisis of democracy" afflicting democracies across the globe. This has revived projects similar to the Italian one. For instance, in 2016, Belgian publicist David Van Reybrouck proposed to solve the decline of party-electorate linkages by shedding the various useless recipes devised by "electoral fundamentalists"[7] and instead using sortition to select public officials. American philosopher Alexander Guerrero argues that after decades of

---

[3] Guerrero, *Lottocracy*, 4-5.

[4] Alexander Guerrero, "The Epistemic Pathologies of Elections and the Epistemic Promises of Lottocracy," in *Political Epistemology*, ed. Elizabeth Edenberg and Michael Hannon (Oxford: Oxford University Press, 2021), 156–69.

[5] Landemore, *Open Democracy*, 115; Dowlen, *The Political Potential of Sortition*, 4.

[6] Nadia Urbinati, "Anti-Party-ism within Party Democracy," in *Multiple Populisms: Italy as Democracy's Mirror*, ed. Paul Blokker and Manuel Anselmi (Oxford: Routledge, 2020), 67–85.

[7] Van Reybrouck, *Against Elections*.

representative government, it is difficult to imagine the quality of deliberation that the lottery would produce, but that this is the challenge for contemporary democracies if they are to solve the structural problems of elitism, bad decisions, and corruption. As Giannini wrote in 1945, as in any political system in a lottocratic system citizens still depend upon the service of the few and a division of labor; therefore, the problem for institutional planners would be "how not to give the few who govern the opportunity to corrupt themselves." This could be achieved, Giannini suggested, by short mandates and by making government activity merely technical and managerial. This would make it unattractive to power seekers and a burden rather than a pleasure. Eliminating competition achieves these outcomes. Purely managerial issues can more easily be translated into objective data and assessments. Dispassionate technocrats and experts would be able to convey such assessments to an assembly that was drawn by lot far better than politicians. Then, much like a jury that is made up of randomly selected citizens, the assembly would verify such proposals and give feedback to the government.[8]

Guerrero proposes a broad, society-wide system of allotted assemblies and devises a new legal, administrative, and institutional order that could completely replace representative institutions. His central arguments are shared by proponents of much less radical proposals. These arguments claim that we should reasonably expect an assembly that has been selected by using competitive agendas or party proposals to be characterized by debate *rather than* deliberation. But in an assembly selected by lot genuine discourse would take place. Agenda setting is crucial in structuring and orienting public deliberation and decisions because it defines what is "considered or taken up as a problem" in the first place. Yet, "[m]any problems in the electoral representative system stem from not even having issues on the legislative agenda."[9] In short, the electoral system is the wellspring of all manner of problems because it conditions the entire political system and its methods of decision-making. In fact, the winning party has the power to impose its agenda on the assembly and to condition not only deliberation in parliament but also the tone and style of the deliberative process both inside and outside formal institutions. If the majority is a coalition, then the discussion in the assembly will depend on mediation and compromise, but these are not transparent methods; if a party has a solid majority (as in a first-past-the-post electoral system), then it will tend to impose its agenda in a quasi-tyrannical way, as it has no need to compromise with forced outside the majority. In both cases, deliberation is simply absent. Thus, the strategy of substituting elections with lotteries tries to get rid of the entire system of parliamentary politics and force the social issues to speak for themselves.

Elections do much more than select a political representative. Elections create and deeply structure a decision-making space wherein strategic reasoning is the driving force that turns deliberation into a relativistic debate over preferences for certain

---

[8] Guglielmo Giannini, *La Folla. Seimila anni di lotta contro la tirannide* (1945), abridged, with a debate between G. Orsina and V. Zanone and afterword by S. Sette (Soveria Mannelli: Rubettino, 2002), 198–9 (our translation).

[9] Guerrero, *Lottocracy*, 161.

agendas and policies; in this space, it is ultimately impossible "to resolve conflicting interests and disagreements *impartially*."[10] Lottocrats claim (just like Schmitt) that the rule of fair play in parliament is misleading since it pretends that there is room for everyone to talk and that impartiality is a criterion that leads deliberation. But, an equal opportunity to raise arguments so as to convince others and attain a majority is simply not the same thing as resolving "conflicting interests ... impartially."

One may object here that in order to have deliberation that is thoroughly dispassionate, the entire society (not simply political institutions) would need to be radically changed such that equality were extended well beyond the legal order. In a society like ours that is socioeconomically unequal, citizens may very much need parties and partisan narratives. To deliver its promise of impartial deliberation, the institutional transformation would need to follow a revolutionary change across the entire society; thus, the issue transcends the type of selection mechanism that we use. But this is not the path lottocrats take. For instance, rather than focusing on the fact that political action takes place in a society that is anything but fair and equitable, Guerrero seems to think that the central driver for biased judgments or differences in interpretation is the selection system itself. For him, conflict and diversity of interpretation are a weakness. It is not the case that conflict and diverse interpretations are a possible source of innovation that requires the engagement of as many citizens as possible, and which sets the whole society in motion. Instead, thoughts like this are a pathology generated by elections. Once elections were removed, politics would finally be what it should be: a technical matter of decision-making based on certain data that had not been manipulated or skewed toward one agenda or another. Politics as we know it seems to be the problem.

Guerrero's argument is interesting since it helps us critically analyze less radical proposals; indeed, if elections and lotteries are institutional forms that each shape two opposite ends of a deliberative spectrum, then any attempt at "mixing" them or having them complement one another would be doomed from the start. As discussed in the following section, supporters of a model in which they complement one another are keenly aware of the fact that these two selection systems pull in different directions. Advocates of complementarity suggest that the allotted chamber should play a monitoring role over an elected body so as to contain the conflicting interests that elections bring into deliberation.[11] According to Guerrero, this division of labor between strategic reasoning and impartial deliberation would be fatal for lottocracy. As allotted members would be monitoring and judging the elected assembly rather than their own agendas (which are, ex ante, not a product of any party), such a division would end up subtly encouraging allotted members to subject their judgments to the partisan logic of the elected assembly that they

---

[10] Arash Abizadeh, "In Defense of Imperfection: An Election-Sortition Compromise," in *Legislature by Lot: Transformative Designs for Deliberative Governance*, ed. John Gastil and Erik Olin Wright (London: Verso, 2019), 250.

[11] "When we add regular elections on top of this, particularly given the use of single-member districts and voting rules that ensure two dominant political parties, we get deeply divided, us versus them dynamic in ordinary political life." Guerrero, *Lottocracy*, 11.

100   The Lottocratic Mentality

are supposed to monitor. Mixing elections and lotteries in the process of lawmaking would engender precisely what a lottocratic polity aims to avoid: increasing the power of the elected and making the sorted assembly dependent on them. Instead, the goal of lottocracy should be to ensure that the allotted assemblies are autonomous bodies that place their own agenda at the core of deliberation and that they do not receive any such agenda from others—certainly not from a partisan assembly. Guerrero encourages lottocrats to abandon the idea that electoral representative democracy is the final step of innovation in the realm of political institutions: "I introduce and defend a broad family of alternatives to electoral representative systems of government—namely, *lottocratic* systems of government—which put lottery selection of political representatives, rather than elections, at the center of the political system."[12]

Landemore proposes a less radical substitution model. Her model is not purely lottocratic insofar as it includes some mechanisms of direct democracy. She proposes that a central national assembly selected by lot should have lawmaking power but not (always) the last word; her nonmixed proposal (e.g., all deliberation should be made by an allotted assembly) uses a national referendum in order to uphold the legitimating principle of popular sovereignty. This feature marks an important departure from Guerrero's model—as he advocated a diffusion of many sorted assemblies across the country to both deal with individual issues and produce a decentralized locus of decisions (e.g., he itemizes 20 "issue areas"). In contrast, Landemore retains the idea of a collective popular entity or what one might term "centralized" collective sovereignty. Thus, while Landemore is opposed to parties, electoral representation, and suffrage, she nevertheless proposes a central national assembly selected by lot that has lawmaking power but that does not always have the last word. This is quite different than Guerrero's proposal for numerous sorted assemblies that lack a centralized locus of legitimacy like a national legislature. He advocates something akin to a federalization of assemblies and issues.

Landemore develops a comprehensive argument against elections. She sees elections as an unreformable system that routinizes the selection of an elite and that disempowers citizens. She claims that when the entire political system is grounded in elections, it tends to generate epistemic distortions that favor the interests of the elected and their stronger supporters in society. At the conclusion of her antielection argument, Landemore resorts to the idea of an "open minipublic" democracy, which would be a "large, all-purpose, randomly selected assembly of between 150 and a thousand people" that would engage in "agenda-setting and law-making of some kind."[13] She does not define the exact powers and abilities of this open minipublic and, in the end, proposes "a generalist kind of assembly."[14] As we noted, Landemore falls back on the idea of a referendum and, in doing so, tacitly acknowledges the legitimacy deficit that crops up with a reliance on lotteries. She knows that, even if

---

[12] Guerrero, *Lottocracy*, 4.
[13] Landemore, *Open Democracy*, 12.
[14] Guerrero, *Lottocracy*, 145.

it occurs by chance rather than choice, lotteries still exclude the vast majority of citizens from decision-making and put the drawn assembly in a position of dominance. As such, Landemore comes to the conclusion that "minipublics should not be run as secretive lab experiments in complete disconnection to the larger public sphere and society-wide deliberation" and she advocates using referenda, although "not necessarily always." After criticizing the consent-based logic of voting, she still admits that regardless of how "open" the justificatory process is, "sometimes" an "authorization moment" (e.g., a referendum) would still be needed.[15]

Landemore puts her finger on the problem we seek to highlight in this book: the lottocratic alternative to elections leaves the problems of an unequal influence and a legitimacy deficit unresolved. Yet, strangely, the architecture of a substitutionary approach entirely rests on a supposedly mutually exclusive dualism between elections and lotteries. As discussed in the next chapter, the lottocratic mentality maintains that (a) electoral competition generates unequal levels of influence that universal suffrage does not eliminate; (b) voting puts a temporary brake on disagreement in society by transferring it to parliament; and (c) even in those fortuitous instances where a decision is good or is reached by a large majority, the electoral system is fundamentally unable to overcome disagreements. Finally, this mentality continually emphasizes the fact that voting in elections fails to resolve these problems because it legitimizes the strategic insincerity that dominates the electoral logic of promises. The maxim guiding the lottocratic mentality seems to be that the more the citizens are engaged in politics the more they develop a "false sense of their own level of understanding of the issues. This leaves them ill prepared for the meaningful give-and-take of deliberation."[16]

In effect, lottocracy targets party politics and the widespread power this system gives to the media, demagogues, and spin doctors. Indeed, the endogenous flaws in party politics are so glaringly obvious that even some political scientists have begun to wonder whether it might be a good thing if certain unskilled citizens were to simply stay home and abstain from voting (though, we cannot accurately know whether the ignorant or the disillusioned would abstain). The pernicious role of parties seems to present an intractable problem. However, if this is so, then why would one want to mix good and evil, and lotteries and elections? Evidently, one cannot. In the end, lottocrats maintain that the only way to solve the problems that elections create is to eliminate them altogether. "Sortition avoids electoral campaigns, demagoguery, and factions, though it cannot guarantee that those do not form after" lotteries are used if the electoral system is not completely eliminated.[17] Hence, Guerrero's conclusion that representative democracy can only be overcome. *Hic rodus hic salta.*

---

[15] Landemore, *Open Democracy*, 116. Landemore brings up referenda in response to Cristina Lafont's objection about the legitimacy deficit that besets the decision power of the minipublics (ibid., 115–7).

[16] Terrill Bouricious, "Why Hybrid Bicameralism Is Not Right for Sortition," in *Legislature by Lot*, ed. Gastil and Wright, 315.

[17] Dimitri Courant, "Sortition and Democratic Principles: A Comparative Analysis," in *Legislature by Lot*, ed. Gastil and Wright, 240.

3.2 Complementarity Proposals

Complementarity proposals are much more numerous and varied than replacement proposals. Over the past two decades, there have been an increasing number of proposals that would change existing institutions and even constitutions so as to legalize a "mixed" legislature or to give drawn assemblies power in matters that have traditionally been handled by elected bodies. Within this complementarity camp, we include all the various proposals that have recently emerged for a bicameral parliamentary system in which one chamber is selected by election and the other (generally the Senate or lower house) is selected by lottery. These proposals were conceived with a view toward establishing a new type of representation that could fix three particular problems that the current political system creates: the formation of a political class separated from the citizenry, the deepening political divisions that party loyalty causes, and the deepening discrimination toward marginalized minorities.

As we noted in previous chapters, scholars have plumbed the ancient past and the early modern age in order to propose several stylized models that might achieve a type of indirect democracy that would nip these problems in the bud.[18] Their proposals also aim to play an educative role and introduce citizens to a new paradigm of participation that might gradually convince them to move beyond the hegemony of elections. In this long-term perspective, if lottery-based institutions were to begin to be implemented, they would slowly encourage changes in citizens' mindsets until the electoral model would finally show up as not simply undesirable or bad but also superfluous and anachronistic. "Historically, most peoples have chosen—either explicitly at the founding moment or more subtly by accretion—systems that mixed different forms of representations. The time is probably ripe for adding more institutions chosen by lot into the mix."[19]

The appeal of this mixing strategy transcends academia and is encountered in several recent policy proposals. In his 2017 presidential election platform, the leader of the French leftist populist party *La France Insoumise*, Jean-Luc Mélenchon, proposed a constitutional reform that would select members of the upper house by using a national lottery (the constituent assembly that would implement the reform would also have 50% of its members chosen by lot). Similarly, in 2018, the leader of the Italian *Five Star Movement*, Beppe Grillo, proposed to draw the members of the Senate in the Italian Parliament by lot.[20] The proposals by Mélenchon and Grillo were not

---

[18] Bouricious, "Democracy through Multi-body Sortition."

[19] Jane Mansbridge, "Accountability in the Constituent–Representative Relationship," in *Legislature by Lot*, ed. Gastil and Wright, 203. While "we cannot get rid of elections . . . lottocratic institutions may be an important corrective of the oligarchic drift of electoral institutions" (Simone Chambers, *Contemporary Democratic Theory* [Cambridge: Polity, 2024], 161).

[20] The mentor and founder of the 5SM, Gianroberto Casaleggio, had already proposed utilizing lotteries as far back as 2004, when he linked lotteries to new innovations induced by digitalization: "The term direct democracy describes a new relationship between citizens and their representatives. . . . Current democracy operates on the principle of delegation, not direct participation: with the vote, the relationship of voters with candidates and the choices that will be implemented by them comes to an end. . . . The Net redefines the relationship between citizen and politics by allowing access to real-time information about any fact,

particularly novel. As discussed in Chapter 1, Marie Collins Swabery already staked out this same goal in 1937. In 1985, the American scholars Ernest Callenbach and Michael Phillips proposed to randomly select 435 members of the US House of Representatives so that political representation could be freed from the power of lobbies and large financiers.[21] More recently, after Tony Blair proposed dissolving the hereditary principle in the British House of Lords, the founder of *OpenDemocracy.net*, Anthony Barnett, and Peter Carty suggested replacing it with a lottery.[22]

Moving from politics to academia, several scholars have endorsed this mixed mode. Ethan Leib has proposed a scheme for adjudicating public policy through randomly selected assemblies of citizens. These assemblies would be convened to discuss and vote on particular issues, and their discussions would culminate in laws that were enacted but then subjected to both a court review and a possible veto by the executive and legislative branches. Leib argues that this "popular branch" would serve a similar function to legislative initiatives and referenda, while avoiding the flaws associated with these forms of direct democracy. He explicitly argues that this "popular branch" could be included within existing governmental and political institutions, and that lotteries could supplement rather than supplant traditional representative democracy.[23] Following a similar line of thinking, Arash Abizadeh has proposed that the Canadian Senate (now appointed by the Governor General on the advice of the Prime Minister) should be replaced by a body that is selected by sortition which should then work in tandem with the elected Chamber. He surmises that the distinctive advantage of such mixing is that it takes the "best of both worlds": sortition upholds the values of political equality, genuine responsiveness, and impartiality, whereas elections are the best mechanism for accountability. "Elections and sortition instantiate this trade-off institutionally . . . . The upshot is that realizing, at least to some degree, each of democracy's two constitutive commitments requires some combination of elections and sortition."[24] Finally, John Gastil and Erik Olin Wright launched an initiative of mixed representation based upon the idea that a dual selection system could be applied to *both* chambers and not just one. To simplify this intellectual trajectory, we should also mention Amar's work on "lottery voting" (briefly referenced in Chapter 1) and Alex Zakaras's more recent

---

and control over the processes activated by central or local government. Direct democracy introduces the centrality of the citizen." Gianroberto Casaleggio, *Web ergo sum* (Milan: Sperling & Kupfer, 2004), 23–5 (our translation).

[21] Ernest Callenbach and Michael Phillips, *A Citizen Legislature* (Berkeley, CA: Banyan Tree Books, 1985).

[22] Anthony Barnett and Peter Carty, *The Athenian Option: Radical Reform of the House of Lords* (Exeter: Imprint Academic, 1998). In 1998, Connan Boyle published an essay on the use of lotteries to select electoral colleges ("Organizations Selecting People: How the Process Could Be Made Fairer by the Appropriate Use of Lotteries," *Journal of the Royal Statistical Society*, ser. D, 47, no. 2 [1998]: 291–321). In that piece, he stressed how other methods had disadvantages and argued that a lottery would confer a democratic legitimacy upon the second chamber.

[23] Ethan Leib, *Deliberative Democracy in America: A Proposal for a Popular Branch of Government* (University Park, TX: Penn State University Press, 2004).

[24] Arash Abizadeh, "Representation, Bicameralism, Political Equality and Sortition: Reconstituting the Second Chamber as a Randomly Selected Assembly," *Perspectives on Politics* 19, no. 3 (2021): 792. For overviews of the initiatives, see John Gastil and Katherine R. Knobloch, *Hope for Democracy: How Citizens Can Bring Reason Back into Politics* (New York: Oxford University Press, 2020).

104   The Lottocratic Mentality

"modest proposal" to have the US state and federal Senates "abolished and replaced with citizens' chambers, filled by lot."[25]

Several famous deliberative polls involving universities and expert-led research groups—such as those in British Columbia or the Ontario Citizens' Assemblies—generated findings that spurred public law theorists and political scientists to formulate a variety of proposals in this vein. The most dramatic experience was that of the Five Star Movement (M5S). As part of its 2018 election platform, M5S proposed to reform the Italian parliament along lottocratic lines and this apparently resonated quite well with the public at large. With financial support from the parliament itself, the movement has sponsored research and simulations on the possibility of two mixed systems: one with a drawn Senate and an elected Chamber of Deputies and another that mixes lotteries and elections when forming both chambers. We discuss later some of the problems that arise in parliamentary deliberation and processes when party and nonparty agents are conceptualized as complementing one another in these ways. However, at present, we want to draw attention to two implications that emerged from the M5S proposal simulations.

First, although the M5S pool of experts concluded their analysis without specifically recommending which model to adopt, their simulations clearly showed that having drawn and elected bodies interact with one another does not necessarily produce a more efficient or even a desirable deliberative environment. Nearly all mixed-system scholars favor proportional forms of representation, and some believe that lotteries introduce better proportionality than what can be achieved through elections. However, the M5S simulations showed that in order for cooperation within drawn representatives to be effective, a mixed parliament could not use proportional representation. This is because cooperation between nonparty-aligned (drawn) and party-aligned (elected) representatives seems to yield better results (decisions with broader consensus) when only two parties make up the elected House such that they can both impose party conformity and discipline on their members. In short, the elected chamber can better interact with the drawn chamber if its composition is simplified into two compact and thus highly polarized collectives; only the drawn chamber can afford the luxury of having a wide variety of opinions that pull from stratified samples rather than from parties.

These simulations showed that party pluralism creates a coordination problem that the drawn chamber simply cannot solve because of its lack of "structuring" organization and its consequently weak power of initiative (we return to this point shortly). M5S leaders were not particularly concerned about sacrificing pluralism in the elected chamber since they considered party pluralism as a problem rather than an asset anyway; in their view, the simulations simply confirmed that democracy had to completely rid itself of parties and party pluralism in order for parliament to produce good deliberation. Containing party pluralism was essential in making

---

[25] Alex Zakaras, "Lot and Democratic Representation: A Modest Proposal," *Constellations* 17, no. 3 (2010): 456–7.

their proposed mixed-system work. The paradox here is that while a two-party system seemed to facilitate more successful mixing, that same system simultaneously enhances the power of party politics rather than limits it. As explained below, the mixed system can actually exacerbate the problems it seeks to correct.

The M5S simulations also showed that the "diversity" principle works best for deliberation purposes if it refers to "objective" data or sociological information free from partisan judgments. In short, the simulations tell us that not all "diversity" is good for lottocracy—certainly not a partisan-based diversity that generates a type of persistent and polemic pluralism that can often be solidified and radicalized via discussion. The simulations also confirm the antiparty lottocratic attitude: party diversity must decrease (as parties need to impose discipline on their members in parliament if a mixed system is to function well); then, a good type of diversity is created by bringing nonparty-affiliated citizens into parliament. Paradoxically, the complementary or mixed system seems to work only if the elected chamber is less pluralistic and more clearly simplified into a binary choice. These observations confirm Guerrero's skepticism about proposals for institutional mixing.

As mentioned earlier, Guerrero stresses how it is inappropriate to have lotteries cooperate with elections. This applies not only when the cooperation is split between two separate chambers but also when it takes place within both chambers. This is because the mixing would *worsen* the pathologies of electoral democracy, since the elected part of the chamber would end up feeling "more dominant and less deferential" than the one that was drawn, and also because its authority derives from the expressed will of the citizens. Guerrero admits that it is difficult to decide which of these two types of mixing is better since they produce decidedly ambivalent results: on the one hand, it is true that direct personal relationships between different types of representatives in the same assembly could mitigate the impacts of their inherent inequality, but, on the other, direct personal relationships between the two types of representatives could radicalize the unequal regard the two groups have for themselves and each other (the elected body may come to think that they are endowed with some sort of qualitatively better or superior authority).[26] Therefore, while forcing party representatives to engage in personal relationships with nonparty representatives could perhaps diminish the dominance of parties, the result would not necessarily be positive. However, in order to cooperate with their drawn peers, the elected representatives' deliberation would have to be even *less* accountable to constituents and they would fail to follow the will of these constituents even *more often* than they generally do now. When elected representatives cooperate with unelected partners, they run the risk of even more radically departing from their promises to their constituents. In a mixed model, the deliberative environment becomes only partially promissory. The combination of lotteries with elections would lead to a general decline in accountability.

We discuss this specific problem at length in order to highlight the main argument in this chapter: the lottocratic mentality inspires institutional models that undermine

---

[26] Guerrero, *Lottocracy*, 142.

106 The Lottocratic Mentality

representative democracy even when (as in the case of mixing) such proposals are "moderate." This is because lotteries generate insurmountable accountability problems. After illustrating the main arguments that are used to support a mixed system, we then itemize the main deficiencies of such a system.

In the introduction, we noted that proposals that endorse allotment are part of a trend that seeks to deal with the current "crisis" of democracy. Moreover, such proposals are rooted in the conviction that this crisis cannot be overcome if democracies remain wedded to electoral selection. Nearly all scholars who share the lottocratic mentality agree that the flaws and limitations of elections can only be solved by narrowing the hegemony of elections over the legislature. All these scholars think elections are inextricably tied to corruption. By "corruption" they mean a way of doing politics that bends to the logic and practice of competing for votes, and that fosters noxious compromises and strategic reasoning both before and after elections. Like it or not, electoral politics is Machiavellian.

According to the lottocratic mentality, corruption arises from politics when it (a) only embraces the principle of impartiality at the procedural level (the rules of the game) and not at the substantive level; (b) uses political freedom to seek and gain power; and (c) interprets equality as a starting point (e.g., the equal right to vote), which then favors only a certain type of candidate. Lottocracy promises to defeat political corruption by subverting the entire process and thereby minimizing or eliminating the role of choice and will in selection. Within such a system, "only chance distinguishes us, so we remain equals" while we deliberate. This is in contrast to elected officials who are never equal. In this vein, Gil Delannoi claims that the use of lottery would foster a change in mentality that would be paramount since "everyone knows that he or she can or cannot be selected."[27] Thus, the first and most important thing lotteries promise is to overcome precisely the kind of equality that we associate with suffrage: the equality of the right to authorize. This will be replaced by an equalization of the (currently unequal) opportunity to become a candidate. Similarly, the current conceptualization of equality in the right to freedom of speech and association will be replaced by an equalization of the (currently unequal) weight that is given to various ideas and opinions within an electoral democracy. The lottocratic mentality claims that the main flaw in representative democracy is that its notion of political equality is not truly inclusive and therefore its outcomes reflect media-dominated opinions rather than free and open deliberation.

Proponents of the complementarity model accept the genuinely "democratic" nature of a probability-based equality. They then propose to counter the type of equality of opportunity to compete that currently breeds partisan pluralism with a type of equality that enhances the plurality of independent information. How can such diverse conceptions of equality cooperate fruitfully in the legislative process? From the perspective of democratic sovereignty, the problems seem insurmountable. However, in a drawn assembly it is not only the case that no one should "lose" or "win," but also that decisions should have an *identical* impact on all the individuals

---

[27] Gil Delannoi, *Le retour du tirage au sort en politique* (Paris: Fondapol, 2010), 19.

who belong to the groups from which the drawn representatives were chosen. This majorly impacts sovereignty since stratifying demographics according to "appropriate criteria" so as to include gender, age, socioeconomic status, and geography, as well as race, ethnicity, and indigeneity would yield laws that would differentially impact individual citizens; while the law would be crafted with respect to people belonging to each of these groups, this would not be the case with respect to all other citizens. The generality of the law would be severely compromised.

Moreover, with a transition to lotteries we are only left with one kind of equality: equality of probability. This type of equality is not immediately associated with political freedom. The idea that runs through the arguments of both radical and moderate lottocrats is that political participation in a democratic society should never produce forms of inequality—not even those that result from the indirect influence of political opinions in decision-making; words and ideas must serve the function of independent and dispassionate discussion and not be used for rhetorical persuasion. Lottocrats value a type of formalistic equality that mimics what is operative in the spheres of justice and administration, where impartiality and the principle of neutrality are crucial values. Can legislative democracy be animated by this type of nonpolitical paradigm?

Lottocrats praise ancient Athens and describe it as if all political activity were carried out by drawn bodies. In Chapter 1, we explained that lotteries were applied alongside elections to achieve direct participation in decision-making within the Assembly. Yet, the vast amount of speeches, rhetorical texts, and pamphlets that have come down to us from ancient Athens reveal how the competition of ideas, victory in the agora, and the study of trying to convince the assembly or a jury were all utterly crucial factors in Athenian democracy. Rhetorical speeches were also vital in the tribunal of the people (whose many members were drawn by lot) even though Aristotle's point from the *Art of Rhetoric* was also undoubtedly true: their raison d'être was to prove to the jury that the acts or facts on trial had occurred in the manner demonstrated.

In ancient democracy, speeches and votes were linked—but the way rhetoric was deployed in the legislative process was different from the way rhetoric was deployed in the judiciary. This difference corresponded to the difference between deliberation in making laws and deliberation in administering justice. Aristotle argued that these differences reflected the good in relation to what speeches were supposed to convince an audience about. On the one hand, there were deliberations concerning things and courses of action that were to come (legislating), and on the other, there were deliberations concerning the implications of things and events that had happened in the past (justice). Here, we see two different forms of judgment that belong to two different institutional functions and that are based on two different virtues—in one case, justice as prudence and utility and, in the other, justice as impartiality. In both cases, the role of individuals was crucial. Hence, individuals repeatedly played a vital role beyond those instances when the Athenian people elected a magistrate or voted in the assembly. The importance of the individual was felt throughout the political life of the city, where different kinds of equality were instantiated in different forums:

108   The Lottocratic Mentality

equality before and under the law, to speak publicly, to demand justification, to have a voice in the assembly, to compete in elections, or to put themselves forward for specific kinds of service to the city and be chosen by lot.

In modern democracy, electoral contests, parliamentary debate, and participation in civil associations and parties are some of the places where equal political freedom is expressed through direct and indirect presence and through speeches, petitions, and public displays of ideas that bear the very personal and individual imprint of the participants: we vote individually and our votes are counted individually, one by one. As discussed in the next chapter, this is so despite the fact that elections define a *collective* moment that includes and is carried out by all citizens simultaneously and which is conducted with a view toward projects that will have a collective impact. These collective moments and impacts are what the lottocratic mentality tries to "overcome" by proposing to use lotteries within legislative activity: "The deliberative input principle does not require dispensing with traditional forms of speech" that end up preferring certain actors and making others hesitant to speak. Rather, in the sorted assembly in order for all citizens to talk equally it is utterly crucial that their speech be straightforward communication concerning data, the exchange of raw information, requests for clarification, and attempts to propose a sound interpretation—speech that lends itself to being driven and ordered by tutors or online technologies.[28] As Terrill Bouricius writes when criticizing the partisan type of disputation that often arises from public and free speech: "we shouldn't believe people are more expert simply because they assert as much. A feeling of certainty that one is right just as often signals a lack of intellectual humility."[29] Such sentiment leaves one with a question: should democratic citizens only feel free to speak publicly when or because they have something competent to say? Lottocrats are confident that those who currently hesitate to speak or who simply have no desire or ability to speak publicly would be more comfortable speaking in an assembly that does not require anyone to try to convince or persuade others. If we want to apply equality as probability to political decisions about laws, then the entire structure of deliberation must change along with the style and format of public performance and participation.

But complementarity models do not necessitate replacing parliaments; they can also function by distributing very specific and sensitive issues across drawn assemblies, thereby establishing a third body that is selected by lot and then added to the existing parliament or congress. For instance, John McCormick has proposed creating a "People's Tribunal": a body composed of 51 private citizens (who are neither registered with parties nor elected to any local or national bodies) chosen by lot from a pool of people that excludes economic elites ("elites" are defined with respect to a predetermined annual income—a line that must be set by a state body). This Tribunate would have several types of powers both related to the legislative arena and outside of it. For instance, such a body could decide on fiscal policies,

---

[28] Delannoi, *Le retour du tirage au sort*, 14–5.
[29] Bouricious, "Why Hybrid Bicameralism," 318.

The Clash Between Electoral Democracy and Lottocracy   **109**

initiate impeachment proceedings against a federal official in the three branches of government, call national referenda, and "veto one piece of congressional legislation, one executive order, and one Supreme Court decision."[30]

In his critical assessment of complementarity models, Guerrero notes how, although these councils "introduce interesting complications," in the end "almost everything [that can be said] about mixed election-selection bicameralism" applies to other assemblies. ."[31] His point is that neither of these models seems to acknowledge a fact that we have known since ancient Athens: institutions that use the lottery should answer to the law rather than initiate policy. In Athens, making sure that ordinary, nonwealthy citizens were involved in the distribution of political functions proved insufficient to realize a principle of horizontal equality; rather, it was also necessary to make sure that society itself was not structured by class. Cleisthenes redesigned constituencies territorially and according to residence in order to break clientelism and kinship networks—*only then* could democracy be based on the equality of every citizen before the law. Lottery, rotation, and short terms of office were then used to avoid a consolidation of power and to prevent alliances between classes of citizens that would threaten political equality.

This background helps explain why it is deeply antidemocratic to propose reviving lotteries within a context in which people divided into social groups (e.g., defined according to income, gender, age, etc.) as if these groups were indicators of who citizens are and what they think. While some scholars insist that sortition from statistical samples would serve goals of information and proportionality, it is worth noting that lotteries must make an extra effort to include marginalized groups. The use of a lottery by itself does not guarantee that it would pick marginalized groups out in a proportional manner. Regardless of how democratically cogent or realistic specific proposals are, the central idea that underlies all systems of the complementary variety is what is so problematic: on the one hand, these systems assume that lotteries can produce a form of representation that is descriptively better than electoral representation, and on the other, they combine a selection method that they think is superior with a method that they do not think represents the citizenry all that well. To paraphrase Guerrero's comments, rather than having the virtues of one add to the virtues of the other, the way that the lottery + election formula shows up within a complementarity system is primed to combine the vices of one with the vices of the other. We focus on the core problems that arise in complementarity systems: veto power, capture, plurality without pluralism, leaderism, arbitrariness, censorial power, and partisanship in disguise.

Veto power: Mixed systems seem to want to assign veto power to the drawn assembly. This makes sense at first blush given the conceptual link that lotteries have to neutral judgment and impartiality. But the censorial function of a veto is not a trivial power: it has the final say. Yet, this final say is only considered to be fair when it is sovereign in the sense that it answers to no particular person but rather only answers

---

[30] John P. McCormick, *Machiavellian Democracy* (Cambridge: Cambridge University Press, 2011), 184.
[31] Guerrero, *Lottocracy*, 138, footnote n. 16.

to the law (we return to this in the next chapter). For all intents and purposes, this makes a drawn Senate into a counterdemocratic body since it limits the legislative power of the democratic majority and adds yet another institutional limitation to those that already exist in constitutional democracies. Moreover, this further limitation upon a democratic will is deployed by a body that, since it is drawn, claims superiority over all other elected and appointed organs in that it can claim to be based on "true" democratic equality. Finally, unlike other organs of control, it exists within the legislature but with a twist: once judgments are separated from a democratic will, they end up accruing a type of power that is superior to that will. In essence, what we get is that one assembly is charged with proposing matters and another is tasked with censuring them. This is somewhat similar to the scheme devised by James Harrington in his *Commonwealth of Oceana* (1656). However, Harrington took his proposal in a different direction: since he wanted to moderate *both* the aristocratic *and* democratic elements, his idea was that the Senate would function to judge among and advise upon the best proposals, which would then be passed on to the popular assembly that (without debate) had the power to render final decisions. The lottocrats appear to be less democratic than an explicitly nondemocratic republican like Harrington: while claiming to honor democracy to the utmost, they put their trust in a body that does not answer to the people and that can block expressions of the popular will in the assembly.

Capture: A drawn assembly is composed of individuals who are dissociated from each other or who do not voluntarily align themselves with any group, political or otherwise. The geography of the assembly is therefore an important factor. As we know from the French Revolution, the national assembly physically organizes its space in a way that mirrors ideological commitments—along the lines of the right, left, and center. How should the drawn members of the Senate sit? Will they sit wherever they like, in alphabetical order, or in groups that are deemed to be statistically relevant to the initial population sampling and the lottery setup (e.g., gender, socioeconomic, age, location, etc.)? The first two possibilities would make sense, while the latter would not. In such a case where they were seated by group, the spatial proximity of equals could ignite a partisan spirit. This would not be in accord with values such as "unpredictability," "impartiality," and "not knowing each other's position on issues"—values that fit hand and glove with the atomistic character of the perfect equality of probability that a lottery makes manifest. A lottery-based assembly must avoid groupings. The question is whether the dissociative individualism of a lottery makes it easy prey for unscrupulous groups and individuals. "Sortition avoids electoral campaign, demagoguery, and factions, though it cannot guarantee that those do not form after the fact—especially if paired with an elected body."[32] Some scholars predict that the "distance between sortition representatives and represented might grow ex post" but that could be curbed by making shorter terms and regular rotation integral parts of lotteries.[33]

---

[32] Courant, "Sortition and Democratic Principles," 240.
[33] Ibid., 243.

The Clash Between Electoral Democracy and Lottocracy **111**

But how short should the terms be? Senate members should have the time and opportunity to exercise their power, but this means they also may be captured by those with an agenda. A short term is never short enough. Thus, it is simply unwarranted to think that a drawn assembly is not exposed to corruption since there are no parties. First, associating based on preferences is sufficient for people to interact and create parties: taken individually, sample members have their own opinions. Moreover, there are many opportunities to bribe or be bribed, and it is naive to think that only elections make citizens corrupt. In fact, in a mixed context, indirect forms of capture are even more difficult to control and regulate since they inevitably arise when the citizens selected by lottery relate to one another and discuss the partisan agendas of the elected representatives. As we have mentioned, in the simulation analysis carried out by the M5S the interaction among elected and unelected legislators makes the former *more* "independent" from (less accountable to) their constituents since they must be able to interact fruitfully with their selected partners whose positions are (or at least *should be*) completely unpredictable. Moreover, why should one not contemplate the possibility that interest groups outside the assembly might "reach out" to the drawn members and bribe or otherwise unduly influence them? After all, in theory, citizens who do not act with an eye toward re-election and who do not have a predetermined agenda are open to all kinds of influence and are perhaps even more exposed to human "vices" than partisans—whose individual wills are limited by their partisan positions. Unless the collective is very large (much larger than the few hundred people that typically make up a Senate), then its members can be targeted by powerful citizens not only outside but probably also from inside the assembly as well. Elites can therefore pilot this Senate even more easily than they were able to guide an assembly that was structured by parties. As discussed in the next chapter, parties act as a substitute for the imperative mandate and are thus critical to making representative democracy work.

Plurality without pluralism: Pluralism reigns in elective assemblies alongside the majority principle; it emerges from elections that put forward agendas and party platforms rather than individual contenders. Pluralism seeks to secure representation that is neither total nor complete; it animates an assembly characterized by groups rather than a heterogeneous collection of isolated individuals. Political pluralism is not to be conceived of as a casual sum of the scattered "many" but rather as a bringing together of groups (at least two: the majority and the opposition) that recognize themselves and one another. Political pluralism does not establish an uneven terrain of collected individuals but rather a structured and level plurality that lends itself toward making alliances, compromises, and taking the initiative through the coordination of decision-making and voting. But a sorted Senate is made up of a plurality of individuals that saps collective agency: "all representatives drawn by lots have the exact same position, instead of being in the majority or the opposition."[34] Yet, when they are asked to cast a vote on a law or proposal that comes to them from the elected Chamber, they have to somehow find a point of coordination or focus that

---

[34] Ibid., 238.

112 The Lottocratic Mentality

can transform their causal plurality into a functional pluralism. Given the endogenous and individualistic plurality characterizing the sorted assembly, the elected assembly would predictably exert its influence over it, and the parties would come to shape the work of the Senate. While lottocrats constantly emphasize the way in which parties and elections exert a corrupting influence, they fail to see how a dispersed plurality of individuals would lend itself even more to dynamics of manipulation and corruption.

Leaderism: Lottocrats value a drawn House because they claim it nullifies leaders and frees deliberation from rhetoric and demagoguery: every voice is heard and carries equal weight in deliberation. But, an equal right to speak does not mean that every voice will have equal weight. Deliberation does not depend upon equality conceived of in terms of probability but rather upon an equality of opportunities to speak and influence each other. This type of equality is proportional to people's interactive potential. Moreover, as Mansbridge demonstrated several decades ago, since all assemblies require and produce leaders, it is not difficult to imagine that those who are good at speaking in the context of a drawn forum have an outsized opportunity to influence the opinions and votes of their peers. Therefore, leaders may have much more power in this context than in an elective assembly where parties regulate and discipline representatives who are their members and also limit the number of potential leaders. Regardless of how they are selected, any assembly is a natural place for leaders to emerge and compete. In both theory and practice, democracy offers two responses to any potential elitism: a political space that allows for the circulation of leadership and a pluralism that encourages many leaders. This is one reason why electoral systems based on proportional representation have often been seen as more democratic since they are abler to spread power and break leadership by increasing the number of competing groups and leaders.

Arbitrariness: Let us return to the issue of the veto or, as Montesquieu put it, "the power to render null a resolution taken by another." As we noted, in ancient Rome this power was given to the tribunes. Montesquieu divided the legislature into two chambers and gave one of them the power of the veto *without* any power of initiative.[35] In contrast, some lottocrats argue that the drawn House should have both the power to initiate and to veto. After acknowledging that this chamber could not generate the "traditional forms of discourse" that grow within an electoral practice of promises and proposals, Gastil and Wright proposed linking drawn parliamentarians to outside society so as to solicit proposals from the public that would restrain the power of speakers within the assembly. "Were this elected body accountable to campaign contributors and party leaders, such input [from the public] might carry little weight, but a sortition legislature comes into being without a fixed agenda. Its members may prove more receptive to public input, particularly if the voices it hears

---

[35] "I call the right to order by oneself, or to correct what has been ordered by another, the faculty of enacting. I call the right to render null a resolution taken by another the faculty of vetoing, which was the power of the tribunes of Rome." Montesquieu, *The Spirit of The Laws*, 161 (bk. 11, chap. 6).

The Clash Between Electoral Democracy and Lottocracy **113**

come from the same kind of deliberation now asked of the citizen legislators."[36] But if the nature and character of the lottery is to produce unbiased, nonpartisan decisions, then trying to make a body chosen by lot "more receptive" to the outside public could be an open door to arbitrariness. In fact, efforts to establish just the opposite would be highly likely: as citizens have no accountability mechanisms to control a body chosen by lot, the citizenry would likely want to ensure that those few who were drawn *do not* communicate all the freely with the public. But if an assembly is selected from predetermined samples, then even if no one knows in advance exactly how many citizens will be selected from each of these sample groups, the condition that Gastil and Wright describe should still be deeply concerning to us.

This problem concerns both radical and moderate lottocrats. Both think that sociological representation is the best form of representativeness and that such representation can only be secured by sorting. If horizontal accountability is conceptually absent in this way (and not absent simply through an imposition by "campaign financiers and party leaders"), then it is not at all clear how communication between those who are drawn and those who are outside the assembly can even be a desirable goal. Parties and elections empower citizens; lotteries do not. Suppose I am drawn by lottery and that I belong to a social group that is numerically underrepresented in the assembly: should I try to ally myself with representatives of other groups in order to have more of a voice? Even by posing this question, we seem to be back in the business of parliamentary politics that mixes strategic and deliberative engagement, but now we lack any grounding that would guide us what those drawn by lottery should do in this situation since a "mirroring" model of representation is meant to reproduce us and not to give us advocates. As explained in the next chapter, making representation into a lottery with winners that simply mirror parts of the population excludes any kind of action that "promotes the interests of the represented" since it does not seek "good" representation (e.g., it is not reactive) but rather a sort of sociological or mirror representation. Lottocrats want to represent people objectively and without bias, but if the drawn assembly is to play a decision-making and proactive role, then the risk of arbitrary and unforeseen influences is inevitable.

Censorial power: Since lotteries do not involve political accountability, the state should design strong mechanisms of control. Current parliamentary regulations already censure "the behavior of their members." Yet, while elective chambers allow their own members to participate in the process of censure, a Senate chosen by lot would need additional regulations: a committee would need to examine citizens who had applied to enter the lottery or who had accepted the burden once they were chosen; a national statistical committee would need to "sort" each citizen into a particular group that they reflect and then periodically revise the statistical composition of groups so as to reflect changes in society; and there would need to be a committee

---

[36] John Gastil and Erik Olin Wright, "Legislature by Lot: Envisioning Sortition within a Bicameral System," in *Legislature by Lot*, 15.

114   The Lottocratic Mentality

to hear appeals from citizens who wanted to challenge their inclusion in or primary designation as reflective of a particular group.[37]

Among these institutions of control, the final committee that drew up the appropriate criteria for stratified samples would hold considerable power to determine the character of the drawn Senate. Lottocrats suggest that drawing up the census in a particular way already has outsized importance in virtue of how the electoral body is currently divided into constituencies. In one sense, they are undoubtedly right insofar as the way that a constituency is divided up is a contentious issue in many countries and we might see less contentiousness if this division were achieved via lotteries. However, the issue is that dividing members of a powerful sorted body by relaying on criteria of gender, race, age, socioeconomic status, etc., would create *other* sources of contention and sow strong public doubts about the arbitrary nature of such divisions. "We are wary of including explicit criteria for stratifying the sample that could have the side effect of reinforcing divisions that limit the deliberative capacity of the assembly."[38] Indeed, individual equal freedom would be at stake.

Partisanship in disguise: The fact that members of the Senate are drawn by lot and treated as samples of social groups does not mean that they do not have political ideas or that their political ideas are not similar to those that are represented electorally. It is unwarranted and abstract to assume that lotteries send people into the Senate without any political ideas, not the least because this assumption ignores the fact that, in a democracy, parties exist both inside and outside parliament and that partisan judgments and ideas would emerge even if parties did not exist. All citizens participate in forming of public opinion both before and after it passes through formal institutions and they do so in a much more continual and widespread fashion than occurs through their participation in election campaigns. Parties and partisan views circulate among the many various "publics" that coalesce into the broader "public" in any truly open society. This means that senators who were selected via lottery would presumably share many ideas with elected representatives. This fact would predictably imply that they would reproduce partisan divisions within the drawn assembly. Moreover, since partisan views are not supposed to exist in the drawn Senate, they may operate there in the shadows and present greater risks of manipulation. In this vein, Guerrero concludes his critical examination of the complementarity proposals with a persuasive observation: "in addition to the concern that mixed sortition-election institutions might get the worst of both, rather than the best of both, there is also the concern that either the electoral side will simply dominate (making the sortition side irrelevant) or that the sortition side will be powerful but also an unattractively designed model of a sortition institution."[39] On his account, Landemore's centralized assembly chosen by lot is hardly a solution because it would end up swapping out the central parliament for a central allotted assembly.

---

[37] The last problem would not arise in the case of assemblies constituted by pure random selection instead of stratified random sampling; the problem with assemblies constituted by pure random selection is that they must be exceedingly large to ensure minimum descriptive representativeness of all citizens.

[38] Gastil and Wright, "Legislature by Lot," 17.

[39] Guerrero, *Lottocracy*, 145.

The Clash Between Electoral Democracy and Lottocracy **115**

This assembly would certainly be much larger than traditional parliaments but it would still not be large enough to avoid corruption and partisan capture. Guerrero also points out an even more worrying possibility: we may give minipublics "far too much power to give to too few people via random selection, and . . . the epistemic burden on those randomly chosen would be far too great for such an institution to do well by sensibility. It might do decently well at those issues it takes up, but it would seem difficult for it to cover adequately all the moral political problems a community might face."[40]

The most radical lottocrat of all put his finger on precisely this problem: is it desirable for the lottery to change representative democracy or to even redesign it such that we replace elections and voting? The root of all problems is the assumption that lotteries can give us democratic representation. As discussed in Chapter 1, even an appreciation of some of the advantages offered by lotteries does not automatically lead one to assume that they can simply stand in for and do the job of elections. Dahl recognized that the use of lotteries would disempower citizens and he thought that lotteries could, at best, function as auxiliary institutional mechanisms. Lotteries cannot perform all the selection tasks a democracy may need; because they select by chance and without regard to the specificity of candidates, lotteries are most useful for staffing judicial and administrative positions. For this very reason, lotteries are not suited for institutional contexts where a collective political will is formed nor are they appropriate for contexts where sovereign decisions are made in an atmosphere of pluralism, dissent, and political freedom. Deciding on matters of war and peace or whether health care should be a public or private good, to give some concrete examples, generates differences in assessment and vision about the kind of society *we* want. These differences cannot be resolved with neutral datasets and information, nor are they distributed in accordance with census categories. Political issues cannot be left to chance and to assemblies that are not accountable to the citizens who must obey their decisions.

3.3 Auxiliary Proposals

Several governmental institutions that do not play a part in political representation such as Constitutional Courts, parliamentary or congressional committees, and the European Commission itself[41] have stressed the inadequacy of both electoral and co-optation methods for appointing representatives.[42] Since the mid-twentieth century

---

[40] Guerrero, Ibid.

[41] Many years ago in Germany, lotteries were proposed in order to choose constitutional judges from among all the magistrates of superior courts (K. A. Bettermann, "Die Aufgabe: Fachgericht für Verfassungsrecht," *Frankfurter Allgemeine Zeitung*, December 20, 1996); a similar proposal was also made in Italy. Elster argued that, thanks to lotteries, it would be possible to "break the system of entrenched power by seniority, which has been a major obstacle to rational policy making in the United States" (*Solomonic Judgments*, 92).

[42] It may refer to the process of adding members to an elite at the discretion of members of the body, usually to manage opposition and so maintain the stability of the group.

the United States has experimented with important institutional designs to combat discrimination in the context of trial juries. Such experimentation intensified in the 1990s with a wave of experiments to improve the quality of opinion formation on sensitive issues that directly and indirectly impact the lives of citizens. These experiments have produced a variety of lottery-based participatory avenues such as deliberative polls, citizen juries, consensus conferences, and citizens' assemblies.[43] Today, all democratic countries possess at least some norms and institutionalized forms of citizen consultation that are based on representative sampling. These lottery-based institutions are part of our conception and practice of democracy whether it be at the local, regional, national, or supranational levels.

In 2009, Hubertus Buchstein and Michael Hein proposed that the European Union should add an auxiliary commission chosen by lottery which would be staffed by mixing members of the European Commission with members selected by lot from both European Union member state governments and from among all European Union citizens. Their complex proposal was an attempt to respond to the democratic deficit in the EU by bypassing the traditional institutional models of legitimacy that apply to national democracies ("presidentialization, parliamentarization, and output") and to turn instead to lottery-based mechanisms that could help redress problems of non-transparency and inefficiency. Buchstein and Hein claimed that the democratization of the EU "can only be achieved by developing new institutional forms."[44] They also proposed that lottery could serve as a method for allocating "the committee memberships" among the members of the parties and groups so as to avoid "the influence of lobbyists."[45] We classify their project as an auxiliary model because they do not propose to use lotteries to dampen the electoral power of European citizens but instead propose the use of lotteries to make that power even more substantial.

Across many contexts and experiments, it has been shown that, outside the context of legislatures, lotteries can function well to allocate scarce goods among a community of equals (e.g., through land or land usage rights in Swiss cantons)[46] and that they can also be used to staff posts in administrative domains where discrimination must be avoided between equal competitors (e.g., choosing between Amsterdam and Milan when deciding on the location of an important EU agency). Finally, lottery has been used in contexts where concord was scarce and cleavages could not be easily tolerated. These contexts have included constitutional redesign (Iceland), constitutional reform (Ireland), and democratization after regime change (the republics

---

[43] In 1971, Ned Crosby invented citizens' juries. At the same time but entirely independent of Crosby, Peter Dienel created consensus conferences. On citizens' juries, see Ned Crosby, *In Search of the Competent Citizen* (Plymouth: Center for New Democratic Processes, 1975); Graham Smith and Corinne Wales, "The Theory and Practice of Citizen Juries," *Policy and Politics* 27 (1999): 295–308. On consensus conferences, see Dienel, "Planning Cells."

[44] Hubertus Buchstein and Michael Hein, "Randomizing Europe: The Lottery as a Political Instrument for a Reformed European Union," in *Sortition: Theory and Practice*, ed. Gil Delannoi and Oliver Dowlen (Exeter: Imprint Academic, 2010), 119–55.

[45] Hubertus Buchstein, "Democracy and Lottery: Revisited," *Constellations* 26, no. 3 (2019): 370–1.

[46] Antoine Chollet and Aurèle Dupuis, "Kübellos in the Canton of Glarus: A Unique Experience of Sortition in Politics," in *Sortition and Democracy: History, Tools, Theories*, ed. Sintomer and Lopez-Rabatel, 267.

that had formerly made up Yugoslavia). Within deeply divided societies, or in the absence of organized parties, lotteries have been able to secure two important goods: a sufficient guarantee that equality will be respected and the inhibition of illicit influences in the selection process.[47] In the 2000s, citizens' assemblies were launched in British Colombia (2004), Ontario (2006), and the Netherlands (2006) in order to discuss proposals for electoral reform. They offered a model for subsequent assemblies that have been established with broader mandates such as the recent Irish Citizens' Assembly (2016–2018) or the Citizens Convention for Climate in France (2019 and 2020). Institutions that include both randomly selected citizens and other political actors are an even more recent development. The best-known examples are the Convention on the Constitution in Ireland (2013–2014) or the G1000 Citizens' Summits in both Belgium (2011) and in the Netherlands (2014).[48]

In all these contexts, the attractive aspects of lottery were accentuated, and they proved to be incredibly helpful. In particular, the randomness of lotteries and the way that they are blind to the intentions and agendas of those involved proved to be two key factors that allowed selection by lot to be less exposed to manipulation than elections would have likely been. Lotteries "can contribute to political order" and be very effective in "proto-political contexts that either predate or operate independently of any centralized state decision-making apparatus. . . . In these conditions there is a strong case for the introduction of non-partisan political organs and the use of sortition could be an important means of guaranteeing impartiality."[49] Political experiments in domains like justice or administration (or even constitution-making) that are not directly "political" in an everyday sense have led some scholars to the conclusion that lotteries have qualities that can be very useful in domains where decisions must be insulated from parties and partiality. The lottocratic mentality dismisses this auxiliary use of lottery. This is incredibly unfortunate since this auxiliary use could potentially play an important role in revitalizing our representative democracies.

Pierre Rosanvallon has recently coined the term "counterdemocracy" in order to identify those institutional forms and types of agencies that counter majoritarian decisions. Forces of counterdemocracy would include formal organs such as juries and courts as well as informal groupings such as minipublics composed of randomly selected citizens, social movements, and nongovernmental organizations (NGOs). In Rosanvallon's most recent book, *The Populist Century*, he advocates the use of drawn lots alongside voting as one possible way to make sure that people "feel" they are

---

[47] Oliver Dowlen, "Sortition and Liberal Democracy: Finding a Way Forward," in *Sortition: Theory and Practice*, ed. Delannoi and Dowlen, 65–6. See also John Durant, "An Experiment in Democracy," in *Public Participation in Science: The Role of Consensus Conferences in Europe*, ed. Simon Joss and John Durant (London: Science Museum, 1995), 75–80.

[48] On citizens assemblies, see among others Min Reuchamps et al., "Le G1000: Une expérience citoyenne de démocratie délibérative," *Courrier Hebdomadaire du CRISP*, nos. 2344–5 (2017): 5–104.

[49] Oliver Dowlen, "Random Recruitment as an Element in Constitutional and Institutional Design: A Dialogue between Means and Desired Outcomes," in *Sortition and Democracy*, ed. Sintomer and Lopez-Rabatel, 410; Dowlen, "Sortition and Liberal Democracy," in *Sortition: Theory and Practice*, ed. Delannoi and Dowlen, 66.

118 The Lottocratic Mentality

represented and that, apart from the traditional linkages that political parties make possible, representatives are receptive to new and innovative ways of being connected to the citizenry at large. He does not suggest that we use lottery to form one of the two chambers of the parliament or to exercise any lawmaking power; he suggests lottery be used for "constituting citizens' councils, for example, or setting up procedures for challenging the existing authority." Making lottery play a monitoring or censuring role effectively recognizes how lotteries can fruitfully serve politics by securing impartial judgment, and perhaps do so in a way that reasserts the nonpartisan posture that lotteries had enjoyed in ancient Athens. For Rosanvallon, these functions of counterdemocracy can also be responded to populism in that they remind citizens that their sovereignty can "broaden beyond its narrowly electoral formulation" without seeking some unified (e.g., personalist or sociological) embodiment of some kind. Rosanvallon thinks sorted councils could play the role that theorists of representative government have traditionally thought that public opinion should play as the so-called "eye of the people." His conceptual move shows how extra-institutional means that were agents of political opinion formation in the past (parties, movements, organizations of interests, and media) now are no longer effective; citizens have either lost faith in them or they need to be refurbished and integrated with newer institutional forms and types of agencies. The "entropy" of traditional intermediary bodies means that we need to fall back on a variety of new procedures and institutions such that we are not instituting "a democracy of authorization—in other words, not simply using elections to deliver a license to government."[50] It is not enough to rely upon eligibility, accountability, and responsiveness (which elections promise to provide); it is necessary to deepen *trust* in democracy. Lottery can precisely do that.

Decades of experience with minipublics have convinced scholars that involving ordinary citizens who are chosen by lot in addressing "important topics, including critical thinking, working with experts, facilitation, and making decisions" increases people's feeling of satisfaction with the work they have done together and that it raises their level of trust in the entire system.[51] On the other hand, creating institutions that give the citizens the "feeling" and perception that the government listens to them can have the unpleasant unintended consequence of legitimizing the power of a certain majority. Randomly selected bodies can be strategically used by public rulers and administrators.[52] This possibility must be taken into account when acknowledging the potential of minipublics, especially if they perform an auxiliary function. Committees of experts or sorted councils that are asked to advise on rather than make decisions can be strategically used by public administrators not simply so as to solicit advice but also for garnering more popular

---

[50] All citations are from Pierre Rosanvallon, *The Populist Century*, trans. Catherine Porter (Cambridge: Polity, 2020), 157–9. On the role and decline of intermediary bodies, see Nadia Urbinati, "A Revolt against Intermediary Bodies," *Constellations* 22, no. 4 (2015): 477–86.

[51] Rosanvallon, *The Populist Century*, 159.

[52] Bruce Ackerman, *We the People*, vol. 1, *Foundations* (Cambridge: Cambridge University Press, 1991), 181.

support, taming popular dissatisfaction, and co-opting the pressure groups that most represent important by neglected interests; in a word, by directly "engaging" citizens in minipublics public administrators can increase their own credibility and trust.[53]

Scholars of social movements have also pointed out how minipublics can generate a convoluted relationship between participation and deliberation, insofar as citizen assemblies seek to find (good) answers to problems that do not necessarily organically originate from within social movements, as such movements are often perceived to be obstacles to good deliberation. Minipublics aspire to a society that puts "rational consensus" and independent citizens yet "not activism, at the center of the political scene."[54] Thus, even within auxiliary models or lotteries the results are mixed. As Yves Sintomer writes, these experiences in sorted participation demonstrate a tension between counterfactual deliberation and actual public debate. They prove that the empowerment of some among the ordinary citizenry does not translate into the empowerment of the general public.[55]

If we judge new forms of citizens' deliberative fora from the perspective of democratic participation, we should not neglect the fact that this surplus of representative participation mobilizes only a few citizens while making most of them feel (or be even) more estranged from democratic institutions. If the citizens randomly selected by minipublics are made to rely on voluntariness, then it may turn out that those who have the most intense interest in serving in an assembly or who simply have more free time end up dominating the forum or that they turn out to exert unequal influence.[56] In order to address these problems, we would need to determine the rules and criteria that should ideally guide the process of a lottery within an auxiliary model. Attention to procedures would be particularly important in this context. However, even if lotteries are not applied to the lawmaking process itself, consultative minipublics might have—and indeed, probably *should* have—an impact on the opinions that influence institutional bodies.

As far as rules are concerned, self-selection or voluntariness is certainly a problem. As such, some lottocrats have proposed that public service be made mandatory for those situations where lotteries are applied to areas that are even indirectly related to representation. The thought behind this requirement is that it would avert discrimination and avoid inverting the principle that in a democracy the *many* rule rather than the few (Dahl already raised this issue in 1970). Voluntariness would fatally privilege the most motivated people and in so doing violate both randomness and

---

[53] Mark B. Brown, "Survey Article: Citizen Panels and the Concept of Representation," *Journal of Political Philosophy* 14, no. 2 (2006): 220. See also Archon Fung, "Varieties of Participation in Complex Governance," in "Collaborative Public Management," special issue, *Public Administration Review* 66 (2006): 66–75; Lyn Carson, "How to Ensure Deliberation within a Sortition Chamber," in *Legislature by Lot*, ed. Gastil and Wright, 208.

[54] Andrea Felicetti and Donatella della Porta, "Joining Forces: The Sortition Chamber from a Social Movement Perspective," in *Legislature by Lot*, ed. Gastil and Wright, 148.

[55] Yves Sintomer, "Random Selection and Deliberative Democracy," in *Sortition: Theory and Practice*, ed. Delannoi and Dowlen, 44–5.

[56] Jane J. Mansbridge, *Beyond Adversary Democracy*, with a revised preface (Chicago: University of Chicago Press, 1980), 248–51.

120 The Lottocratic Mentality

the basic condition of equality of probability—this is the context in which Jacques Rancière calls voluntariness "the worst of all evils."[57] If we were to look at the problems and solutions that arose with respect to jury selection in the United States, then we might think this problem could be solved through individual decisions that took place after an initial round of selection such that all citizens would first be in a drawn lottery and then, after selection, they could choose whether to accept or refuse to serve. Moreover, since ex post voluntariness may penalize the most disadvantaged social groups (e.g., who may feel that they cannot take time off work or away from other responsibilities), one proposal would be to pay for service so as to disincentive abstention. These regulations would hold for all kinds of sorted councils, regardless of their missions and regardless of whether they were consultative or representative.[58] Such regulations tell us something important about lotteries: in terms of institutional design and regulatory control they are very demanding; they require a set of ex ante decisions, which presuppose a planning authority that shapes the entire polity in a coherent way. This overarching authority is hardly conceivable as something that would itself be the result of a lottery.

Lottocracy started with concerns about the crisis of representative democracy but has now grown into a movement that identifies elections as the main factor that is responsible for this crisis. Those who support replacement and complementarity models of lottocracy take this reading as a given. They believe that lotteries can regenerate representation and also achieve a form of accountability that is different from electoral accountability yet no less effective or important. Faith in lottocracy supposedly follows from our commitment to democratic experimentation in representative politics. Mansbridge notes that, in the past few decades, several experiments have randomly selected participants for deliberative bodies that then "advise" elected and appointed officials—but still "we have little experience of giving bodies of this sort direct power to legislate rather than just advise."[59] While caution is necessary, it should not halt experimentation that searches for alternative forms of accountability. This search for an alternative model of accountability is the main problem faced by lottocracy.

Electoral and lottocratic accountability are radically different. Electoral accountability is formally sanctioned by periodic elections, whereas lottocratic accountability would perhaps be informally sanctioned by the response of the public. Mansbridge maintains that, in a legislature drawn by lot, the "informal sanctions by the public" will have their own weight. But, as we tried to explain in two early sections of this chapter, this is not necessarily a good thing. In the next chapter, we discuss how lottocrats claim that "morality" and "knowledge" are the sources of incentives and punishments meted out by citizens—who can always propose, criticize, petition, or enter into dialogue with the sorted few. This is the informal accountability of lotteries.

---

[57] Quoted in Courant, "Sortition and Democratic Principles," 235.
[58] Ibid., 233–6.
[59] Mansbridge, "Accountability in the Constituent–Representative Relationship," 189.

Elections also produce informal accountability. They do not solely rely upon an authorization derived from voting, but they also rely on a panoply of citizens' activities that constitute a rich public sphere—a continual process of participation that uses a mix of influence and scrutiny to appropriately stimulate democratic engagement and constrain illiberal or authoritarian impulses so as to maintain a connection between elected institutions and those who are represented. The question is whether, in order to be effective, informal accountability needs to be complemented with formal accountability or whether one of the two is sufficient by itself. In a representative democracy, *informal* and *formal* sanctions are intertwined such that if the former is weak the latter cannot be strong. If informal sanctions are strong but unconnected to formal sanctions, then there is a very real chance that those who participate in the public sphere will have a disproportionally stronger influence than that of all other citizens. Earlier in this chapter, we explained how proponents of complementarity models of lottocracy propose to solve the "problem" of accountability by making lotteries work in tandem with elections. We showed why this would not only help representative democracy solve its crisis of legitimacy but also would perhaps intensify the so-called "democratic deficit" since it would lower the level of accountability that characterizes the entire lawmaking process. The piece of the puzzle that lotteries leave out—accountability—can hardly be functionally replaced by mixing lotteries with elections since this would predictably exacerbate the defects of electoral representation by increasing rather than constraining the power of the elected who would then, as discussed above, end up exerting their influence upon the allotted assembly.

3.4 Conclusion

At the core of the lottocratic mentality is an erroneous assumption that lotteries can produce political representation. Guerrero is aware of this problem and concludes that new forms of arbitrariness or undesirable authoritarian solutions can only be avoided if lottocrats remain steadfastly consistent with and committed to their goal of creating a polis in which institutions and procedures are designed to eliminate precisely what representative government requires: a unitary national sovereignty and the idea that rights are separated from but nevertheless linked up to the exercise of a type of power upon which voting and elections are based. Getting rid of the electoral system and creating a legitimate lottocratic order means radically transforming the identity of both politics and the state. A lottocratic order means promoting a paradigm of knowledge and deliberation that resembles the decision-making process that takes place within a business, where only one kind of issue is to be decided upon rather than the complex mixture of many issues that is typically found in a political community. Not surprisingly, Guerrero proposes to disaggregate deliberation: with an assembly that is assigned the task of discussing each distinct issue. Lotteries can be effectively used as a substitute for elections when the interest that unifies the group of selected citizens is singular or when the assembly is organized around a single issue. Mansbridge seems to corroborate this idea when she mentions that a school or school association would be a good test case for experimenting with the lottery in decision-making. When applied to the political order, this case does not seem to be particularly useful. The case only works well if the institution that the decision-making group serves is specific and uniform (the school) such that both the sample of a few randomly selected people can accurately reflect the whole (representativeness) and that the quality of the outcome can easily be assessed (functional accountability). It seems like the prerequisite for a lottery to enjoy accountability is either homogeneity or unanimity on an issue or else a mirrored collective constituted around a singular and discretely defined theme. This dynamic parallels delegation under a direct mandate, which likewise requires a collective to be united by a single thematic group (as with a school or a union) or that the collective be composed of identical members (as in Rousseau's model).

What we want to emphasize here is that a thoroughly lottocratic system would require a total redesign of the political and social order, not just a simple makeover. In the new order, the popular sovereignty that has traditionally characterized representative democracy—a type of unified and legitimating agency—would simply disappear along with the factors that animated it: voting in elections, representation, and parties. At least according to Guerrero's model, the lottocratic polis that is put forward as an alternative to a traditional representative polis would be a federation of short-lived assemblies. Each assembly would address a specific issue by using lotteries to randomly select people from among those parts of the population that are most directly affected by or interested in a given issue. This system would not want to use some fixed or invariable set of criteria to divide the country's population into predefined groups (e.g., gender, socioeconomic class, occupational status, age, etc.). In order for an issue to become a formal topic for discussion and decision, each issue would need its own "selection pool" of people. This would mean that in a decentralized lottocratic polis proximate localities and thematic issues would be the relevant actors; rather than citizens these amorphous actors would be the protagonists of sovereign power. Instead of a polis of citizens, we would have *a polis of issues*, with councils and assemblies structured to perform the different functions a government needs (justice, administration, information, decision-making, etc.).

In conclusion, we partly agree with Guerrero: a mixture of lotteries and elections can hardly be applied to the legislative process without also calling the democratic nature of popular sovereignty into question. In order to have the desired positive impact on a community, lottocracy must radically redefine legitimacy and must do so against the backdrop of the following conundrum: either lotteries must *only* be applied to those departments where judgment and impartiality are prerequisites for legitimate decisions or else lotteries can *also* be applied to the domain of lawmaking but, in that case, we would need to entirely rethink politics itself and to do so in a way that cuts against democracy, insofar as it would make "some" rule over others even though the "others" have not authorized this rule but yet must obey its decisions. Even in a deeply federated polis, the lottocratic mentality would inspire democratically untenable systems of decision-making.

Chapter 4
The Targets of Lottocracy Revisited

In 1967, Hanna Pitkin revisited Marie Collins Swabey's proposal from three decades prior, which contemplated using "choice by lot" to transform the US Congress into an "accurate or truly random sample . . as truly representative." Pitkin noted that "[s]uch a change would mean an end to political parties, to professional politicians, to the regarding of elections as an occasion for reviewing policy or authorizing or holding to account."[1] The lottocratic mentality embraces this conclusion and envisions a political order that would supposedly empower the people not through reinstating direct democracy but rather through a new mechanism to select lawmakers. This new selection method would make citizens feel less "under the thumb" of a publicity-seeking, self-referential political class. "Representation by lottery" or "lottocratic representation" is a type of indirectness that *resets* the three pillars of modern democracy: elections, representation, and political parties. In this chapter, we articulate the lottocratic critiques of these pillars and defend the democratic credentials of each pillar against those critiques.

4.1 Voting Power and Elections

4.1.1 What's Wrong with Elections?

The popularity of lotteries and the lottocratic theory of representation, in particular, mirror dissatisfaction with elections. "Democratic theory has had an ambivalent relationship with elections," as elections are an aggregative institution that is central to a minimalist conception of democracy but peripheral to participatory and deliberative theories of democracy more broadly.[2] Recently, low voter turnout and polarization in consolidated democracies have deepened skepticism toward elections and, as we just observed, encouraged institutional reform proposals that use lotteries as at least "transitional steps" toward a more extensive reliance on them. Thus, while skepticism for elections is not new, it has recently taken a radical turn insofar as that skepticism has started to challenge universal suffrage itself. Some political scientists who espouse a realist conception of politics propose that elections "prove"

---

[1] Pitkin, *The Concept of Representation*, 75; Swabey, *Theory of the Democratic State*, 25.
[2] Chiara Destri and Annabelle Lever, "Égalité démocratique et tirage au sort," *Raison publique*, no. 26 (2023): 63.

The Lottocratic Mentality. Cristina Lafont and Nadia Urbinati, Oxford University Press. © Cristina Lafont and Nadia Urbinati (2024). DOI: 10.1093/9780191982903.003.0005

124 The Lottocratic Mentality

that democracy is inherently too vulnerable to the influence of citizens' ignorance and tribal identifications such that "the more power they are given, the more we all suffer the consequences." This line of argument often turns nefarious: to "be realistic about democracy" means questioning the deliberative potential of mass participation while admitting that elections are an unfortunate necessity.[3]

This is not the position of lottocrats. They do not blame the citizens; they blame procedures and institutions—voting and elections.[4] Ironically, between theorists who hold a realist conception of politics and lottocrats, *lottocrats* actually turn out to be more averse to electoral democracy. Whereas the complaint of realists lumps democracy together with elections (thereby confirming their relationship), lottocrats think that representation can be disconnected from elections and that democracy can be disconnected from both. This argumentative structure falls back on a dichotomous "representative government versus direct democracy" paradigm from the eighteenth century, whereby "voting for" a candidate is seen as an act of consent that legitimizes the transfer of citizens' legislative power to an assembly. This paradigm does not renounce indirectness but instead promotes a "true" democratic form of indirectness. We shall reveal three radical moves that the lottocratic mentality often makes: breaking the identification of nonelectoral democracy with direct democracy, disconnecting representation from elections, and dissociating democracy from suffrage. The result of these moves would be a type of representation that bypasses authorization by the represented and creates two sets of citizens (the sorted and the nonsorted) who remain separate from one another.

Within this lottocratic model, one of the core premises is that voting in elections creates a political class insofar as it necessarily violates the two main principles of democracy: inclusiveness and equality. When representation solely depends on the choice of voters, then this essentially transforms representation into a social construct subject to representatives' ability to garner votes, be it as a single candidate or through the apparatus of a political party. Lottocrats think that to make the lawmaking assembly representative *and* democratic, we must "dethrone the individual consent" or the electoral function of "voting for" a candidate.[5] For an assembly to be representative, it would be sufficient for it to "stand for" groups conceptualized as miniaturized samples.[6] For an assembly to be democratic (i.e., "inclusive and equal"), it would be necessary for access to be regulated by a selection mechanism that nullifies choice and discourse. If an assembly were reconfigured along these lines, then representation would be democratic insofar as it would not be subjected to any kind of pressure from candidates or voters in order to get or give consent.[7] On the other hand, equality of access and inclusion would not require direct self-government; they could instead

---

[3] Brennan and Landemore, *Debating Democracy*, 10.

[4] "The few minutes it takes to cross or number a ballot cannot be the primary mode of holding rulers accountable for their actions." Brett Hennig, "Who Needs Elections? Accountability, Equality, and Legitimacy under Sortition," in *Legislature by Lot*, ed. Gastil and Wright, 305.

[5] Landemore, *Open Democracy*, 85.

[6] Ibid., 80.

[7] "Tacit authorization" is foreseen "under very specific conditions" such as "large events with high media coverage" or in those communities when "digital access is prevalent." Ibid., 111.

The Targets of Lottocracy Revisited   **125**

be secured if the selection mechanism bypassed the type of mediation that political parties now standardly engage in—a mediation that is the primary source of bad and corrupt decisions. But lottocracy faces a problem: how can a legislature be legitimate if it is composed through a process that neither secures authorization from the citizenry nor holds decision-makers accountable? As we shall see, the "solution" to this problem is the notion of "accountability *stricto sensu*"—a form of legal sanction that does not require the input and judgment of citizens—neither their opinions nor their voting decisions (horizontal accountability).[8]

At the root of this radical revision is the assumption that, structurally speaking, elections are not democratic since they produce elitist outcomes: they do not provide citizens with an equal opportunity to compete as candidates and they transform electoral competition into a game that favors those who start out with advantages: citizens "with extraordinary, socially salient qualities" use their economic and cultural resources to gain visibility, be chosen, and then govern.[9] This assumption about elections shapes the lottocratic mentality. Indeed, lottocrats routinely subscribe to this narrative even when they do not go as far as proposing that elections should be replaced with lotteries. Even the more moderate lottocrats think that "voting for" inevitably violates equality and jeopardizes good deliberation since it involves the criterion of individual preferences to fill political offices, and such preferences are not always enlightened or immune to the promises of the most powerful candidates. From this perspective, elections necessarily create an affluent clique of elites, and this dynamic tends to disproportionately represent only the most powerful and advantaged groups of citizens.[10] According to this framing, electoral accountability itself entrenches these defects since it conceptually depends on elected officials seeking reelection (and thus remaining sensitive to public opinion), and this then focuses attention on short-term goals—which is not necessarily in the best interests of the country over time.[11] Against this backdrop, the claim is that *liberating democracy from the logic of "voting for"* would put an end to competition, elites, political conflict, and bad decisions.

The problem is that "dethroning" elections is not that easy. In the democratic imaginary, suffrage occupies a central place as the focal point of political freedom and emancipation. To discard suffrage, lottocrats must first gloss over the meaning of the specific type of political freedom it involves. They attempt to do this by endowing suffrage with a historically contingent value and then judging it from the perspective of justice as impartiality. As their argument goes, while the struggle for universal

---

[8] Ibid., 100–1. Dunn defined *stricto sensu* accountability (criminal law) and stressed its very imperfect character: "will only handle a fairly modest proportion of the hazards we face from our rulers and which it is reasonable for us to wish to minimize." John Dunn, "Situating Democratic Political Accountability," in *Democracy, Accountability, and Representation*, ed. Adam Przeworski, Susan C. Stokes, and Bernard Manin (Cambridge: Cambridge University Press, 1999), 338.

[9] Brennan and Landemore, *Debating Democracy*, 3–4; Tom Malleson, "Should Democracy Work through Elections or Sortition?," in *Legislature by Lot*, ed. Gastil and Wright, 173: "Electoral democracy . . . will always be somewhat biased toward the rich."

[10] Guerrero, *Lottocracy*, 140.

[11] Ibid.

126 The Lottocratic Mentality

suffrage was able to motivate the emancipatory aspirations of millions in its initial phase, this imagery dissolved once this goal was achieved.[12] The right to suffrage lost its significance at precisely the moment that it achieved a nearly universal scope and stabilized; today, it has entirely exhausted its emancipatory force. Low electoral turnout supposedly proves this point.[13] Apart from referenda, the right to vote "does not count as a genuine right of participation" nor does it even create representative institutions with broad or enriched "deliberative capacities."[14]

This criticism waters down the distinctive value of voting and dissociates it from the many instances of participation it generates and sustains over time. In this narrative frame, voting gets identified with consent that delegates power rather than with a power that institutes a legitimate legislature. Moreover, voting and elections are no longer judged from the perspective of political freedom.[15] Instead, they are judged through the lens of justice as impartiality. This is a specific conception of justice governed by equality of probability, which, as discussed earlier, lottocrats take to be the most genuine form of democratic equality. "Legitimacy by virtue of impartiality is distinct from legitimacy by virtue of election" because it is interested in preventing anyone from benefiting disproportionately from a given practice—the logic is the same as that ruling independent authorities, whose procedures are also based "on the project of destroying individual advantages."[16]

This criticism of suffrage and elections has produced three general lottocratic models.[17] The first is *lottery voting*. As discussed in Chapter 1, this seeks to bypass majority rule through a mixture of voting and lottery that provides justice to minorities and fairness to all candidates.[18] The second model is *suffrage by lottery*. The goal is to secure efficiency and stability by using a lottery to select those who can exercise competently the right to vote. The idea here is that "while in universal suffrage every citizen has one equal vote, in [suffrage by lottery] every citizen has equal eligibility to vote."[19] This is a form of justice related to (in)exclusion. This basic framework yields proposals that are explicitly antidemocratic and paternalistic. The third model is

---

[12] Landemore, *Open Democracy*, 130–1.

[13] Ibid.

[14] Ibid., 134; Brennan and Landemore, *Debating Democracy*, 6; Mark Warren, "Citizen Representatives," in *Representation: Elections and Beyond*, ed. Jack H. Nagel and Rogers M. Smith (Philadelphia, PA: University of Pennsylvania Press, 2013), 54.

[15] A corollary of political justice in elections goes as follows: a democratic goal is to establish and preserve an equilibrium between potential candidates so that they can compete on a fair basis while providing voters with a chance to enter the competition if they so choose and to make their voices heard. Charles Beitz, *Political Equality* (Princeton, NJ: Princeton University Press, 1989), 194–5. A critical discussion on the extension of justice as impartiality to politics has been recently proposed by Ian Shapiro, *Uncommon Sense* (New Haven, CT: Yale University Press, 2024).

[16] Rosanvallon, *The Populist Century*, 132.

[17] For a thorough discussion of these three proposals, see Lachlan Montgomery Umbers, "Against Lottocracy," *European Journal of Political Theory* 20, no. 2 (2021): 312–34.

[18] See chap. 1, above, wherein, along with Elster, we cite Saunders, "Democracy, Political Equality, and Majority Rule," and Amar, "Choosing Representatives by Lottery Voting."

[19] Jason Brennan and Lisa Hill, *Compulsory Voting: For and Against* (Cambridge: Cambridge University Press, 2014), 36; Claudio López-Guerra, "The Enfranchisement Lottery," *Politics, Philosophy and Economics* 10, no. 2 (2011): 214–5. For a criticism of López-Guerra's exclusionary use of lottery, see Peonidis, "On Two Anti-democratic Uses of Sortition," 29–31, 35–9. For a critique of this exclusionary use of lottery, see Guerrero, *Lottocracy*, 116 foonote n. 2.

representation by lottery. Here, the goal is to protect equality by replacing aggregative decision-making through elections with a multitude of randomly selected bodies that are each representative in their own ways and with respect to their own issues.[20] Models within this third camp share a desire to minimize political power and design institutions according to the criterion of impartiality in the distribution of public functions. They attempt to realize this goal (a) by closing the main avenues that people use to achieve unequal influence, (b) by attaining accountability through statistical samples, and (c) by breaking the monopoly of parties.

We agree with lottocrats that problems of electoral justice and fairness in representation affect virtually all existing democracies. Over the decades, major reforms have been put forward (with varying degrees of success) to ensure that underrepresented minorities have a voice (e.g., proportional versus first-past-the-post representation, group representation, and special seats or quotas) as well as laws to regulate electoral colleges, ballot access, and control over regulation for the distribution of financial resources to parties and campaigns. Lottocrats are skeptical about the possibility of improving electoral representation since they think that no reform can mitigate the flaws of a system that structurally breeds an elite and that also fails to ensure that citizens vote according to their reasoned preferences. They especially believe this in light of the fact that neither the media nor political parties help citizens understand what their true preferences or interests even are (or ideally should be).[21] Elections also stand in the way of meaningful change because they are based on "promises" that involve political hypocrisy, "dirty hands," and the risk of "corrupting the legislative process as a whole"—a corruption that can include the very anticorruption laws that parliaments endlessly seek to enact.[22] If this is what elections are about, then voting power is worth little; it should not cost us all that much to give it up.

4.1.2 Our Argument

Any response to these critiques must address two main assumptions: that voting is a form of consent (in that it transfers decision-making power) and that elections are aristocratic or oligarchic (in that they discriminate among equals). Although lottocrats do not renounce referenda, they question the supposedly "individualistic" principle of "one-person/one-vote" because it fosters a self-congratulatory passivity

---

[20] Along with Guerrero's and Landemore's work, see also Stone, *The Luck of the Draw*; Zakaras, "Lot and Democratic Representation"; and McCormick, *Machiavellian Democracy*.

[21] "The basic argument is simple. Voter ignorance undermines meaningful electoral accountability. An absence of meaningful electoral accountability results in capture. And capture results in what might well be described as epistemic disaster" (Guerrero, "Pathologies," 163); which meets with the detailed description of the election entrepreneurs in Christopher H. Achen and Larry M. Bartels, *Democracy for Realists* (Princeton, NJ: Princeton University Press, 2016), 3–79.

[22] Bouricius, "Why Hybrid Bicameralism Is Not Right for Sortition," in *Legislature by Lot*, ed. Gastil and Wright, 323; David Runciman, *Political Hypocrisy: The Mask of Power, from Hobbes to Orwell and Beyond* (Princeton, NJ: Princeton University Press, 2008); Michael Walzer, "Political Action: The Problem of Dirty Hands," *Philosophy & Public Affairs* 2, no. 2 (1973): 160–82.

128   The Lottocratic Mentality

among citizens: when voting is made into an expression of consent, it gets transformed into something akin to a conjuring trick that gives citizens the *illusion* of self-government at the very moment that it is taken away from them.

It is our basic argument that elections primarily pertain to the exercise of both individual and collective political freedom and that voting is a power that catalyzes the lawmaking function in its entirety, from the raising of issues to the elaboration of proposals to the approval of law and then its comment by the public and eventually its reconsideration and change. While certain types of elections can indeed occur outside the context of a democracy, "democracy cannot endure without elections," which rest on "the fundamental idea that the democratic process should regard citizens as free and equal persons."[23] By the same token, while it is true that not every form of democracy is representative, it is also true that "not every representative state is democratic by virtue of being representative," and universal suffrage is the minimal determinant threshold that makes a state democratic; as a threshold, it is "a question of take it or leave it."[24] Currently, if leaders refuse to acknowledge their electoral defeat, then they very publicly call the entire power of the vote into question and send a strong signal that democracy is at risk. Yet, what would the similar threshold be in a lottocracy? This question is not merely rhetorical but rather fundamental. It reveals what the lottocratic mentality does and does not ask democracy to provide. The lottocratic mentality asks for "equality, justice, stability and efficiency," but these values can also be secured by nondemocratic regimes.[25] Yet, the lottocratic mentality does not seem to ask for or expect political freedom to be secured.

A theory of voluntary consent recast as voluntary subjection to an elected body is conveniently traced back to the contractarian story of political legitimacy and natural law and to John Locke in particular. As we know, Locke emphatically did *not* merge the consent to be part of the "body politic" with electoral consent. He assumed that everyone has natural and equal rights to property, life, and liberty, and he only introduced elections once the agreement to form the body politic was made to produce enforceable laws by which citizens could better protect the interests that were associated with their rights. Voting in elections emerged as a power, and it was also an issue of freedom because it represented a mark of power limitation. Voting originated as an artificial power to legitimize the exercise of another artificial power—lawmaking—whose task was to protect a fragile good: the individual. De facto, the power of voting started as a function to protect the interests of some *particular* group of people or a certain predetermined class. Yet, when understood as a power, it could be and was used by democrats as well.

---

[23] Dennis F. Thompson, *Just Elections: Creating a Fair Electoral Process in The United States* (Chicago: University of Chicago Press, 2002), 1 and 8.

[24] Norberto Bobbio, *The Future of Democracy: A Defence of the Rules of the Game*, trans. Roger Griffin (Minneapolis, MN: University of Minnesota Press, 1987), 46 and 66; Boagang He, "Deliberative Citizenship and Deliberative Governance: A Case Study of One Deliberative Experiment in China," *Citizenship Studies* 22, no. 3 (2018): 294–311.

[25] Brennan and Landemore, *Debating Democracy*, 7; Malleson, "Should Democracy Work," in *Legislature by Lot*, ed. Gastil and Wright, 171, also adds public control, deliberation, impartiality, and competency.

The claim that voting is a type of power has become especially true for democracy. Indeed, in antiquity, democracy was born out of ordinary people making a revolutionary choice to claim decision-making power as an essential condition for being and remaining free. In the context of nineteenth-century suffragist movements, when labor unions, socialist and democratic political parties all asked for suffrage, they did not make their demands to either give consent to the rulers or to protect specific interests (they were propertyless and economically weak). They wanted a power that could allow them to promote valuable policies and protect themselves from those who had power. Voting had to be a personal right precisely because it was a power, and that power was made secure in direct proportion to its equal distribution. Those who are supposedly "protected" by a law that they do not participate in making and who cannot check and judge in its implementation are in actuality not protected at all: "we know what legal protection the slaves have, where the laws are made by their masters."[26]

Theories of voting mirror conceptions of democracy. Voting is one of the most important expressions of political freedom, but it does not yield electoral democracy by itself. Even if voting is an essential and nontransferrable right, it is far from the only component of democracy. As a power, voting is more comprehensive than electing—for, to elect, one has to vote, but one can vote to deliberate, yet not necessarily to elect. Voting is the natural conclusion of deliberation and the most natural expression of democracy. On the other hand, electing seems to be the source of many problems within democracy since the technique (and its several modes of application) used to elect someone deeply determines the nature of the assembly and the course of deliberation within and outside it.[27]

What makes for an electoral democracy is the universal right to "vote for" exercised in the context of something more than a two-party system. Citizens should not only enjoy the possibility of forming a majority and an opposition, but they should also be able to exercise an effective choice over proposals concerning the general government and direction of their country over and above serial choices that merely involve this-or-that decision or this-or-that candidate. While voting in a plebiscite for a leader seeking acclamation and voting for candidates from a single-party list are cases of consent, they are not cases of electoral democracy.[28]

---

[26] John Stuart Mill, *The Subjection of Women* (1689) in *On Liberty and Other Essays*, ed. Nadia Urbinati (New York: Norton, 2023), 204. For a compelling argument in favor of the centrality of "voting" (for someone and/or on something) or *psephocracy* (the ancient Greek practice of voting by dropping *psēphos* – pebbles – into urns) see Ferris, "Lottocracy or Psephocracy?."

[27] For a comparative analysis of the impact on extra-institutional participation within electoral systems, see Arend Lijphart, *Patterns of Democracy: Government Forms and Performance in Thirty-Six Countries* (New Haven, CT: Yale University Press, 1999) and G. Bingham Powell Jr., *Elections as Instruments of Democracy: Majoritarian and Proportional Visions* (New Haven, CT: Yale University Press, 2000).

[28] A plebiscite can also be held on issues in order to give legitimacy to a new regime; in 1860 Italy had a plebiscite in its northern regions to decide whether to merge under the realm of Savoia, and then again in 1946 to decide on whether to remain a monarchy or to become a republic; in 1992 a plebiscite was then used to decide on the dissolution of Czechoslovakia and the formation of two independent states, the Czech Republic and Slovakia.

130   The Lottocratic Mentality

The lottocratic mentality's conception of voting and elections echoes a minimalist conception of democracy that sees elections as an exercise of individual choice that responds to individual preferences and treats voting like an arbitration that resolves a dispute between competitors over government. According to this conception, the arbitration yields a choice of an elite group and, in so doing, stabilizes society (indeed, such arbitration keeps the "few" at bay who, if left to themselves in the absence of any popular checks, would tend to generate factionalism). In contemporary political science, the most common approaches to elections stem from these "individualist" and "competitive" views. Both these views simply ignore considerations of electoral justice and neglect the institutional dimension of elections or how, alongside shaping decision-making, they shape and structure the public sphere of opinion, language, and participation as well.[29] Both views start from an assumption that the private interests or preferences of individuals constitute the true "agency" of politics, and this predictably turns politics into a sort of "game" whose fairness can be articulated in terms of the fairness of competition (the rules of the game) among candidates and interests. Both views overlook how citizenship constitutes a dimension of political freedom that is not simply individually but collectively enjoyed.

Joseph A. Schumpeter criticized the idea that elections (or even democracy) could serve political freedom or other normative values. He denied the ability of the people to govern themselves and consider elections as a mechanism to divide labor to get around the scarcity of time and expertise among citizens. In his view, the function of elections is "to produce a government" through "a competitive struggle for the people's vote"; elections give citizens a passive role in politics that is, at best, akin to that of a consenting audience.[30] In sum, voting is consent to being ruled, and it is democratic because it relies on an ad hoc system (elections) through which consent is expressed, assessed, and checked with computational certainty.

This conception reemerges in the lottocratic view that elections (a) expel the citizens from political decisions, (b) serve to legitimize those who rule, and (c) stabilize the conviction that democratic representation consists in the whole body of the citizenry consenting to be subjected (albeit temporarily) to the few. This view is put forward as an objective description of representative democracy, but it fails to consider that the electoral *process* is also constituted by agenda setting, that citizens select their preferred political proposals and not just isolated candidates, and that elections project the idea of a *collective* (e.g., the country, the society, and the people) that is not typically thought of as merely the sum total of votes.[31] Yet, the lottocratic mentality persists in casting elections as a contract between those with equal natural

---

[29] Thompson, *Just Elections*, 4–8.

[30] Neither equality nor inclusion is defining characteristic here because democracy always entails some degree of discrimination in suffrage—against foreigners at the very least, but also against citizens, since no universal suffrage is truly universal: Joseph A. Schumpeter, *Capitalism, Socialism, and Democracy* (London: Allen & Unwin, 1943), 269. This explains why Schumpeter has been a key author for the contemporary renaissance of plebiscitary democracy; see, for instance, Jeffrey Edward Green, *The Eyes of the People: Democracy in the Age of Spectatorship* (Oxford: Oxford University Press, 2010), 171–7.

[31] See Robert A. Dahl, "Procedural Democracy," in *Contemporary Political Philosophy: An Anthology*, ed. Robert Goodin and Philip Pettit (Oxford: Blackwell, 1996), 107–25.

rights, which legitimizes the transfer of decision-making power from voters to the elected. Such a view locates representative government on a spectrum somewhere between domination and democracy. As such, the lottocratic mentality invites citizens to conclude that elections strip representation of its representative function and inhibit democracy's promise of an impartial and equal opportunity to serve the public.

However, elections have a normative and participatory value. They work for and guarantee political freedom and the permanence of the conflictual dimension of politics, a goal that has inspired global struggles for democracy over the past two centuries at least. How lottocracy underestimates political freedom as the normative justification for elections is also puzzling since the whole idea that democracy is a self-enforcing mechanism implies that freedom must be protected as a collective good.[32] Democracy's capacity for self-limitation is confirmed by its ability to internalize threats of rebellion and induce moderation in incumbents *without* suppressing dissent and political conflict. It is undoubtedly true that elections allow the majority to impose its preferences for a while. However, this dominance is limited by the very existence of an opposition that could become a majority in the foreseeable future and which, in the meantime, is active in the representative assembly and society. Therefore, electoral democracy not only prevents violence, as the minimalist conception reasonably argues, but also limits power through its process and, in this sense, enhances and protects political freedom.[33] When we vote, we do two things at once: we contribute to forming a government or opposition and we seek representation of our positions and preferences. This means that elections are not just a race that some win at the expense of others, but rather that they are a way of participating in creating the representative body and government.

Emilee Booth Chapman suggests *three key features* of popular voting in a modern democracy that can be taken as a reference point: (1) "the standard of universal participation" (which low turnout *does not* call into question) means that the "expectation" of universal turnout "operates as a public norm that shapes election administration as well as private activity and public discourse around elections."[34] This gives a sense of the importance of this right, which is internalized as a duty to the point that the public and citizens routinely treat low turnout as a problem. This normative standard sustains the principle of electoral justice and suggests some specific conclusions: "registration procedures should be eased, campaign expenditure controlled, regulatory authority strengthened."[35] (2) The criterion of "discrete, attention-grabbing moments of participation" makes voting both a collective decision and an

---

[32] Realists' classification of political regimes explicitly excludes the extent of popular participation in elections as a criterion for distinguishing democracies from nondemocracies: Adam Przeworski, Michael Alvarez, Jose Antonio Cheibub, and Fernando Limongi, *Democracy and Development: Political Institutions and Well-Being in the World, 1950–1990* (Cambridge: Cambridge University Press, 2000).

[33] Maria Paula Saffon and Nadia Urbinati, "Procedural Democracy, the Bulwark of Equal Liberty," *Political Theory* 41, no. 3 (2013): 456.

[34] Emilee Booth Chapman, *Election Day: How We Vote and What It Means for Democracy* (Princeton, NJ: Princeton University Press, 2022), 24.

[35] Thompson, *Just Elections*, 17.

individually exercised power at the same time; as "a call to participate" in the same moment, voting opens a long-lasting process that lives on beyond election day, from agenda setting to campaigning to analyzing the results and projecting the future.[36] This panoply of activities means that elections are not simply a method for choosing governments but also that they possess an "expressivist function," which explains the permanent effort to fight all forms of disfranchisement in a consolidated democracy (the struggle for enfranchisement is never over).[37] Finally, (3) there is aggregative equality or equality "among participants [that] is realized through symmetry" and is "impersonal and anonymous." The impersonal character of this equality makes it different from deliberative equality, which is interpersonal, although it does certainly generate deliberative participation since it activates important "mental states of citizens": attitudes of reciprocity, openness to deliberative contributions, and tolerance.[38]

In sum, voting rights and elections open the door to an endless process of direct and indirect participation through which people see certain issues that previously might have been widely seen as "natural" or nonexistent or unchangeable, to be taken up as problems that affect them and that should be addressed by the entire political community.[39] Elections also have an ethical impact on citizens' behavior insofar as they are a procedure that constitutes the players and regulates their interaction: the citizens who participate in the electoral process (whether as candidates or voters) conceive and structure their language and behavior in a way that respects their adversaries without deference, and which orients judgments toward the future. This creates reciprocity and inculcates respect for the freedom to express ideas publicly and thus also for values like pluralism and tolerance. We shall illustrate this dynamic when analyzing the democratic role of political parties.[40] This dynamic applies both when we compete and after everybody knows (and accepts) the outcome of elections. Such behavior is paramount, and it confirms how, rather than being mere formalities, elections are *essential* to democratic agency and political freedom.[41] They are not a method to choose the individuals who rule above us but rather a method to create and assess representative majorities and groups within the opposition. Elections contribute to democracy by encouraging the open expression of collective and individual dissent in society. As Habermas puts it, these are "anarchic" forms of self-reflection that are not subject to institutional regulation and which continually produce the majority/opposition divide in shifting iterations that respond to the morphing internal "borders" among parts of the citizenry and their associated

---

[36] Chapman, *Election Day*, 30.

[37] Thompson, *Just Elections*, 24.

[38] Chapman, *Election Day*, 33.

[39] Pierre Rosanvallon, *La contre-démocratie: La politique à l'âge de la défiance* (Paris: Seuil, 2006).

[40] "Mutual respect expresses a constructive attitude toward, and willingness to engage in good faith with, one's political opponents." Amy Gutmann and Dennis F. Thompson, *The Spirit of Compromise: Why Governing Demands It and Campaigning Undermines It* (Princeton, NJ: Princeton University Press, 2012), 34.

[41] Bobbio, *Future of Democracy*, 65–7; Joshua Cohen, "Procedure and Substance in Deliberative Democracy," in *Democracy and Difference*, ed. Benhabib, 407–37.

political groups. In creating occasions for participation and decisions, an election "creates distinct moments in which the political community is rendered salient to its members."[42] In short, elections entail (and strengthen) civil and political rights, that is to say, freedom.[43]

Indeed, the conceptual *contrast* with lotteries can help to articulate the sense of democratic agency that is involved in elections: "While the use of sortition guarantees democratic 'breadth,' in the sense of ensuring extensive participation by average citizens, election could introduce greater democratic 'depth,' in the sense of candidates running on agendas that attempted to give voice to the will of the *dêmos*, considered collectively. Election could provide policy direction and ideological coherence in a way that the widespread involvement of random, uncoordinated individual citizens (many of whom might have held no particularly strong feelings about polis-wide issues) could not."[44] This confirms our idea that bringing lotteries into an auxiliary relationship with elections turns out to be more beneficial to democracy than their mutual exclusion.

Therefore, in response to the lottocratic assumption that voting and elections are nothing more than mechanisms of consent to select a ruling elite whose decisions we are then simply subjected to, we argue that in electing political representatives, we *do not* consent to be ruled such that the rulers, once elected, can just decide what to do as they see fit until the next election. This view treats democracy as if it were a chronological series of majorities that were garnered every few years and that, in between, citizens were largely passive, and the work of the government was more or less arbitrary (apart from constitutional checks that are not in the hands of the people anyway). Elections and voting are not like traffic rules that a policeman is charged with enforcing, and they are not like an autopilot that, once put into action, will navigate on its own, while citizens are just the potential inhabitants of a state of nature that needs to be regulated.[45]

Along with Jane Mansbridge, we argue "against interpreting the act of casting a vote in an election as 'consent.'"[46] Voting is a simple gesture that involves a vibrant menu of knowledge and judgments, of association with others, and of initiating deliberative trials and possibly even decisions upon new or rediscussed issues and agendas.

---

[42] Chapman, *Election Day*, 31.

[43] Kelsen wrote: "A democracy without public opinion is a contradiction in terms. Insofar as public opinion can arise only where intellectual freedom, freedom of speech, press, and religion are guaranteed, democracy coincides with political—though not necessarily economic—liberalism." Hans Kelsen, *General Theory of Law and State*, trans. Anders Wedberg (Clark, NJ: Lawbook Exchange, 2007), 288.

[44] Matthew Simonton, "Ambition for Office and the Nature of Election in Ancient Greek Democracies," Forthcoming (2025) in *Journal of Sortition*.

[45] Thus, rather than the militaristic image of voting as "flexing muscles," Jeremy Waldron aptly proposes "experience of rotation in and out of office and the empowerment of opposition." Waldron, *Political Political Theory* (Cambridge, MA: Harvard University Press, 2016), 107. The "one-person, one-vote" principle is the strongest recognition that in a democracy each person's judgment counts equally; Melissa Schwartzberg, *Counting the Many: The Origins of Supermajority Rule* (Cambridge: Cambridge University Press, 2014), 111.

[46] Jane Mansbridge, "Accountability in the Constituent–Representative Relationship," in *Legislature by Lot*, ed. Gastil and Wright, 192; see also Emanuela Ceva and Valeria Ottonelli, "Second-Personal Authority and the Practice of Democracy," *Constellations* 29, no. 4 (2021): 460–74.

134 The Lottocratic Mentality

Through elections, we participate in and reason in terms of collective decisions about what political program we want to be implemented. But we also signal our perennial possibility of mobilization and defection from previous decisions, and this reminds the elected that the office they received in the last election can be taken away from them (indeed, in parliamentary systems, it can be taken back even before their term naturally expires). As we discuss in more detail when we analyze representation as a form of political mandate, voting is not a blank check. Beneath the lottocratic view of elections lies a simplistic and inadequate conception of the democratic authority that disclaims the anti-monopolizing role of political freedom.

To paraphrase Étienne de La Boétie, elections cannot simply be identified with consenting to "voluntary servitude" such that we suffer the yoke of the victors. Helping to form an opposition is an important power that does not come to an end simply because there was an election, as making laws is itself a collective process in the assembly (that reverberates outside), which, either directly or indirectly, both the majority and the opposition participate in. Any majority decision needs to pass through a process of discussion. This process is often a gymnastic of compromise with the opposition, particularly if the opposition is not all that weak. Indeed, this dynamic between the majority and the opposition illustrates why the choice of an electoral system is so important.[47] It is important because it amounts to an issue of justice within representation: elections entail numerical justice, but representation seeks a type of proportional justice since its role is not merely to form a majority but also to give political expression to social plurality and give the opposition more of an ability to influence lawmaking. "Political equality requires not only weighing votes equally in the drawing of districts but some assurance that the process is representative of the entire country."[48] For this reason, an election is not just a contest to win the majority or, as Gerry Mackie aptly puts it, "rooting" for one's team; it is also playing on the team itself, so to speak, since the proposals to be voted on are not simply thrown into the marketplace of the ballot from outside and above. Elections are a way for citizens to participate in building the representative environment itself, and this means more than just a parliamentary seat.[49]

4.1.3 History Rethought

Democratic voting in elections tells us some important things about the use of elections in history. These lessons can help us revise the lottocratic story. It is certainly

---

[47] Hans Kelsen, *The Essence and Value of Democracy*, ed. Nadia Urbinati and Carlo Invernizzi Accetti, trans. Brian Graf (Lanham, MD: Rowman and Littlefield, 2013), 70.

[48] Thomas Christiano, *The Rule of the Many: Fundamental Issues in Democratic Theory* (Boulder, CO: Westview, 1996), 218–24; Fabio Wolkenstein, "Party Reforms and Electoral Systems: Proportional Representation Is More Hospitable to Internal Democratization," *Journal of Representative Democracy* 57, no. 3 (2021): 313–28.

[49] James S. Fishkin, *The Voice of the People: Public Opinion and Democracy* (New Haven, CT: Yale University Press, 1997), 142–4; see also David Plotke, "Representation Is Democracy," 19; Gerry Mackie, "All Men Are Liars: Is Democracy Meaningless?," in *Deliberative Democracy*, ed. Elster, 69–96.

true that many eighteenth-century thinkers and political leaders mistrusted ordinary citizens (and democracy) and that they thought elections could be strategically deployed to exclude them from lawmaking (Federalist no. 63 spoke of "total exclusion of the people, in their collective capacity" of making political decisions). Yet despite that old plan, elections gave birth to a dynamic form of public and political "presence" that made the people "included" and powerful, both directly and, above all, indirectly. The turning point in democratization coincided with voting transitioning from a function (as in Locke) to a right—a right that the most democratic French revolutionaries thought of as "attached" to each citizen. This change marked the transition from liberal representative government to representative democracy, which began when voting ceased to be conceived as a tool to protect the interests of some by selecting the best representatives from among them and was instead conceived as a right to give voice and power to the various claims and proposals that citizens raised with their representatives.[50] In this new formulation, voting power made its appearance in the pamphlets of the Levellers, was theorized by democratic republicans like Thomas Paine and le Marquis de Condorcet, and was sought by several generations of democrats, republicans, and socialists over the next two centuries.[51] Since then, those who wanted to attack democracy started by attacking the right to vote—either by abolishing it or by making it hard for citizens to practice it, or by using elections to either represent corporate interests or to acclaim a leader.

From the moment the right to vote began to be applied and theorized as a personal/political right, voting ceased to be associated with either the choice of a "natural aristocracy" of competent and virtuous rulers or with the selection of certain individuals based on the individual evaluation of their specific virtues and qualities. One reason why elections are anachronistically conceived of as a form of "aristocratic selection" is that they have been analyzed without any emphasis or attention to how they are bound up with the right to vote.[52] Voting in elections entails *both* having the right to vote for a broad proposal *and* having the right to campaign for it freely. Voting simultaneously constitutes a formal and an informal set of activities; this complexity activates a society that is querulous and vibrant, composed of movements and contestation, proposals and petitions, and other forms of representative claim-making we are familiar with, and that do not necessarily end in elections.[53] After citizens have voted, they "do not stand by helpless, without resources. They can organize with allies to depose, or at least fight against, their elected representative in the next election."[54] Voting is a tonic to participation rather than a depressant; it keeps the minds

---

[50] Suffrage—distribution of the right to vote on the basis of one-person/one-vote—"is the first step toward the equal protection of interests. But, the traditional arguments for universal suffrage can always be extended to demands for equal power because an equal vote will not protect one's interests unless it is backed by equal power." Mansbridge, *Beyond Adversary Democracy*, 30.

[51] For a reconstruction of that history, see Nadia Urbinati, *Representative Democracy: Principles and Genealogy* (Chicago: University of Chicago Press, 2006).

[52] See Chapter 1 for a synthesis of this view, from Montesquieu to Manin.

[53] Daniel Carpenter, *Democracy by Petition: Popular Politics in Transformations, 1790–1870* (Cambridge, MA: Harvard University Press, 2021).

[54] Mansbridge, "Accountability in the Constituent–Representative Relationship," 193.

of citizens alert to what the legislature is up to and focused on how they will use their voting power in the next election. It invariably comes along with other rights—rights that no specifically *democratic* election could ever exist without: the right of associating together within political parties, of freely contesting and publicly opposing decisions and politicians, of freedom of speech, and of gathering information and openly expressing ideas. Thus, if an internally raucous polity is taken to be a sign of the "crisis" of democracy, then this is only because it has somehow been decided that the "functionality" of elections should be measured by the level of apathy among the citizenry. This is indeed the picture proposed by the economic theory of democracy. However, the fact is that democracy works in just the opposite manner as the market: we leave home not so much when we need to (as if interests trigger our decisions as citizens) but when, for the most diverse set of reasons, we want to (passions *and* rather than interests often move us).[55] This is the sense of political freedom that the right to vote expresses.

Thus, we concede that the thinkers and leaders of the parliamentary revolutions in the seventeenth and eighteenth centuries regarded elections as an aristocratic form of selection of the most competent and wise and that they praised representative government as a remedy to be deployed against both monarchical absolutism and ochlocracy.[56] When representative government was being shaped, its architects resisted the possibility of a conflictual split within the national community between either parties or the majority and the opposition; such a split was seen as an aberration.[57] Those early generations were marked by a "quest for unanimity," and the hope was that elections would end in the selection of those few who had the time, disposition, and better qualities or temperaments.[58] Elections at that time meant choosing, within a group of like-minded people (constituent identity in interests), individuals with certain characteristics who could administer the government for the good of all. Elections did not immediately go hand in hand with accepting a diverse citizenry and with party divisions in the community (even though, from the very start, they inevitably tended to produce parties).

The transition from elections as a choice between and of individuals in a community of those who were equals in their interests to elections as involving contrasting political groups, and options was a transition that, for whatever reason, was hard

---

[55] We like to mention Albert O. Hirschman, who, in his attempt to question the fascination of political science with the logic of economics, claimed the influence of "intended but unrealized effects" or the force of beliefs and the role of culture in motivating political behavior; see Hirschman, *The Passions and the Interests: Political Arguments for Capitalism before Its Triumph* (Princeton, NJ: Princeton University Press, 1997), 128–35.

[56] Talking about the US Constitution, Schattschneider argued that it was formulated without respect to political parties and a theory of suffrage, and so without reference to democracy. E. E. Schattschneider, *Party Government* (New York: Farrar & Rinehart, 1942), 15–6.

[57] The "practice of elections in the founding period [of the US] closely mirrored [a] communal symbolic expression of consent," in which competition for government and the idea of a legitimate opposition was not yet at the horizon. Andrew Rehfeld, *The Concept of Constituency: Political Representation, Democratic Legitimacy, and Institutional Design* (Cambridge: Cambridge University Press, 2005), 131; see also Hirschman, *The Passions and the Interests*.

[58] Richard Hofstadter, *The Idea of a Party System: The Rise of Legitimate Opposition in the United States, 1780–1840* (Berkeley, CA: University of California Press, 1972).

to achieve and stabilize (was not Fascism a violent reaction against party-pluralism and electoral democracy?). Yet that transition was what allowed voting power to acquire its full democratic potential and show up within the acceptance and practice of opposition to an elected government. It overlapped with the acknowledgment that the polis is composed of two levels: the community as one (the sovereign people in the constitution and the rules of the game) and the political community in which the citizens can freely articulate their plurality in making and remaking the boundaries between the majority and the opposition. Starting with Carl Schmitt, critics of representative democracy opposed this dual-track and its vision of an embodied unity, either through a leader or (as with lottocrats) through descriptive samples.[59] For these critics, elections are a sort of individualistic choice that mimics market behavior; they fit liberal societies rather than democracy. This interpretation might be accurate concerning the start of representative government, but its extension to electoral democracy is anachronistic. Political history changes institutions and practices—not only in terms of their form but also in terms of their meaning as well.

Lottocrats are right when they claim that legitimation by consent is an individual-to-individual rendering of electoral selection that could be and historically has been used by hereditary monarchs or paternal despots.[60] The problem is that they incorrectly identify this process with elections in a democracy. In contemporary China, it would indeed be possible to have the kind of elections that the ancients and the early moderns had when they selected individuals based upon their merit and capacity to fill a post—filtering out any partial and local interests that might inhibit the common good. What would be impossible both in predemocratic Europe and America and in contemporary China is an electoral agonism among proposals that took place in a climate of political pluralism and dissent against the backdrop of the prospect that one "part" of society is going to govern and that the other/s will resist and oppose, thereby generating a public sphere of conflicting views and contestation. Selecting one political program over another, mobilizing in the public sphere to acquire support from the largest possible number of citizens, and then exercising a sort of "surveillance" upon the representatives cannot be meaningfully characterized as merely "consenting." Consent is a yes/no proposition while choosing between political programs is a complex action that requires a public sphere wherein individual citizens can freely associate, help build constituencies, determine the government and the opposition, and, finally, exercise influence and oversight between elections. Consent comes into play at another level, at the level of the rules, procedures, and the constitution—the preconditions for elections. But this consensus, too, is far from a passive or formalistic consensus; it is pragmatic and concrete (and never closed-off to change), conceived and "used" by citizens (who hopefully are themselves the majority) as a grammar

---

[59] The renaissance of the lottery/election dualism in contemporary political theory owes much to Schmitt, who employed it to justify plebiscitary rather than electoral politics: "In comparison with lot, designation by election is an aristocratic method, as Plato and Aristotle rightly say." Schmitt, *Constitutional Theory* § 19.

[60] Landemore, *Open Democracy*, 84.

138 The Lottocratic Mentality

that allows them to participate in the advancement of proposals that can temporarily win and lose.

To conclude, if we closely examine the charges that elections are oligarchic or that voting is an act of consent to transfer power, we can see that political freedom is the "Cinderella" of the lottocratic mentality. Political freedom entails individually and collectively deciding as equal citizens upon the political direction for our country and doing so by choosing among alternative political programs and agendas (at times not even knowing or paying attention to the name of the candidates in the party list, as often happens in proportional representation systems) as well as by discussing, monitoring, and influencing our representatives between elections. Elections create a public space for citizen action and judgment that is predisposed to expand political participation and responsible politics because they activate a transitive (back-and-forth) relationship between citizens and representatives that prompts the former to demand a response from the latter and that makes everyone responsible for obeying the laws that, in different ways and with different responsibilities, they have all contributed to making. Thus, a democracy that is based on voting rights and elections cannot be reconciled with the predemocratic reading of elections as aristocratic selection. Even though the history of representative government resembles a story that has not been substantially edited since its institutional beginning, the adoption of universal suffrage has produced radical changes that cannot be fully apparent or appreciated unless we review how political life itself is generated by the representative process.

4.2 Political Mandate Representation and Accountability

4.2.1 Two Peoples?

"No one has authorized these particular people to be agents"[61] If this sentiment is true, then why should we feel represented rather than dominated by sorted lawmakers? Assemblies that are chosen by lot have an obvious problem: they cannot establish forms of accountability beyond legal sanction (*strictu senso*). While it is true that citizens can follow their activities from the outside if they want, their members have not been voted into office. This makes any legislative activity that these assemblies undertake into a formally self-sufficient (rather than interdependent, as the case under electoral representation) enterprise beyond the reach of citizens. Indeed, it is as if there are two independent peoples: one who decides and the other who obeys. As Richard Tuck wrote recently, sortition "is an unusually pure example of what we might call representation without agency."[62] This then means that the mechanism for monitoring a lottocratic legislature "may need" a censorial system, but this can end up stifling the type of voluntary control that is peculiar to representative

---

[61] Guerrero, *Lottocracy*, 174.
[62] Richard Tuck, *Active and Passive Citizens: A Defense of Majoritarian Democracy* (Princeton and Oxford: Princeton University Press, 2024) 49.

democracy.[63] Doubtless, deficits in responsiveness occur with elected assemblies, as they can blithely ignore citizens' opinions and demands. It is common to distrust and disrespect elected assemblies, and these attitudes fuel recurrent expressions of discontent in our democracies. But while it *makes sense* for citizens to be angry with their elected representatives, it does not make sense for them to be angry with those drawn by lot. This differentiation in terms of which attitudes even make sense within a prevailing selection system highlights a serious democratic deficit that we would run into with representation by lot.[64] Whereas direct democracy more closely embodies self-government than electoral democracy, legislation by lot completely fails to instantiate self-government and disempowers citizens, "save those selected to hold political office."[65] Clearly, our understanding of representation is the real bone of contention between democracy and lottocracy.

Let us first sketch the nature of representation.[66] Etymologically, to represent means to present again or make someone or something present that is absent (e.g., a guardian representing the interests of a minor or an attorney representing a citizen in court). Starting from this technical definition, representation can be articulated along three possible paths: as a *mandate*, i.e., delegation in the juridical/legal sense of a principal/agent relationship; as an instance of *mirroring*, i.e., a sociological likeness that transcends all volitional choice and aims at empirical sameness; and as a *responsibility* that those chosen now have toward the choosers—a model which properly belongs to the electoral or political notion of representation. From among these three possible pathways, lottocracy follows the second. Mirroring or sociological likeness is the most impersonal of the three models since it aims at reproducing the characteristics of a group or a class without any intentional effort to interpret it.[67] This form of representation is disconnected from elections and technically nonpolitical. Representation that is disconnected from elections could be the "virtual representation" that Edmund Burke spoke of (which would include those who did not express their electoral choice) or, as is the case with a "mirroring" conception, it could be a sort of sociological likeness akin to statistical samples. In this latter case, what matters is a procedure that does not itself construct the relationship between representatives and represented since that adhesion is supposed to be factual. Such representation would supposedly yield positive harmony (conflict avoidance) and a broad "cognitive diversity" that organically arose and which was neither premeditated

---

[63] On the "vital function" of political accountability that elections provide and the coercive system that an allotted legislature requires, see Gastil and Wright, "Legislature by Lot," in *Legislature by Lot*, ed. Gastil and Wright, 15.

[64] To recall Dahl's analysis discussed in Chapter 1, to replace enfranchisement with the lot would subvert democracy because, even supposing that a sample of the sovereign body can be made to mirror the population in statistical proportion, "occasionally we might find ourselves with a highly unrepresented legislature subject to no authority except the next lottery."

[65] Umbers, "Against Lottocracy," 321.

[66] For an overview of the conception of representation and the meaning of it about participation, elections, and lotteries, see Nadia Urbinati and Mark Warren, "The Concept of Representation in Contemporary Democratic Theory," *Annual Review of Political Science*, no. 11 (2008): 387–412.

[67] For this reason, it was deemed a condition for legitimacy of elected assemblies in the eighteenth century; see for instance the position of Mirabeau.

140 The Lottocratic Mentality

nor artificially constructed.[68] This is the radical opposite of *political* representation, which is precisely concerned with how to construct the relation between those represented and their representatives.

In this section, we argue that political representation is the most complete form of representation since it reinterprets juridical/legal representation and transplants it into new conceptual ground. Political representation acquires a form of *mandate* through elections that is not merely a legal relationship (as in a principal/agent relation), but that is a genuinely political relationship. Political representation tries to realize a form of *representativeness* that is not passive and sociological but is instead actively constructed by all the relevant actors (candidates/elected, voters/citizens). This form of representation generated an expectation that the citizenry participate in *advocacy* since they are the people who are in the best position to do so and because their judgment and self-assessment of their social situations inform their vote. Finally, political representation generates *accountability* and *responsibility* because the "acting for" process that elections initiate presupposes that the elected will serve a constituency that is a part or a collection of parts of the citizenry at large rather than an identification with the people as an entirety. And yet, while the representatives have ethical obligations to those who put them in office, they *also* have obligations toward the institutional and constitutional system itself. The political mandate that representation entails inhabits this tension between parts and the whole, and its location is the source of the tension that reverberates throughout the laws and the legislature in general. *The concepts of a political mandate, representativeness, and advocacy define the nature of democratic representation and its complex form of accountability.*[69] To preview the topic of this chapter and the next, communicative processes that mediate between institutions and extra-institutional forums constitute the broad meaning of legitimacy in representative democracy. But this mediation naturally cannot be conceived of as some final remedy that can close the gap between representatives and represented. However, while such communicative processes manage this gap they also simultaneously reinsert and amplify citizens' dissatisfaction with those who were elected, and this means that communication can hardly avoid dynamics of partiality in judgment. Thus, while the collective sovereign wants the law to be the will of the whole, electoral representation fragments that will and subjects lawmaking to processes of partisanship and dealmaking. This makes it impossible to insulate the law from the divided interests and partisan politics of society.[70] This mark of partiality is what the lottocratic mentality most wants to resist.

---

[68] "Random lotteries have been recently explored as an alternative to elections on many grounds: equality, fairness, representativeness, anticorruption potential, protection against conflict and domination, avoidance of preference aggregation problems, cost efficiency, among others .... However, it is normatively desirable for specifically epistemic reasons as well. Descriptive representation achieved through random lotteries would not elevate the level of individual ability in the deliberative assembly, as by definition, the expected individual ability of the selected individuals would necessarily be average, but it would preserve the cognitive diversity of the larger group." Landemore, *Democratic Reason*, 109.

[69] See Urbinati, *Representative Democracy*, particularly chap. 1.

[70] Waldron, *Political Political Theory*, 4–5.

The Targets of Lottocracy Revisited   **141**

At first glance, it would seem that accountability is a liberal criterion designed to protect individuals from abuses by policymakers since it serves as a check on power, but that it is not an overriding principle of democracy since democracy prioritizes equality conceived of as the equal probability to have access to power. This framing echoes Schmitt's conviction that freedom is the same as individual liberty and belongs to liberalism, while equality as sameness is a value that is peculiar to democracy. Hence his adage: if "I had to choose between accountability and equality, I would choose equality."[71] Indeed, lottocrats often refer to the model of accountability at work in popular juries, as these operate according to "common sense" in the service of truth and justice—notions that everyone basically understands. These juries have the final say, and, although jury members are not formally serving in an office like elected officials, the thinking is that everyone can easily come to identify with their decisions in virtue of their obvious accessibility to basic moral judgment. This basic model of representation is the main one that is used to defend the rather "impolitic" type of representation secured by lot.

But things are not that simple. First, accountability is not an exclusively liberal exigency. However, democracy is as much about political freedom as it is about political equality: citizens demand an equal distribution of power because they do not want to be dominated. To be aligned with democracy, any lottery must avoid usurping the principle of an equal right to (direct or indirect) self-government. Clearly, for lottocracy the main point of contention is how we conceptualize political representation and the verticality of state functions in general. According to lottocrats, rotation "ensures that the practice of politics as a profession and the view of politicians as a separate caste is not part of democracy."[72] Apparently, this newfound horizontality makes political accountability elusive. Lottocrats "prioritize horizontal over vertical hazards"[73] and, in this way, value directness. Yet, the directness they secure is obtained within the context of the appointment method and *not* within decision-making. Within lottocratic decision-making, a select few decide for all (which creates a form of verticality) but without authorization (i.e., public confirmation of verticality). The lottocratic mentality retains Rousseau's charge that representation transfers the sovereign power to a few yet oddly drops his proposal for direct government (while it makes sense not to bother with accountability in a Rousseauean universe, the same cannot be said of lottocracy since it creates a separate "group" of decision-makers). As such, since lottocracy aspires to create a representative system (verticality), it must demonstrate that sortition can ensure accountability without elections—otherwise, it will simply reproduce another form of domination by some over the rest. The key lottocratic argument seems to rely on impartiality versus partisanship.

Lottocracy claims that it can create a representative democracy and avoid making representation into something that involves either a claim to representativeness

---

[71] Hélène Landemore, "La democrazia funziona meglio col sorteggio," an interview published in the Italian newspaper *Domani*, 11 December 2022.

[72] Landemore, *Open Democracy*, 142.

[73] Dunn, "Situating Democratic Political Accountability," 331.

or advocacy. This is a tall order since representativeness and advocacy are typically defined with reference to the *complex* of *motivational energies* associated with elections and political promises (e.g., to "speak for" or "act for")—energies that generate a request for accountability. While there are citizens who are eager to compete and/or support/propose competing candidates and parties within an electoral democracy, a lottocratic polis apparently expects passions and dispositions to partisan judgment to disappear since the system for deliberation is designed in such a way that citizens do not need to flaunt their opinions to be chosen or be heard. The fact that officials are chosen by the system itself and not their fellow citizens means that the "demand to be heard" simply loses momentum. Lottocracy endorses the sociological category of sameness and assumes there is no such thing as "good" representation that we should strive for. This is because representativeness exists independently of any demands that citizens make and that candidates agree to represent. The "goodness" of representation is a matter of objectively recording social samples. Traditional politics is minimized, if not completely obliterated, and accountability along with it.

Drawing on Philip Pettit, Guerrero writes that those selected by lottery practice "indicative representation" rather than "responsive representation" insofar as they know they do not have to represent any particular constituency. "Rather, the fact that an individual member [of a lottocratic assembly] comes to have certain views about an issue—after hearing from experts, advocates, stakeholders; and engaging in consultation and deliberation—is evidence that members of the political community who share contextually salient characteristics with that individual would also come to have those views, had they gone through the same experiences."[74] Apparently, having the same experience under certain circumstances (as workers, women, senior citizens, etc.) will instill a measure of trust that the assembly members' judgment and decisions will be the same as those outside it. "They can think: I don't know very much about this issue, but this person (or these people) is like me in all these ways, and I imagine that I would have the same views that they do if I had gone through what they have gone through."[75] Representatives should thus be identified with those who are selected and presented as the (objectively) "best" to represent them. The entire notion of "accountability" here is based on a type of experiential similarity since no authorization ever takes place. As discussed below, electoral representation builds its accountability out of extra-legal forms of proximity, which are constructed by parties, movements, and the press. Lottocrats are most distressed by precisely this sort of *constructive work* because it is radically opposed to their preferred option of "indicative representation." The main point of contention between political representation and allotted representation then plays out amid the conceptual terrain of *informal accountability*.

---

[74] Guerrero, *Lottocracy*, 144. Philip Pettit's distinction between "responsive" and "indicative" within the context of representative politics seems to match the distinction we propose here: Pettit, "Representation, Responsive and Indicative," *Constellations* 17, no. 3 (2010): 426–34.
[75] Guerrero, *Lottocracy*, 173–74.

Lottocracy's only accountability is *stricto sensu* accountability that takes the form of legal sanctions.[76] The reference point here is ancient Athens, which, as discussed earlier, embedded sortition within a complex system of legal controls that were all aimed at monitoring the intentions, the agents, and the decisions of the sorted few to protect their roles from both untoward outside interference and bribery and from the malevolence or hidden interests of those who were allotted. Lottocratic representation puts forward no control method beyond legal ones (for instance, "mandatory participation," a combination of lottery, rotation, and administrative decentralization)[77] because its selection mechanism does not rely on incentives. To be sure, criminal law is always a central deterrent for elected and public officials. However, it becomes operative *post factum* and gains its efficacy if the judicial system is strong and reliable; as daily experience in all democracies shows, in actual practice, it can be quite difficult to take politicians to court and obtain this kind of sanction. However, the presence of elections means that the informal component of accountability can often "come to the rescue," so to speak, and that the burden of control is "distributed across the full range of political initiative among the citizens at large, exercising all its rights and liberties."[78] The effectiveness of punishment through elections is therefore significant; it shows up as the stabilization of political initiatives over time, both inside and outside the assembly. As discussed in the following section, parties are like the agents of an "imperative mandate" in electoral democracy.

Electoral democracy thrives on *both* formal and informal channels of accountability. As we argued above, with elections, the entire society is mobilized in one form or another so that representative governments are democratic "not simply because they have free elections and the choice of more than one political party, but because they permit effective political competition and debate" around what kind of politics we do or do not want; political representation is not reducible to the "static fact of electoral politics."[79] We call this comprehensive dynamic *political accountability*. It works to the extent that the political conduct of politicians is always trackable, not only by the law but also by citizens themselves; publicity is one of the most powerful weapons within a representative democracy, and effective intermediary bodies like parties, movements, and civil associations have traditionally wielded it. Publicity demands that representatives' positions are intelligible and that they are ready and willing to change if need be. Unsurprisingly, in contemporary democracies, one of the central battlefronts against the privileges of politicians is over their claim to expand their privacy—as this often turns out to be an attempt to act without scrutiny and with impunity. A crucial component of democratic surveillance stems from politicians who hold the power to act in public and are constantly under public scrutiny. This makes "political groups" and "institutions" into "collective agents" of a broad and

---

[76] Landemore, *Open Democracy*, 100–1.

[77] Ibid., 90–1.

[78] Dunn, "Situating Democratic Political Accountability," 337.

[79] Paul Hirst, *Representative Democracy and Its Limits* (Cambridge: Polity, 1990), 33–4; Michael Saward, *The Representative Claim* (Oxford: Oxford University Press, 2010), 3; Lisa Disch, "The Constructivist Turn in Democratic Representation: A Normative Dead-End?," *Constellations* 22, no. 4 (2015): 487–99.

144 The Lottocratic Mentality

articulated process of accountability.[80] It is this informal process that would vanish the moment that we drop elections.

Above, we explained how the lottocratic mentality views suffrage as a sort of strategy of consent; understood against this backdrop, it is unsurprising that the lottocratic view of electoral accountability is thoroughly negative: electoral consent fails to fulfill its sanctioning role because the vertical system of representation it generates institutionalizes an asymmetry of power that cannot be fully addressed by the citizenry for the simple reason that in such a vertical system those who are subject to control are expected to both rule and regulate systems of oversight, surveillance, and control. Since it is impossible to realize an impartial level of justice among political agents and voters (as elections come with a free mandate), whoever has more power dominates the controlling process. Within such a framework, the endogenous impartiality at the core of any lottery can only function to stop this process. As Guerrero writes, electoral representation offers no "political morality"; its only values are governability (efficiency and division of labor) and selfishness (getting reelected). The merit of the lottery is that it simply cannot offer this more traditional kind of accountability, and for precisely that reason, it does not produce its vices, either.[81] At the bottom, the lottocratic critique of electoral democracy is a moral critique that, as we shall see by the end of this book, bleeds over into a critique of politics itself. This dynamic can easily inspire or lend itself to an idealization of technocracy.

The lottocratic mentality reinscribes a belief that is already taken for granted in much of political science: the belief that electoral democracy cannot generate an equilibrium of power between the elected and electors since it necessarily produces a ruling class, and this sells citizens the illusion that their participation can restrain the power of these elites. Lottocrats also believe that elections are a "typical way of disciplining political agents, [and] a crude and imperfect way of controlling officials" and that, rather than promoting good policies, these mechanisms of party discipline and control function to weed out candidates that would fail to resonate among a suitably wide audience.[82] To escape this "trap," lottocrats propose a type of accountability that can fully realize correct "morality" and "knowledge" since it is not derived from voting.[83] It is important to explain this view to grasp the unbridgeable gulf that lies between political representation and lottocratic representation, a gulf that calls the very meaning of politics into question.

4.2.2 The Data Speaks for Itself

The lottocratic model is supported by a prominent argument that claims lotteries simply record and aggregate facts without partisan evaluations contaminating this

---

[80] Dunn, "Situating Democratic Political Accountability," 334.

[81] Guerrero, *Lottocracy*, 139-47.

[82] John Ferejohn and Francis McCall Rosenbluth, "Electoral Representation and the Aristocratic Thesis," in *Political Representation*, ed. Ian Shapiro, Susan C. Stokes, Elisabeth Jean Wood, and Alexander S. Kirshner (Cambridge: Cambridge University Press, 2009), 273.

[83] Guerrero, *Lottocracy*, 105.

process. They can avoid such contamination since they rely on the commonsensical "morality" that people naturally and indifferently acquire being deployed in the context of an evaluative equality that aims at impartiality (lottery reflects the fact that all people are "morally legitimized to govern"). Lotteries also rely on "knowledge" (obtained from statistical representation) as the objective data over which moral judgment is exercised. This makes government by lottery the opposite of representative democracy, which traditionally either problematizes the social conditions of citizens or makes the social realm into something political by reinterpreting the people's needs, claims, and perspectives and transforming them into issues of political decision and lawmaking. Selecting lawmakers by lot would end the partiality of judgment and political pluralism (which is not the same as cognitive diversity). In effect, partisan affiliations and political conflict would both be lessened by changing the conceptual starting points (e.g., lottocracy starts with facts rather than ideas; it mirrors rather than interprets the social realm). Within a lottocracy, facts and data are supposed to talk by themselves. For example, age, job, residence, educational qualification, gender, etc., are said to be "objective" subdivisions from within which sorted representatives make dispassionate evaluations and objectively derive ideas and proposals that those who are like them simply identify with. The underlying assumption is that there is no relevant difference between a person's social position and their perceptions of it. If knowledge of what we need comes from our social position, then representation is just if it perfectly adheres to people's lives. To paraphrase Marx, one might say that the "class in se" speaks by itself and makes the "class per se" an unwarranted interpretation. Accountability is as much out of place as the attempt to represent is. *Representation ceases to be a political achievement.*

The lottocratic mentality downplays both the role of the individual citizen by essentially making her into a mirror of her social condition and the role of her interpretative judgment by simply putting statisticians in charge of photographing the social world. Such a mentality seeks technocratic knowledge of society that refuses to pass through the mediation of political evaluation. This mentality follows the populist revolt against intermediary bodies (elections and parties), which attempts to secure a *direct* relation between lawmakers and society that is only mediated by lot. The horizontal simplification of descriptive sampling enacts a sort of "live broadcast" type of representation, whose driving logic is to transform representation into a direct presence of a (miniaturized and allotted) object. We might say that this is a kind of trustee relation that is obtained by identifying the represented and the representatives in the substance of their social attributes—"being like" is supposed also to entail "thinking like" and "acting like." Deliberation is radically transformed into a technical rendering of issues. Moreover, trust gives way to faith. If there is no space between representatives and the represented and their will is identical, then this sociological adherence dissolves any reason for distrust and, consequently, any check upon trust. Such representation runs the risk of giving rise to a formidable and arbitrary power by a select few over their fellow people and the community.

Lottocratic writings persistently use adjectives such as "objective," "impartial," and "photographic." These characterizations outline a kind of deliberation that achieves

146 The Lottocratic Mentality

its goals by expunging evaluative judgments. Under this model of deliberation, disagreements and evaluative judgments should ideally disappear. In explaining what makes a majority legitimate within a context of lawmaking without intermediation, Rousseau noted that any such disagreement would be a "mistake." This Rousseauean idea deserves some additional thought: deliberation is legitimate insofar as any discrepancies or differences are only cognitive, based on verifiable data, and thus capable of being effectively corrected. In such a view, disagreements are not the result of genuinely political premises, such as values, interests, and partisan views; instead, they are only cognitive "mistakes." Thus, to achieve a legitimate deliberation, an assembly must be composed of a sort of plurality that, in contrast to elections, is *not* the result of preferences but rather an assembly composed of a plurality of persons whose characteristics are classified and predefined. In effect, the agents of a nonpartisan lottocratic deliberation are not even the sorted persons as such but instead the data or description that the persons stand for; they speak through the drawn samples as if they embodied the social identities that they "stand for."

With the elimination of the principle of choice (voting), lottocracy eliminates the political character of the representation and secures a technocratic kind of deliberation. We have good reason to resist calling this type of deliberation democratic. Under lottocracy, the audience, public, or even polls are seen as important not so much as to stimulate or criticize or influence the representatives and other citizens but rather to "reveal" the real issues: "what counts as valid recognition" is to be discussed in the public in order "to avoid over- and under-inclusion of cases."[84] For the specific solution of the issue at stake, this is the only pertinent type of accountability that counts as a check on the completeness of knowledge with respect to the purpose for which a given assembly has been sorted. Hence, accountability is achieved through the miniaturized completeness of the random sample.[85] *Lottocratic representation is apolitical.*

"This definition," Landemore writes, "allows me to specify *democratic* representation as a species of representation, specifically a kind of 'standing for' that is an activity open to all on an egalitarian and inclusive basis. This is very different from the standard account. For Pitkin, for representatives to be 'democratic' they must (1) be authorized to act; (2) act in a way that promotes the interests of the represented; and (3) be accountable to the represented. As should become clear later, from my perspective, the first condition is a legitimacy condition. The second one is a requirement of 'good' representation but not democratic representation per se. And the third criterion is democracy-enabling rather than democratic per se. In other words, on the view presented here, a democratic representative is not someone who is doing a good job of representing the interests of the people... nor is someone who is authorized by the people... Instead democratic representative is simply someone who

---

[84] Landemore, *Open Democracy*, 86.
[85] Fishkin's deliberative poll is an elucidation of this idea of representation. Fishkin, *The Voice of the People*, 162.

has accessed the position of representative through a selection process characterized by inclusiveness and equality."[86]

In lottocracy, a "democratic representative" will serve the interests of her people not because she wants to listen to them or be consistent with what her party or she herself has promised to them. She is a "democratic representative" because she was randomly chosen and does her deliberative job without any external impulses apart from her commonsense morality and the knowledge she derives from her social positionality; moreover, she is a "democratic representative" because she follows the good procedures of deliberation that govern the assembly. The technicality of the selection method and the rules of deliberation within the allotted assembly make representation free of influence from outside the assembly. *The sorted few do not have to represent, they represent de facto.* As Burnheim puts it, "Let the convention for deciding what is our common will be that we will accept the decision of a group of people who are well informed about the question, well-motivated to find as good a solution as possible and representative of our range of interests simply because they are statistically representative of us as a group. If this group is then responsible for carrying out what it decides, the problem of control of the *execution* process largely vanishes."[87]

Lottocrats always highlight how sorted assemblies get public input from the citizens in a more "spontaneous" manner than elected assemblies do. Yet since the public (individual citizens and/or groups) will, of course, try to interfere with the work of the sorted assembly, it is worth asking what the difference would be between an elected assembly, in which interference is foreseen ex ante and dealt with through parties and social groups, and an allotted assembly that is ex ante programed to avoid interference and to be "protected from the risk of corruption?"[88] It is unclear how the communication between those who are selected by lot and the rest of the citizenry outside the assembly should be regulated. Sociological sameness itself is apparently supposed to orient the thinking of the citizens such that belonging to the same gender or the same age bracket would make people think the same. Yet, presumably, since an aging woman does not think the same as all others in her category, we have to presume that, in a lottocracy, ordinary individual citizens have discordant ideas and make an effort to associate with others to raise their claims with the sorted few.[89]

In distinguishing lottocratic representation from "acting for" electoral representation, lottocrats argue that their representation avoids a kind of acting that "promotes the interests of the represented" since it does not seek "good" (responsive) representation but rather, in their eyes, genuinely "democratic representation."[90] Since selection by lot represents people as they are and not ideas, it makes sense to caricature and critique electoral representation as a method for creating an artificial world wholly subject to the interpretation of the elected and electors. This strain of

---

[86] Landemore, *Open Democracy*, 86–7.

[87] Burnheim, *Is Democracy Possible?*, new ed., 124–5.

[88] Landemore, *Open Democracy*, 89 and 100.

[89] Owen and Smith, "Sortition, Rotation, and Mandate," in *Legislature by Lot*, ed. Gastil and Wright, 293.

[90] Landemore, *Open Democracy*, 86.

148 The Lottocratic Mentality

critique connects lottocracy to a well-established tradition in political science, which criticizes electoral representation from the perspective of a person-to-person relation or the principal/agent model. The argument runs as follows: electoral accountability is purely ideological because, strictly speaking, the sanctioning power of elections cannot subject itself to promissory and retrospective calculations. This is true for the simple reason that, once elected, officials are under no legal mandate to fulfill their promises, and they simply enjoy a type of power (of knowledge and agency) that voters do not. In order to counter this objection and defend the democratic specificity of political representation, we need to go back to the basics of political representation.

4.2.3 The Political Work of Representing

Political representation is not a one-to-one relation, and it cannot be identified with a principal/agent model (although, as we acknowledged above, as a historical matter it did happen to originate in the sphere of private law). As such, political representation simply cannot be criticized by making recourse to this model. But just because it does not fit this specific conceptual type of mandate does not mean that democratic representation lacks any mandate whatsoever. Elections introduce a new, purely political form of mandate. Let us try to clarify this crucial point.

At first glance, a principal/agent relation shows some resemblance to political representation. A broker counsels my financial interests, and I delegate their care to her; as with any political representative I vote for, our interactions generate trust. The strength of that trust reflects my satisfaction with and positive judgment about her service, and it also keeps her somewhat in check and under control. In both the financial broker and political representative cases, reappointment is a "reward" and a sign of trust, the outcome of a considered judgment that is achieved after due consideration based on a detailed knowledge of what exactly one was promised and what one received. Consent and accountability go hand in hand. The question is whether they go hand in hand in electoral representation.

Granted, this contractual scheme has indeed migrated into politics.[91] However, any linguistic similarity is deceptive for the simple reason that political and private (i.e., juridical) forms of representation are incommensurable with one another. One might even say that endorsing the principal/agent scheme within a democracy testifies to a society with rifts that are so deep as to think it makes sense to fragment the collective sovereign into groups. Each group then seeks a lawyer-like delegate to ruthlessly argue for and win its case. But, normatively speaking, the principal/agent scheme is in contradiction with a democratic conception of the sovereign as a collective that is

---

[91] Some years ago, feminists and scholars of minority issues produced a body of work that explicitly linked political exclusion to the betrayal of the principal/agent scheme in a mandate, a scheme that would thoroughly seal a promise between marginalized groups and their representatives; see in particular Lani Guinier, *The Tyranny of the Majority* (New York: Free Press, 1994); Melissa S. Williams, *Voice, Trust, and Memory: Marginalized Groups and the Failings of Liberal Representation* (Princeton, NJ: Princeton University Press, 1998).

made up of free and equal citizens, who each have individual voting power that has identical weight; endorsing contractual delegation and its model of representation would reveal that the sovereign people is thought to be made up of groups (much like the ancient regime in France), and this would gravely violate not only legal and political equality but the rule of law.

In almost all existing democracies, the discrepancy between the representative assembly and society is at the core of current political debates, and this disconnect highlights issues of justice in representation so as to redress the exclusion and marginalization of disadvantaged classes of citizens. Two levels of politics intertwine: *representation of people's opinions* (the principle of one-person-one vote) and *representation of claims and programs in the durée* (the representatives' permanent attention and receptivity to "those changes in public opinion that might [occur] between one election and the next").[92] The former defines how votes are counted and aggregated (and it instantiates the vertical dimension of lawmaking); the latter defines representation as reflexivity and critical adhesion to political programs over time by groups of citizens and their candidates/elected (and it instantiates horizontal accountability). This complexity makes political representation into a mix of *direct* and *indirect* presence and action.[93]

Understanding political representation within the framework of a private contract (principal/agent) does not allow us to see this complexity; moreover, it is problematic because representation can never be corroborated by and rendered in terms of indisputable data concerning what the principal "really" wants or whether the "agent" is individually responsible as in the case of a causal relationship of "input" and "output." People's expectations and their representatives' achievements will never perfectly correspond. Yet, if we agree that representation is a key component of citizenship (and not a trick to keep the people away from government) and if we are persuaded that representation presupposes and inherently promotes forms of participation and control that partly make up for and supplement the *lack* of legal sanctions (or direct mandate), then it turns out that when citizens complain of a lack of representativeness and ask for advocacy they actually raise an exquisite political challenge that involves and pertains to *everyone*, and not simply to the groups to which they belong. Their questioning concerns the citizenry as a whole. This is because the exclusion and injustice that a part of the citizenry suffers and denounces is bound to affect the entire political discourse and civic fabric or to at least broadcast the message that political freedom is being *unequally* enjoyed. The wave that unifies society and institutions

---

[92] Benjamin Constant, "Principles of Politics Applicable to All Representative Governments," in *Political Writings*, ed. Biancamaria Fontana (Cambridge: Cambridge University Press, 1988), 170 and 209. So too see Guinier: the argument for recognition of groups makes three assumptions: "legislators should represent unanimous, not divided constituencies"; "each voter's vote should count towards the election of a representative"; and "the unit of representation should be psychological, cultural, and/or political rather than territorial" (*Tyranny of the Majority*, 140).

[93] This makes sense of the "problematic" character of representation when it is analyzed in relation to democracy. It is problematic because representation can never be corroborated by and rendered in terms of indisputable data concerning what the people "really" want. Structurally speaking, this transforms the accountability of representatives to electors into an ethical and political claim, and it makes elections the most democratic institution since votes are the most reliable public data at our disposal.

150 The Lottocratic Mentality

is precisely what makes political representation a *process of participation*, a kind of "presence" that goes well beyond voting. With political representation, participation is enriched beyond the formal moment of decision-making.

In the past few decades, a number of studies have investigated representation as a part of political justice alongside identity politics and group rights. They have discussed representation with the goal of addressing the representativeness and the deficit in advocacy—the tangible fact that some sectors of the citizenry are given proportionally less attention than others in contexts such as legislation, workplace regulation, and general social, health, and education policies. This has led to a challenging debate over equal representative opportunity, fair representation, and the search for electoral systems that can make representation more expressive of the claims of those who are represented.[94] Interestingly, it has also led to a greater appreciation of the fact that the political category of "trust" is *far* more fruitful than that of a delegate making the case for bringing the role of "ethics" back into representation.[95] The demand for justice in representation is consistent with the actual and concrete possibility for all citizens to participate voluntarily, be heard, have effective advocates for their causes, and be able to check up on their progress. Democratic representation is thus fair or just representation insofar as it involves issues of advocacy and representativity—issues of a *meaningful* presence, not simply a bare presence, in the game of discord and agreement that is democracy.[96]

Unlike representation by lot, political representation seeks "good" representation. The goal here is not to appoint delegates who look after our personal interests or who have interests that are identical to mine but rather to give collective visibility to all "parts" of the citizenry. The goal of political representation is to define what can bring together disparate social groups whose interpretations of politics and communal life may sharply differ. In political representation, the representatives and the represented set the conditions of political deliberation and the circularity of opinions and inputs that keep them in communication. In short, democratic representation does not replicate existential identities because it *does not represent persons but problems, claims, and ideas.*

In conclusion, the lottocratic mentality questions electoral representation from a premise and vantagepoint that belongs to direct self-government—it alleges that elections violate democracy because they cannot create the strict accountability one finds in a principal/actor contract. This premise brings us to the following alternatives: we can either have delegation with an imperative mandate or something like "direct democracy" or else we can have a form of selection that is not based on a

---

[94] I am referring in particular to the works mentioned above by Guinier and Williams and also to Will Kymlicka, *Multicultural Citizenship* (Oxford: Clarendon, 1995); Anne Phillips, *The Politics of Presence* (Oxford: Clarendon, 1995); and Iris Marion Young, "Deferring Group Representation," in *Ethnicity and Group Rights*, ed. Ian Shapiro and Will Kymlicka, Nomos 39 (New York: New York University Press, 1997), 349–76.

[95] Susan Dovi, *The Good Representative* (Oxford: Blackwell, 2007), chap. 5; Jane Mansbridge, "Rethinking Representation," *American Political Science Review* 97 (2003): 515–28.

[96] Urbinati, *Representative Democracy*, 42; Nancy Fraser, "Identity, Exclusion, and Critique: A Response to Four Critics," *European Journal of Political Theory* 6 (2007): 313–4.

"decision" about who decides. In a lottocracy, the question of "how" to select is all that matters. How people live, and what the state of economic inequality is, all this will apparently be solved by changing the system of selection so that it is not dependent on choice and is as nonideological as possible.

But just because representation cannot be cast as a principal/agent relation does not mean that citizens only have a say in the moment that they vote or that representation is essentially alienation, nor does it mean that accountability is a type of "alchemy" or pure myth.[97] Rousseau was right to say that representation cannot be a contract. Yet, precisely because political representation can only exist in the form of a nonlegally bound mandate, another form of "mandate" is both possible and necessary in order to place a check upon representatives. It is thus incorrect to posit a radical dualism between imperative and free mandates. Forms of indirect participation stand in for the role of a legally binding mandate. Because representatives play an active (legislative) role, they cannot be independent of the electors: a relation of *interdependence* must hold between them and the citizens—this is what we call a political mandate. And this is precisely where political parties come in.

4.3 Political Parties and the Partisan Divisions among Citizens

The lottocratic mentality is part and parcel of the antiparty movement; lottocracy aims at a partyless democracy since it views the existence of political parties as a type of pathology that can only be cured by abandoning elections and partisan judgment. The lottocratic mentality is not simply a critique of parties but also an ambitious new conception of politics and citizenship—a vision of a new polis. This vision raises not only functional and practical concerns but major normative concerns as well: lottocracy tries to shape a society wherein political freedom is subordinated to an equality of probability that citizens could be selected to fully participate in formal decision-making processes. From this perspective, a no-party democracy looks rather dystopian. This seems to prove, *a contrario*, that a democracy without parties is, in Robert Goodin's words, "no democracy at all."[98]

The best way to respond to lottocratic antiparty sentiment is to reclaim the role that parties play both in and outside institutions. That is, parties can be reclaimed in their function as intermediary agents that can exercise control over the elected without resorting to legal sanction (or imperative mandate) and also as expressions of political freedom that let citizens play an active part in structuring deliberation in

---

[97] "Empirically, of course, the boundaries between delegation and alienation are not always sharp, and what begins as delegation might end as alienation. But, the theoretical distinction is nonetheless crucial. In a system of full procedural democracy decisions about delegation would be made according to democratic procedures. . . . The criterion of final control completes the requirements for full procedural democracy in relation to a demos." Dahl, "Procedural Democracy," 112.

[98] Robert Goodin, *Innovating Democracy: Democratic Theory and Practice after the Deliberative Turn* (Oxford: Oxford University Press, 2008), 214.

152 The Lottocratic Mentality

the public political sphere and helping others associate around projects and ideas. The role that parties play in motivating civic interest on issues removed from the daily lives of citizens can also be reclaimed in a way that teaches respect for political opponents, pluralism, and the practice of tolerance ("tolerating and being tolerated is a little bit like Aristotle's ruling and being ruled: it is the work of democratic citizens").[99]

We share the lottocratic opinion that parties have become a precipitating factor of the legitimacy crisis in contemporary democracies. But, for several reasons, the solution we propose is in direct contrast to theirs. First, we propose our specific solution since we think that parties exist *because* democracy exists; the two forms tend to live and die together. Second, we argue that the main challenge we face today is to *revitalize* parties rather than sweep them away entirely. Parties only work by pursuing concrete political goals such as winning a majority and governing or structuring an opposition; they cannot be conceived and implemented in the abstract. They belong to "a network of pragmatic considerations, compromises, and discourses of self-understanding and of justice" that are not mere instruments in the pursuit of power.[100] Historically, *vanguard* parties were created and organized as instruments of this kind, but they cannot be a model for democratic parties more generally since they tended to close the flow of information and, once they came to power, tended to obstruct the process of (re)conceptualizing state and society. More than any other political form, parties are an expression of democracy in action: they mirror the actual conditions, the needs, and the dispositions of a society at a given time. Moreover, unlike a country's constitutional order, theorizing about them in purely a normative manner would be unwarranted.[101] Our intent in this chapter is to propose a comprehensive defense of parties that starts from these self-limiting and pragmatic premises, that is aware of the context-based nature of parties, and that is clear-eyed about their deficiencies and transformations. Our defense is not based on solely functional grounds but is instead an expression of political freedom. Let's first outline the main arguments against parties, party democracy, and partisanship, which we encounter in the writings of lottocrats. These arguments are central components of the lottocratic mentality.[102]

---

[99] Michael Walzer, *On Toleration* (New Haven, CT: Yale University Press, 1997), xi.

[100] Jürgen Habermas, *Between Facts and Norms: Contribution to a Discourse Theory of Law and Democracy*, trans. William Rehg (Cambridge, MA: MIT Press, 1996), 296–7.

[101] For useful overview of conceptions of parties and partisanship, see Russell Muirhead and Nancy L. Rosenblum, "The Political Theory of Parties and Partisanship: Catching Up," *Annual Review of Political Science*, no. 23 (2020): 95–110.

[102] Partisanship and parties are generally treated as identical, even if the former has recently met with more positive judgment than the latter; in effect, reevaluating partisanship has also been a way to stress the negative role of parties. Some scholars, therefore claim that partisanship is a method for empowering otherwise marginalized social groups or groups that have disproportionally small political influence by facilitating political education or by connecting them with experts who share the same values. Yet, they also simultaneously recognize that if it were merged with party, partisanship would be used in a group of likeminded citizens, and this would increase the polarization between the parties and citizens alike, and decrease the epistemic value of partisanship. See Ivan Cerovac, "The Epistemic Value of Partisanship," *Croatian Journal of Philosophy* 18, no. 55 (2019): 99–117. We think that the dualism between partisanship and parties is problematic because making partisanship the tool of identity groups can deepen political

4.3.1 What's Wrong with Parties?

The lottocratic mentality is part of the burgeoning literature on the crisis of democracy, and it shares that literature's critique of partisanship and polarization. Lottocrats fluctuate between, on the one hand, radical proposals to redesign the system of deliberation and decision so as to dispense with parties and, on the other, less radical designs that would reduce the role of parties to a bare minimum—for instance, electing the chief executive in a presidential system.[103] Common to all of this is the belief that party politics violate the key values that lottocrats ascribe to democracy: political equality, popular control, good deliberation and impartiality, competence, and well-informed decisions. Political freedom does not figure among their values. Yet, political freedom is essential to explain their growth and the problems their rejection would create.

Historically speaking, parties have come in many different forms: parties of notables, of opinion, mass parties, parties internal to the legislature, parties that are largely absent from society between one election and another, parties that have a direct relation to the citizens, parties that are capable of mobilizing not only their affiliates but larger sectors of society as well, and so on. Regardless of these variations, lottocrats and critics of political parties tend to subscribe to Robert Michels's characterization of parties as like-minded citizens united "into a coherent political platform," which is piloted by leaders' "greed of power." These critics therefore think parties "would by definition have no place in a purely nonelectoral open democracy."[104] On the other hand, several generations of democratic thinkers see parties as primarily voluntary associations that bind (and divide) citizens along the lines of their evaluative interpretations of matters that are general and of "equal importance for all parts of the country."[105] Within this framework, a good democracy should offer citizens real and feasible political alternatives and, to repeat a much-used saying of late, parties should not simply be as "different" from each other as Pepsi Cola and Coca Cola.[106]

In effect, the closer parties get to one another with the intent of grabbing more votes from the center (a behavior that Otto Kirkheimer ascribed to "catch-all parties"),[107] the more problems they create for democracy since the similarity between parties may discourage citizens from going to vote, alienate them from politics, and

---

divides and jeopardize the resolution of marginal claims. Parties play the important function of unifying claims, coating them with a political language that can make concrete proposals, and creating the right political battles to then implement them.

[103] Landemore, *Open Democracy*, 145; Guerrero, "Pathologies."

[104] See Guerrero, *Lottocracy*, 60, 90, 122; Landemore, *Open Democracy*, 146.

[105] Alexis de Tocqueville, *Democracy in America*, trans. J. P. Mayer (New York: Harper Perennial, 1969), 174–5.

[106] This is Chantal Mouffe's line in Inigo Errejón and Chantal Mouffe, *Podemos: In the Name of the People*, preface by Owen Jones (London: Lawrence and Wishart, 2016), 64. Also Bobbio, *The Future of Democracy*, 25: "those called upon to take decisions, or to elect those who are to take decisions, must be offered real alternatives and be in a position to choose between these alternatives."

[107] Electoral competition ceases to project alternation as a goal, in favor of the goal of achieving social integration of all parties. Otto Kirchheimer, "The Transformation of the Western European Party Systems," in *Political Parties and Political Development*, ed. Joseph La Palombara and Myron Weiner (Princeton, NJ: Princeton University Press, 1966).

expose politics to more charges of being subject to corruption.[108] Many former mass parties in several established democracies have become "liquid" parties without a nonmoderate "militant" wing, and this points toward a democracy where a minority of citizens is in a de facto position of control over the rest.[109] The term "partitocracy" (or "particracy") underscores this pathology.[110] The more parties move to a "catch-all" mode, and the more their organization becomes "fluid," the more their internal life resembles that of "one large party" in which only one distinction is visible: that between the few who govern and the many who acquiesce through elections.

We have good reason to believe that such a system is not a model for democracy. The recent series of wins scored by populist leaders and far-right movements can also be seen (at least in part) to be a side effect of party fluidity and the dissolution of people's perceptions of partisan identifications.[111] Peter Mair described this phenomenon as "post-party democracy" or a democracy made of "cartel parties." Such "cartel parties" are like consortia of power seekers that live on state resources and use parties as taxis to get in through a selection process that stresses the personal qualities of politicians as the sole indication of a difference among party rosters. This is the specific context in which political scientists lament the growth of polarization. These reactions interpret polarization in one of two distinct ways: as either caused by the parties themselves yet not by rational preferences, or instead as evidence of "partisan dealignment"—the way that parties have lost their grip upon voters. The first approach is followed by traditional realists who are skeptical of the normative value of democracy and to whom "group" psychology shows up as a form of participation that is inferior to individual psychology; the second approach is followed by critical realists who take parties to be an important condition of democratic participation since they allow citizens to interpret their preferences, identify with others, and take sides.[112] Lottocrats tend to have more sympathies with the first perspective: they agree with traditional realists that polarization is not caused by slimmed down or cartelized parties but that it is instead caused by parties themselves, irrespective of whatever form they take. Yet, lottocrats are importantly different in that they see this assessment not as a reason to lower their expectations about what electoral

---

[108] Peter Mair, "Populist Democracy vs. Party Democracy," in *Democracies and the Populist Challenge*, ed. Yves Mény and Yves Surel (New York: Palgrave Macmillan, 2002), 81–98.

[109] Christian Blum and Christina Isabel Zuber, "Liquid Democracy: Potentials, Problems, and Perspectives," *Journal of Political Philosophy* 24, no. 2 (2016): 162–82; Nadia Urbinati, "Liquid Parties, Dense Populism," *Philosophy and Social Criticism* 45, nos. 9–10 (2019): 1069–83.

[110] Partitocracy was a term coined in Italy in mid-1940s (during the Fascist regime notoriously opposed to parties), and it was used alongside criticism of parties; see Giovanni Sartori, *Democratic Theory* (Detroit: Wayne State University Press, 1962), 120.

[111] To fill the gap of legitimacy, cartel parties make a classic "establishment" move: they go "to the state to get more resources" and become "state-centered organizations" because the core of their activity is mainly "anchored in, and performed through, the state." Piero Ignazi, *Party and Democracy: The Uneven Road to Party Legitimacy* (Oxford: Oxford University Press, 2017), 175.

[112] An example of the former is Achen and Bartels, *Democracy for Realists*, in particular chap. 9; and of the latter, Schattschneider, *Party Government*, in particular chap. 1. For a thorough discussion of both, see Lisa Disch, *Making Constituencies: Representation as Mobilization in Mass Democracy* (Chicago: University of Chicago Press, 2021).

The Targets of Lottocracy Revisited   **155**

democracy can deliver but rather as a reason to think that it is desirable and possible to overcome party democracy itself.[113]

Scholars who take polarization to be at least partly caused by "partisan dealignment" generally focus on two dynamics within parties. First, "weak collegiality" makes interparty relations more "problematically conflictual" since parties have a shaky hold on their opinions and leaders, and so they tend to *respond* to social "inputs" rather than proactively selecting and framing the social issues to be taken up and thematized. Second, parties can have an "excess of collegiality" insofar as they become "cozy" strongholds for a political elite. The Tea Party seems to play this role insofar as it mimics traditional organization-based parties but behaves like a vanguard faction that is recalcitrant to tolerance, dialogue, and compromise.[114] The two extremes that scholars have suggested a democratic party system should avoid are either too much democracy (with primaries) or too much oligarchy (cartelization).[115] In any case, for whatever reason weak parties have little control over social identity claims and they cannot provide stability to the political system; they cannot govern partisanship or moderate polarization.[116] In contemporary democracies the kind of polarization we are seeing tends to develop outside of parties, but it is not generally antiparty itself. Such partisanship is fueled by identity politics, partisan media, sectarian social forces, and populist leaders. According to many political scientists, this dynamic is symptomatic of the weak grip that parties currently have on the narratives, political ambitions, and emotions running through society. Weak parties are disposed to yield to external pressures, be more reactive and less accountable, and also be more apt to intensify and exploit sharply divergent impulses rather than to try to filter and channel them.

Now, if the weakness of parties (or their lack of control) is a factor in the deterioration of representative democracy, one might expect that, in order to correct this trend, we should want to revitalize parties while also leaning on small groups who deliberate together as occurs in minipublics. While minipublics cannot claim

---

[113] Guerrero relies extensively on Achen and Bartels's book to prove his points about the systemic ignorance produced by elections and the irrationality of demanding party government to be responsive government. See also the collection of essays edited by Gastil and Wright, *Legislature by Lot.*

[114] For the two forms, see Matteo Bonotti and Zim Nwokora, "Who Should Pay for Parties and Elections in a Democracy?" (unpublished manuscript), 104; Richard S. Katz and Peter Mair, "Changing Models of Party Organization and Party Democracy: The Emergence of the Cartel Party," *Party Politics* 1, no. 1 (1995): 5–28; Susan E. Scarrow, "Party Subsidies and the Freezing of Party Competition: Do Cartel Mechanisms Work?," *West European Politics* 29, no. 4 (2006): 619–39. The Tea Party, a mix of "collegial" and "cozy," is unique within this liquid parties category since it is well organized yet without a strong leader, able to capture militants, and relies on faith and loyalty more than interests; this makes it almost unique in the US party system landscape but similar to other far-right parties in Europe. See Brigitte Nacos, Yaeli Block-Elkon, and Robert Y. Shapiro, *Hate Speech and Political Violence: Far-Right Rhetoric from the Tea Party to the Insurrection* (New York: Columbia University Press, 2024); see also Cas Mudde, *The Far-Right Today* (Cambridge: Polity, 2019).

[115] Frances McCall Rosenbluth and Ian Shapiro, *Responsible Parties: Saving Democracy from Itself* (New Haven, CT: Yale University Press, 2018), 236.

[116] Moderate parties in a polarized environment can do very little to reverse the trajectory because they have to follow the current if they want their candidates to be elected; parties are not strong enough to be in control. Gary C. Jacobson, "2008 Presidential and Congressional Elections: Anti-Bush Referendum and Prospect for the Democratic Majority," in *Perspectives on Presidential Elections, 1991–2020*, ed. Robert Y. Shapiro (New York: Academy of Political Science, 2021), 246–53.

156   The Lottocratic Mentality

electoral representation they can play an auxiliary role to parties by offering them a plurality of points of view and inputs that can enrich a party's initiative. However, this is not what lottocrats propose, as they see the mixture of elections and parties as an obstacle to improvement. This is because, in their eyes, elections and parties tend to gravitate toward one another since they are both driven by the same "logic" of winning.

From the lottocratic perspective, modern democracy jettisoned the use of lotteries either for blatantly antidemocratic reasons or for practical reasons that today's technology can easily surmount. In short, parties continue to exist not for any normative reason but rather as a form of mediation that is only "fitting" for or suited to outdated assumptions about technology and what is "practical." As such, defending party democracy in a contemporary context seems to entrench dysfunction and, if anything, signal a conservative mindset that has simply become accustomed to a sort of reasoning that selects the elites to rule. The main obstacle seems to be empirical limitations on imagining a different yet workable model of democracy that confirms rather than denies the value of a democracy—wherein the gulf between real and ideal could be bridged, perhaps by a no-party polity.[117] This seems to be the vision held by various lottocratic depictions and proposals, regardless of whether they are "radical" or more moderate. Therefore, we must focus on whatever empirical limitations there might be in imagining a no-party democracy and whatever functional concessions lottocrats might make to parties, the animating impulse of lottocracy is to go "beyond parties" by tapping into "the new spirit of sortition."[118]

4.3.2 Antiparty-ism, Old and New

The lottocratic mentality is at home within an old and varied antiparty lineage that has ancient and modern roots: on the one hand, the problem is how to seek or protect the concord of the republic; on the other, the problem is how to assert and defend the independence of the individual citizen's mind from an attempt by politicians or would-be politicians to gain consent through persuasion and manipulation. The first position (rooted in the ancient city) accepts the idea that politics involves rhetoric and conflict and, as a response, seeks to protect concord by limiting the forms of participation (both conflict and parties are seen as "taboo"). The second position questions whether politics necessarily involves rhetoric and conflict and seeks to and intervene in public deliberation in order to make it as resistant as possible to irrational motivations; its primary goal is the quality of deliberation. Lottocracy shares elements of both positions insofar as it casts partisanship as responsible for

---

[117] Landemore confesses that she does not have "knock-down arguments against what seem like consensual, compelling objections to a no-party democracy . . . . Presumably, an open democracy [based on lottery] would offer different incentives, some of which we have yet to imagine . . . . And finally, couldn't be that the lack of an electoral incentive would actually free such 'think tanks' from the temptation to lie, smear, and generally confuse rather than enlightened the public debate?" *Open Democracy*, 147–79.

[118] Dimitri Courant, "From Kleroterion to Cryptology: The Act of Sortition in the 21st Century," in *Sortition and Democracy: History, Tools, Theories*, ed. Sintomer and Lopez-Rabatel, 365.

bad deliberation and reveals its trust in an ideal community wherein harmony wins over divisions and concord over conflict (see below, Chapter 7).

The idea of a political party and the reaction against parties arose in tandem in the ancient republics, where sovereign power was not formed out of individual citizens but rather out of socially stratified groups or "parts" that each sought power in order to exercise commanding control and positively undermine the pluralistic bases of political authority—in ancient Greece and Rome as well as in the Italian humanist republics tyrannical coups and civil wars underscored the very real fear of parties. As discussed in Chapter 1, in socially divided sovereignties like both the ancient and humanist cities, parties were identical to factions or militant groups in that they attacked those who ruled in order to replace them and, eventually, rule against them. Protecting political freedom meant protecting the city from party conflicts. Discord was the opposite of constitutional order, and constitutional order only persisted in direct proportion to its ability to expunge conflicts from the life of the city. This explains why, in Aristotle, turmoil and conflict occupies the intermediate space between regimes. As with his humanist followers, Aristotle's study of politics is in fact a study that tries to understand the causes of sedition in order to identify the virtues that a community should cultivate and enhance so as to suppress the vices that fuel it.[119]

A conception of sovereignty as an impersonal legal order based on individual equal subjects, written constitutions, and the institution of elections changed that scenario and it also changed the traditional criticism of parties.[120] In a constitutional commonwealth that dissolves once prominent social groupings and "orders" from within the state, parties manage the game of political contention in the service of a new kind of (constitutional) consent so that their claim to exercise power is never *merely* an expression of the will of the voters from whom they receive consent.[121] A political party "never put itself above the state, the part above the whole."[122] Thus, in 1971 John Rawls argued that in a well-ordered society, parties are not "mere interest groups" petitioning the government on their own behalf. Indeed, just ten years prior Schattschneider had proposed a clear dualism between "pressure politics"

---

[119] As Finley observed, ancient Athenians tried to keep conflicts at the margin of their political narrative; as shown by the uses of strategies of oblivion, denial, and pardon, they thought "tumults" (státis) were undesirable but always imminent; the "sense of community . . . fortified by the state religion, by their myths and their traditions" had the educative function of inducing "self-control" that was far different from apathy. M. I. Finley, *Democracy Ancient and Modern*, rev. ed. (New Brunswick, NJ: Rutgers University Press, 1988), 29–30; see also Nicole Loraux, *La cité divisé: L'oubli dans la mémoire d'Athènes* (Paris: Editions Payot & Rivages, 2005). This was the task of the republican virtues as we learn from Cicero, who condemned the Gracchi as pestilential because they introduced the denunciation of economic inequality in political life (asking for land distribution). This move upset the social order because it sparked radical disagreements (factional) since the quest for social equality would nourish the passions of envy and mistrust, in opposition to liberality and justice.

[120] Nancy L. Rosenblum, *On the Side of the Angels: An Appreciation of Parties and Partisanship* (Princeton, NJ: Princeton University Press, 2008), 35.

[121] Jonathan White and Lea Ypi, *The Meaning of Partisanship* (Oxford: Oxford University Press, 2016), 34.

[122] Johan Caspar Bluntschli, "What Is a Political Party?" (1869), in *Perspectives on Political Parties: Classic Readings*, ed. Susan E. Scarrow (New York: Palgrave Macmillan, 2002), 80.

158 The Lottocratic Mentality

(by interest groups) and "party politics."[123] Parties are supposed to advance conceptions of the public good from a perspective that is shared by a sizable part or parts of the citizenry.[124] Parties became an expression of political freedom and stability. But while they emancipated themselves from factions, "it would be wrong to forget, on the other hand, that parties have long been preceded by factions and ... that may well relapse into something resembling faction."[125] Democratic citizens and critics of parties have long been disturbed by the dialectics of "parts and the whole" or the fear that "factions may conquer the whole"—hence the recurrent demands that we dissociate deliberation from parties or even overcome parties and party government.

Yet, the kind of antiparty-ism we want to discuss here arose with the institutionalization of representative government in the seventeenth and eighteenth centuries, when candidates no longer "opposed each other for personal reasons" as in ancient Athens but rather "represented something more than themselves"; this "shift from the social to the political" made the franchise into the apex of an "expansion of political participation" and of political freedom.[126] In the age of representative government, political and democratic theorists of various generations and stripes— epistemic and realist, followers of Rousseau, Schmitt, and Schumpeter—have all been united by their shared criticism of parties. The specific way that party critique becomes fashionable in a given period tells us what "the good" is thought to be that the political community should want and preserve—whether it is the general will of the republic (Rousseau), the unchallenged unity of state command (Schmitt), or the stability of a government that does not renounce pluralism (Schumpeter). Hence, parties have been criticized for violating public reason or good deliberation (Rousseau), for making the sovereign divided and out of control (Schmitt), or for aiming at monopolizing power (Schumpeter). These answers alone point to the roots of modern parties: the roots are elections. As a result, elections have either been ruled out ex ante (direct government or an imperative mandate as with Rousseau) or turned into a sort of acclamation for a plebiscitary leader (Schmitt), or minimized into a method for selecting an elite (Schumpeter). Whatever the approach or orientation, it is clear that the problem of parties arose the very moment that candidates began to represent "something more than themselves"—since, at that point, parties became not only a necessary part of the system but also a problem as well.

---

[123] John Rawls, *A Theory of Justice* (Cambridge, MA: Harvard University Press, 1999), 195; E. E. Schattschneider, *The Semisovereign People: A Realist's View of Democracy in America* (Chicago: Holt, Rinehart and Winston, 1960), 20.

[124] "The criterion of autonomy therefore cannot demand, even as an ideal, a wholly unencumbered legislator, one who acts utterly unswayed by political pressures and partisan loyalties." Dennis F. Thompson, *Political Ethics and Public Office* (Cambridge, MA: Harvard University Press, 1987), 113.

[125] Giovanni Sartori, *Parties and Party Systems: A Framework for Analysis* (Cambridge: Cambridge University Press, 1976), 25.

[126] "The depersonalization of the process of parliamentary selection is one of the most important elements" of the transformation of election from selecting individual leaders to selecting members of the legislature. Kishlansky, *Parliamentary Selection*, 21.

The Targets of Lottocracy Revisited   **159**

Thus, if party denial was understandably once seen as "radical" since it often went along with power seizures that threatened survival (of certain factions, of the community as a whole, and the citizens individually), opposition to parties took on a very different tone under representative government since parties were no longer identical to subversive factions; a desire to eliminate parties now shows up as something akin to the desire to suppress political freedom. Thus, quite unlike in the past, parties and political conflicts today are conditions and expressions of citizens' political freedom. Parties do not jeopardize unity and stability. On the contrary, stability would be jeopardized by their weakness and narrowness with respect to their capacity to involve as many citizens as possible.[127] As Goodin has argued, precisely because of their disposition to translate sectarian and identity-based interests into policy proposals and political language, parties are able to bring citizens with different identities together, get them to think in terms of general policies, and facilitate compromise and collaboration on programs that, while they may not totally please everyone, do not just please one part alone.[128] Herein lies the significance of the part/whole dialectic that representation is able to enact thanks to parties. Herein also lies a possibility for containing political corruption—for instance, types of corruption that stem from "patronage politics" which are more difficult to resist when parties are cartelized or "liquid" or weak than when they are stronger and more in command of not only social cleavages but also their own ambitious leaders.[129] Moreover, even though they do generate a political class, well-structured parties can contain more "personalistic" politics because their internal governance and organization are able to contain the thirst for power.[130] The perfect storm of weak parties and contemporary populism offers a vivid a contrario exemplification of a lesson: *if* parties save themselves from the "monarchical" drive of a leader, then they can also save democracy from the downward spiral of personalistic politics.

However, the lottocratic mentality invites us to draw different conclusions. It extends this invitation despite the fact it can neither "prove" that lotteries would combat personalistic politics or corruption, nor that the elimination of parties would *eo ispo* eliminate rhetoric from deliberation and secure impartiality. If lottocrats think otherwise, it is because they assume that even when parties are created for a good cause they are fatally prone toward oligarchic solutions and "systemic corruption"— the infamous antidemocratic force that, as ancient Athens proves, only lotteries can avert. Yet, as Madison made clear more than two centuries ago and the experience of fascism confirmed, once parties are already embedded in representative government it seems like suppressing them is self-defeating since this would also simultaneously

---

[127] In 1960, the intertwining of democratization and the party system's stabilization induced Schattschneider to write in *The Semisovereign People* that parties are the best answer to partial vested interests (whose intention cannot be made public if they are to be satisfied) since they "tend to socialize conflict" and make conflict the political language through which free and equal citizens participate and compete in public to shape the politics of their country.

[128] Goodin, *Innovating Democracy*, 213.

[129] Ibid., 210–1.

[130] See Mauro Calise, "The Personal Party: An Analytical Framework," *Italian Political Science Review* 45, no. 3 (2015): 301–15.

160 The Lottocratic Mentality

suppress basic freedom of speech, expression, and association. Thus, while antiparty sentiment is as old as representative government, we cannot prevent the formation of parties or simply eliminate them without jeopardizing the entire system. Older routes toward achieving a "partyless" polity must be avoided. But what if we use new tools to get parties "out of the way," so to speak, without falling back on nakedly tyrannical solutions? *This* is the challenge that the lottocratic mentality poses to us today. Any answer we give needs to be *far* more challenging than a mere "counterargument," not least because the opposition to parties is not just a practical or functional matter.

This points toward something that contemporary attempts to justify partisanship and parties do not emphasize nearly enough, namely, that the justification of parties is not simply or solely that they make political representation or governing institutions possible, but rather that they are inextricably bound up with political freedom as well. Parties spring up as soon as citizens are free to express themselves in the light of day. And even when citizens are repressed by dictatorial regimes, they simply hide their divisions—but this does not make them magically go away. A populace's struggle against dictatorial regimes is never that of a homogeneous people without internal dissent. Freedom is the midwife of parties because it is the essence of politics. This is precisely why "political parties appear in a state whenever political life is freed."[131] Presumably, parties would also spring up even if lotteries came to replace elections.[132]

Even in the hypothetical case where a perfect lottocracy existed, we would still see the emergence of political groups, differences in interpretation, conflicts, contestations, rhetorical expressions of views "for" and "against," and, ultimately, a desire to *change* the decisions made by (hypothetically) impartial allotted assemblies so as to tell those few who were selected by lottery how they should best decide.[133] A lottocracy must reckon with the possibility of political groups and political contestation that demand a voice and want to be heard by the randomly selected assemblies or by a general one, and who do not simply assent to being ruled by institutions that are operationalized by "professional" tutors of deliberation who seek to implement goals that they decide are good. Given that parties and elections are not supposed to exist, how would this discontent be represented? Through which institutional and procedural means would dissatisfactions, protests, or other forms of counterlottocratic pushback be actualized? Moreover, how could we continue to foster a feeling of belonging to a singular, unified national community through a collective process of communicating political ideas and projects if people are now supposed to explicitly run for office as individuals completely on their own, with the expectation that they will vote on the basis of their own personal sense of morality and independent judgment, that is, as private individuals?

Evidently, there seems to be some sort of tacit understanding that those within lottocratic allotted assemblies *could* (or should?) listen to protests and grievances

---

[131] Bluntschli, "What Is a Political Party?," 75.

[132] "What is certain is that, as is already the case in electoral democracies, a plethora of associations and intermediary bodies not primarily motivated by electoral goals would still exist." Landemore, *Open Democracy*, 148.

[133] This possibility is contemplated by all lottocrats, even the more or less radical ones.

from citizens and political groups and, crucially, that they could do so while *avoiding* falling back into old habits of political representation or compromise or some even more radical form of arbitrariness than the sort that lottocracy criticizes. Indeed, in the absence of channels of political representation such as parties and elections, drawn assemblies will be subject to influence by the "strength" (or outright coercion) of groups who have "more say" or who are better organized or whose activists have more spare time. Thus, even in the best of all possible political worlds, political freedom would find a way to worm in and break the order—even an order born from good and impartial deliberation that, in theory, should be able to *prevent* (and not simply resolve) dissent and conflict. The problem would be that once such a system is disconnected from electoral forms of accountability, parties would pose the following dilemma to the polis: they would either fall in an arbitrary system of political influence or they would catalyze a censorious and repressive system. Lottocrats admit that it would be possible to have "groups interested in influencing" the public "absent the electoral incentive to provide exactly the kind of bundling platforms parties provide today." But such acknowledgement is not enough. For our part, we doubt that those "other [kind of] incentives" would be safe for the general interest and the political freedom of the citizens without the types of checks offered by electoral dynamics.[134] Eliminating parties runs the risk of resurrecting the sort of factionalism that characterized early modern Italian republics.

Thus far, theorists of lottocracy have not thoroughly reflected on these issues and they do not seem to consider the implications that eliminating parties and elections would have for political freedom—whether its importance is cast in terms of nondomination or either individual or collective political agency. Lottocrats *are* certainly concerned with civil and economic liberties.[135] Yet, political freedom is not the same as these liberties since within the formation of the country's opinion and the will it plays out both on the individual and associational levels; political liberty is embodied in *both* the right to serve the public under established and shared procedures *and* in the right to intervene so as to object to or influence public opinion and decision-makers. In this framework, parties do not merely respond to judgments of functionality. Partisanship brings normative issues directly into play that

---

[134] Landemore, *Open Democracy*, 148.

[135] Guerrero proposes a theory of "political functionalism" that addresses "the practical problems of moral significance" and socioeconomic significance. The basic issue is that of both knowing problems and then choosing means and procedure to solve them. Systems are judged according to how they respond and which institutions might be better because they better respond to "moral demands of justice, equality, autonomy, and so on." This general reasoning pertains to the rule of law and functionality. The answers are relative and "this relativity is due to the differences in the practical problems encountered by particular communities, not due to some more general relativism about these concepts of political morality" (*Lottocracy*,37). Compliance and moral behavior of members of society are what should be expected if we reason according to "concepts of political morality." However we are told nothing about political freedom unless this is included in the category of "political morality" and therefore identified with individual liberty and morality whose goal is "respect and equality and social harmony." Here, liberty refers to an *interpersonal* relation among citizens and institutions that is to be conceived so as to "ensure that no members of the society stand in relations of domination or oppression to each." Thus, individual as well as civil liberty and the rule of law are the parameters of Guerrero's norms inspiring the organization of the decision-making process. In this liberal and moral picture, any attention to political freedom as a collective and individual relationship of power and influence among citizens is simply absent.

162 The Lottocratic Mentality

are associated with the value and practice of *isegoria*. Isegoria can be characterized as the right that best expresses distinctively democratic political freedom, and it is certainly not the same as enjoying civil liberties or trusting that luck will see to it that we get our turn to participate.

A functionalist defense of parties carries a lot of water to the lottocrats' mill, so to speak, especially when one considers that the Internet and AI offer digital alternatives to traditional associationism and deliberation. It is urgent that we use the perspective of political freedom to challenge and correct the lottocratic construal of democracy precisely because implementing a lottocratic system is increasingly feasible with modern technology. This is why we argue that lottocracy is not just another critique of parties and partisanship. Instead, it is a project that seeks to realize an alternative form of politics that needs to be neither direct nor electoral. Above all, this new form of politics has no need for parties. How should one respond to such a radical vision?

4.3.3 How to Defend Parties?

Political parties have more often than not been studied as obstacles standing in the way of realizing both public and private morality as well as the epistemic qualities that democratic decision-making procedures promise.[136] Historians have shown how most of their rehabilitation came from functional considerations about how space could be made for a legitimate opposition within a republic that was supposed to be united by a spirit of concord fixed in a written constitution. Richard Hofstadter reconstructed this trajectory in American history. He showed how early republicans had views that resembled "modern authoritarian conceptions of [a] one-party state." Indeed, they thought that party conflict was evil and a single-party republic would be laudable.[137] Today, scholars studying the role of parties in democratic government can rely on a rich body of research that has integrated the work of political historians and scientists over the past several decades and which has contributed to a normative political theory of parties as separated off from vested interests and a component of the public good.[138] Important as it is, this research does not give us the tools we need to address the radical challenge posed by the lottocratic mentality.

---

[136] Thomas C. Atchison, "Distrusting Climate Science: A Problem in Practical Epistemology for Citizens," in *Between Scientists and Citizens*, ed. Jean Goodwin (Iowa City, IA: Great Plains Society for the Study of Argumentation, 2012), 61–73; Geoffrey C. Layman, Thomas M. Carsey, and Juliana Menasce Horowitz, "Party Polarization in American Politics: Characteristics, Causes, and Consequences," *Annual Review of Political Science*, no. 9 (2006): 83–110; David W. Brady, John Ferejohn, and Laurel Harbridge, "Polarization and Public Policy: A General Assessment," in *Red and Blue Nation?*, vol. 1, *Characteristics and Causes of America's Polarized Politics*, ed. Pietro S. Nivola and David W. Brady (Washington, DC: Brookings Institution, 2008).

[137] Hofstadter, *The Idea of a Party System*, 23.

[138] Matteo Bonotti, *Partisanship and Political Liberalism in Diverse Societies* (Oxford: Oxford University Press, 2017); Russell Muirhead, *The Promise of Party in a Polarized Age* (Cambridge, MA: Harvard University Press, 2014); Rosenblum, *On the Side of the Angels*; White and Ypi, *The Meaning of Partisanship*.

The Targets of Lottocracy Revisited   **163**

Indeed, those who defend selection by lottery agree with political scientists and historians about the function of political parties: they agree that parties helped stabilize democracies after the collapse of totalitarianism. But they argue that these honorable historical achievements should not make us lose sight of the main flaw of parties, which is that their sole purpose is to extract and extend both consensus and resources. Therefore, according to this line of thinking, the noble role that parties have played at certain historical moments tells us very little about their true nature. For lottocrats, this nature is decidedly oligarchic and has remained unchanged. It is simply the case that parties are chameleon-like and adapt to social contexts in order to satisfy their thirst for power; their propensity to survive at any cost makes them "the dinosaurs of our times."[139] The target here is partisanship. Particularly in two-party systems and first-past-the-post elections, the partisan spirit ensures that the entirety of political life—from the construction of electoral platforms, to the creation of a binary mindset, to the promotion of sentimental loyalty to a party—is permeated with divisive and polarized dynamics that corrode the community and which cannot be undone.[140] The partisan spirit humiliates any independent citizen because it renders facts and information worthless since everything that happens and should happen is framed in the logic of "us" versus "them," and no truth holds up to the logic of partisan identification. The function of party control over elected officials (parties as informal agents of the imperative mandate in the assembly) also backfires on voters since it turns out not to be about control but rather about the imposition of party conformity and domination.

The novel feature of the lottocratic mentality is that it does not use direct democracy as a model but rather starts from an *indirect* form of government which it proposes can overcome the obstacles to rational and impartial deliberation that have arisen from elections and parties. In effect, the target of this view is popular participation in both its direct and its electoral forms since the masses are mobilized in either. The uncompromising response to the structurally nonepistemic nature of a type of representative democracy that deploys partisanship is the ideal city without parties. In the scramble to expel parties from deliberation, we can see some troubling echoes of a Platonist dystopia ("holistic antiparty-ism"[141]): a conception of the political order in which drawn guardians who are devoid of partisan judgments can decide for all the citizens in an atmosphere of concord and do so without generating partisan opinions or animosities.

Some recent work on parties and partisanship has developed important arguments that stress the *positive* contribution of partisanship to deliberation in terms of motivating cognition, teaching respect for adversaries, and extending the logic of public justification to partisanship itself.[142] These arguments are meant to show the contribution parties make to collective deliberation conceptualized as a process that

---

[139] Brett Hennig, "Who Needs Elections?," in *Legislature by Lot*, ed. Gastil and Wright, 309.

[140] Guerrero, "Pathologies," 176–7.

[141] Rosenblum, *On the Side of the Angels*, 35.

[142] White and Ypi have proposed their "circumstances of political justification" of partisanship: "a comparative perspective, an adversarial posture, and a basic level of public visibility" thus claiming a "structural

164 The Lottocratic Mentality

makes *politically relevant* reasonable disagreement possible without fragmenting or otherwise "disaggregating" society. This is possible for the simple reason that parties "formulate issues and create, not just reflect, political interests and opinions."[143] Other research has convincingly shown the role that partisanship can play in articulating *inclusiveness and proximity* among citizens who live in a large territory or in training partisans in the art of *compromise and self-control*—parties approach electoral aggrandizement with modesty since there are always several of them and, if they are democratic, they simply do not want to become one large and amorphous party.[144] Scholars have also shown how, in identifying with a party and expressing their political beliefs in public to others, citizens *practice pluralism* and *commend themselves to be informed and seek knowledge* about matters that are removed from their own everyday lives and naturally "closer" interests.[145] In expounding the normative and ethical values of partisan thought, these various contributions offer an important defense of party affiliations for civic, functional, and deliberative purposes.

The problem is that some of these arguments are and remain contested. Other arguments can be shared by lottocrats, as they claim that their system can also secure many of these qualities, particularly in the areas of deliberation, information, cognitive diversity, and respect for others. As discussed in Chapter 2, scholars who advocate for deliberation by lottery have often built their arguments and alternative models of democracy from *within* the deliberative conception of democracy in order to both improve that conception and enlighten its participants.[146] While many such scholars started from an interest in deliberative democracy—how to make democracy more deliberative and inclusive—lottocrats have slowly moved toward experimenting with small group selection and decision-making mechanics that foster good discussion. Yet, in so doing they have almost forgotten that democracy is a *collective* enterprise of free and equal citizens and not simply an exercise in good deliberation among a few people.

The same ideal criteria of good deliberation and the spirit of concord seem to be present in the lottocratic mentality. Echoing what Simone Weil wrote in 1943, the argument is that allotted assemblies or minipublics can achieve what parties, despite efforts to improve their internal organization, would like to achieve but cannot: simultaneously having good deliberation and wide participation. This has been unachievable for the simple reason that, in elections, a partisan citizen votes for her party's candidate while ignoring and opposing candidates of the other parties;

---

affinity between practices of partisanship and public justification . . . . Partisanship is a catalyst of public justification." *The Meaning of Partisanship*, 57.

[143] Muirhead, *The Promise of Party*, 96; Rosenblum, *On the Side of the Angels*, 259.

[144] "Not only is a part without a counterpart a pseudo-part, but a whole that does not contain parts (in the plural) lacks the completeness of a real whole—it is a 'partial' whole, in both senses: It excludes and it takes side." Sartori, *Parties and Party Systems*, 40.

[145] Democratic citizens who are involved in a party are loyal to their party and to its "borders which are the expression of both pluralism and respect of others." White and Ypi, *The Meaning of Partisanship*, 36–7 and 79; see also Muirhead, *The Promise of Parties*, 91–2.

[146] Ken Newton, "Curing the Democratic Malaise with Democratic Innovations," in *Evaluating Democratic Innovations: Curing the Democratic Malaise?* Brigitte Geissel and Kenneth Newton (London: Routledge, 2012), 3–20.

partisan citizens "cannot be deliberatively minded and politically engaged at the same time."[147] In the end, parties exalt misinformation and make it difficult for citizens to keep up on all of the relevant information and training, "even if one had reason or desire to do so."[148] A zero-sum win/lose mentality and various judgmental practices are entrenched in elections and parties. "In light of this contemporary understanding of what makes groups smart, one way forward in dealing with the crisis of democracy could thus be, instead of rationalizing away the electoral democracy we have inherited from the eighteenth century, to start imagining different institutions, which could aim to maximize cognitive diversity of the law- and policymakers and whose attendant civic virtue would be open-mindedness rather than partisanship."[149]

4.3.4 A Question of Freedom

We think there is a basic normative principle of democracy that the lottocratic mentality does not satisfy—namely, political freedom as an essential element not only of deliberation but of democratic legitimacy itself. This comes before any question about the conditions conducive to good deliberation. We observed in analyzing criticisms of elections and accountability that some lottocrats express doubts as to whether freedom is essential to good deliberation, whether it is a truly democratic good and not a liberal one instead. We think it is important to stress the meaning of political freedom in all its manifestations and not to confuse or identify it with liberty. Hannah Arendt wrote that in a very imperfect polity such as representative government, "only the representatives of the people, not the people themselves, had an opportunity to engage in those activities of 'expressing, discussing, and deciding' which in a positive sense are the activities of freedom."[150] Arendt's words were a polemical tirade against the minimalist conception of representative government, conceived of as the selection of an elite—a conception that was hegemonic among political scientists when she wrote. Like minimalist democracy, the lottocratic model would keep the majority of citizens in a state of nondeliberation while reserving the "expressing, discussing, and deciding" for a select few (no matter how numerous they could be). But, what these few could do seems perhaps even *more* limited. Indeed, the forms of expression and overarching processes of decision-making in the sorted assemblies seem to be out of the hands of the allotted protagonists because, if the goal is to produce good deliberation, each moment must be regulated so deliberation is not swayed by the mood or "anarchic" expressiveness of the participants. Indeed, Arendt's critique of elections as the selection of an elite can be extended to lotteries as another form of elite selection.

---

[147] Landemore, *Open Democracy*, 39; Simone Weil, "On the Abolition of Political Parties," https://theanarchistlibrary.org/library/simone-weil-on-the-abolition-of-all-political-parties.
[148] Guerrero, *Lottocracy*, 52.
[149] Landemore, *Open Democracy*, 42.
[150] Hannah Arendt, *On Revolution* (London: Penguin Books, 1990), 235.

166 The Lottocratic Mentality

A further problem would be how to bring a multitude of citizens together without neutralizing them but instead enabling them to be free to associate and activate their political pluralism. Elections are an institution that responds to this problem, while lotteries do not. As Elster noted, lotteries are consistent with a kind of anomic individualism that jeopardizes the transmission of institutional memory from one assembly to another, and which makes decisions characterized by a permanent form of presentism. Elections in a representative government are not just a method to choose individual candidates on the basis of personal qualities or a mechanism that performs monocratic functions. Instead, they stimulate the formation of convergences and divergences with respect to ideas and projects, transform candidates into speakers and advocates for different political platforms to which citizens have the opportunity to identify with or reflect on and through which they can articulate their different visions of the public good, and they confer legitimacy through voting and opinion formation. In this way, citizens have the opportunity to see the public as their own because they construct it while simultaneously acting in both concert and disagreement (that is, associating with some and not others). In the previous session, we observed that, without elections, one cannot know the "will of the people." Instead such a will would be akin to something like a horizontal and indeterminate multitude of atomized personal opinions. On the contrary, the "will of the people" is *created* through the formulation of contestable solutions in a step-by-step manner and through processes freely constructed by the citizens themselves, and not simply concocted by visionaries with a view about a rational good that seems to be somehow "outside of" or "above" the boundaries of conversation and conflict. We could therefore say that the role that was played by semiprofessional orators in ancient Athens, the *rhētores*, is played by parties in our democracy.

A final contribution that parties make to political freedom emerges once we reflect on party organization—the power any party has to guard its gates, as it were, and expel even its own elected members. Party discipline plays an important controlling role insofar as it limits the autonomy opened up for representatives by free mandates, not by violating or opposing free mandate representation itself but rather, as discussed in the previous section, by activating a "political" form of mandate. While legal coercion (imperative mandate) cannot be justified in a representative government, the power that parties hold over their elected members in the legislature (their internal discipline) can trigger an informal imperative mandate. Several decades ago, Schattschneider wrote that parties operate in a "no legal man's land" in the sense that they do with their own representatives what no law could ever do if the state is to avoid becoming authoritarian.[151] *Parties play an auxiliary role in citizens' political freedom* as they afford them an important measure of controlling power over the elected without resorting to the sanctioning force of law, which would effectively nullify representation. Parties induce representatives to stick to the promises that they made to the electors; in a way, they help actualize the ethical obligation that representatives make to be responsive to their constituents' interests.

[151] Schattschneider, *Party Government*, 12.

The Targets of Lottocracy Revisited 167

Thus, while the imperative mandate cannot be constrained in its legal form, democracy must make room for some forms of limitation on the power of representatives, for example, by constraining their freedom to change parties once in parliament or by taking their immunity away.[152] At any rate, parties become *agents* of political freedom in a broader sense, and their agency is more valuable and consistent the more they positively attract citizens and are not merely catchall "cartel" parties. It is no coincidence that some democratic constitutions (like those in Germany and Italy) contemplate not only the right to free association for political purposes but also the right to participate *through parties* to help craft the politics of the nation.

After illustrating the value of parties and party association in relation to political freedom, we can understand how they are connected to voting, elections, and representation. While the lottocratic mentality suggests that this connection is a problem for democracy, we claim that a "no-party" democracy would be highly problematic. We make this claim for two main reasons.

The first reason pertains to *democratic empowerment*. Representatives make laws that all citizens, and not simply those who elect them, must obey. Thus, a political mandate entails that representatives represent the *entire* nation, and not just the constituency that elected them. This not only means that their mandate is non-contractually based or that it is an individual act of transfer; it also means that the representatives cannot ignore the "will of the people" and simply concentrate on their relationship with their own constituency and those who have elected them; both the *particular* and the *general* constitute democratic representation in a democratic party system.[153] Without the mechanism of elections and parties, the connection between society and broader political institutions would simply fade away. Without intermediary institutions and practices, any remaining "thread unifying the intention of the various independent actors"[154] would vanish, and the democratic empowerment of the citizenry would vanish along with it.

The second reason pertains to *political agency*. Political representation denies that we should rely on mere sociological similarity since it offers an artificially created similarity among (some) citizens and their representatives. The seed of the democratic character of representation germinates from the paradox that although representatives are supposed to make decisions about things that affect *all members* of the polity, they are supposed to have a sympathetic relation *to a part* of it

---

[152] Kelsen, *Essence and Value of Democracy*, 58.

[153] This view questions the politics of presence versus politics of ideas dualism, which seems to presume that the "particular" and the "general" loiter about separate from one another. Yet, both of them are essential components in the work of judgment and not substantially separable as if "particularity" were ideas-blind and "generality" were facts-empty. For a critical examination of the issue of presence in the dynamic of representation, see Susan Dovi, "Preferable Descriptive Representatives: Or Will Just Any Woman, Black, or Latino Do?," *American Political Science Review* 96 (2002): 745–54. The idea that representation is not merely a one-to-one relation between constituents and a legislator also gives rise to the idea that legislators "could not justify representing particular claims of established groups without taking into account the state of representation of less-established groups in the legislature." Thompson, *Political Ethics*, 107.

[154] Goodin, *Innovating Democracy*, 212.

168 The Lottocratic Mentality

in particular.[155] In essence, a partisan relationship of sympathy and communication obtains between representatives and their electors. This relation is necessary precisely because political representation rules out formal or legal "checks" that would force a representative to do one thing or another, and it is also a far different relation than the type of relation set up by a contract. Instead, this relationship lives off of the currency of political accountability.[156] This is why, if they are viewed in isolation, the conditions of representative democracy and the practices of elections and parties in particular "seem to violate formal requirements of political equality. Viewed in the context of a democratic system as a whole, they can be seen as equalizing democratic representation, and ensuring that representative institutions function as they should."[157]

Ironically, the ideal of a lottocratic polis is actually what makes us appreciate the normative value of parties—it helps us appreciate how they enable pluralism and both activate and protect political freedom. In the sort of society which that lottocratic mentality envisions, this value would be absent. We therefore agree with the lottocrats that parties have become a key factor which has set off a crisis of moral legitimacy within contemporary democracy. But we argue that, if we want to remain consistent with the principles and norms of democracy, we should seek a solution that is diametrically opposed to theirs. This is for several reasons. First, parties are not simply functional tools or a "second-best" option that stands in for some mythical direct self-government that we do not and have never had. Instead, parties exist because democracy exists. Indeed, *even* in an idealized direct democracy, divisions among the citizens would emerge. Therefore, it makes perfect sense to claim that parties and democracy live and die together. Second, the challenge for democracy today is to revitalize informal political intermediary institutions such as parties rather than (as we observed in our analysis of polarization) trying to wipe them out. In questioning the lottocratic mentality, we argue that the decline of moral legitimacy accorded to parties is both a factor in and a sign of the decline of the political value of democratic participation and the equal opportunity of citizens to associate in order to exercise political influence freely. We, therefore, conclude that the best way to respond to antipartisanship is to understand its meaning genuinely and to defend the ethics of taking sides in public. We can do this with the peace of mind that comes from the knowledge that by doing so we are securing political freedom. Recovering the value of political associations and forms of the collective political agency may require new rules and laws (e.g., on party financing and running election campaigns or different regulations on parliamentary groups) as well as new organizational forms (forms that are attentive, for example, to the physical rather than simply the digital interaction of members and to the effective authority that party members

---

[155] See Kelsen, *Essence and Value of Democracy*, chap. 2.

[156] "The criterion of autonomy, therefore, cannot demand, even as an ideal, a wholly unencumbered legislator, one who acts utterly unswayed by political pressures and partisan loyalties." Thompson, *Political Ethics*, 113.

[157] Chapman, *Election Day*, 36.

exercise in both decision-making and in the development of political programs and candidacies). These decisions are in the hands of citizens.

4.4 Conclusion

In this chapter, we have defended the democratic value of elections, representation, and parties. Of course, these are not the only forms of politics that are found within a democracy, and none of these forms is free of malfunction or immune to justified criticism. Throughout their history, democracies have endlessly sought to create, reform, regulate, and revitalize these political forms in a Tantalus-like task that reveals how important they are to democratic politics and how risky their abolition would be. Although far from perfect, not to say satisfactory, none of these institutions has only a functional value; elections, representation, and political parties are among the substance of democracy itself and not some "second-best" practices that we are forced to follow under nonideal circumstances; they are not merely functional stratagems. They are expressions and forms of political freedom and, as such, fundamentally democratic goods. Clearly, if we accept the lottocratic mentality with respect to elections, then representation and parties are worth very little, and it should not cost us much to give them up. This rhetorical argumentative strategy is reminiscent of Thomas Hobbes's *Leviathan*, which depicts the condition of liberty in the state of nature as so depressing and miserable that not much would be lost by giving it up in exchange for security and obedience. In this chapter, we have set out to demonstrate the democratic value of each of the three main components of democracy. In Part II, we intend to show how the alleged benefits associated with their renunciation are undemocratic elements harbored by the lottocratic mentality.

II

WHAT'S WRONG WITH THE LOTTOCRACTIC MENTALITY?

Chapter 5
Disempowering The People
The Lottocratic Reinterpretation Of Political Equality

The rallying cry of lottocrats is the claim that lottocracy will give power to the people. In the context of the current crisis of democracy, this is undoubtedly what makes lottocracy seem particularly appealing. Such sentiments also bolster the claim that lottocracy is more democratic than electoral representative democracy. According to lottocrats, the people are empowered when they select ordinary citizens by lottery, whereas electing representatives is an oligarchic process that necessarily generates an elite group of political officials whose interests are different than those of the people.

There is some irony to this claim. For lottocracy would in fact disenfranchise the citizenry in its entirety. Citizens would have no opportunity to vote, and there will be no elections, no political parties, and no venues for exercising effective influence over political decisions on a regular basis. In contemporary electoral democracies, all citizens have the power to regularly make important political decisions—either by voting for political parties and policy agendas in periodic elections or by voting on specific issues in ballot initiatives and referenda.[1] Yet, in a lottocracy only a few randomly selected people are empowered to make political decisions as they see fit and the overwhelming majority of the citizenry would be excluded from exercising political power. It is true that in the context of more moderate proposals that envision lottocratic institutions complementing instead of replacing electoral ones, the situation would be less dire. But it is important to keep in mind that this would be so only to the extent that (some) electoral institutions remain available. In other words, if the citizenry can still exercise some power, it would be *despite* and not *by virtue of* having lottocratic institutions. For whichever political decisions lottocratic institutions have authority over, it would also be the case that only the few randomly selected members will have the power to make those decisions and the rest of the citizenry would be excluded from exercising any power over them.

---

[1] Just in case readers need to be reminded of the important political decisions that citizens regularly make in elections, let me mention a couple of highly consequential examples. In the USA, citizens are about to decide whether to vote for Harris or Trump in the next presidential election. It can hardly get more consequential than the choice between the right-wing political agenda of MAGA Republicans and the center-left agenda of the Democratic Party. In recent years, citizens in Bolivia, Chile, Colombia, and Brazil have voted for parties with a leftist political agenda, whereas citizens in Paraguay recently voted in favor of the conservative party by a big margin. In Argentina, citizens elected the most far-right candidate in decades. Such fundamental decisions about the general political direction of a country can have consequential effects that last over decades.

The Lottocratic Mentality. Cristina Lafont and Nadia Urbinati, Oxford University Press. © Cristina Lafont and Nadia Urbinati (2024). DOI: 10.1093/9780191982903.003.0006

174   The Lottocratic Mentality

Since the democratic ideal of self-government seeks to include citizens in decision-making, the lottocratic empowerment of the few and disempowerment of the many seem straightforwardly antidemocratic. If this is so, how can it then be claimed that lottocracy is a "radical" form of democracy? How is this illusion of democracy created? To answer this question, we need to analyze the lottocratic reinterpretation of political equality in detail, which is a core feature of the lottocratic mentality. As such, it is not only endorsed by defenders of the most radical proposal of replacing electoral democracy with lottocracy, but also equally endorsed by defenders of less radical proposals for using lottery-based institutions whether as complementary or auxiliary to electoral institutions. In fact, it is widely assumed that one of the main attractions of lottery-based institutions over electoral-representative institutions is that the former do a better job at promoting "political equality."[2] Since political equality is an essential component of the democratic ideal, this is surely an important claim to consider when evaluating the democratic credentials of different political systems and institutions. Unfortunately, the lottocratic reinterpretation of political equality is problematic. Despite its superficial plausibility, as it is often the case, the devil is in the details. Under closer inspection, it turns out that it has two problematic features: (1) it severely weakens the political rights and power that citizens in electoral democracies collectively exercise as equals (under the "one person, one vote" principle) on a regular basis; and it does so for the sake of (2) equalizing asymmetric relationships of power among citizens which are objectionable from the perspective of democratic equality. Although these are problematic features for any defense of lottery-based institutions on grounds of political equality, its negative implications are most obvious in the radical proposals that favor replacing electoral institutions with a lottocracy. Let's take a look at each of these features in detail.

5.1 Levelling Down for the Sake of Equality?

The democratic ideal of political equality is about having an equal say on collective political decisions. However, lottocrats transform the democratic requirement of having equal access to the exercise of political power into the remarkably weaker requirement of "having equal chances to be selected" to exercise political power. If we change the example from political rights to another type of rights, then it becomes obvious why the lottocratic "reinterpretation" of what political equality requires is so objectionable. Following the lottocratic formula, the right of "equal access" to health care, for instance, would be reinterpreted as the right to "equal chances to be selected" to have health care. Securing a lottocratic right to health care would be remarkably cheap since only a few randomly selected citizens would

---

[2] Abizadeh, "Representation, Bicameralism, Political Equality and Sortition," 792ff.; Landemore, *Open Democracy*, 89–90; Alexander Guerrero, "Against Elections: The Lottocratic Alternative," *Philosophy & Public Affairs* 42, no. 2 (2014): 168; Sintomer, *The Government of Chance*, 5, 229–33.

actually enjoy access to it. This cannot plausibly count as a way of providing equal rights to health care to everyone.[3] Political rights are no different. Being included in a lottery can be a way of securing procedural equality or fairness, but it does not provide the substantive political equality that the democratic ideal of inclusion in decision-making requires. Excluding the bulk of citizens from effective opportunities to exercise decision-making power can hardly count as a "democratic" strengthening of the political rights that citizens currently enjoy in democratic societies.[4]

To see where the problem originates, one needs to keep in mind that a lottery is a fair procedure for distributing a good only when it is not possible to provide the good in question to everyone who has a proper claim to it. Indeed, that it is perfectly possible to give everyone access to health care is precisely why it seems utterly unacceptable to propose that, instead of providing for everyone, we just randomly select a few who will have access to it. In contrast, for the specific case of providing access to, say, organs, a lottery could in some particular context be a fair procedure of distribution precisely and only because there are not enough organs available for everyone who needs a transplant. However, this is not the case in the political context. Since access to the ongoing exercise of (some important form of) political power can be provided to all citizens through voting (on elections, referenda, etc.), there is no obvious reason for limiting its distribution to only a few citizens through a "fair" procedure such as a lottery.[5] The problem is not with the fairness of the lottery procedure per se but with the artificially generated "scarcity" that prompts the need for a "fair" distribution of unequal access. It took centuries of political struggle to expand the franchise in democratic societies so that most adult citizens (women, ethnic minorities, those without property, etc.) could exercise the right to make some important political decisions on a regular basis. To convince citizens that unilateral political disempowerment is a risk worth taking, let alone an attractive political project, we would need *extremely* compelling reasons. We should closely scrutinize the democratic credentials of lottocracy before giving up our current rights to collectively exercise political power as equals and establishing a lottocratic form of "rule by the few." We can do this by examining the second problematic feature of the lottocratic reinterpretation of political equality.

---

[3] For an argument along these lines, see Thomas Christiano, *The Constitution of Equality: Democratic Authority and Its Limits* (Oxford: Oxford University Press, 2008), 109.

[4] Obviously, this problem is at its worst for lottocratic proposals that envision conferring *all* decision-making on allotted assemblies. But the problem also persists for proposals that confer only *some* legislative authority upon such institutions. The fact that such proposals would leave *some* decision-making in the hands of electoral institutions in no way justifies why (any) decision-making power should be conferred upon allotted assemblies over which the citizenry has no capacity for democratic control.

[5] The lottocratic proposal to lower everyone's current access to the exercise of decision-making power for the sake of political equality would seem to fall afoul of the leveling down *objection to egalitarianism*. But, as discussed in the next section, the situation is worse than that. For it turns out that the leveling down in question is proposed for the sake of equalizing *unequal* relationships of power and this is objectionable *on egalitarian grounds*.

5.2 Equalizing Asymmetric Power Relations

Lottocrats' main argument against electoral democracy is that it cannot secure political equality because elected officials necessarily have more opportunities to exercise political power than ordinary citizens.[6] By contrast, lottocrats argue that the use of lotteries better respects fundamental ideals of equality and particularly political equality. Guerrero justifies this claim as follows:

> Even in electoral systems in which each person gets one vote to elect their representative—and the ideal of equality thus plays some role—the election of some individuals to "rule" over others is less egalitarian than random selection. One reason for this is that, although it may be true that all have an equal say in the electoral process, only a select few actually have political power, and (for reasons having to do with resources and the influence of the powerful) not everyone has anything close to an equal chance of having political power. Lottery selection thus arguably better reflects egalitarian ideals since anyone might wield political power and everyone has an equal chance of doing so.[7]

Certainly, elected officials have more opportunities to exercise political power than ordinary citizens because of their role as political representatives. However, it is important to note that, since this is an intrinsic feature of representative democracy, it does not help the lottocratic case. The lottocratic proposal would generate an even more extreme form of political inequality between the few randomly selected decision-makers and the rest of the citizenry since the latter would have no power to influence or shape the decisions of the former or to hold them accountable. It is certainly true that, in electoral democracies, the right to vote does not in fact secure equal access for all citizens to the effective exercise of political power. There are very good reasons to improve the system. But *eliminating access to the effective exercise of political power for nearly all citizens virtually all the time* can hardly be an improvement on that score!

A defender of direct democracy could argue that no improvement of representative democracy could ever eliminate the political inequality built into the differential access to political power that is intrinsic to the distinction between elected representatives and the rest of the citizenry. Only a direct democracy in which all citizens equally exercise political power, so the argument would go, could effectively secure political equality.[8] Note, however, that this line of argument is not available to lottocrats since lottocracy is a form of representative democracy rather than direct

---

[6] Similarly, in his book *Against Elections*, Van Reybrouck criticizes elections as "a procedure that was not invented as a democratic instrument but as a means of bringing a new, non-hereditary aristocracy to power. The extension of suffrage made that aristocratic procedure thoroughly democratic without relinquishing the fundamental, oligarchic distinction between governors and governed, between politicians and voters" (66).

[7] Guerrero, "Against Elections," 168–9.

[8] We are reconstructing this argument only to clarify the lottocratic position, but we are not endorsing it. A direct democracy in which all political decisions are made by majority rule could easily fail to secure equal opportunities to influence policy decisions for permanent minorities.

democracy. Far from advocating that all citizens make all political decisions collectively through aggregative procedures such as voting, the lottocratic proposal is to have a few randomly selected citizens in charge of making political decisions for the rest of the citizenry. Since lottocracy is a form of representative democracy, the political inequality created by the existence of a group of decision-makers that is separated from the group of decision-takers is equally intrinsic to lottocracy.[9] In what sense then can it be claimed that lottocracy promotes political equality better than electoral representative democracy? Lottocrats offer a normative and an empirical line of argument. (1) From a normative perspective, they argue that inequalities of access to the effective exercise of political power in a lottocracy would be equalized over the long term through opportunities "to rule and be ruled in turn." (2) From an empirical perspective, they argue that electoral democracies generate more inequalities of political power than lottocracy would. Let's examine each of these arguments in turn.

5.2.1 Ruling and Being Ruled in Turn. Can Rotation Secure Political Equality?

Since lottocracy is a form of representative democracy, the randomly selected decision-makers necessarily have more political power than the rest of the citizenry. However, lottocrats argue that these inequalities may be equalized over time. Guerrero argues as follows:

> although at a particular time some will have more political power than others in the lottocratic system, this is less pronounced than in the electoral representative system (since the heightened power will be for a much shorter average duration), and it may not even be true when measured over lifetimes (depending on the numbers and the resultant likelihood of each person being chosen randomly at some point during her lifetime).[10]

Lottocrats are aware that, in large countries, citizens would have an *equal but, unfortunately, close-to-zero* chance of ever being chosen to a lottocratic assembly. Lottery may be a "fair" selection mechanism, but it does not provide the losers, who are *the overwhelming majority* of citizens, with *any access* to the exercise of political power. For this reason, lottocrats argue that, over time, it is the combination of sortition and *rotation* that equalizes the stark inequalities of access to the exercise of power that are created by having a few randomly selected members of the lottocratic assembly make all political decisions for the rest of the citizenry. Lottocrats maintain that

---

[9] We are analyzing the democratic credentials of lottocracy as a replacement for electoral democracy. Some defenders of lottocracy, like Landemore, add to their proposals some features of direct democracy such as referenda, rights of deferral, etc. However, Landemore agrees (in fact it is a central argumentative goal of her book) that lottocratic institutions are a form of representative democracy and not of direct democracy. This is also true of electoral democracies. Although they often include such mechanisms as referenda, citizen initiatives, etc., as a political system they are a form of representative democracy.

[10] Guerrero, "Against Elections," 168–9.

178 The Lottocratic Mentality

political equality is secured by the equalizing effect of rotating political offices among all citizens, whereas this is simply not the case in electoral democracies. Landemore explains the normative importance of rotation as follows:

> The combination of sortition and rotation . . . ensures equal access to all citizens over time. Lottocratic representation is thus a more open form of representation than electoral representation. Given the limited life expectancy of human beings, however, some thought needs to be given to the size of these assemblies, the number of citizens they are meant to represent, and the exact frequency with which they are renewed if we want citizens to have a meaningful chance (though not necessarily a certainty) of being chosen over the course of their lifetimes. Indeed, if the number of seats and the frequency of rotation are insufficient for everyone to plausibly expect to rule someday, then the comparative democratic advantage of lotteries over elections becomes quite thin.[11]

Let's take a closer look at the role of rotation in the defense of the democratic credentials of lottocracy. The idea seems to be that so long as citizens can meaningfully expect to "rule" someday, they can see themselves involved in a democratic project of self-government. In other words, it is democratic to be ruled by others most of the time so long as you get to rule at least once in your lifetime. But is this claim plausible? Over time, rotation equalizes the chances of being randomly selected as a "ruler." Following this idea, one may claim that it is "fair" to be ruled by others so long as everyone has (1) the same chances of being selected as "ruler" and (2) a meaningful chance of being selected at least once. So long as not everyone can get to rule, distributing "ruling" in this way may be indeed "fair." But why would such an arrangement be democratic? Imagine that I am a citizen of a populous country. I would be expected to blindly obey all the political decisions lottocratic assemblies happen to make during my entire life, so long as I have a meaningful chance of becoming a member of such assemblies at least once in my lifetime so that I can effectively influence the few political decisions this assembly happens to make. In other words, throughout my life, I am supposed to obey any and all political decisions that randomly selected citizens happen to make about everything that affects me (from taxes to education, health care, climate change, abortion, vaccinations, and so on), and this is because of the bare fact that I have a chance (though not necessarily a certainty) to exercise decisive influence in making a few political decisions at least once in my lifetime—whether or not these decisions happen to be of any particular relevance to me. In contrast to the *ongoing* opportunities to influence political decisions that electoral systems provide, the problem with the *temporal* opportunities that rotation provides is that decisions made by a lottocratic assembly here and now are binding for everyone regardless of what other decisions future assemblies may make. If I oppose

---

[11] Landemore, *Open Democracy*, 91.

a decision on education policy, say, because of the way it affects my children's schooling experience, the fact that I may be randomly selected to a lottocratic assembly after my children are out of school in no way provides me effective opportunities to influence the political decisions to which I am subject *at the time when it matters to me.* In an electoral system, I can immediately mobilize against proposals on educational policy that I disagree with: I can protest, I can send letters to my representatives, I can vote for the party with the proposals that I agree with and can hold the representatives accountable for their decisions, etc. Certainly, there is no guarantee that these actions will succeed but, if enough fellow citizens join the cause, they may. By contrast, in a lottocratic system with rotation, I can only wait until I am lucky enough to happen to be randomly selected to a future assembly which may or may not make decisions that are of any concern to me. This system may be "fair" if there are not better options, but how is it democratic? In what sense would citizens be engaged in democratic self-government if they had no way of regularly shaping the political decisions to which they are subject? Something seems deeply wrong with this picture. Let's take a closer look.

5.2.2 Two Requirements of Political Equality

In electoral democracies, citizens' political rights aim to guarantee political equality in two dimensions. Citizens should have equal opportunities to (1) hold public office and (2) influence the outcome of political decisions.[12] By contrast, in a lottocracy, these requirements of political equality are pit against each other so that, in order to enjoy the first type of equality, citizens must relinquish the second. This leads to a very problematic form of *political inequality.*

As we have seen, adding rotation to sortition aims to equalize citizens' chances of holding office. But it is unclear why this is important or needed. Having "equal chances" to hold political office is a much stronger requirement than having "equal opportunities" to do so. The latter only requires that "the political process is open to everyone on a basis of rough equality,"[13] but, due to electoral competition, the chances of holding office of different candidates will vary.[14] But why should this be a problem? Perhaps lottocrats assume that political equality requires citizens to have not just equal opportunities but also equal chances to hold political office because this is *morally due* to them. But this is an extremely counterintuitive assumption since giving all political candidates equal chances to hold office would undermine

---

[12] We follow Rawls's wording here, although he uses the term "fair" instead of "equal" to highlight that the political liberties should have their fair value and thus require *substantive* and not merely formal equality. As he puts it, the fair value of our political liberties requires that "everyone has a fair opportunity to hold public office *and* to influence the outcome of political decisions." John Rawls, *Political Liberalism* (Cambridge, MA: Harvard University Press, 1993), 327.

[13] Ibid., 330.

[14] We are grateful to Peter Niessen and Palle Bech-Pedersen for pointing out the need to clarify this point.

the political freedom of citizens to elect candidates according to their interests, values, and policy objectives.[15] Moreover, it is far from clear why citizens should have a fundamental interest in holding office. Citizens are certainly interested in ensuring that the political decisions to which they are subject are right, fair, reasonable, acceptable, or whatever the case may be. But this is a very different interest from being directly involved in making the decisions in question. If anything, the latter interest would seem to be parasitic on the former. Being directly involved in making political decisions can help ensure that the right decisions are made (i.e., the decisions that one finds acceptable, reasonable, or whatever the case may be). The problem with the idea of combining sortition and rotation is that it gets these priorities *exactly backward*. For in order to someday have the chance of being directly involved in making a few political decision/s, citizens would have to blindly defer to all the political decisions made by random others during their entire lifetime—whether they find them right or wrong, reasonable or unreasonable, etc. This seems to be the wrong trade-off to make.

In a lottocracy, citizens are asked to trade the ongoing opportunities to influence political decisions that they enjoy in electoral democracies (e.g., by voting on elections or referenda) for the equal chance ("though not necessarily a certainty") of holding office at least once in their lifetimes. Democratic citizens have an interest in collectively shaping the political decisions to which they are subject. But this is very different from having an interest in fairly distributing the chances to directly make a few decisions while having to blindly accept the overwhelming majority of decisions that are made by random others, whatever they are. This is not to deny that in a democracy citizens should have a fair opportunity to hold office if they so wish. But the price of this opportunity should not be relinquishing their ongoing opportunities to shape the political decisions to which they are subject. Even more important, this trade-off undermines the lottocrats' claim that the combination of sortition and rotation secures political equality.

---

[15] Umbers, "Against Lottocracy," offers additional arguments against the view that having equal chances to hold office could be *morally due* to citizens: "Political equality does not fundamentally require that citizens enjoy equal chances for political office because citizens do not have positive claims to hold political office. . . . There are two reasons to reject the idea of claims to political office. First, it is deeply counterintuitive. Each representative is one of a small number of individuals with the power to exercise control over decisions to be coercively imposed upon the entire citizenry. Representatives—especially under systems like representation by lottery in which citizens have no means of holding them to account—thereby enjoy substantially greater power and authority than ordinary citizens. The political community does not intuitively owe asymmetric power and authority of that kind to anyone. We do not typically think, for example, that losers in fair elections have some legitimate complaint against the citizenry for failing to satisfy some claim of theirs. Second, such claims would conflict deeply with Social Equality. Asymmetries of power and authority are constitutive of relations of social inequality, and representatives enjoy asymmetric power and authority over the citizenry. I think, then, that it is implausible that individuals have positive moral claims to hold such offices" (317). We agree with this argument. However, we also would like to emphasize that, from the point of view of political equality, not all forms of asymmetric power are equally problematic. In contrast to direct democracy, all forms of representative democracy have a built-in asymmetry of power between representatives and those they represent. However, as discussed in the next section, in a lottocracy the asymmetry of power is objectionable because power is *unilaterally exercised* by the few and the rest of the citizenry can only blindly obey their decisions, whatever they are. This is not the case in electoral democracy and is contrary to any democratic idea of self-government.

5.2.3 What's Wrong with Excluding the Citizenry from Decision-Making?

In contemporary democracies, citizens possess an ongoing power to influence decision-making by choosing their representatives and holding them accountable. The fundamental problem with eliminating this power is that it transforms the power relationship between citizens and representatives into a fundamentally *unequal* one. In contrast to elected representatives, randomly selected "rulers" make political decisions as they see fit and citizens must in turn blindly defer to their decisions. Far from securing political equality, this is an asymmetric relationship in which the former exercise *unilateral power over* the latter. Equalizing citizens' chances of "ruling" at least once in their lifetimes at the cost of being ruled over for most of their life *is not a plausible interpretation of political equality* any more than equalizing the chances of being a master once in their lifetimes at the cost of being slaves most of their life would be a plausible interpretation of social equality.

As a mechanism for equalizing the chances of "ruling," rotation perpetuates asymmetric relationships of power instead of enabling symmetric relations and is, from this perspective, incompatible with political equality.[16] What the democratic ideal of political equality and inclusion in decision-making requires is not *to equalize the chances of "ruling"* (i.e., of exercising unilateral power over others) but rather *to equalize citizens' opportunities to collectively exercise the power of making political decisions as equals.* To be politically equals, citizens must be able to exercise political power *omnilaterally*, instead of letting a few citizens unilaterally impose their political decisions on the rest of the citizenry.[17] To appreciate the difference between these two ideas, it is helpful to shift the focus from the political power exercised by office-holders to the political power exercised by ordinary citizens in electoral democracies. Indeed, lottocrats mischaracterize and downplay the latter form of political power to such an extent that its democratic significance entirely falls out of view.

In electoral democracies, citizens' power to influence and shape the political decisions to which they are subject is ongoing. Instead of having a chance to shape a few political decisions at least once in their lifetime, they collectively exercise power over decision-making on a regular basis. They do so in two ways. First, they *directly* (and collectively) make decisions about the political parties and programs

---

[16] Guerrero recognizes a concern about political inequality, at least in the case of instituting a powerful generalist legislative chamber that he does not recommend. He argues that "even if everyone has an equal chance to be selected, if that chance is incredibly small, there is a case that the difference in actual political power between those selected and those not selected is too great to comport with considerations of political equality, *given how small the chance is that people will be selected*" ("Lottocracy," 105–6). However, his argument only attends to the unequal frequency in the exercise of power among citizens while disregarding the deeper problem of the unequal relationships of power that are established between decision-makers and decision-takers.

[17] According to Landemore, "self-rule means that individuals are entitled to participate in making the laws that bind them. Equality means that they should be able to do so on equal terms" (*Open Democracy*, 6). We agree. The problem with lottocracy is precisely that the citizenry *never exercises power on equal terms*. Neither sortition nor rotation offer the citizenry any venue for *collectively exercising power over political decisions as equals*.

182 The Lottocratic Mentality

that they favor by periodically voting in elections (they may also make direct decisions about specific political issues by voting on initiatives or referenda). Second, through their power to vote for some political parties and programs rather than others, they also *indirectly* influence the political decisions that their representatives make.[18] This form of political power enables citizens to hold their representatives accountable.

By contrast, in a lottocracy, citizens have no way to hold the randomly selected few accountable. They may disagree with the decisions and may criticize them, but they have no formal accountability mechanism at their disposal to constrain the discretion of the randomly selected assembly or to steer it in one political direction rather than another. Whereas the relationship between citizens and their elected representatives is based on *accountability*, the relationship between citizens and the randomly selected representatives is based on *deference*.[19] Randomly selected representatives are supposed to make decisions as they see fit, and the citizenry is supposed to blindly defer to them; citizens have no formal tools for holding them accountable for their decisions. For this reason, they have no power to influence or shape the decisions that their "rulers" make. Thus, in a lottocracy, political power is wielded exclusively by the "rulers" (e.g., the members of the lottocratic assembly) and the rest of the citizenry is simply expected to "be ruled" by them. Note that having to *blindly defer* to the coercive political decisions of others is a quintessential form of *political inequality*. It can hardly get more unequal than that! Yet, lottocrats assume that this type of unequal political relationship is also the norm in representative democracies. This explains why, for them, political equality can only be about equalizing the chances of "ruling" since, apparently, *there simply is no other form of political power that citizens could exercise as equals*. This problematic assumption about political power is salient in Guerrero's characterization of electoral democracy. As discussed before, on his view:

> in electoral systems in which each person gets one vote to elect their representative—and the ideal of equality thus plays some role—*the election of some individuals to "rule" over others* is less egalitarian than random selection. One reason for this is that, although it may be true that all have an equal *say* in the electoral process, *only a select few actually have political power.*[20]

---

[18] These are not the only opportunities to exercise political power that citizens have in electoral democracies. In addition, citizens can influence political decisions by exercising their rights to political and legal contestation, even if they are in the minority. They can legally contest decisions that they deem unconstitutional (e.g., that violate fundamental rights and freedoms) through the courts. They can also organize protests to demand policy changes and can expect to be listened to. For, even if they are not a very large or powerful group, they nonetheless may be able to gather the needed power to remove the targeted officials or political parties from office in the next election if they convince enough of their fellow citizens to endorse their demands (Umbers, "Against Lottocracy," 20).

[19] In *Democracy without Shortcuts*, I offer an in-depth analysis of the antidemocratic underpinnings of the expectation of (politically blind) deference in lottocratic systems. See also Dimitri Landa and Ryan Pevnick, "Is Random Selection a Cure for the Ills of Electoral Representation?," *Journal of Political Philosophy* 29, no. 1 (2021): 46–72.

[20] Guerrero, "Against Elections," 168–9, our italics.

It is quite strange to characterize electoral systems in which citizens vote to elect their representatives as "the election of some individuals to 'rule' over others." In contrast to authoritarian regimes, citizens in a democracy can elect their representatives based on their political preferences. In so doing, citizens give their officials an implicit mandate to promote and advance the policies, programs, and priorities that they favor and can hold them to account if they do not. No matter how imperfect this delegating process may be in practice, it is decidedly odd to simply describe it as a process whereby citizens elect individuals to "rule" over them. Since political officials can only stay in power as long as citizens continue to vote for them, it would be quite inaccurate to describe the relationship between citizens and their representatives as one in which the latter exercise unilateral power over the former, as is the case in authoritarian regimes. Perhaps the fact that Guerrero uses the term "rule" with quotation marks could be taken to mean that he does not endorse the view of elections as a process in which citizens choose their "rulers." However, his second characterization of elections is crystal clear in that regard. In his view, although it may be true that all citizens "have an equal *say* in the electoral process, *only a select few actually have political power*."[21]

Oddly, this claim suggests that having an equal say in elections is not having any actual political power. Under the standard understanding of competitive elections, citizens are understood to have the power to choose which political parties and programs they endorse. This is a very strong form of political power that citizens exercise collectively as equals every few years by participating in elections (under the "one person, one vote" rule).[22] By choosing some political programs and parties over others, they shape the political/ideological space within which the elected representatives must operate until the next election. Only the citizenry as a collective body has the power to make that fundamental overarching decision about the political direction of their government and to revise it or maintain it every few years.

---

[21] Landemore shares a similar conception of political power. For her, when citizens vote in elections they are not themselves exercising any power over political decision-making. They are only selecting who gains access to power. This is why, for Landemore, electoral democracy is exclusionary: "electoral representation has by construction exclusionary effects in terms of *who gains access to power*" (Landemore, *Open Democracy*, 23). Landemore's conception draws from Manin's interpretation of representative democracy. As she explains, "For Manin, whereas the direct democracy of the Ancients used to mean the ability for all citizens to hold offices, representative government thus means instead the ability to consent to power exercised by an elected subset and put some sort of discursive pressure on it between elections" (ibid., 34). As we argued in Chapter 1, Manin's characterization of representative democracy may fit the representative systems of the 18th century, but it is not equally plausible with respect to multiparty democracy. By relying on an account of representative democracy that mischaracterizes current democracies, lottocrats adopt a problematic conception of political power that consists exclusively in "ruling," i.e., "wielding power over others." In so doing, they mischaracterize or downplay forms of political power that citizens collectively exercise as equals, e.g., by voting for specific political parties and programs, voting in referenda, etc. Under the (implausible) assumption that when citizens vote in elections they do not exercise power over decision-making but simply "consent to be ruled" and select "their rulers," lottocratic systems can be seen as more attractive since only they provide citizens an equal chance to "actually exercise political power."

[22] The "one person, one vote" rule indicates that in elections citizens exercise their power collectively, but as individuals (i.e., based on their own free will). There is no assumption of a collective actor (e.g., "the people") making a homogeneous decision. The collective electoral decision results from the aggregation of individual (politically heterogeneous) votes that gives rise to majorities, oppositions, coalitions, etc.

Representatives, certainly, do not have such power since they lack the power to ensure that their own political party or program wins out over the other parties, and they also cannot predetermine the margin by which each party wins or loses. They acquire power only after they have been voted into office and can lose this power in the next election cycle.

The power to determine the political/ideological direction of the government is precisely the kind of political power that authoritarian regimes refuse to give to their citizens. If it were true that having an equal say in elections is not having any actual power over substantive decision-making besides having a say on which "rulers" will have such power, it would be hard to understand why "elections" in one-party authoritarian regimes that let citizens choose among various "rulers" of the same party should be called "undemocratic." But, leaving aside for the moment the question of whether this view of elections is justified, what it clearly reveals is that the lottocratic conception of political power is one of "ruling over others." If having an equal say in the electoral process is not itself an exercise of political power over decision-making by the citizenry—if only the "rulers" have actual political power—then it seems accurate to understand their relationship as one in which the latter exercise unilateral power over the former. Indeed, as discussed before, it is precisely because lottocrats assume that only rulers have political power that they think political equality must be about equalizing the chances of "ruling."

This conception of political power seems suitable for nondemocratic regimes. For instance, in one-party rule systems, citizens may be able to vote for different "representatives" but, since they cannot choose them according to the political programs and policies that they favor, they have no power to influence the political decisions to which they will be subject. Their votes have no power to steer decision-making in one political direction rather than another. Since there are no genuine "alternative" political programs and policy proposals for citizens to choose from, officeholders do not receive any political mandate from the citizenry whatsoever. There is no sense in which they are bound to pursue some specific political goals or policy objectives rather than others. Thus, they can make political decisions entirely unconnected to citizens' political preferences. It seems accurate to claim that in such systems, "although it may be true that citizens have an equal say in the electoral process, only the select few actually have political power." Indeed, since there is no sharing of political power between citizens and their "representatives," all that citizens can do in elections within one-party systems is select those who will "rule" over them. Note that a view of political power as something that is exclusively exercised by the "rulers" is not questioned or criticized by lottocrats. Lottocrats endorse "rule by the few." They just favor equalizing everyone's chances to become a "ruler" at least once in their lifetime.

What the lottocratic conception of political equality lacks are *forms of political power that are collectively exercised by citizens as equals*, like those exercised when citizens vote in elections (under the "one person, one vote" rule).[23] In contrast to

---

[23] See footnote 29.

one-party authoritarian regimes, in electoral representative democracies, citizens collectively exercise *direct* political power by choosing from among *political programs, policies, and priorities* in periodic elections (or on specific policy issues in referenda, citizens' initiatives, and so on). They also have the political power to exercise control over officeholders (by regularly voting them in and out of office) and, in so doing, to *indirectly shape the political decisions* to which they are subject. Instead of "being ruled" by officeholders, as they would be in a lottocracy, *citizens in an electoral democracy have actual power over their "rulers."* They can (and, in fact, regularly do) remove these rulers from power as part of the process of deciding *which political parties and programs* they favor in any given election.

Most importantly, by choosing some political programs and parties over others (and by being able to change their choices in periodic elections), citizens do more than simply hold officeholders accountable for their individual behavior. Citizens also indirectly *shape and guide* the political decisions to which they are subject toward some ideological direction and away from others. As the saying goes, elections have consequences. Citizens periodically decide among the political agendas and programs of different political parties. Their collective choice gives a stronger or weaker mandate to the winning party and correspondingly empowers or disempowers opposition parties. This in turn determines how far winning political parties can go in implementing their policy agendas and what types of compromises and/or trade-offs will need to be forged with opposition parties, which coalitions to form, and so on. Whereas in multiparty, competitive elections citizens regularly choose among different political projects and agendas (e.g., conservative, progressive, social-democratic, environmental, neoliberal, etc.), citizens in one-party systems do not have *any* say on such fundamental political decisions about the political direction of their government. For Chinese citizens, for instance, "socialism with Chinese characteristics" is the only political program on the table, whether they like it or not. Shaping and guiding the general political direction of their government is an extraordinarily important political power that citizens in electoral democracies collectively exercise as equals. It is not the power *to rule over others* but rather the collective exercise of self-government. This is precisely the power that authoritarian regimes are not willing to share with their subjects. Indeed, they are willing to commit the most egregious human rights abuses to prevent citizens from gaining the power to collectively determine the political direction of their country as equals. It is also the power that participants in democratic movements (from Hong Kong to Myanmar to Thailand, and beyond) are willing to risk their lives for. How can lottocrats be missing it?

Lottocrats downplay the political power that citizens in electoral democracies exercise over decision-making in a variety of ways. First, as discussed above, they rely on a problematic view of representative democracy, according to which the sole function of elections is to give citizens the power to select their rulers. Landemore, for instance, claims that "elections are meant to identify individuals who differ from ordinary citizens by their 'superior' or at least 'extra-ordinary' qualities."[24] She relies on

---

[24] Landemore, *Open Democracy*, 89.

186 The Lottocratic Mentality

Manin's characterization of representative democracy as based on "the principle of distinction." As discussed in Chapter 1, this characterization may accurately describe representative systems in the 18th century, but it is not particularly plausible for multiparty democracies. Before the emergence of multiple, competing national political parties, selecting "representatives" may indeed have been a matter of selecting "superior" individuals. However, in contemporary multiparty democracies, citizens can vote for political parties and programs according to their own political preferences and priorities—even without any knowledge of the specific candidates, let alone a belief that they are "superior" to them. Yet, this outdated view of electoral democracy is quite widespread among lottocrats.[25] Abizadeh argues *explicitly* against the view that elections give citizens any power to influence or shape the political decisions to which they are subject. He argues as follows:

> in representative democracy, elections do not decide legislation or policy: they select those who decide. The significance of this simple fact has not been adequately appreciated in the literature on political equality. One might think elections treat people as equals in their capacity as selectors of officeholders, and helping to select representatives can provide a mechanism for indirectly influencing political decisions. But without imperative mandates, participating in selecting those who decide is not equivalent to participating in deciding legislation or policy.[26]

Abizadeh's argument against the idea that competitive, multiparty elections enable citizens to indirectly influence political decisions seems problematic. Now, there is obviously a difference between being directly involved in making specific decisions and indirectly influencing them. But precisely because they are not the same, pointing out that citizens are not directly involved in making decisions, as Abizadeh does, does nothing to undermine the obvious point that through elections citizens clearly do indirectly influence political decisions by choosing between different political parties and programs. Citizens collectively decide *how much* power representatives of *which* political party have for implementing *their respective political agendas*. They determine which political party wins and which political party (or parties) lose/s,

---

[25] See also Guerrero, "Against Elections," 169. There is a long tradition of *elite democrats* (Schumpeter, Downs, Caplan, Somin, etc.) arguing that citizens are so politically ignorant that they should not make any substantive political decisions. They should only choose among the rulers. Correspondingly, these authors see elections exclusively in terms of mechanisms for leadership selection. But it is important to keep in mind that this is a *normative* recommendation and not a descriptive claim about how actual electoral democracies work (many of which allow for initiatives and referenda). Authors in this tradition are also skeptical of citizens' capacity to impose a *desired* direction on political decisions through elections. A recent defense of this type of skepticism is offered by Achen and Bartels, *Democracy for Realists*. However, these authors do not deny that citizens impose some direction through their votes (after all, it is hard to deny that they do so in initiatives or referenda). What they are skeptical of is that the direction that citizens impose reflects their "real interests," given citizens' massive political ignorance. This is a normative claim that we are not disputing here. We do not mean to deny Achen and Bartels's claim that when ordinary citizens are allowed to shape policy "the results can be distinctly counterproductive" (15). This may be true. But note that this claim *presupposes* rather than *denies* citizens' capacity to shape policy in electoral democracies. Lottocrats seem to deny this capacity.

[26] Abizadeh, "Representation, Bicameralism, Political Equality and Sortition," 796.

how strong a mandate the winning party has, which candidates get power and which candidates lose power, and so on. Their collective choice gives a stronger or weaker mandate to the winning party and correspondingly empowers or disempowers opposition parties. This in turn determines how far representatives of the winning party can go in implementing their political agendas and what types of compromises, coalitions, and trade-offs will need to be forged with representatives of other parties, and so forth.

This is a powerful way in which citizens collectively shape and constrain the political/ideological space within which representatives exercise discretion. The fact that there is no "imperative mandate" does not mean that there is no political mandate at all. This would only be the case if representatives were randomly selected. Whereas randomly selected officials have *total* discretion, elected political parties and officials must operate within the political space that the citizenry has collectively shaped and continues to shape in each election cycle. Far from being a (politically) "blank check," the political decisions of the citizenry shape and constrain the actions of their representatives. It is true that, once elected, representatives exercise (sometimes considerable) discretion and, in so doing, they may disregard citizens' political preferences—though they do so at their own peril. Yet, the representatives voted out of office do not get to exercise *any discretion at all*. Their political agenda is simply "out" and will have to wait for another day. This is a clear way in which citizens' votes positively *influence* political decisions.

Paying attention to the difference between competitive, multiparty elections and "elections" in one-party authoritarian regimes is a helpful exercise in this context. Whereas in electoral democracies citizens have the power to shape political decisions one way or another by choosing between different political parties and programs, in one-party authoritarian regimes citizens are in exactly the situation that Abizadeh describes. They may select "those who decide," but the process of doing so provides no mechanism for indirectly influencing their political decisions. Unfortunately, in a lottocracy, citizens are in the same sad situation. Since there are no political parties and programs for citizens to choose from, those few who are randomly selected make political decisions as they see fit and the rest of the citizenry has no power to shape the general direction of the policies and programs to which they will be subject.[27] This is not to deny that lottocracy would be an improvement over one-party, authoritarian regimes. Equalizing everyone's chances of ruling over time would avoid the formation of a permanent "caste" of rulers. But this improvement is not enough to make lottocracy democratic, as the citizenry does not have any say over the political decisions to which they are subject—only a few randomly selected people have such a say.[28]

---

[27] Lottocrats often highlight the many venues of consultation and advocacy that would allow the citizenry to try to influence the decisions of the randomly selected assembly. However, these opportunities do not change the fact that only the randomly selected members have the power to make decisions as they see fit.

[28] In *Open Democracy*, Landemore suggests that democratic legitimacy does not require citizens to directly authorize their representatives. They can also authorize the use of lottery as a selection mechanism. But this view seems to conflate consent with democratic self-government. Following this view,

188 The Lottocratic Mentality

To sum up, in contrast to electoral democracy, lottocracy fails to realize political equality in two ways. First, in a lottocracy, citizens lack equal ongoing opportunities to influence political decisions by *collectively exercising power as equals*, as they do in elections (under the "one person, one vote" principle).[29] This in turn has problematic consequences for the type of power that they do have opportunities to exercise. Second, since in a lottocracy political power can only be exercised asymmetrically, the fact that everyone has equal chances of "ruling" *does not mean that citizens stand in a relationship of political equality with one another.* To the contrary, it means that they have equal chances to *exercise unilateral power* over others. Since "rulers" are randomly selected, there is no sense in which those "being ruled" can, as is the case in electoral democracies, exercise some degree of political power over them and hold them accountable for the political decisions that they make. To the contrary, they can only blindly defer to their decisions. The power relationship goes in only one direction. By contrast, in electoral democracies, citizens choose their representatives based on political programs and policy objectives and have the power to remove them from office. This establishes a *bilateral* power relationship between them. On the one hand, elected representatives have some degree of discretion in their exercise of political power—and this is as it should be given changing circumstances, the need to negotiate and forge compromises with representatives of other political parties, etc. But, on the other hand, citizens elect their representatives based on the political goals and policy objectives that they are expected to promote. If citizens do not like the political decisions their representatives make or if they simply find other political programs more attractive next time around, then they can vote for other parties/representatives in the next election. Because citizens can exercise political power over their elected representatives, there is a clear sense in which the latter are their delegates, not their "rulers." By contrast, in a lottocracy, citizens can only stand in unequal relationships of power with one another. From a normative point of view, the claim that lottocracy is more consistent with political equality than electoral democracy does not seem very plausible. However, as we mentioned at the beginning, lottocrats offer additional empirical considerations in other to defend their claim. Let's turn to these now.

---

citizens who authorize a dictator to make all political decisions for them would also live in a democracy so long as the authorization is not revoked.

[29] In *Open Democracy*, Landemore illustrates the antidemocratic roots of current representative democracies with references to the American Founders. She indicates that they "famously wanted to create a 'republic,' as opposed to a democracy" (3) and refers to Madison's view of "representation serving to filter and refine the raw judgments of the people" (ibid.) and his claim (in Federalist 63) that the American republic would be characterized "by the total exclusion of the people *in its collective capacity* from any share" in government (4, her italics). We agree that, from a democratic perspective, these are worrisome characteristics. Yet, lottocracy fits this characterization better than electoral democracies. In a lottocracy, the people *in its collective capacity* are excluded from any share in the exercise of power. By contrast, through elections, citizens can exercise power collectively as equals. Second, the reason the people in its collective capacity are excluded from any decision-making authority in a lottocracy is precisely that the few randomly selected members of the assembly can have access to high-quality information and deliberation and thus can "filter and refine the raw judgments of the people" to make better political decisions.

5.3 Would Lottocracies Generate Fewer Political Inequalities Than Electoral Democracies?

Lottocrats admit that in electoral democracies representatives are accountable to citizens whereas they would not be in lottocracies. However, they argue that, in practice, it is very hard for citizens in electoral democracies to hold their representatives accountable because they do not have (and cannot easily acquire) the kind of knowledge and information needed to do so.[30] Consequently, representatives, once elected, often cater to (and are captured by) powerful actors and special interests. Instead of being responsive to the interests, values, and policy objectives of ordinary citizens, their ability to remain in power slowly comes to depend upon appeasing these powerful actors.[31] If that is the case, voting in elections does not *in fact* provide citizens equal opportunities to influence outcomes. This is a serious problem that afflicts electoral democracies where representatives are often "captured" by strong special-interest groups whose support they need for reelection. This in turn generates substantive political inequalities in terms of the outsized power that wealthy elites have to influence political decisions in their favor and the comparative lack of power and inability of ordinary citizens to make sure that their interests and political preferences are reflected in the political decisions to which they are subject. These are well-known problems of electoral democracies. What is new is the claim that lottocracy is a better option for solving them. Let's take a closer look at this claim.

A difficulty in addressing this type of empirical argument is that no lottocracies exist that could be analyzed and compared to existing electoral democracies, so one can at best speculate about whether, if they were ever created, lottocracies would work better or worse than electoral democracies. Yet, even in the absence of empirical examples, it seems counterintuitive to assume that nonaccountable members of lottocratic assemblies would be less susceptible to corruption or capture by powerful actors than elected representatives. Having *no* democratic accountability can hardly be better than having *some* democratic accountability, however deficient it may be.[32] Since citizens cannot hold the randomly selected representatives accountable for their decisions, lottocracy seems likely to fare *worse* than electoral representation in terms of responsiveness.[33] As discussed in Chapter 1, in *Solomonic Judgments*, Elster highlights the lack of accountability to citizens as a strike against selecting representatives by lottery: "having to think about reelection is not simply a source

---

[30] See, e.g., Abizadeh, "Representation, Bicameralism, Political Equality and Sortition," 795; Guerrero, "Against Elections," 140.

[31] See, e.g., Guerrero, "Against Elections," 142; Zakaras, "Lot and Democratic Representation," 455.

[32] Even lottocrats admit that a limited level of meaningful, informed electoral accountability does exist in electoral democracies. See, e.g., Guerrero, "Lottocracy," 79.

[33] In this context, we are focusing on the lottocrats' contention that the ability of citizens to hold their representatives accountable through elections is in fact too deficient to secure that the representatives' decisions are responsive to citizens' interests and preferences. We use the term "democratic accountability" to highlight its connection to *responsiveness* to citizens' political preferences. Electoral democracies and lottocracies can have many other forms of accountability (fiscal, legal, reputational, deliberative, etc.) but, since they are unrelated to the mechanism of elections, they are not the target of the lottocrats' argument that we are discussing here.

190 The Lottocratic Mentality

of vulnerability to special-interest groups. It is also a form of accountability to the electorate without which the temptation to plunder the spoils of incumbency might be overwhelming."[34] Indeed, since lottocratic systems have no accountability-based constraint to prevent officials from taking personal advantage of their position, it seems unlikely that the problem of *capture* could be better solved in a lottocratic rather than an electoral system. To the contrary, such system seems likely to generate powerful incentives for interest groups and partisan elites to try to manipulate lottocratic assemblies.[35] In "Is Random Selection a Cure for the Ills of Electoral Representation?" Landa and Pevnick articulate this point in detail:

> given what is at stake in policy debates, it seems fanciful to expect that simply changing the mechanism for selecting legislators will prevent wealthy and well-organized interest groups from being willing and able to influence what policies emerge from that process with greatest support, even if details of their favored strategies are likely to change ... It is reasonable to suppose, for instance, that representatives who advance the interests of wealthy groups or individuals while in office will be supported by them afterward (perhaps, for instance, through lucrative job opportunities)—as a kind of implicit, if rarely provable, quid pro quo. With this expectation in place, those selected by lottery will have a strong personal interest in catering to the needs of wealthy and powerful groups—indeed, doing so may well be their best strategy for taking personal advantage of having been selected in the lottery. Since lottocratic systems have no accountability-based constraint to prevent officials from using their positions to effectively sell public policy to the highest bidder, *there is no protection from this source of unequal opportunity for political influence.* This is one of the worrisome implications of the deference model, which underlies lottocratic regimes. . . . Whereas elected representatives' desire to stay in office limits the extent to which they can use the powers of public office to reward wealthy supporters at the expense of ordinary voters, winners of lotteries know that they will not hold office in the next period regardless of how they perform. This gives legislators in lottocratic systems a much freer hand than elected officials to "sell" their legislative influence to the highest bidder.[36]

This argument is based on the intuitive idea that the ability to translate social and economic power into political influence is not simply a feature of the mechanism of selecting representatives. Rather, that ability is above all a consequence of social conditions (e.g., social and economic inequalities, freedom of speech, etc.) that will

---

[34] Elster, *Solomonic Judgments*, 89.

[35] For an argument along these lines, see Michael A. Neblo, *Deliberative Democracy between Theory and Practice* (Cambridge: Cambridge University Press, 2015), 181.

[36] Landa and Pevnick, "Is Random Selection a Cure?," 8–11, italics added. In response to this worry, lottocrats could reply that it is possible to introduce mechanisms of accountability, including severe forms of punishment, for abuses of office by randomly selected representatives. However, as Landa and Pevnick plausibly argue, this is likely to affect who is willing to serve in a lottocratic assembly, given the risks attached to do so. This would in turn undermine the claim of descriptive representativeness of the randomly selected assembly on which the case in favor of lottocracy is based. We leave aside the concerns related to the claim of descriptive representation here. These are discussed at length in the next chapter.

be present no matter which selection mechanism is in place. Keeping this in mind, the incentives for preventing capture seem comparatively stronger in electoral rather than lottocratic systems. In addition to the important incentive of reelection, party membership offers additional defenses against capture of elected representatives. Owen and Smith cite the ways in which political party membership reduces the exposure of particular representatives to "external targeting" as a comparative advantage of election over sortition as selection mechanism:

> Sortition is intended to guard against the negative impact of expressions of economic power and social influence, but once members of the sortition chamber are selected, they are vulnerable to traditional lobbying activities that transmit the inequalities of civil society to the formal political domain. They are left exposed in the same way as elected legislators—but without the defenses that membership of a political party can offer. Being a representative who is part of an organized political party reduces the scope of individual discretion over agenda setting, party discipline reduces discretion over voting, and party competition provides incentives for monitoring the conduct of legislators. While parties may undermine the deliberative potential of legislatures, as collective organizations they can, at their best, exercise power over their legislative representatives in ways that counter incentives for external targeting of individual representatives and their susceptibility to such targeting, while the accountability of party leaders to the wider membership acts as an obstacle to successful external targeting of the leadership.[37]

Apart from the incentive structures and constraints to which elected legislators are subject, it is important to also keep in mind that the economic imperatives that condition the political system in each country are a crucial way that economic power translates into political influence. Responsible politicians need to secure economic prosperity, energy and food independence, sufficient tax revenues for addressing social needs and provide essential services, etc. Certainly, different political parties can address these economic imperatives in different ways. But such imperatives are not simply caused by the rent-seeking behavior of representatives, and they would not magically disappear if we used a different mechanism for selecting them. Regardless of how they are selected, the economic power generated by the strategic importance of certain sectors of a country's economy produces opportunities for political leverage that responsible officials can neither ignore nor wish out of existence, no matter how they are selected. This observation is not meant to justify current social and economic inequalities but rather to make it clear that superficial changes in the political system—such as replacing elections with sortition as the selection mechanism of representatives—are woefully inadequate for reducing the inequalities of political influence that result from economic power. Fundamental social and economic changes would be needed instead.

---

[37] David Owen and Graham Smith, "Sortition, Rotation, and Mandate: Conditions for Political Equality and Deliberative Reasoning," in Gastil and Wright, *Legislature by Lot*, 278.

192   The Lottocratic Mentality

There is a different source of inequalities in political influence that may also be worse in lottocracies than in electoral democracies. As discussed in Chapter 1, in *After the Revolution*, Dahl points out how the inevitably lack of continuity across various lottocratic assemblies coupled with the lack of expertise of randomly selected representatives could yield a dramatic and dangerous increase in the political influence of bureaucrats: "If elected officials were all replaced by citizens chosen by lot for short terms, I fear the contest between expert bureaucracies and legislative bodies would be even more unequal than at present. Far from increasing citizen control, as a simplistic advocate of democratization might contend, it would very likely increase the influence of skilled bureaucrats by a wide margin."[38] Similarly, in *Solomonic Judgments*, Elster points out that because of the lack of continuity among randomly selected representatives: "disproportionate power would accrue to the bureaucracy, which would, even more than today, be an element of stability in ceaseless flux of politicians coming and going. On balance, therefore, populist goals would be badly served by the system."[39] Landa and Pevnick explain the problem of *bureaucratic capture* in more detail:

> there are reasons to think that lottocratic systems would be much more vulnerable to bureaucratic capture than electoral systems. This vulnerability stems from the fact that lottocratic systems would typically move representatives in and out of office more frequently than electoral systems (because incumbents would be returned for subsequent terms at far higher rates in electoral systems). Since those selected by lot would have extremely limited knowledge and expertise in particular policy areas, they would be forced to heavily rely on members of the civil service (or lobbying firms) for information about existing laws, their effects, and other important information. Their relative lack of independent information would make it difficult to control the much better-informed bureaucracy. Further, given the short periods for which those selected by lot would hold power, influential members of the bureaucracy would have incentives and ability to resist policy changes that they dislike by dragging their feet or even refusing to implement selected policies, with the knowledge that a new group of officials would soon come to power. While this kind of bureaucratic capture certainly occurs in electoral systems, the quicker rotation of legislators in lottocratic alternatives heightens the problem, again undermining confidence in the view that overall concerns about capture are likely to be less problematic in lottocratic systems.[40]

These arguments are, of course, tentative and cannot be taken to provide conclusive evidence against the claim that lottocracies would generate fewer political inequalities than electoral democracies. A knockdown argument is hardly possible here,

---

[38] Dahl, *After the Revolution?*, 124.

[39] Elster, *Solomonic Judgments*, 89.

[40] Landa and Pevnick, "Is Random Selection a Cure?," 13. For a similar argument, see Stuart White, "Citizens' Assemblies and Republican Democracy," in *Radical Republicanism*, ed. Bruno Leipold, Karma Nabulsi, and Stuart White (Oxford: Oxford University Press, 2020), 91.

not only because no lottocracies exist whose actual workings could be analyzed and compared to the workings of existing electoral democracies, but also because institutions can be modified, complemented, and improved in an almost limitless variety of ways. Since that is true of both lottocracy and electoral democracy, it is simply not possible to provide a final verdict one way or the other. However, what we hope that these arguments show is that it is *far from obvious* that a political system without accountability to the citizenry would in fact better promote political equality and lead to political decisions that are more responsive to citizens' interests and preferences than electoral democracy. In light of this, why are lottocrats not worried about lottocracy's lack of democratic accountability? Why are they confident that lottocracy would nonetheless lead to political decisions that are more responsive to the citizenry than electoral democracy? The key to answer these questions lies in the conception of political representation and the understanding of political decisions that shape the lottocratic mentality and motivate the defense of lottocracy. We now turn to these fundamental questions. The conception of political representation is analyzed in the following chapter, and the conception of politics is analyzed in Chapter 7.

Chapter 6
A Sample Embodying Everyone
A New Populist Conception of Representation

As discussed in Chapter 4, lottocrats reject electoral forms of political representation and interpret representation as a matter of sociological likeness. Selection by lot aims to generate a descriptively representative sample of the population that can be said to represent the people, not because the citizenry has authorized or selected them through the mechanisms of electoral representation, but simply because they are *like* them. Thus, in contrast to the political representation of electoral assemblies, lottocratic assemblies represent the people in the descriptive sense of "mirroring" or "embodying" the people. A brief historical overview of the emergence of representation as political mandate and its contrast with representation as embodiment can be helpful to understand what is at stake in endorsing the latter instead of the former, as lottocrats do.

Embodiment and mirror representation, on the one hand, and mandate representation, on the other, make up the triangulation that portrays the struggle for and against representative democracy. Before elections politicized it, representation was applied to the system of decision (in religious and civic domains) under three guises: juridical, descriptive, and embodiment; none of which entailed a relationship of interdependence through an explicit expression between representatives and represented.[1] As old as the history of sovereignty and the legitimation by popular consent, representation as embodiment takes us back to the Middle Ages, although it never disappeared from the political West.[2] As to the descriptive paradigm, which acquired prominence in the age of representative government, Hanna Pitkin has explained that its character is "being like" and its task is "standing for" or making an absent entity present in a pictorial sense, "a phenomenon which may be accomplished equally well by inanimate objects."[3] Neither embodiment nor mirror is endogenously associated with "acting for."[4] Beginning with the anti-Federalists in the eighteenth century, the principal task of representation as mirroring was that of having people recognize society when looking at the House of Representatives or the

---

[1] Lorenzo Tanzini, "Représentation et décision politique dans les assemblées communales italiennes du 13ᵉ siècle," *Raisons politiques*, no. 72 (2018): 54.

[2] Yves Sintomer, "La représentation-incarnation: Idéaltype et configurations historiques," *Raisons politiques*, no. 72 (2018): 21–52.

[3] Pitkin, *The Concept of Representation*, 11.

[4] Ibid., chap. 4.

The Lottocratic Mentality. Cristina Lafont and Nadia Urbinati, Oxford University Press. © Cristina Lafont and Nadia Urbinati (2024). DOI: 10.1093/9780191982903.003.0007

parliament;[5] this recognition would give them the sense of legitimacy with no need for action. Mirror and embodiment could go thus together, yet not with mandate representation, which was their alter as it required quite explicitly "acting for" by the representatives, a condition that injected advocacy and the quest of responsibility in the political arena, at the state level and society as well. The gap between represented and representatives emerged at that point and became the main difference that would from then on distinguish representation as a mandate from embodiment and mirror. This transformed representation from a mere institution to a political process open to all, in which ideas constructed claims and created constituencies led to the decline of pictorialism and embodiment. At this point, the question became one of "who" should be represented, whether individual citizens (Mill) or "communities and corporations" (Hegel). As soon as it became established through elections, representation as a mandate suffered a split within it between a corporatist and an individualist trajectory. The (partial) solution to this split and the stabilization of representative democracy thereafter came from the leading role of political parties, which made possible a functional mediation between ideas and social divisions, between general and particular interests, individualism and a corporate perspective.[6]

Mandate representation could adjust to both "acting for" and the pluralism of claims from society vindicating action thanks to a broad process of public deliberation and discourse, which became the sole terrain of unification in a political order based on legally free and equal citizens and absolutely equal electors. As discussed in Chapter 4, this was the most important alternative to the kind of society foreshadowed by the mirror strategy: a checkerboard of corporate entities in the ancient regime model before the French Revolution and a balkanized society of ascriptive entities (the estates or *les corps*) that naturally needed a centralized authority to embody the nation. This helps us see how incarnation (or embodiment) and mirror were connected and how they served to contain rather than help the expansion of the right to vote.

As Gregory Conti shows with Victorian England, an argument used against extending the right to vote was that the parliament could be better legitimized by reproducing in miniature those parts of society that more prominently participated in the nation's wealth with trickle-down effects on the excluded.[7] During the Revolution cycle of 1848–1849 in France, embodiment and mirror were claimed by antidemocrats in order to give the people an identity that the National Assembly reflected and a supreme chief embodied.[8] In the fatherland of the *peuple-roy*,

---

[5] As John De Witt said in 1789, summarizing John Adams's ideas, the representative assembly "is the sense of the people, and the perfection of the portrait, consists on the likeness." *The Complete Anti-Federalist*, ed. Herbert Storing, vol. 4 (Chicago: University of Chicago Press, 1981), 3.14.

[6] For a sharp and synthetic overview of the two conceptions of constituency, see Rehfeld, *The Concept of Constituency*, 30–4.

[7] Gregory Conti, *Parliament the Mirror of the Nation: Representation, Deliberation, and Democracy in Victorian Britain* (Cambridge: Cambridge University Press, 2019).

[8] Samuel Hayat, "Incarner le peuple souverain: Les usages de la représentation-incarnation sous la Seconde République," *Raisons politiques*, no. 72 (2018): 137–64.

196   The Lottocratic Mentality

the myth of embodiment met more easily with a pictorial collection of the nation than it did in England. Since the 1830s, the French republicans construed their criticism against embodiment and mirror by denouncing both of them for lacking advocacy: "Here is the monarchy, here is the state of a people which is not represented, of a people that does not appoint its own representatives . . . . To say that we are represented, it is to play with us, it is to insult the nation with an audacious irony."[9] In England on the other hand, a stubborn diffidence toward democratic uniformity signaled a conception of sovereignty that mistrusted political equality in the name of a pluralist corporate society and an idea of representation that pitted mirror against centralized embodiment. In effect, the tension between predemocratic representation (when suffrage was designed to mirror social groups in the parliament) and democratic representation (with the vindication of suffrage as a right) was eloquently visible in John Stuart Mill, who greatly valued the political participation of laborers' and women's social movements, but also thought that only a few virtuous advocates (not yet organized parties, which he despised) would represent them proficiently. Precisely because of the "acting for" that he thought representation should seek to attain, Mill proposed proportional representation, not mirror representation.[10] To him, representation could be neither an issue of identification with the whole people nor an issue of mirroring the people's parts because representation in the assembly required "passionate" and "intelligent" advocates, who were neither blind partisans nor bureaucratic placeholders.[11]

Thus, embodiment and mirror marched together, and universal suffrage never defeated them. They were (and still are) ready to re-emerge every time the decline of advocacy and representativeness plagued mandate representation.[12] The more the parliament became active in lawmaking—and lawmaking achieved prominence in a growing civil society needing more laws and regulations—the more the descriptive aspect of representation was supplemented with advocacy; mirror representativeness was no longer sufficient yet not meaningless either. In effect, the attempt to link "standing for" with "speaking for"—advocacy and representativeness—was (and is) a never-finished work.[13] The more the "voice" of representatives in the parliament acquired prominence, the more the issue of the character and quality of the representatives became relevant. Yet, the more "advocacy" achieved momentum,

---

[9] From a text by Georges Sand of 1848, cited in Hayat, "Incarner," 144 (our translation).

[10] John Stuart Mill, *Considerations on Representative Government* (1861), in *Collected Works*, ed. John M. Robson, vol. 19 (Toronto: University of Toronto Press; London: Routledge and Kegan Paul, 1977), particularly chap. 8.

[11] Ibid., 432.

[12] Phillips, *The Politics of Presence*. On "advocacy" and "representativity" as the character of mandate representation, see Urbinati, *Representative Democracy*, 44–52.

[13] Pitkin, *The Concept of Representation*, chap. 5. More recently, the issue re-emerged in relation to ethnic minorities and unrepresented groups as a form of fair accommodation and justice in representation: Kymlicka, *Multicultural Citizenship*; Williams, *Voice, Trust, and Memory*; Jane J. Mansbridge, "Should Blacks Represent Blacks and Women Represent Women? A Contingent 'Yes,'" *Journal of Politics* 61 (1999): 629–57.

the more descriptive representation proved inadequate, and another form of proximity of the representatives to the represented was needed.[14] The triangulation of parliamentary government—a deliberative assembly, competent speakers, and the public debating and surveilling—showed that proportional representation could be a viable strategy (although not the only available one) to ensure the selection of an engaged few in an electoral environment approximating democracy.[15] In the context of democratization, the "speaker" was meant to perform as an intermediary actor, and at that point a new kind of "similarity," a constructed, not a pictorial one, was needed so that the assembly could perform efficaciously and acquire legitimacy, not because it resembled society but because it acted in its citizens' favor. Preferences and their representations are not "prior to acts of representation" but are constructed by the representative process itself, which acquires democratic significance as it brings citizens to share their interests and demands in response to "political communication that occurs over the course of the representative process."[16] Yet the problems remain and are far from simple because, while it makes a lot of sense to say that "lunatics" are not the best representatives of "lunatics," it makes no sense at all to apply this logic to people whose differences are not a reason for justifying representative paternalism.[17] Representative assemblies that are largely made by one of the two sexes or by the most numerous ethnic groups in a multiethnic nation are short of politically adequate, although formally legitimate. "The underlining preoccupation is not with pictorial adequacy—does the legislature match up to the people?—but with those particularly urgent instances of political exclusion which a 'fairer' system of representation seeks to resolve."[18]

Going back to Pitkin, while she made clear that mirror and embodiment models were endorsed by those who regarded democracy as a poor second best, she made clear the unsolved tension between mandate representation and the other two forms when she argued that in representative democracy, the representatives are authorized (formal representation through elections) and their mandate is to act for the representatives (although within the frame of rights and constitutional limitations) so as to answer to their expressions and claims. The tension between mirroring and constructing representative claims circulates undercurrent in the never-resolved dualism between formal and substantive representation that simultaneously separates and unites assembly and citizens. This tension is kept alive by regular and free elections and moreover by the open and rich public space they set in motion. Yet, none of this is expected to resolve that tension. In the dynamics of participation and representation (which is what we call representative democracy), then both representation as

[14] Mill, *Considerations on Representative Government*, 459.
[15] On parliamentary deliberation in Victorian Britain see also William Selinger, *Parliamentarism: From Burke to Weber* (Cambridge: Cambridge University Press, 2019).
[16] Disch, *Making Constituencies*, 16.
[17] On the example of lunatics representing lunatics, see A. Phillips Griffiths and Richard Wollheim, "How Can One Person Represent Another?," *Proceedings of the Aristotelian Society* 34 (1960): 190.
[18] Phillips, *The Politics of Presence*, 47.

embodiment and representation as mirror are displaced but never entirely erased. What role do they play in representative democracy?

From the moment suffrage became the condition of elections by free and individual choice, representation as embodiment played the function of blocking democracy by means of a charismatic leader claiming to incarnate the whole nation, against and above dissent and participation alike. Starting with the plebiscitary dictatorship of Napoleon III to fascism and the authoritarian regimes of the twentieth century in Europe and Latin America, embodiment representation made this claim successful on several occasions and for a few decades. In contemporary societies thus, if representation as embodiment plays a democratic role, it must be mostly outside the institutions, in the sphere of public discourse and the movements of contestation, like for instance with Occupy Wall Street, which did not claim representation as embodiment when opposed the 99% to the 1%, but used this sociological-embodiment symbolism to denounce the condition of factual lack of representation as advocacy by large sectors of the population. On the other hand, the claim of going back to pictorial representation in order to give voice to underrepresented minorities and recognize their presence in the assembly has also achieved democratic momentum as a form of denunciation that has not been useless at all. The denunciation of the discrepancy between ideas and presence in mandate representation, wherein ideas (party proposals) are no longer or not always capable of being representative of many pressing claims, may be capable of playing the function of vindicating voice and visibility by appealing to forms of pictorial representation (like quota for example or other strategies of special representation). In sum, in representative democracy, embodiment and mirroring are indications of dissatisfaction with and malfunction of political mandate representation. They may thus play an important role in denunciation and emendation and, although they are an alternative to mandate representation, they never disappear.

It is possible to argue, as did the editors of the special issue of *Raisons politiques* dedicated to representation as embodiment, that the current crisis of political mandate representation has a dual face that renders quite well the challenges coming from embodiment and descriptiveness—populism and lottocracy. Embodiment returns not only through the apex figure of the dux incarnatus but also through lottery, a novel and radical contestation of electoral selection that purports itself capable of providing pictorial representation and embodiment. We situate the lottocratic mentality within this context, that is to say, as a challenge of political mandate representation that pivots on the appeal to a new form of embodiment by means of the statistical composition of the pool on which to apply selection by lot. We thus detect two ideas/proposals of embodiment in contemporary democracy, one based on a plebiscitary kind of leadership and the other based on an antileadership descriptive conception of representation, the first populist and the second lottocratic. As discussed in the next sections, for all the differences between populism and lottocracy, their conceptions of representation as embodiment have some striking and worrisome similarities.

6.1 Traditional Populism: The Leader as an Embodiment of the People

In their criticism of representative democracy, populists and lottocrats give themselves two major tasks: (1) seeking unification of the represented with the representative(s), thus avoiding the formation of a political elite; and (2) neutralizing the role of responsibility of the rulers toward the recipients of their decisions. The fulfillment of these tasks defines representation as embodiment, the most radical alternative to political mandate representation, and is what relates populism to lottocracy. Indeed, although they achieve these tasks in different ways—as populism uses elections and rhetoric while lottocracy avoids both of them—they situate the problem of representative democracy in the gap that elections create between the inside and the outside of state institutions. Thus, before turning to embodiment we need to clarify the normative meaning of the gap these critics want to fill since their problematic impact on democracy comes precisely from this move.

The gap that political representation creates between the elected and the citizens is an indispensable condition for institutions and procedures to preserve their impersonality and openness, to remain autonomous from any performing agent including the majority, and to remain a permanent object of control and surveillance by the citizens.[19] The gap that elections create is among the most remarkable aspects of the modern *res publica*. It makes representative democracy a process of continually checking on and blocking the risk that the elected or any ruling agent will capture state power. That this gap is indispensable does not mean that is not open to abuses and corruption or that it does not facilitate representatives' indifference toward their constituents' needs and opinions. But these weaknesses cannot be amended by "shortcuts" of the kind we are discussing here, namely through a providential leader or by taking away the rule of choice in the selection of the decision-makers.[20] Both "solutions" make the problems worse since they disempower the citizens of the opportunity to monitor those who make decisions, to surveille them, and to impose changes in the process if they so wish.

Historically, the representative gap materialized in constitutions written by elected conventions or assemblies and was part of the emancipation of the people from the myth and authority of a lawgiver or an absolute monarch. This process of humanization and immanence of sovereignty made politics open to contestation and conflict and made representation a name associated with constitutional government or power limitation in intensity, performance, and tenure. It engaged philosophers and politicians beginning in the seventeenth and eighteenth centuries and facilitated two revolutionary moves: the denaturalization and depersonification of the sovereign power, and the redescription of politics as a process that belongs to nobody and consists in making, justifying, and remaking laws and decisions—with the citizens

---

[19] Manin, *The Principles*, 174–5.
[20] On lottocracy as "shortcut," see Lafont, *Democracy without Shortcuts*.

200 The Lottocratic Mentality

participating through votes and opinions, elections, and movements in the entire political enterprise. In other words, representation has historically been the means for expunging the category of *possession* from politics, which became ipso facto a process of *making* (creating immaterial things, such as rules and laws) and *instituting* (shaping and stabilizing political and social behaviors through rules and laws).

Institutions and procedures can certainly close off the democratic process to the citizens' will and voice. Claude Lefort grasped this risk when he argued that in a constitutional democracy the sovereign power is a modus operandi that is located neither in an organ nor in a function of the state. Modern democracy was "born from the collective shared discovery that power does not belong to anyone, that those who exercise it do not incarnate it, that they are only the temporary trustees of public authority."[21] This is the democratic credential of representative democracy. Contemporary populism—which we consider a technology of power rather than just a movement of opinion and contestation—wants to reinstall representation as the incarnation of a determined people in a leader; in doing so, it affirms the priority of possession over process and plans to fill the empty space of power by the part of the population that a leader defines as "the people." Populism is a new form of patrimonialism as it were or an appropriation of the levers of politics by those who convince a majority of electors that they embody the "good" people (the characteristic of the "good" people varies from country to country and, as political scientists have shown, tends to include the most distressed parts of a society for reasons as diverse as economic and cultural; the populist people is a recognition of the failure of political parties and more generally of democratic representation). Populism reaches this end by contesting ex ante the inclusiveness and indeterminacy of the people as explained later; hence, the outcome of representation as embodiment (or incorporation) is first the substantializing of sovereignty and second the nullifying of the impersonality of power. Populist leaders consider impersonality as a stratagem that the political elite devises to dominate politics with the acquiescence of the majority and the illusion of holding a limited power. In a speech he gave during the electoral campaign of 1946, Juan Domingo Perón (the father of Argentinian populism) styled himself a *true* democrat, in contrast to his adversaries, whom he accused of being *liberal* democrats: "I am, then, much more democratic than my adversaries, because I seek a real democracy whilst they defend an appearance of democracy, the external form of democracy."[22] According to populists, the kind of democracy elections install produces two ruinous consequences: it pluralizes and therefore weakens popular sovereignty, and it makes the representatives independent of the will of the people, thereby creating a self-referential elite. If elections are an aristocratic selection, as the populist mantra goes, the role of the electors is that of expressing consent through their choice, not that of making their authority prior. The irony is that as we shall see in using elections as a plebiscite the populist leaders are the most consistent

---

[21] Claude Lefort, *Complications: Communism and the Dilemmas of Democracy*, trans. Julian Bourg (New York: Columbia University Press, 2007), 114.

[22] Quoted in Ernesto Laclau, *Politics and Ideology in Marxist Theory: Capitalism, Fascism, Populism* (London: Verso, 2011), 189.

"aristocratic"! After winning the elections in 1949, Péron declared: "We have given the people the opportunity to choose.... The people have elected us, so the problem is resolved."[23]

Criticizing populism's goal does not entail abandoning the normative value of popular sovereignty or dismissing the populist diagnosis of the malfunctions and corruption in representative democracy. The problem is that populism does not solve the decline of democratic legitimacy, nor does it deliver political power back to the people as promised. In effect, it does not eliminate the political elite but substitutes it instead. "The notion that 'the people' are one; that divisions among them are not genuine conflicts of interests but are merely self-serving factions; and that the people will be best looked after by a single unpolitical leadership that will put their interest first—these ideas are antipolitical, but they are nevertheless essential elements in a political strategy that has often been used to gain power."[24]

Who is the "good" or "true" people the populist leader asserts to embody? Populism does not rely upon a normative view of politics and does not accept the people to be a fictio iuris or foundational of the constitutional legitimacy. Populist politics is structurally factional as its dominion is made of two homogenous predefined groups: the ordinary people and the elite; consequently, populist representation is always sectarian because it is either concerned with the interests of those who play politics directly (the few) or it is connected to those whose interests "are disregarded by established elite groups" and unwisely rely on indirect ways of representation like parties.[25] Changing representation from political mandate to embodiment entails bringing the people into politics yet without returning to direct self-government but by using elections as a plebiscitary investiture of the people's leader. Thus, populism aspires to achieve power through electoral competition. But instead of using elections to assess the various representative claims, it uses them as plebiscites that serve to prove the force of the winner to the public and the audience. Elections do not make the majority/opposition divide; they *reveal* instead what already exists: the "good" people waiting to rule and be installed in the state through its leader. Thus, populism consists in dissociating "the people" from any pretense of impartiality and staging the identification of a part (the "good" people) with the legitimate ruler (*the part operates for its own good and although conquers the whole it remains a part nonetheless*). The engine of populist politics is based on this dualism that is rooted in the ideology of the antiestablishment, the engine of populist rhetoric. What legitimates the antiestablishment is the visible status of superiority of one part over the other, which breaks the unity of the sovereign and violates the democratic principle of inclusion. The emotion associated with this hierarchy is resentment of "good" or "true" people toward the few or the elite—a feeling that a representative leader intercepts, exalts, and narrates.

---

[23] Ibid. In a style that reminds us of the constitutions "granted" by kings to their subjects in nineteenth-century Europe, Peron's elections were *octroyées*, or conceded to the people by their paternal ruler; elections played a confirming, rather than a selecting, function.

[24] Margaret Canovan, *Populism* (New York: Harcourt Brace Jovanovich, 1981), 265.

[25] *Oxford English Dictionary*, s.v. "populism."

202   The Lottocratic Mentality

The antiestablishment is the engine that keeps populism alive; in Montesquieu's language, it is the "spirit" of populism and as such it shapes the populist government. It works like an internal frontier that allows the leader to pose the people as a part that defines itself by excluding another part, which is numerically a minority—it does not need to be the richest or more affluent part though because what interests populism is attacking the political elite or the establishment and this can be done quite proficiently by affluent citizens who start their political career as political outsiders and thus as ordinary as any other nonpolitical citizen.[26] The people of the populist leader achieve consciousness of their strength and legitimate request of power by means and through a radical opposition against an externality (the elite) that never disappears and will never be included as such—its persistence is in effect very useful to the populist leader's projects. The residual presence of the elite is never resolved or eliminated although populism in power makes it weaker and humiliates it through propaganda. This dualism and enmity are a rhetorical construction that pivots on a leader who captures the claims of dissatisfied groups and unifies them around and under her or his person and through an alter to be blamed. As discussed above, the validity of this conception is certified by the electoral victory and the support of the people through the entire process. Hence, Ernesto Laclau wrote that all populist governments take the name of their leader. This is the meaning and symbolism of embodiment. "The construction of a popular subjectivity . . . reaches a point where the homogenizing function is carried out by a pure name: the name of the leader."[27] "An assemblage of heterogeneous elements" succeeds when the face of a leader works "a surface of inscription" that literally constitutes the collective. With the decline of the political role of classes and class politics, the disorganization and heterogeneity of society finds its principle of identification in the "name of the leader." This leader carries (out) the people and becomes its voice and figuration.[28]

Based as it is on embodiment, the leader's main plan is that of *remaining close to the people* and filling the representative gap we have defined above—this is the reason of his opposition to party politics and competitive elections that generate it. Representation as embodiment (of the people and the leader) resists relying on intermediary collective actors (parties) and is actualized and managed by the leader herself in a kind of direct representation. If parties exist in a society that is exposed to populist politics, they are structurally weak, elusive, and incapable of attracting the large public and electorate. In effect, as we see in today's populist countries, democracy based

---

[26] A populist leader can be an outsider in relation to an ethnic majority or a ruling elite, as with Alberto Fujimori in Peru and Evo Morales in Bolivia; an outsider in relation to a political (but not social) elite, as with Silvio Berlusconi and Donald Trump; an outsider–insider, as with Jorg Haider of Austria or Corneliu Vadim Tudor, the founder of the Greater Romania Party, or as with an actor who leaves one party to create his or her own, new party, like Fernando Collor de Mello, president of Brazil, or Geert Wilders, the Dutch conservative who established his own populist party. "Populism can be thought of as *politics for ordinary people by extraordinary leaders who construct ordinary profiles.*" Cas Mudde and Cristobal Rovira Kaltwasser, eds., *Populism in Europe and the Americas: Threat or Corrective for Democracy?* (Cambridge: Cambridge University Press, 2013), 78.

[27] Ernesto Laclau, "Populism: What's in a Name," in *Populism and the Mirror of Democracy*, ed. Francisco Panizza (London: Verso, 2005), 40.

[28] Ernesto Laclau, *On Populist Reason* (London: Verso, 2005), 99–100.

on parties is in the minority or it attracts a minority of voters. Not only populism does not revoke elections but actually also uses them to make them do what they are not supposed to do, namely, working like plebiscites, thus showing along with the strength of the leader the meagerness of the opposition and the parties that represent it. Thus, while traditional parties practice elections according to competitive and deliberative means of persuasion that recognize the plurality of options and reasons pro and against and relate to the losers without humiliating them (since they are recognized as possible winners), populist politics is a permanent movement toward overcoming that style through propaganda and rhetoric. A populist majority humiliates the opposition in the attempt to make it powerless and ideally permanently an opposition, yet without revoking elections (a move that would decree a regime change and thus put an end to populism itself along with constitutional democracy). The populist embodiment is primarily a rhetorical fact.

We have seen that the engine of populism is the antiestablishment. But how can the leader avoid becoming part of the establishment once in power? While lottocracy eliminates political accountability at the outset by replacing elections with sortition, populism preserves voter choice but, as discussed earlier, in order to make the electoral investiture the passport to political de-accountability. This is what representation as embodiment is for. Let's explain this puzzle with reference to empirical cases.

The president of Argentina, Juan Domingo Perón, used to say that he wanted to appear pope-like, if needed. "I always follow the rule of greeting everybody because, and you must not forget it, I am now something like the Pope."[29] The president of Venezuela, Hugo Chávez, employed salvific and apocalyptic symbols to prove that the people were the protagonist and the true agent of transformation rather than him who had no will of his own. He asked for lealtad absoluta (absolute loyalty), declaring, "I am not myself . . . I am not an individual, I am the people," and claiming, "Only the people can save the people, and I will be your instrument."[30] In one of the speeches that Donald Trump delivered on the evening of his presidential victory, he said that it was not he who had won and in fact claimed that it was not even he who was talking: the people had won the White House and the people were talking through him that night. Whence this invocation of the populist leader as merely a means?

Claiming to be the voice of the people's will is both a way to seal an alliance with the represented based on faith and a way to anticipate that the leader will never be a new elite anyway. To the contrary, if anything, it will be under the permanent threat of a never disappearing elite. Like the "true prophet" in political theology, the leader claims to have no will of her own (she refuses free mandate, at least in her narrative)

---

[29] Quoted in ibid., 216.

[30] Speech delivered on January 23, 2010; "Chavez exige 'lealtad absoluta' a su liderazgo," *El Nuevo Diario*, January 23, 2010, http://elnuevodiario.com.ni/internacionales/66703-chavez-exige-lealtad-abs oluta-su-liderazgo/. See also Margarita Lopez Maya and Alexandra Panzarelli, "Populism, Rentierism, and Socialism in the Twenty-First Century: The Case of Venezuela," in *Latin American Populism in the Twenty-First Century*, ed. Carlos de la Torre and Cynthia J. Arnson (Baltimore, MD: Johns Hopkins University Press, 2013), 250.

204   The Lottocratic Mentality

but simply be the vessel of the people's will—the mouth from which the vox populi manifests itself directly without the intermission of his will. This is the symbolic of representation as *incarnation* of the people in the leader, the most radical alternative to political mandate representation since it takes away from elections what they are supposed to instantiate: first that no majority is superior, and second that the elected have responsibility toward the electors because they ask for trust not faith, which is a principle of unity but not of representative control. The filling of the gap by the embodied leader brings us precisely to the formidable outcome of exalting the role of the chief by annulling his responsibility.[31]

This makes sense of the authoritarian role that representation as embodiment played in the struggle against parliamentary democracy in the name of the reconstruction of the authority of the state above and against its conflicting parties. We need only mention Carl Schmitt's accusation of the parliament to be an assemblage of elected delegates who bring social and economic interests within the state so as to demote the latter's supreme authority. Plebiscite versus party pluralism is a strategy for unity that translates into a visual reproduction of the whole nation at both the symbolic and institutional levels. "The President, by contrast [to the fragmentation of parliamentary grouping] has the confidence of the entire people not mediated by the medium of a parliament splintered into parties. This confidence, rather, is directly united in his person."[32] We can trace this view directly to populism through Canovan's words: "A vision of 'the people' as a united body implies impatience with party strife and can encourage support for strong leadership where a charismatic individual is available to personify the interests of the nation."[33]

The condition of *incarnation* means that the leader is never truly responsible, for better and for worse. Using elections as a plebiscite it makes the leader not responsible to the voters because a plebiscite is an affirmation of power against the limitations imposed by mandate representation. Populists welcome the overcoming of mandate representation in the name of a more inclusive politics that fills the gap separating the "outside" and the "inside" of the state. In effect, this turns out to be a scheme that allows the leader to avoid responding to the quest for responsiveness by the people, which would be primed to open a breach in the embodiment construct. Accountability is a currency that has no circulation in populism.[34]

To wrap up, embodiment shares with pure delegation with imperative mandate the ambition of preserving the unity between the people and the representative. In addition, it aims at overcoming pluralism in representation. Its goal is to translate proximity into unison and move from communication between elected and electors

---

[31] Sintomer, "La representation-incarnation."

[32] Schmitt, *Constitutional Theory*, 370.

[33] Margaret Canovan, "'Trust the People!' Populism and the Two Faces of Democracy," *Political Studies* 47 (1999): 5.

[34] Many cases of populism seem to confirm that the ability of a dominant personality "to penetrate state institutions [and] shape and contest public policies" is less successful if popular subjects are "relatively autonomous, self-constituted, and mobilized from below." Kenneth M. Roberts, "Populism and Democracy in Venezuela under Hugo Chávez," in *Populism in Europe and the Americas*, ed. Mudde and Rovira Kaltwasser, 143–4.

as in representative democracy to fusion. Its ambition is not to represent citizens' claims and give them advocacy but is to affirm the unity of the collective will above its parts and under the symbolic unifier. Whereas "speaking for" and "acting for" are the characteristics of political mandate through elections, "talking and acting as if" the representative and the people were one is the character of embodiment, whose task is not making citizens partake in the political action of the government but rather subjecting them to it with enthusiasm. "If the main goal to be achieved is the welding of the nation into a unified whole . . . then it is tempting to conclude that a single dramatic symbol can achieve this much more effectively than a whole legislature of representatives."[35] The question is that, as we have mentioned, the main goal of representation is not achieving the unity of the people but giving the people's claims and ideas voice and participation in making and evaluating decisions. It is thus reasonable to say that representation as embodiment is the most prominent reaction against party politics along with mandate representation. Thus, while applicable to a symbolic figure of the nation (like an elected president or a constitutional monarch), embodiment is hardly consistent with parliamentary democracy because it tends toward an *irresponsible leader* who bypasses accountability through a quest of faith in his person, independent of (and at times against) the limits that institutional checks impose on him and also of parties (in effect an instrument in his hand).[36]

Returning to the goal of embodiment as filling the gap that distinguishes/relates representatives and represented, preventing the formation of a representative group of citizens has the effect of annulling the means to contain and control the elected, without reuniting the people with politics. Thus, embodying the people is voiced as *being and acting as* the people but ends by meaning acting *in place of* the people (without this replacement be acknowledged). Representation as embodiment is successful insofar as the people's faith in their leader remains undivided and unreserved; this is of course the opposite of mandate representation, which generates and profits from mistrust and dissent. The engine of populist representation is trust through faith, rather than trust through free and open debate among citizens and between them and their representatives. The continuous flux of judgment and criticism that connects and separates society and institutions—that gap that populists so much despise—is endogenous to representative democracy.[37] Opposite to the populist unison is the osmosis and permanent communication between institutions and society, which was paramount for democratization as marked the transition from representation as giving "presence" (*being like*) to representation as promoting "activity" (*acting with and speaking for*).[38] This is crucial for the perception of accountability, which would be an empty word if it were disconnected from the climate of mistrust and

---

[35] Pitkin, *The Concept of Representation*, 106–7.

[36] Nadia Urbinati, *Me the People: How Populism Transforms Democracy* (Cambridge, MA: Harvard University Press, 2019), chap. 3.

[37] Habermas, *Between Facts and Norms*, 483–8.

[38] Marcel Gauchet, *La révolution des pouvoirs: La souveraineté, le peuple, et la représentation, 1789–1799* (Paris: Gallimard, 1995), 48.

206 The Lottocratic Mentality

denunciation that characterizes a democratic society.[39] The assumption that elections reinforce is that a political leader is not like us anyway, and can be defenestrated; hence, elections are not the mark of an aristocratic tenor as critics of elections claim but the most effective injection of trust/mistrust that keeps democratic politics always open to change. Low faith in political leaders, no matter their claims about being closer to the people than their rivals, is a tonic for mandate representation, but not for embodiment representation, which does not have access to any safety valve against the *capopopolo*.

6.2 Lottocratic Populism: Citizens' Assemblies as an Embodiment of the People

As pointed out in the previous section, the conception of representation deployed by traditional populism is based on the idea of an "embodiment of the people." In contrast to electoral representation, the populist leader does not represent the people in virtue of a political authority that has been transferred to him by the people. To the contrary, the populist claim is that the leader *embodies* the people because she is "one of them," and it is in virtue of this direct, unmediated relationship that the leader can be said to represent the people. This direct relation between the leader and his people is what renders intermediary actors such as political parties, the independent media, institutional rules, the bureaucracy, monitoring agencies, and so on "suspicious." Obviously, the relationship of "embodiment" only makes sense under an assumption of homogeneity. The leader can only be "like the people" if the people themselves constitute a homogeneous, unified body that can stand in a relationship of identity (or at least sufficient similarity) with her so that the claim of embodiment can be justified. If the people were divided in plural or disparate groups with conflicting values, interests, and political objectives then it would be impossible for the leader to simultaneously be *like all of them* in the politically relevant sense. By being *like some* of them, he would necessarily be *unlike others*. It is often noted that this assumed homogeneity is nothing other than a fictional construction of the alleged "real people" by populist leaders themselves—a construction that, in turn, justifies the political exclusion of dissenting minorities by casting them as "the enemies of the people."[40] Be that as it may, what matters in our context is to note that the assumption of *homogeneity* of the people and the attendant *exclusion of heterogeneous minorities* are key components in the idea of "embodied representation."

Now, although lottocracy relies on the populist conception of representation as an embodiment of the people, it also differs from the traditional populist conception in important respects. First, since lottocrats aim at increasing citizen participation in political decision-making, the populist reliance on a leader is wholly absent from the

---

[39] Rosanvallon, *La contre-démocratie*, 19–28.

[40] See, e.g., Jan-Werner Müller, *What Is Populism?* (Philadelphia, PA: University of Pennsylvania Press, 2016), 35, 40, 42.

lottocratic model. Yet, like populists, lottocrats harbor a deep suspicion of political elites and they also "strive to appeal to ordinary people who feel that their concerns are disregarded by established elite groups."[41] Second, from a purely formal point of view, the main difference is that, under the populist model, the representation of the leader supposedly "embodying" the people is a one-to-many relationship whereas, under the lottocratic model, there is a many-to-many relationship in the way that a random sample of citizens supposedly "mirrors the people." This formal difference has significant consequences. While those citizens who cannot see themselves in the leader can quite straightforwardly contest the populist claim that the leader embodies the people because she is "like them," it is trickier to challenge the claim that a random sample of ordinary citizens embodies the people because their members are "like them." This is particularly the case when stratified random sampling techniques are used with the explicit intention of generating a sample that "mirrors the people." Thus, the problematic features of the notion of "embodied representation" are equally operative within lottocratic conceptions but much harder to spot than they are in traditional populist conceptions. No leader, political party, or organization can match the similarity between a stratified random sample of ordinary citizens and the citizenry that they mirror. Indeed, precisely because random samples of ordinary citizens are so much *like* the rest of the citizenry that they mirror, they harbor the possibility of becoming the "ultimate usurpers." In what follows, we explore this worry through a close analysis of the specific features of the notion of "embodied representation" that underlies lottocratic conceptions of democracy and its potential negative consequences.

6.2.1 Citizens-Representatives: The Ultimate Usurpers?

Although the notion of a "citizen-representative" is essential to the lottocratic model it has not yet been fully accounted for.[42] For instance, it is unclear how a citizen can simultaneously play the role of a citizen and a representative with respect to one and the same political decision. Are citizens-representatives supposed to act in the role of citizens who speak for themselves and who only represent themselves, or are they supposed to act as political representatives of all those who are *like them* in a descriptive sense? It is also unclear which obligations citizen-representatives have toward the rest of the citizenry who do not participate in the decision-making process. Can they be meaningfully accountable to nonparticipants while continuing to exercise their rights as citizens to make their own free decisions? If they are not, in which sense can they be taken to represent "the people"? Our analysis does not aim to answer these intricate questions. We mention them only to indicate that, until we have such answers, the democratic credentials of the lottocratic

---

[41] *Oxford English Dictionary*, s.v. "populism."
[42] For some interesting work, see Brown, "Citizen Panels and the Concept of Representation"; Warren, "Citizen Representatives"; Landemore, *Open Democracy*.

208 The Lottocratic Mentality

conception of representation cannot be properly evaluated. In the absence of such answers, we would like to explore the worrisome implications involved in the notion of "embodied representation" that underlies the lottocratic conception.[43]

According to the lottocratic conception of "embodied representation," citizens should accept the decisions of lottocratic assemblies because the participants are *like them*. Since participants are ordinary citizens, they can "speak *like* the people rather than *for* them."[44] In other words, lottocratic assemblies should have decision-making authority not because the citizenry has authorized or selected them through the usual mechanisms of electoral representation. Instead, they should have such authority simply because they are a "mirror of the people." Guerrero justifies the lottocratic claim of representation on this basis. He explains that members of the type of lottocratic assemblies that he favors "will be—at least over a long enough run—broadly descriptively and proportionately *representative of the political community, simply because they have been chosen at random*."[45] Since those who are randomly selected "mirror the people" we can expect that their political decisions will reflect the interests of the people. The more representatives descriptively resemble their constituents the more likely it is that they will make political decisions that are *responsive* to citizens' interests, instead of serving the particular interests of the elites. Abizadeh explains this connection as follows: "sortition selects for a gyroscopic set of representatives collectively disposed to act in constituents' interests *because* random selection tends to produce an assembly that, if large enough, is descriptively representative of them."[46] In sum, citizens should accept the decisions of the randomly selected assembly because their members are *like them*. In *Is Democracy Possible?*, John Burnheim makes this lottocratic claim explicit:

> Let the convention for deciding what is our common will be that we will accept the decision of a group of people who are well informed about the question, well-motivated to find as good a solution as possible and representative of our range of interests *simply because they are statistically representative of us as a group*. If this group is then responsible for carrying out what it decides, the problem of control of the *execution* process largely vanishes. (124–5; our italics)

Whether using pure random selection or applying techniques of stratified random sampling, the idea is to generate a descriptively representative sample of the population so that it can be assumed that their views, interests, and values reflect those

---

[43] We take the expression "lottocratic representation" from Landemore, *Open Democracy*, 80.

[44] See Yves Sintomer, "The Meanings of Political Representation: Uses and Misuses of a Notion," *Raisons politiques* 50, no. 2 (2013): 21. For an empirical study testing the hypothesis that citizens think that minipublics participants are "like them" and the consequences for legitimacy, see James Pow, Lisa van Dijk, and Sofie Marien, "It's Not Just the Taking Part That Counts: 'Like Me' Perceptions Connect the Wider Public to Minipublics," *Journal of Deliberative Democracy* 16, no. 2 (2020): 43–55. For a discussion of their findings, see Cristina Lafont, "Against Anti-democratic Shortcuts: A Few Replies to Critics," *Journal of Deliberative Democracy* 16, no. 2 (2020): 101–3.

[45] Guerrero, "Against Elections," 159, our italics.

[46] Abizadeh, "Representation, Bicameralism, Political Equality and Sortition," 798; McCormick, *Macchiavellian Democracy*, vii.

of the citizenry at large. In addition, since the members of the lottocratic assembly have access to high quality information and have the opportunity to deliberate under good epistemic conditions, it can also be assumed that their judgments after the deliberative experience reflect *what the people would think if they were informed and had the opportunity to properly deliberate about the matter.* They represent "the considered judgments of the people."[47] This view is often associated with a selection model of representation in contrast to a sanction model.[48] Whereas a sanction model expects representatives to accurately track the views of their constituents on pain of losing their office, a selection model expects constituents to choose representatives with interests, values and objectives that are largely aligned with their own such that representatives have self-motivated, exogenous reasons to enact their constituents' will.[49]

In our context, the question is whether the selection model's characteristic congruence or "match" between the interests and values of representatives and those of the citizens who select them also holds between the interests and values of those in the stratified random sampling group and those of the nonparticipating citizens that the sample "mirrors." Since the lottocratic proposal is justified on the grounds that its participants are *like us* (or at least more like us than political elites, interest groups or other political actors in electoral democracies) we need to examine this assumption of *congruence.* There are several claims involved in this argument.

Participants in lottocratic assemblies can be said to be *like us* in that they are ordinary citizens. Thus, in contrast to politicians, lobbyists, and other political actors they are unlikely to have hidden agendas or conflicts of interest in their deliberations about the public interest. We can trust them as our representatives in that we do not need to monitor them or threaten them with sanctions because they are independently motivated to figure out what's best for the polity. However, following the selection model of representation, it is claimed that participants in lottocratic assemblies are *like us* in a *stronger* sense as well: they supposedly share our interests, values, policy objectives, and so on.[50] This is why we are supposed to trust them not only in that we do not need to threaten them with sanctions to keep them accountable,

---

[47] Fishkin, *When the People Speak*, 28. In this and the following sections, we draw from Lafont, *Democracy without Shortcuts.*

[48] For an in-depth analysis of the contrast between the selection and sanction models of representation, see Jane Mansbridge, "A 'Selection Model' of Political Representation," *Journal of Political Philosophy* 17, no. 4 (2009): 369–98. For the contrast between the selection and sanction models regarding minipublics such as Deliberative Polls, see Jane Mansbridge, "Deliberative Polling as the Gold Standard," *The Good Society* 19, no. 1 (2010): 55–62. For an interesting analysis of the contrast between these two models of representation under the rubrics "responsive" and "indicative," see Pettit, "Representation, Responsive and Indicative."

[49] Mansbridge, "A 'Selection Model,'" 371. It is important to keep in mind that both the selection and the sanction models are *electoral* models of representation whereas in the case of minipublics, there is no election involved at all, i.e., citizens do not select any of the participants. For an application of the selection or "indicative" model of representation to randomly selected bodies such as minipublics, see Pettit, "Meritocratic Representation."

[50] As Mansbridge indicates with respect to the alignment of objectives between agent and principal under the selection model, "the alignment of objectives can take place not only on the high ground of similar understandings of what is best for the nation as a whole but also on what is best for particular individuals or communities such as farmers, miners, or inner-city residents" ("A 'Selection Model,'" 380).

210 The Lottocratic Mentality

but also in a stronger sense where we assume that their decisions *coincide with what we would have decided if we had participated*. Guerrero argues along these lines to answer the pressing question of why the citizenry should accept the decisions of the lottocratic assemblies:

> The hope is that if SILLs [single-issue lottery-selected legislature] are seen as descriptively representative—and if those chosen are seen as indicative representatives—even those not selected to participate will see the decisions arrived at as the product of a well-designed process. And they might reason that although they do not have the same view on the issue, *someone who is in important respects like them* (from their neighborhood, profession, and so on) has come to that view after hearing from experts and talking with others, after having devoted time and thought to the problem—and that *this provides a powerful reason for them to think that they would have that view if they had gone through the same process. This provides a basis for them to accept the ultimate decision*, even if it differs from their initial view.[51]

Now, the *stronger* mirror claim that Guerrero defends here seems problematic. Unless one makes the highly implausibly assumption that lottocratic assemblies will invariably reach unanimous decisions, regardless of the issue at stake, the expectation of congruence is obviously unfounded. Indeed, since there is so much ethical and political disagreement among citizens in pluralistic societies the stronger mirror claim can hardly be true of a genuinely representative sample of the population. The more that diverse evaluative perspectives (concerning need interpretations, value orientations, worldviews, etc.) are included in the sample, the less sense it makes for nonparticipant citizens to assume that their own interests, values, and political objectives will invariably coincide with those of *the majority of the sample* regardless of the issue. Nonparticipants cannot assume that the decisions of the majority of the assembly reflect what *they would have thought if they had participated*. For, in principle, the opposite is equally possible. After all, the dissenting minority has reviewed the same information and deliberated as much as the other members and yet reached the opposite conclusion. Even if citizens can trust that all participants were genuinely interested in figuring out what is best for the polity, they know that in pluralistic democracies there is ongoing contestation over a variety of social, moral, ethical, religious, and economic views and values, and that this significantly influences political questions and policy objectives. Far from constituting a homogeneous body, citizens in pluralist societies committed to maintaining free institutions have ongoing political disagreements with their fellow citizens.

In pluralist societies, the selection model of representation seems plausible at a smaller scale. Citizens can trust some political party, civil society organization, or other individuals who share their interests, values, and policy objectives. But, for that same reason, it would not make sense for them to also trust those political parties,

---

[51] Guerrero, "Against Elections," 171–2, our italics.

organizations, and other individuals that endorse the opposing views, values, and policy objectives, whatever those may be. If I trust Oxfam's recommendations on poverty relief then I cannot also trust the countervailing recommendations of, say, the Chamber of Commerce. If I trust Planned Parenthood's recommendations on women's reproductive health then I cannot also trust the opposing recommendations of, say, the Pro-life Action League. Since I cannot simultaneously trust the conflicting views, values, and policy objectives of all these different actors, I also cannot trust the decisions of the majority of the lottocratic assembly without first knowing whether *they took the side in the political spectrum that I would have taken if I had participated.*

Of course, if the background policy information and the content of the deliberations are made public then citizens could check whether this is the case. But, once they do, *many* citizens will predictably find that the majority of the sample is *not like them*, since they actually oppose their views, values, and policy objectives on the issue in question. At this point, the claim that nonparticipants should accept the decisions of the lottocratic assembly *because* their participants are *like them* predictably collapses. For the fact that the random sample is a microcosm of *the people taken collectively* means that, with respect to contested issues, there will be a majority defending one view and a minority defending the opposite view. This means that it cannot be true of *all the people considered individually* that the majority of the sample is *like them*. But if this is so, then in what sense can we say that sample participants are *their representatives*? If the majority of the sample is neither *like* them nor *accountable to* them then, what is the justification for expecting nonparticipating citizens to *blindly defer* to the decisions made by *this majority*? Since citizens have not selected their own representatives to participate in the assembly none of them has any reason to assume that the views of either the majority or the minority are those that coincide with what they would have thought if they had been informed and thought about it on their own.

But let's consider an alternative argument that Guerrero does not offer.[52] In contrast to the standard selection model of representation where citizens choose their own representatives according to their own interests, values, and policy objectives, perhaps the argument regarding lottocratic assemblies is not that citizens should accept the decisions of the majority because they are *like them*, as Guerrero argues, but rather because they are *like the majority of the people*.[53] If this were the case, then

---

[52] Since this chapter concerns the lottocratic conception of representation, here we only analyze lottocrats' justifications for why citizens ought to accept the decisions of the lottocratic assembly that are based on the representative links between assembly members and the rest of the citizenry. In the next chapter, we will address lottocrats' justifications related to the high epistemic quality of lottocratic assembly's decisions. This type of argument may be implicit in Guerrero's contention that nonparticipating citizens will see the decisions arrived at by the lottocratic assembly "as the product of a well-designed process" ("Against Elections," 172). We are grateful to Ryan Pevnick for pointing out this possible reading of Guerrero's argument.

[53] It is hard to think of any interpretation of the selection model of representation according to which it would be plausible to claim that citizens should trust that the considered opinion of a majority of random others will invariably coincide with what they would have thought if they had been informed. For an analysis of the difficulties of this claim, see Lafont, "Deliberation, Participation and Democratic Legitimacy," 54–7. Yet, regardless of whether this view of representation could be considered plausible, the problem in our context is that the "modified" mirror claim on which it is based is false. In the postdeliberative

212   The Lottocratic Mentality

the democratic legitimacy of majority rule could provide a reason for acceptance. Citizens whose views, interests, and values, are aligned with those of the dissenting minority in the lottocratic assembly would accept the assembly's decisions, not because it is the decision that they themselves would have made if they had participated, as Guerrero and other lottocrats contend, but simply because they have been outvoted by the majority. Yet, this argument only works if it is the case that the majority of the assembly is like the majority of the people.[54] But are they?

6.2.2 Are the Majority of the Lottocratic Assembly Like the Majority of the People? The Problem of Blind Deference

Before the deliberative experience, it may be trivially true to claim that participants in the lottocratic assembly were *like the people* in that the views of the random sample were likely to reflect the views of the whole population. This is why regular polls can be used to (more or less reliably) track the views of the people despite the fact that only a handful of randomly selected citizens are actually interviewed. However, once the "deliberative filter" is deployed, the views of participants undergo significant and at times drastic transformations. As a consequence of getting better informed and of having a chance to deliberate with their fellow citizens under good conditions, participants often change their minds on important political issues.[55] But, precisely for that reason, it would be a clear case of usurpation to claim that the voice of the participants in the lottocratic assembly after deliberation is the voice of "the people,"[56] especially in those cases when they are on record as *dissenting from the actual people* about the issues in question. The populist temptation to "speak for the people" is common among political actors of all kinds, but the blatant dissimilarity between populist actors and the *actual people* helps to undermine such claims. By contrast, the similarity between the participants in the lottocratic assembly and the people at the initial, predeliberative stage makes their dissimilarity at the *empowered stage* harder to spot. As mentioned before, for that reason they could become the "ultimate usurpers." Let's see why.

---

empowered stage, often the majority of the sample *no longer mirrors the opinions of the majority of the people.*

[54] To see why this is so, the analogy of an authoritarian one-party system that makes political decisions by majority rule among the members of the ruling party is helpful. The reason why merely using majority rule fails to confer democratic legitimacy to the decisions of that type of political system is precisely that there is no reason to assume that the views of the majority of the party members coincide with those of the majority of the citizenry.

[55] For a variety of examples, see Fishkin, *Democracy When the People Are Thinking.* An example that he discusses at length concerns a dramatic change of opinion (a drop of support from 69% to 35%) among minipublics' participants regarding legislation to privatize the Japanese pension system (172–3).

[56] Although this claim is often made. See, e.g., Crosby and Nethercut, "Citizen Juries"; Fishkin, *The Voice of the People*; Fishkin, *When the People Speak*, 176, 196. Since Deliberative Polls often use a control group to track changes of opinion after deliberation, Fishkin's claim that the voice of the deliberative participants is "the voice of the people" is particularly implausible when such changes of opinion occur. Thanks to Fishkin's accurate tracking, we know perfectly well that the views of the people are those of the control group, not the deliberating group.

Participants in the lottocratic assembly are supposed to be representative of the citizenry at large in the *descriptive* sense of the term. Unfortunately, this is true (if at all) only with respect to the "raw" opinions they have *before* the deliberative process since the whole point of going through that process is to elicit a transformation of their initial judgments into qualitatively different judgments that are *for this very same reason* no longer representative of the actual views of the citizenry. Indeed, participants are supposed to make up their minds based on the information available and the deliberative process itself. Thus, they are not supposed to act as representatives of the groups that they represent in a descriptive sense. There is no sense in which female participants are supposed to defend the views of women or Californians the views of other Californians. They participate as individual citizens with total freedom to express whichever views and opinions they have and to change them in whichever way they see fit. As ordinary citizens, they represent only themselves. But, *for that very same reason*, they are in no way accountable to citizens outside the lottocratic assembly. The reason lies in the peculiar nature of representation involved in random selection.

To the extent that the randomly selected sample is supposed to "mirror the population" as a whole, their members are taken to be *reliable indicators* of the considered judgments of the citizenry (i.e., what the citizenry would think about a particular political issue if they had the chance to become informed and had deliberated under good conditions).[57] But, precisely for that reason, there is no space left for nonparticipants to hold the participants in the lottocratic assembly to account for their decisions any more than one can hold a thermostat to account for the temperature that it reliably indicates. Moreover, since the decisions of the lottocratic assembly are not supposed to reflect the actual judgments of any particular citizen or group but instead the considered judgments of the people as a whole, the fact that any number of nonparticipants disagree with these decisions would offer no basis for questioning the reliability of the participants in the lottocratic assembly. After all, they are not selected to reliably indicate actual but rather *counterfactual* public opinion, i.e., what the people *would think* if they were well informed and had thought about the matter under good conditions. If they are "accountable" to anyone at all then it would be to the counterfactual citizenry whose considered judgments they are supposed to mirror or reliably indicate, not to the actual citizenry. The problem here is that the deliberative "filter" undermines the "mirror" claim. Precisely because the members of the lottocratic assembly are better informed and have had the opportunity to deliberative under good conditions, their judgments no longer "mirror" those of the citizenry. Consequently, there is no good reason to expect that the judgments of the majority of the lottocratic assembly will coincide with those of the majority of the people. We are left yet again without a justification for the claim that citizens should blindly accept the decisions of the lottocratic assembly, especially when the majority of the citizenry actually opposes these decisions. If the lottocratic assembly

---

[57] See Pettit on "indicative" vs. "responsive" representation in Pettit, "Representation, Responsive and Indicative" and "Meritocratic Representation." Also Guerrero, "Lottocracy," xx.

is allowed to make decisions against the opinions and will of large majorities, then the legitimacy of majority rule cannot be used to justify the expectation of blind acceptance of the decisions of the lottocratic assembly nor can the lottocratic assembly's authority be justified on the democratic ground of its responsiveness to the people's demands.

Precisely because lottocrats expect the lottocratic assembly to make better, more informed decisions than ignorant citizens, the question of whether and why citizens would blindly *accept* decisions that they cannot identify with and may be directly against their own views, interests, and policy objectives becomes all the more pressing. Guessing the best answers to political questions is one thing, and getting the citizenry to comply with them *against their own opinions and will* is quite another. Lottocrats seem to assume that, once decision makers hit on the right political answers, agreement by decision-takers will simply follow. This assumption eliminates a task (and an epistemic dimension) of political deliberation that is quintessential to democracy, namely, the need to reach agreement with others by justifying political decisions to them with reasons that they can reasonably accept so that they can identify with them and endorse them as their own. The latter task, however, is crucial to the aim of reaching better political outcomes. Whereas it is an open question how inclusive deliberation ought to be in order to best fulfill the epistemic function of figuring out the best answers to political questions, it is quite clear that only fully inclusive deliberation can fulfill the epistemic function of tracking the justifiability of the policies in question to all those who must comply with them and without whose cooperation many of the policies' intended outcomes will not materialize. Thus, if the goal is reaching better political outcomes, and not just guessing the best answers to political questions (according to someone or other), then bypassing the citizenry and expecting them to simply defer to the decisions of the majority of the lottocratic assembly is simply not an option. In a lottocracy, the bulk of the citizenry may be excluded as decision-makers, but they cannot be excluded as decision-takers. It takes two to tango. To reach sufficient acceptance and compliance, citizens need to be convinced that the sacrifices, the trade-offs, and the general impact of the laws and policies in their life choices and opportunities are necessary, fair, reasonable, or whatever the case may be. They need to be convinced so that they do their part and the expected policy outcomes materialize. Unfortunately, convincing just a random sample of the citizenry will not do. However, once we account for the epistemic aim of justification toward those who must do their part in realizing such outcomes, it becomes clear that the proper scope of deliberative inclusion is not just the few randomly selected members of the assembly but the set of citizens to whom justification for their compliance is owed, namely, the citizenry as a whole.

In sum, the problem with claiming that nonparticipating citizens should accept the decisions of the lottocratic assembly *because* the random sample is *like* them is that this claim is incompatible with the claim that the random sample mirrors "the people." Indeed, the more plausible the mirror claim is—the more the sample descriptively resembles the plurality of views, interests, and values of the population—the less it can be the case that all nonparticipating citizens are *like* the majority and unlike the minority of the sample. Thus, *the mirror claim cannot justify a blanket recommendation to accept the decisions of the majority of the lottocratic assembly.*

This difficulty points at a problematic feature of the notion of "embodied representation" that we highlighted in the previous section. In order to assume, as lottocrats do, that the decisions of the majority of the lottocratic assembly invariably reflect what is in the best interest of "the people," and should therefore be blindly accepted by the citizenry at large, one would need to embrace the exclusionary majoritarianism characteristic of populism and assume that the interests and values of the disagreeing minority in the lottocratic assembly are *not congruent* with those of the "real people" and should therefore simply be rejected or disregarded by the citizenry. Without the populist assumption of *homogeneity* of interests, values, and political objectives among the people and the attendant *exclusion of heterogeneous minorities* as contrary to the interests of the real people, the conception of representation as embodiment cannot do the justificatory work that lottocrats expect it to do.

6.3 What's Wrong with Lottocratic Representation?

Lottocrats claim that a lotted assembly can effectively represent the entirety of the people because of the way sortition works. If random selection makes sure that all parts of the society are proportionally represented, then the assembly is like a bonsai, a miniaturized mirror of the whole, or a statistical sample that is accurate in relation to the entire citizenry. The dimension or scale changes but not the composition. Now, suppose I try to identify those members of the lotted assembly that "mirror" me. What should I look for? A senior citizen, a white middle-class woman, an academic, or an atheist? These questions point toward a panoply of problems that are bound up with the ascription of lotted persons to groups; in particular, with the underlying assumption that citizens' social and political perspectives are just a function of their ascriptive characteristics (i.e., conventional identity markers such as gender, profession, geographical location, etc.). Discussing the example of citizen panels, Mark Brown summarizes the obvious difficulties with such an attempt:

> First, any particular panel member will belong to multiple statistical categories, and it is impossible to know in advance how particular individuals rank their various identities in their self-conception and behavior. Second, one can always find people who experience themselves as members of a social group but lack at least some of the allegedly group-defining attributes and vice versa. Third, casting panelists selected on the basis of their social identity as representatives of group interests falsely suggests that people are only capable of representing the interests of their own social group. Fourth, even people who define themselves as members of a particular social group may differ greatly in their political values and interests. And finally, assuming that participants have fixed interests associated with particular social categories forecloses the very process of informing and transforming

216   The Lottocratic Mentality

interests that deliberation aims to foster. In short, not all identity groups are interest groups, and group identity often exists prior to and conflicts with any sense of shared interest.[58]

As these difficulties make clear, the problem with the lottocratic conception of representation as an "embodiment of the people" is that it essentially depends on an assumption of homogeneity. Only if "the people" are homogeneous (or composed of distinct homogeneous groups) does the idea of "mirroring the people" with a randomly selected sample make sense at all. This essentialist idea is reminiscent of the ancient regime's "estates," which represented their members as if they were identical (in ideas, interests, and values). In July 1789, the French Revolution started when one of the three estates summoned to the general assembly objected to the procedure of deciding by group (one vote, one estate). These dissenters refused to think of all eligible voters as being synonymous with the ascriptive features of an estate. Instead, they claimed that each individual person was entitled to a vote. This was a revolutionary conceptual move because it defied the principle of ascription and the logic that went along with it. Instead, it inaugurated a new way of thinking: When I vote, I am a citizen with the complexity that belongs to me. I freely decide which part of that complexity is politically relevant to me; the assembly does not mirror any of the parts that compose me. Indeed, I might have so many identities or be part of so many groups that no aggregative microcosm can represent them all. Any "mirroring" achieved by random selection mechanisms is partial, and it is partial in a way that is decided by a statistician rather than by me. By contrast, the principle of "one person, one vote" reflects the fundamental complexity and political freedom of citizens. When I vote for a political party or program, I get to decide what my political priorities, my values, and my policy objectives are in the context of the current political situation, and so do my fellow citizens. Thus, in representation by election the parliament is not representative of the nation, and it does not act in the name of citizens *because* it "mirrors" the parts of the nation. Rather, it is representative because it is an expression of the *political will of the citizenry* at the exact moment of the election. By choosing representatives based on their political programs and agendas, citizens collectively shape the political space within which their representatives must operate until the next election. This fundamental political decision is made by the citizenry, not by their representatives. The political composition of the elected assembly reflects *the political will of the citizenry*. Alarmingly, in a lottocracy, it is the other way around. The lottocratic assembly reflects *the political will of its members* who have absolute discretion to make political decisions as they see fit, whereas the citizenry has no say and no power to make any decisions. As Guerrero tellingly indicates, members of lottocratic assemblies "would be instructed to do what they think is best with regard to the particular policy question, after having heard from experts, stakeholders, members of the community, and other SILL members. They would not be required to see themselves as 'representatives' of any particular community

---

[58] Brown, "Citizen Panels and the Concept of Representation," 218.

or group."[59] But if members of the lottocratic assembly are not representatives of any particular community or group, it is unclear how citizens from such communities or groups can see them as anything other than usurpers of their sovereignty.

This democratic worry is absent from the lottocratic mindset because of the assumption of homogeneity at the core of the conception of representation as embodiment. For, of course, only if the citizenry is politically homogeneous, and only if the interests, values, and policy objectives of the random sample coincide with those of the citizenry at large, does it make sense to assume that the former will make the *same decisions* as the latter because they are *like* them. This is why citizens supposedly do not lose democratic control by blindly deferring to the lottocratic assembly's decisions. Like populism, lottocrats traffic in the mistrust of "political elites." On their view political conflicts, polarization, and contestation are basically blamed on the corrupting influence of elites trying to make their particular interests prevail in the political process. In contrast to the elites, the members of the lottocratic assembly are *like* their constituents and, for that reason, are "collectively disposed to act in constituents' interests" (Abizadeh). This, in turn, is why the citizenry can blindly trust them to make the right political decisions for them.

It is important to note that rejecting the lottocratic conception of representation does not mean rejecting demands for greater representation of marginalized groups. These justified demands can be properly addressed without undermining the priority of political representation and going back to a retrograde model of representation based on ascriptive characteristics. When excluded or marginalized groups (women, indigenous groups, religious minorities, African Americans, Hispanics, etc.) demand greater representation, even quotas—whether in political party lists, government, the courts, corporate boards, or sports committees—they are not thereby questioning the priority of political representation or demanding that it be replaced by descriptive representation. Rather, they are demanding that this dimension should also be included within the existing structure of representation. This is perfectly compatible with prioritizing whichever selection criteria are deemed most appropriate in each context (political orientation, competence, experience, etc.) while demanding that, among the candidates who meet the criteria in question, choices are made to ensure that the composition of the group reflects the diversity of the relevant population.

By contrast, lottocrats who advocate using lottery to select political representatives are asking for a return to the obsolete model of representation based on ascriptive characteristics. Indeed, the proposal of subsuming citizens into predetermined groups (using stratified random sampling) is retrograde from a democratic point of view since it robs them of the political agency that universal suffrage gave them (with the principle of "one person, one vote"). Instead of citizens choosing their representatives based on the political programs and agendas that they favor, they should let themselves be represented by a random sample of individuals who are supposed to be *like them* in virtue of their ascriptive characteristics. The fundamental problem with this assumption of homogeneity is that it obliterates political freedom.

---

[59] Guerrero, "Lottocracy," 17.

Indeed, if citizens are free to shape their social world in genuinely different and mutually incompatible ways, regardless of their ascriptive characteristics, then it is to be expected that, under conditions of freedom, they will develop different and mutually incompatibles ideas, interests, values, and policy objectives. In that case, who should decide the political direction of their community from among the many possible alternatives? Who should set the political agenda? The democratic response is that the citizenry should be able to make these consequential decisions. After all, they are the ones who are collectively taking the risks involved in such decisions and who will have to live with the consequences. In electoral democracies, citizens make that decision collectively as equals by choosing among different political parties and programs during periodic elections under the "one person, one vote" rule, whereas in authoritarian regimes the citizenry has no say whatsoever in this dimension. But if the latter system is deemed undemocratic for that reason, then how can lottocracy be democratic if the few members of the lottocratic assembly are the only ones in charge of setting the political agenda and the rest of the citizenry has no say? The assumed homogeneity among citizens' interests is again the answer. Under the assumption that the citizenry shares homogeneous interests and values, it is sufficient if a few randomly selected people do the thinking, deliberating, and deciding for the rest of the citizenry who do not need to form their own political opinion and will. Reaching political goals does not require that citizens resolve political conflicts among themselves, convince one another, or change one another's hearts and minds. All that is needed is the disposition and the epistemic resources to figure out the best political decisions. Consequently, any random sample of the citizenry can get the job done equally well. The flipside of a homogeneous citizenry is a depoliticized conception of politics. As discussed in the next chapter, this is the missing piece without which the lottocratic puzzle cannot be solved.

Chapter 7
The Technocratic Conception Of Politics

Within the lottocratic mentality, politics is conceptualized as problem-solving. Answers to political questions are ultimately a matter of *knowledge*: of knowing what the world is like and, based on that, finding out the right solutions to objectively existing problems.[1] Lottocrats take political questions to be just like technical and moral questions that have a single right or best answer. They often endorse "epistemic democracy."[2] This is a view broadly characterized by three core assumptions, namely (1) political questions have single right answers, (2) there is a procedure-independent standard by which we can evaluate whether a political decision is right or wrong, and (3) democratic procedures tend to track the "truth" (or what is "right," "correct," etc.). Within this conceptual framework, the actor who ought to have decision-making authority is simply whoever is most likely to make the right decisions. Indeed, so long as the right decisions are made, it does not matter so much who makes them. Anyone who can reliably identify the right or best solutions to the problems we face would be as good as any other.

It is important to note that challenging the technocratic assumption that all political questions have a single right answer does not entail endorsing the opposite view that no political questions have right answers. It may be the case that some of them do, and others do not. For example, it may be true that within the domain of what is morally required whether a political decision is right or wrong does indeed have a single answer whereas within the domain of what is morally permissible the question of whether a political decision is right or wrong can have multiple, mutually incompatible answers for different political communities or at different historical times. Landemore, for instance, explicitly endorses the weaker claim, namely that "at least for some political questions there are right or correct answers."[3] However, her epistemic defense of lottocratic institutions seems to tacitly rely on the assumption that all political questions do indeed have a single right answer, given that these institutions are supposed to make political decisions on *all kinds of questions* and not only on a

---

[1] Guerrero, "Lottocracy," xx; Landemore, *Democratic Reason*. Landemore also speaks of "better" decisions; as she (and Scott Page) put it: "By better decisions, we mean decisions that are as empirically accurate, socially desirable, and as morally correct as possible" (Hélène Landemore and Scott E. Page, "Deliberation and Disagreement: Problem Solving, Prediction, and Positive Dissensus," *Politics, Philosophy and Economics* 14, no. 3 [2015]: 230).

[2] See Landemore, *Democratic Reason*; David Estlund, *Democratic Authority: A Philosophical Framework* (Princeton, NJ: Princeton University Press, 2008); Estlund and Landemore, "The Epistemic Value of Democratic Deliberation," in *Oxford Handbook of Deliberative Democracy*, ed. Bächtiger et al., 113–31.

[3] Landemore, *Democratic Reason*, 233.

The Lottocratic Mentality. Cristina Lafont and Nadia Urbinati, Oxford University Press. © Cristina Lafont and Nadia Urbinati (2024). DOI: 10.1093/9780191982903.003.008

220 The Lottocratic Mentality

specific subset of them (e.g., those that are supposed to have a single right answer). This is a problematic feature of lottocratic proposals of all types, not just of radical defenses of lottocracy. Proposals for conferring decision-making authority on deliberative minipublics almost never distinguish between different types of political questions or suggest any restrictions on which questions these institutions should be able to address. To the extent that no distinction is made, these proposals are *most plausible* under a technocratic conception of politics, even if not all their defenders explicitly endorse such a conception.

What the technocratic view of politics misses entirely is that political decisions are never only a matter of *knowledge*. They are always *also* a matter of *freedom*: the freedom to decide in which political direction a community would like to go; which values and goals it aims to prioritize; which risks it is willing to take in which cases; which trade-offs, compromises, and sacrifices it is willing to make; and so on. Since we have to make political *choices*, politics concerns not only *opinion formation* but also *will formation*.

When citizens make up their minds about which political goals, values, and interests to prioritize and decide to vote for one political party or program over another, they are not simply forming their opinions on how to vote but also forming their political *will*: a willingness to accept the consequences of the collective choice to follow the course of action endorsed by particular political parties as opposed to others, a willingness to take on the risks involved in making certain political choices to the exclusion of others, a willingness to make the lifestyle chances and even sacrifices that might be necessitated by pursuing this political program and not another, and so on.[4] For this reason, deliberation about political choices is never simply about figuring out what the best political decisions are, *according to someone or other*. Rather, political deliberation is always also about justifying the political decisions that one favors to those who will be subject to them, namely, *one's fellow citizens*. This justification makes it possible for them to come to endorse these decisions, of their own accord, such that they can not only form their opinion accordingly but also, above all, their political will. It can foster a willingness to accept the consequences, trade-offs, and differential impacts in their lives that will flow from the collective choice among the different political paths that are available at a specific historical juncture. In sum, by deciding on which political choices or programs to endorse, citizens are not only forming their *opinion* as decision-makers but also forming their *will* as decision-takers.

Once we recognize that we have genuinely political choices, that different democratic societies can choose different political paths (and, in fact, do so on a regular basis), and that this choice has a tremendous impact on citizens' lives and future prospects, it becomes clear what we would lose if we were to deny the citizenry the freedom to collectively decide upon the political direction of their country as

---

[4] Part of accepting the consequences of the collective choice to shape the political space in a particular way may include contesting or protesting specific political decisions with the aim of changing the hearts and minds of fellow citizens. These types of actions presume that the collective choice is legitimate, even if it leads to decisions that some citizens think are wrong on the merits and ought to be contested.

equals through regular elections. Since we have the freedom to shape the social world in different (mutually incompatible) ways, political decision-making always requires both opinion and will formation. To participate in a democratic project of self-government, the citizenry must *form its political will* and exercise its political freedom. In order to participate in democratic self-government, it is simply *not sufficient for a few randomly selected citizens to form an opinion and impose their political will on the rest of the citizenry.*[5] Indeed, it is hard to see how a lottocratic system can count as democratic if it only grants political freedom and agency to a few randomly selected citizens while simultaneously expecting the bulk of the citizenry to blindly defer to the political decisions of the few.

Now, if we are politically free to choose the political programs, values, and goals that we want to realize, then there are only two options: either *all* citizens make that fundamental decision collectively as equals (e.g., through regular elections) or *only* some individuals decide the political agenda as they see fit, and the rest of the citizenry must blindly defer to their decisions. Whereas electoral democracy exemplifies the first option, lottocracy exemplifies the second.[6] In electoral democracies, citizens form their political will and regularly exercise their political freedom by participating in elections. With their vote, citizens decide which political party or program to endorse among the available alternatives. They exercise this power collectively as equals. In so doing, they shape the political/ideological space within which the elected officials must operate until the next election. By contrast, in a lottocracy, the citizenry is subject to the political will of a few randomly selected people who are the only ones with decision-making authority and, consequently, the only ones who can exercise their political agency and freedom. This problem is certainly *less acute* in the case of complementarity proposals that would confer legislative authority on allotted assemblies only for *some* and not for *all* political decisions. Yet, the problem *persists* for those political decisions that allotted assemblies would have the authority to make.

7.1 Lottocratic Epistocracy: Technical Problem-Solving vs. Political Freedom

Political freedom is the main casualty of the lottocratic view of politics as technical problem-solving. Oddly, lottocratic proposals are never evaluated or defended in terms of how they impact the political freedom of a community. While political equality is foregrounded in defenses of such proposals, political freedom simply disappears as a significant issue entirely. Within the framework of lottocratic

---

[5] This problem affects not only the radical proposal of establishing a lottocracy but also the less radical proposals of conferring decision-making authority to lottery-based institutions only for some legislative decisions, even if not all.

[6] Doubtless both options can be exemplified by more than one political system. Direct democracy is an alternative example of the first option whereas meritocracy, oligarchy, or dictatorship are all examples of the second.

222   The Lottocratic Mentality

assumptions, there is simply no space to ask questions about whether and how citizens can exercise their political freedom collectively as equals. By contrast, if we recognize that we always have choices about how to shape our social world—that we can always choose among different values, priorities, and policy objectives—it becomes abundantly clear that selecting legislators among different parties necessarily involves citizens freely making a fundamental political decision about the different political programs and visions of their social world that they would like to endorse. Political decision-making is never merely a matter of exercising technical "competence" to identify the best solutions to problems that objectively exist. It is precisely because citizens themselves are free to choose among different political programs, goals, and policy objectives that they must make such a decision. They cannot defer to others or be represented by others in this matter. No one can exercise *their* political freedom for them.

But why do not lottocrats see any problem in asking the bulk of the citizenry to relinquish their political freedom (e.g., through elections)? Why is it that lottocrats are unconcerned about limiting the exercise of political freedom to only a tiny subset of randomly selected individuals? The technocratic conception of politics offers a *partial* answer to this question. As noted above, if political decision-making is simply a matter of technical problem-solving—if politics is about knowing what the world is like and, based on that, finding out the right solutions to objectively existing problems—then there is simply no genuine or significant space for freedom in politics. The right political decisions are simply those that are morally or technically required in order to solve the objective problems that we face. The "freedom" to deviate from the right decisions seems to have as little value as the freedom to do what is morally wrong or to fail to solve the problems that we face. Since the goal of a legislative assembly is to accomplish the epistemic task of problem-solving, what matters is that the right or the best solutions are indeed *found* and anyone who can acquire the requisite competence and skills to do so is as good as any other. There is nothing lost in letting competent others do the thinking and deciding for us. Indeed, from a technocratic perspective it is difficult to see value in the democratic ideal of self-government. Why should it matter so much whether we govern ourselves or whether some competent and reliable "others" govern us, so long as the right political decisions are made, and the problems are solved?

A clear implication of the technocratic conception of politics as problem-solving that prevails among lottocrats is the in-principle interchangeability of decision-makers. So long as the right epistemic properties are exemplified in the legislative assembly (e.g., cognitive diversity, quality of information and deliberation, etc.), any randomly selected subset of the citizenry can do the job of problem-solving as well as any other. Landemore's argument in *Democratic Reason* makes the reason behind this assumption apparent. A central aim of the book is to justify lottocratic decision-making on the basis of cognitive diversity. To do so, Landemore applies Hong and Page's "Diversity Trumps Ability Theorem" to the political domain. She makes it clear that Hong and Page stipulate a necessary condition to establish their claim that "diversity trumps ability" and that she incorporates this into her approach—namely,

The Technocratic Conception Of Politics   **223**

the relevant participants "think very differently, even though the best solution must be obvious to all of them when they are made to think of it."[7] Given the deep political disagreements that characterize pluralist democracies, this condition might seem out of place in the context of politics. But, Landemore does not see it that way. Her conceptualization of politics as technical problem-solving is the key to understanding why she thinks this condition is plausible. Let's see why.

In her article "Deliberation and Disagreement," Landemore discusses political decision-making in what she calls "pure problem-solving contexts." She indicates that in these contexts "individuals evaluate proposed solutions identically." As she explains, the reason is that "participants have already reached consensus on the criteria for evaluation and how those criteria will be weighted. A problem-solving task consists then of generating potential solutions and identifying the best from among them."[8] If this is the case, then it follows that "in what we call problem-solving contexts . . . consensus would be the only possible end. Disagreement would mean that at least one person ignores or refuses to accept another person's better solution."[9] Naturally, once there is agreement on a political goal (and on the proper criteria of evaluation, the proper balance among criteria, etc.), figuring out the best way to realize it can indeed be seen as a purely technical question of problem-solving. Unfortunately, the problem in politics is precisely that citizens disagree on the goals, values, priorities, criteria of evaluation, and so forth. This is why political questions cannot be reduced to technical ones. Yet Landemore disagrees. Addressing the objection that the problem-solving model is only suitable for technical questions, she states: "We do not deny that our problem-solving framework resonates particularly well with technical and operational problems (how to design environmental policies or how to fund a public utility). However, we believe that the logic of the problem-solving framework applies to a much larger set of domains, which includes the normative side of at least some political disagreements."[10] Thus, she insists that "the values of competing solutions even in contexts of a more social or political nature can be relatively *self-evident*, at least with the benefit of hindsight, given enough time, and in relative if not absolute terms."[11]

In order to justify applying a problem-solving paradigm to political disagreements, Landemore discusses an example that can be helpful in our context. A neighborhood faces a recurrent safety issue on a dark bridge that separates it from the city's downtown. Muggings occur on the bridge so often that people fear walking home alone after dark. Potential solutions to this problem run the gamut from stationing a police car near the bridge, to installing public lighting, or even having neighbors sign up to

---

[7] Landemore, *Democratic Reason*, 102.

[8] Landemore and Page, "Deliberation and Disagreement," 234.

[9] Ibid., 235.

[10] Ibid., 236. Although Landemore's wording leaves open the possibility that *not all* political disagreements fit the model of technical problem-solving, this possibility is never reflected in Landemore's proposals for democratic reform. The technocratic conception of politics prevails since she leaves decision-making *on all kinds of political questions* in the hands of the few randomly selected members of lottocratic assemblies.

[11] Ibid., our italics.

224 The Lottocratic Mentality

take shifts to walk each other home. Landemore explains that "even assuming that all deliberators value safety, some may consider that having the police stationed on the bridge at night every night is too much surveillance and object to it on libertarian grounds. Other citizens may be opposed to spending money on treating the symptoms of insecurity—muggings—rather than their deep-rooted causes, such as poverty, socioeconomic inequalities, and lack of education."[12]

This is an excellent example of how different political values, interests, and priorities can lead citizens to disagree not just on how to solve a particular problem but also, above all, on what the actual problem that the community faces even *is*. Is "safety" the problem the community faces or is it "poverty, socioeconomic inequalities, and lack of education"? Moreover, is personal safety a problem that should be solved by the government or instead a matter of personal responsibility? What's the right trade-off between safety and surveillance, between government protection and personal freedom?

In that context, Landemore points out that such disagreements do not have to be intractable. For instance, she notes that citizens who do not want to spend money on supposedly superficial solutions like more public lighting could potentially be convinced by arguments that, given strict budget constraints, it is better to do something feasible in the short term (lighting) rather than nothing. Alternatively, citizens who think that the muggings are actually symptomatic of deeper systemic problems could convince everyone else that starting to address the underlying problem of poverty is actually the right way to use what little funding there is. Libertarian-leaning citizens may be persuaded that stationing a police car near the bridge at certain times is not such a big deal in terms of surveillance or matters may turn out the other way around: they may persuade their fellow citizens that any increases in public safety are not worth the potential cost to civil liberties that comes with increased surveillance or an armed police presence.

It seems very plausible that the debate could develop in any of these directions. However, the mere possibility of agreement on political values, priorities, and goals in no way shows that such political questions can be reduced to technical questions that have a single right answer. Since different political values, priorities, and agendas may be equally legitimate, political disagreements are not an indication that one side or the other is making a mistake. Rather, what they indicate is that there is more than one reasonable way to use politics to shape our social world and thus that citizens are free to decide among genuinely different political paths as they see fit. If this is the case, then it makes no sense to assume that when citizens think very differently about the relevant political values, priorities, and policy agendas "the best solution must be obvious to all of them when they are made to think of it."[13] To the contrary, what Landemore's example shows is that political agreement on the values, goals, priorities, and criteria of evaluation are necessarily located at a *prior* step within any overarching search for technical "solutions." So long as there is no agreement on what

---

[12] Ibid.
[13] Landemore, *Democratic Reason*, 102.

the political problem even is "the best solution" would certainly *not be obvious* to all citizens: not because they are unreasonable or making a mistake but rather because, depending on their interests, values, priorities, and policy objectives, they are free to choose among many reasonable but different (often mutually incompatible) political paths.

The problem with assimilating political questions about values, priorities, and policy objectives to technical problem-solving is that, by assuming that *all* political questions have a single right answer, such an approach undermines the legitimacy of political pluralism. If political questions did have a single right answer in every case, then it would indeed not matter much who makes political decisions so long as the right (or best) decisions were made. But if we are free to prioritize some interests, values, and political objectives over others by choosing among different political agendas and paths—to decide which risks, compromises, and accommodations are acceptable and which are not—then the question of *who* gets to make that fundamental decision becomes pressing. The technocratic conception of politics tacitly undermines the legitimacy of freedom of choice. In a slight of hand, any dimension of genuine choice in political decision-making is transformed into a matter of epistemic "competence" at identifying the right solutions to the objectively existing problems. This depoliticized way of thinking about political questions gives the impression that there is only one (right) way to shape the social world and consequently, from among the many different political ideals and priorities, there is only a single objectively "better" (or "right") one.[14]

This assumption is worrisome enough. But, the technocratic conception of politics has another highly problematic implication in that *it stipulates political disagreement away* by assuming that, once decision-makers hit upon the right "answers" (or "solutions") to political questions, everyone else's agreement (decision-takers included) will simply follow. This assumption expunges a political task that is quintessential to democracy, namely, *the need to reach agreement with fellow citizens who have different interests, values, priorities, and policy objectives.* Since they have equal rights to exercise their political freedom, we need to justify our political decisions to them with reasons that they can reasonably accept so that they may identify with those decisions and come to endorse them as their own. Naturally, this task would be superfluous if one were to assume that the best "solution" to a political question "must be obvious to all of them when they are made to think of it." Indeed, if political decisions could generally meet that condition, then blindly deferring to the decisions of randomly selected others would not be problematic at all. *Lottocrats assume political homogeneity as a given rather than acknowledging it as an uncertain and fragile political task to be achieved* under conditions of political pluralism that characterize democratic societies.

---

[14] There is no need to deny that many political questions have single right answers (e.g., slavery is wrong, rape is wrong, and poverty is wrong) in order to recognize that many others do not (e.g., joining the European Union or remaining an independent nation, dismantling nuclear energy or reducing use of fossil fuels, eliminating all forms of surveillance or the risks of cyberattacks, expanding marked-based mechanisms or public provision for some goods and services, etc.).

226 The Lottocratic Mentality

The assumption of a politically homogeneous people is not only rooted in the technocratic view of politics, but this assumption, as discussed in Chapter 6, also plays a central role within the populist conception of representation that lottocrats endorse. Indeed, the populist assumption of "homogeneity" among citizens' interests, values, and preferences fits hand in glove with the technocratic assumption that legislation is a matter of accurately responding to a community's objective (prepolitical and homogeneous) "common good."[15] In her account of traditional populism, Canovan highlights the deep affinity between the technocratic view of politics and the populist assumption of homogeneous people: "The notion that 'the people' are one; that divisions among them are not genuine conflicts of interests but are merely self-serving factions; and that the people will be best looked after by a single unpolitical leadership that will put their interest first—these ideas are *anti*political, but they are nevertheless essential elements in a political strategy that has often been used to gain power."[16]

If we focus on lottocrats' criticisms of electoral democracy, the underlying similarities between traditional and lottocratic populism are hard to miss. According to lottocrats, competitive elections among different political parties do not reflect the plural, often mutually incompatible political values, priorities, and objectives of the citizens themselves. To the contrary, political conflicts and disagreements among citizens are actually *caused* by the perverse incentives of elections (of the two-party ingroup/outgroup dynamics, elite manipulation, etc.) that threaten to break down the political community.[17] Like populists, lottocrats assume that if it were not for the perverse incentives of the elites—and the politicians, political parties, lobbyists, and the media that serve them—the citizenry would have no fundamental conflicts between interests or ideological disagreements. They would just be able to see the objective problems that they face and come to an agreement upon their optimal solution. After offering a grim diagnosis that elections within a two-party dominant system are the real culprit for the current levels of polarization, division, and dysfunctionality that we see in the United States,[18] Guerrero tellingly contends, "the division

---

[15] The assumption of homogeneity among citizens' interests, values, and policy objectives also explains the relative insignificance given to freedom of choice. As we pointed out in Chapter 1, in *The Social Contract*, Rousseau makes this connection explicit when he claims that "elections by lot would have few disadvantages in a true democracy, in which, as equality would everywhere exist in morals and talents as well as in principles and fortunes, the choice would be almost indifferent" (bk. 4, chap. 3). Rousseau distances himself from this view by adding: "But I have already said that a true democracy is only an ideal" (ibid.).

[16] Canovan, *Populism*, 265.

[17] Guerrero, "Lottocracy," 68.

[18] In our opinion, the lottocratic contention that elections are the fundamental cause of the dysfunctionality in current electoral democracies is not very convincing. Nevertheless, we do not deny that elections are an imperfect mechanism that generates perverse incentives and which can exacerbate dynamics like polarization, divisiveness, etc. Given the many ongoing and serious threats to which democratic societies are currently exposed, we recognize the urgent need to improve our electoral systems. However, the problem with the lottocratic proposal is that it throws the baby out with the bath water, so to speak. Elections are a tool that enables citizens to exercise their political freedom both collectively and as equals. Lottocrats are right that the tool is defective in many ways and that it generates all kinds of problems, perverse incentives, etc. Perhaps they are even right in claiming that the tool cannot be significantly improved. Yet, the problem with their proposal is that, instead of offering a better tool for achieving the same goal, *they offer*

and disharmony is not real. We really aren't all that far apart. Perhaps because I personally know many people on the other side from me, I do feel that we aren't all that far apart. I think the forces described above [the perverse incentives produced by elections] are real and powerful, but they are also distorting all of us, on both sides, from thinking about the moral–political problems we actually face and engaging them in a serious way that is good for the whole political community and the broader global community." He explains further: "Fundamentally, if elections are causing these divisions through the creation of ingroup/outgroup dynamics and partisan mega-identities, the most natural response, it seems to me, is to consider what our ingroup/outgroup divisions and dynamics might look like if we removed elections."[19]

The lottocratic response is clear. If the plurality of political views, interests, values, and priorities among citizens should not be seen as a valuable result of citizens exercising their freedom but rather as the regrettable consequence of the perverse incentives set up by elections, corrupt political parties, and other powerful actors who manipulate and polarize an otherwise homogeneous people, then dismantling elections and establishing a lottocracy would seem like a necessary step to restore the natural homogeneity of the people: "avoiding short-term electoral influences and having a less captured process is likely to result in *somewhat similar, broadly compatible ideas*" about political questions among the citizenry.[20]

If citizens' interests, values, priorities, and policy objectives are sufficiently homogeneous, then it makes sense to think of political decisions as basically a matter of technical problem-solving. Indeed, if citizens fundamentally agree on what they collectively want, then the only question left is how to best get from here to there; politics becomes indeed a matter of knowing what the world is like and, based upon that, finding the right solutions to the "objectively existing" problems standing in the way of realizing what the citizenry wants. Surprising as it may be, the populist assumption of homogeneity and the technocratic conception of politics are not only compatible but in fact mutually *reinforce one another*. They are the two sides of the same lottocratic coin. The combination of a technocratic conception of politics and a populist conception of representation that the lottocratic mentality fuses together exemplifies the logic of a type of political action that Bikerton and Invernizzi have characterized as "technopopulism":

> within this new political logic, populism and technocracy do not function merely as opposites of one another. Even though appeals to the popular will and competence are often rhetorically deployed against each other, there is also a deep

---

a tool whose use sacrifices the goal itself. The lottocratic system no longer enables the citizenry to exercise their political freedom and agency collectively as equals. Instead, the exercise of freedom and agency is limited to a few randomly selected citizens who impose their political opinion and will on the rest of the citizenry, who is then supposed to blindly defer to their decisions. Thus, with the lottocratic proposal, we are not simply facing a choice between two different tools or selection mechanisms for achieving the same goal. What we face is a choice between entirely different political goals.

[19] Guerrero, "Lottocracy," 69–70.

[20] Ibid., 182, our italics.

> affinity between them, which consists in the fact that they are both *unmoored from the representation of specific values and interests within society* and therefore advance *an unmediated conception of the common good*, in the form either of a monolithic conception of the "popular will" or the specific conception of political "truth" technocrats claim to have access to. This sets both populism and technocracy at odds with the traditional conception of party democracy as a system of "regulated rivalry" between competing social interests and values that are all in principle equally legitimate.[21]

Although Bikerton and Invernizzi's analysis of the technopopulist logic behind new political formations, parties, and actors does not focus on lottocratic proposals in particular, the contrast they establish between technopopulism and the traditional conception of party democracy is still quite illuminating in the lottocratic context. The institutions of electoral democracy are predicated upon the assumption of political freedom. Citizens have different interests, values, and policy objectives and this is why we need competitive elections among political alternatives that can appeal to different citizens so that we can foster agreement (through competition, negotiation, coalition building, and so forth) on legislation that a majority of citizens can rally behind or at least find acceptable such that they are willing to do their part and live with the consequences of such political choices. By contrast, under the populist assumption of homogeneity among citizens' interests, values, and political objectives, political decision-making can be seen as a technical matter of accurately responding to the objective (homogeneous) "common good" of the community by "competent" legislators. Certainly, populism and technocracy share a deep affinity in that they both rely on the assumption of a homogeneous "common good." But one should also not lose sight of the many incompatibilities between the two approaches that ultimately render lottocratic technopopulism inherently unstable. If put under justificatory pressure, lottocrats must choose between the populist and technocratic justifications of lottocracy. Let's see why.

7.2 The Tensions within Lottocratic Technopopulism

As mentioned earlier, lottocrats justify the exclusion of the overwhelming majority of the people from political decision-making through a peculiar blend of populist and technocratic assumptions. Like populists, lottocrats are suspicious of political elites and think that ordinary citizens must take matters into their own hands in order to solve current democratic deficits. Citizens must enter the political system and do the job that the nonresponsive political elites and political parties are unable or unwilling to do. Moreover, as analyzed earlier, lottocrats also share the populist view of political representation as embodiment. Like the leader in traditional populism,

---

[21] Christopher Bikerton and Carlo Invernizzi, *Technopopulism: The New Logic of Democratic Politics* (Oxford: Oxford University Press, 2021), 3, our italics.

the lottocratic assembly is supposed to embody "the people" because its members are *like* them. It is because the assembly "mirrors" the people that nonparticipants, who are the overwhelming majority of the citizenry, should *trust* the few randomly selected, let them do the thinking and deciding for them, and blindly accept whatever decisions they make. Against the backdrop of a highly problematic assumption about political homogeneity, it is claimed that citizens should trust that the decisions of the majority of the assembly will invariably reflect their own interests, values, and policy objectives. Thus, by following the decisions of the assembly members, the people would actually be following themselves. But there is a catch. Like technocrats, lottocrats are suspicious of letting the citizenry as a whole actually make its own political decisions, for example, through voting. They endorse the epistocratic assumption that political decisions should be made by the knowers—by those who are well informed and have deliberated about the issues under sufficiently good conditions. This is why, instead of having all citizens make decisions, for example, through elections or referenda, they claim that political decisions should be made by a few randomly selected assembly members whose views have been properly "filtered" through a careful deliberative process. Like technocrats, they expect that the (randomly selected) few will make *better* political decisions than the (ignorant) citizenry.

Unfortunately, lottocrats cannot have it both ways. The "mirror" claim and the "filter" claim are mutually incompatible. Either the few participants in the assembly will make the *same decisions* as the rest of the citizenry because they are *like* them, and this is why citizens do not lose democratic control by blindly deferring to them. Or the participants in the assembly are expected to make *better decisions* than the rest of the citizenry because they have become properly informed and have deliberated about them and *this* is why the ignorant citizenry ought not to have democratic control over political decisions. Instead, they should blindly defer to the assembly so that better political outcomes are achieved. Both claims cannot be simultaneously true. Lottocrats must choose between the technocratic and the populist claim as the ultimate normative justification for their proposals. Yet, no matter which option they choose, both end up excluding the bulk of the citizenry from decision-making and require them to blindly defer to the randomly selected few. Both options are equally antidemocratic, although for different reasons.

This internal tension at the core of the lottocratic mentality is relevant for anyone interested in the democratic potential of lottery-based institutions. As mentioned earlier, the populist conception of representation as embodiment and the technocratic conception of politics are essential elements of the lottocratic mentality that lends support to and inspires the radical proposals of replacing electoral democracy with lottocracy. However, it would be a mistake to think that only advocates of lottocracy endorse these elements of the lottocratic mentality. In fact, populist claims to the effect that deliberative minipublics "mirror" the people, that their participants speak *like* the people, and that, for that reason, the rest of the citizenry should blindly trust their recommendations or decisions are ubiquitous in the literature on deliberative minipublics. Similarly, technocratic claims to the effect that citizens should blindly defer to minipublics' participants because the deliberative "filter" would lead them to make better political decisions than the (ignorant) citizenry are equally ubiquitous in the literature. Indeed, these claims are made again and again by scholars and practitioners interested in lottery-based institutions regardless of the specific institutional proposals that they happen to endorse.[22] This situation raises two distinct concerns.

On the one hand, the spread of the lottocratic mentality is a worrisome development in its own right, regardless of the fate of lottery-based institutions in the foreseeable future. As discussed earlier, questioning the priority of political representation over descriptive representation by endorsing the populist conception of representation as "embodiment" undermines citizens' political agency and freedom. Indeed, it brings back the antidemocratic idea that it is fine to let others make political decisions for us, so long as they share some ascriptive characteristics with us (e.g., profession, gender, or geographical location). The same is true of technocracy. Questioning citizens' rights to make political decisions by endorsing a technocratic view of politics undermines citizens' political agency and freedom. It brings back the antidemocratic idea that we should let others make political decisions for us, so long as they have been properly informed and deliberated about the issues. Either way, the spread of the lottocratic mentality in our societies would weaken the commitment to democratic self-government regardless of whether lottery-based institutions are ever established in one form or another. This concern with the antidemocratic effects of the lottocratic mentality is precisely what motivates the critical analysis that we have articulated so far.

Yet, there is another, separate concern that we should also briefly address before concluding. If the argument we have offered so far is plausible, anyone interested in the democratic potential of lottery-based institutions such as deliberative minipublics faces the challenge of justifying proposals for using these institutions *without embracing the lottocratic mentality*. Can proposals for using lottery-based institutions be crafted and justified without relying on a populist conception of representation as embodiment or a technocratic conception of politics? This question is the focus of the next chapter.

---

[22] As we indicated in Chapter 2, the deliberative democracy paradigm is ambiguous enough to enable different lines of argument among those interested in deliberative minipublics. All authors agree that what is special about these institutions is the peculiar combination of being a "mirror" of the people and being subject to a proper deliberative "filter." But they can offer very different accounts of each of these elements. Authors who prioritize the populist "mirror" are likely to have a less technocratic view of politics (e.g., Fishkin). However, those who emphasize the technocratic "filter" (e.g., Landemore) can justify the populist "mirror" on epistemic grounds of cognitive diversity and thus defend a thoroughly technocratic conception of politics while rejecting technocracy in the specific sense of "rule by experts" (technocratic elites). There are, of course, many more combinations and variations among deliberative democrats.

III
LOTTERY WITHOUT THE LOTTOCRATIC MENTALITY

Chapter 8
The Democratic Alternative

Institutionalizing Minipublics to Empower the Citizenry

Proposals for institutionalizing deliberative minipublics—whether they follow the auxiliary, complementarity, or substitution models discussed in Chapter 3—are typically justified as a way of reaching democratic aims. Institutionalized minipublics are expected to function as vehicles for empowering the citizenry in various ways: from increasing the venues of political *participation* available to citizens; to improving the *responsiveness* of the political system to citizens' concerns, interests, and policy objectives; to enhancing citizens' *democratic control* of political institutions; and so forth. While radical proposals to substitute or complement electoral assemblies with lottocratic ones have not yet been implemented, over the past decades many auxiliary proposals have been implemented that use different types of minipublics to supplement or assist electoral-representative institutions. In fact, their increasing popularity is generating a huge variety of proposals for their institutionalization. It would be nearly impossible to analyze and discuss all the proposals that are currently on offer. The aim of this chapter is much more limited. We would like to show that it is perfectly feasible to craft and justify proposals that would institutionalize minipublics as auxiliary supplements to representative institutions *without* embracing the lottocratic mentality. More importantly, we would also like to show that doing so is compatible with *strong democratic ambitions*. While we do not consider deliberative minipublics to be a panacea for overcoming the current crisis of democracy, we do think that they could help overcome many of the democratic deficits of current institutions.

8.1 Deliberative Minipublics as Auxiliary Institutions: Two Approaches

As we indicated in Chapter 3, in contrast to the replacement and complementarity models, the auxiliary model recognizes the sovereignty of the collective citizenry and their voting power both with respect to issues and the choice of representatives. Thus, on this model, the point of institutionalizing minipublics is to help the citizenry exercise its political power more thoughtfully and effectively. However, even if minipublics only serve electoral-representative institutions in an auxiliary or supplemental fashion, in order to make an actual impact, they would obviously

The Lottocratic Mentality. Cristina Lafont and Nadia Urbinati, Oxford University Press. © Cristina Lafont and Nadia Urbinati (2024). DOI: 10.1093/9780191982903.003.009

234 The Lottocratic Mentality

need to have some *effective power* to influence the political process. Indeed, democratic theorists and practitioners involved with minipublics often complain about their relative lack of impact. So far, the record shows that the relevant political actors (government officials, administrators, or voters) often fail to take up and implement the recommendations of minipublics. This is not to say that an increase in the power of minipublics to influence the political process would be without problems. Any significant increase in minipublics' political power is likely to generate "powerful incentives for interest groups and partisan elites to try to manipulate deliberative forums."[1] However, this is a general worry that arises for any institution with a significant level of political power. If minipublics became politically influential, then this problem would arise regardless of the specific way in which they were embedded in the political process. Needless to say, the more political power that is conferred upon minipublics the more acute this problem is likely to become, as discussed in Chapter 5.

If we focus on the level of empowerment, proposals for institutionalizing minipublics can be situated on a spectrum. On the weakest side of the spectrum, minipublics have no agenda-setting capacity or decision-making authority conferred on them and are simply consulted about policy issues that have already been determined. This minimal political role reflects most current practice where minipublics have the power of influencing political actors (such as legislatures or administrative agencies) through nonmandatory, one-off processes wherein they are convened to discuss some preselected policy issues. Since minipublics are not yet permanent institutions, most citizens are unfamiliar with them and any recommendations they make can easily be ignored. With very few exceptions, the political impact of minipublics has been quite limited. On the strongest side of the spectrum, we find the proposals for substitution and replacement that were described in Chapter 3. Such proposals would confer full decision-making authority onto minipublics. However, it would be a mistake to think that only these stronger proposals face the legitimacy concerns discussed in previous chapters. Certainly, legitimacy concerns arise with respect to proposals that would empower minipublics to directly make binding political decisions while bypassing the citizenry. Yet, even weaker proposals that seek to institutionalize minipublics for merely consultative purposes (the more popular variety among deliberative democrats) can give rise to legitimacy concerns as well. This is because the central question surrounding the democratic legitimacy of minipublics is not about *how much power* they ought to exercise but rather about *the capacity* in which they are supposed to exercise that power.

This concern is unavoidable with minipublics because, in contrast to other political actors, minipublic participants can easily be taken as *proxies for the entire citizenry*. In comparison to other political institutions, minipublics are special in that they are composed of ordinary citizens who are supposed to act exclusively in their capacity as members of the citizenry itself. The composition of a minipublic is supposed to reflect or descriptively represent the composition of the citizenry as a whole.

---

[1] Neblo, *Deliberative Democracy between Theory and Practice*, 181.

At the same time, members of the minipublic have neither been selected by the citizenry nor are they required to act as political representatives of the individuals or groups that, in a descriptive sense, they represent. There is no sense in which female participants are supposed to defend the views of women or doctors the views of other doctors. They are and remain members of the citizenry who, as such, represent only themselves. They participate as individual citizens with total freedom to express whichever views and opinions they happen to have and to change them in whichever way they see fit. But, for that very same reason, they are in no way accountable to citizens who are outside of the minipublic.

In the context of public consultation, this is problematic in light of the potential differences of opinion between participants and nonparticipants. The purpose of having a process of public consultation is for officials to be able to find out the citizenry's opinion and will regarding certain policy decisions. But if minipublic participants and nonparticipating citizens disagree about the decisions at hand, then who is supposed to speak in the name of the citizenry? Whose views ought to count as the views of "the public" that officials are supposed to consult? John Parkinson illustrates the problem with a real example of a citizens' jury convened to consider hospital restructuring in Leicester, England. In that case, decision-makers were confronted with the results of a deliberation by a citizens' jury that recommended one course of action and a petition of 150,000 signatories demanding another.[2] The citizenry neither elected the minipublic participants nor had any way of holding them accountable. As such, the normative basis upon which officials should take the opinions of the minipublic to have more recommending force than the opinions of the citizenry is unclear. In such a situation it is normatively unclear whether and why officials should just follow the judgment of a minipublic over the judgment of the citizenry at large. Of course, this problem is not unique to minipublics. It can also arise with other forms of public consultation (e.g., town hall meetings, focus groups, and so on). Thus, it is possible that, in some cases, the recommendations of a minipublic might be better aligned with the views of the relevant constituency than the recommendations defended by participants in other fora or activist movements and organizations which may be less representative, more polarized, or "captured" by particular interests.[3] However, just because this *can* be the case does not mean that it will *always* be the case. Indeed, given the extensive empirical evidence about drastic changes of opinion among minipublics' participants on contested political issues,[4] the legitimacy concerns remain for all cases in which there is a conflict between the recommendations of minipublics and the opinions of the relevant constituency.[5]

---

[2] John Parkinson, *Deliberating in the Real World: Problems of Legitimacy in Deliberative Democracy* (Oxford: Oxford University Press, 2006), 33.

[3] See, e.g., Edana Beauvais and Mark E. Warren, "What Can Deliberative Mini-publics Contribute to Democratic Systems?," *European Journal of Political Research* 58, no. 3 (2019): 893–914.

[4] See, e.g., Fishkin, *When the People Speak*.

[5] It is true that, according to deliberative democrats, only postdeliberative, considered judgments, and not just raw preferences and opinions, provide the legitimate basis for justifying political decisions to all those who are bound by them. However, as we argued in Chapter 2, unless and until the considered judgments of a minipublic *become* the considered judgments of the actual people who will be bound by the

236 The Lottocratic Mentality

From a democratic point of view, these proposals face a dilemma. After the consultation process concludes, if the actors with decision-making authority (e.g., politicians, administrators, voters, etc.) are expected to follow their own judgment, rather than the recommendations of the minipublic, then minipublics would seem to lack impact and purpose: consulting them would be at best redundant (when there is agreement) and at worst useless (when there is disagreement).[6] By contrast, if these actors are expected to blindly follow the recommendations of the minipublics instead of following their own judgment, then an alienating disconnect will eventually result between the citizenry's own views and the political decisions to which they are subject. The long-term effect of making political decisions based on the considered judgments of minipublic participants *instead of upon the actual judgments of the citizenry* is that the latter would have difficulty identifying with and endorsing the decisions to which they are subject, as the democratic ideal of self-government requires. Institutionalizing minipublics in the hope that they would do the thinking and deciding for the rest of the citizenry would not be a way of increasing the citizenry's democratic control over the political process. The problem with this way of thinking about the potential uses of minipublics is that it focuses on increasing the involvement and impact of *a few randomly selected citizens* in the political process, while nonparticipants—the citizenry as a whole—are simply ignored. However, if minipublics are to have a democratizing effect, then the focus needs to be on ways that we can use minipublics to improve the involvement and impact of *the whole citizenry* within the political process.

This signals two fundamentally different ways of thinking about why we might want to use minipublics: either to *empower the (few) minipublic participants* to do the thinking, deliberating, and deciding for the rest of the citizenry or to *empower the citizenry as a whole* to have greater influence over the political process. As such, proposals for institutionalizing minipublics may follow two different approaches:

(1) The *lottocratic* approach aims to give minipublics advisory or even decision-making authority while bypassing deliberation and decision-making by the citizenry.

(2) The *participatory* approach aims to empower the citizenry to initiate public debate, influence policy making, set the political agenda, and/or have final say on certain political decisions.

---

decisions in question they cannot accrue any legitimacy under the criterion of public justification. There can be different interpretations of how this criterion can best be satisfied, but justifying political decisions to only a few members in a random sample cannot be one of them.

[6] This reflects the current situation in which the authorities that organize minipublics have wide discretion to decide what to do with their recommendations (which is, very often, to simply ignore them). This calls the legitimacy of the process into question leading to the understandable suspicion that the organizing authorities engage in cherry-picking (following the recommendations they like and ignoring the ones they dislike), co-optation of their opponents, silencing of critical voices, and other forms of manipulation. For an overview of these issues, see, e.g., Stephen Elstub and Zohreh Khoban, "Citizens' Assemblies: A Critical Perspective," in *De Gruyter Handbook of Citizens' Assemblies*, ed. Reuchamps, Vyrdagh, and Welp, 116–7.

It is hard to see how the first approach can lead minipublics to have a positive *democratic* impact. Giving decision-making authority to the few who are well informed and who have access to good-quality deliberation while simply expecting the rest of the citizenry to blindly defer to their decisions would predictably increase the disconnect between citizens' beliefs and attitudes and the political decisions to which they are subject. Far from having a positive democratic impact, it could exacerbate the problem that citizens' assemblies are meant to solve; citizens' alienation from the political process would grow rather than shrink.[7] By contrast, if citizens' assemblies are institutionalized with the participatory aim of empowering the citizenry to catalyze public debate, set the political agenda, and have the final say on important political decisions, then such institutions could clearly contribute to democratization.

The key difference between the two approaches is therefore not *how much power* minipublics can exercise but *who is empowered* by using minipublics: either its few participants or the citizenry as a whole. As analyzed in the next section, levels of power can vary among proposals that follow each of the two approaches. The fundamental difference is *how they are integrated into the political system* in each case. In that regard, we can distinguish between a vertical or "top-down" approach versus a horizontal or "bottom-up" approach.[8] The first approach would aim to integrate citizens' assemblies directly into the political system—either as advisory bodies or as a supplement to or replacement for some of the functions and decision-making authority of existing political institutions.[9] Minipublics would be *directly coupled with formal political institutions* with varying degrees of decision-making authority *while bypassing the citizenry*. In contrast, the second approach would institutionalize minipublics as *mediating bodies between formal political institutions and the wider public* with the aim of making these institutions more responsive to the interests, values, and policy objectives of *the entire citizenry*.

When understood as intermediary institutions, there are many democratic functions that minipublics could fulfill. We would like to focus on two general functions that minipublics are distinctively suitable to serve and which are particularly important for overcoming current democratic deficits. First, minipublics could help *improve* the quality of public deliberation in distinctive ways such that the citizenry

---

[7] It is both naive and dangerous to assume that political communities can afford to leave their citizens politically ignorant (misinformed, fragmented, polarized, etc.) in the hopes that they will blindly follow the enlightened few (be they elite experts or minipublic participants). As the current rise of populism is showing, misinformation, fragmentation, and polarization make citizens feel justified in prioritizing and affirming their own interests, rights, and freedoms and those of the groups that they identify with while subordinating those of "the other side." Without an inclusive process of collective opinion and will formation, solidarity among groups of citizens cannot be generated, citizens' willingness to share the burdens of achieving collective goals correspondingly diminishes, fair compromises cannot be reached, and democracy cannot be sustained.

[8] The distinction between top-down and bottom-up approaches to minipublics can be understood in different ways. According to some, a "bottom-up" approach merely requires minipublic participants to influence the political process even if the rest of the citizenry is entirely disconnected from that process (see, e.g., Sonia Bussu and Dannica Fleuß, "Citizens' Assemblies: Top-Down or Bottom-Up?—Both, Please!," in *De Gruyter Handbook of Citizen's Assemblies*, ed. Reuchamps, Vrydagh, and Welp, 141–4). In our usage, a "bottom-up" approach requires minipublic to enable the citizenry as a whole (and not just the few minipublic participants) to influence the political process.

[9] Maija Setälä, "Advisory, Collaborative and Scrutinizing Roles of Deliberative Mini-publics," *Frontiers in Political Science* 2 (2021): 1–10. doi:10.3389/fpos.2020.591844.

could reach considered opinions on important political decisions that they are bound to obey. Second, they could also help make the political system more *responsive* to considered public opinion for the political decisions at hand. With respect to this latter function, we want to challenge the impression that minipublics could only have a *weak or limited democratic impact* in virtue of the fact that they play merely an *auxiliary* role. As such, we shall focus our discussion on proposals that would use lottery-based institutions in the most democratically significant context—legislative decision-making—and will ignore potential uses for other purposes (e.g., redistricting, oversight and monitoring functions, etc.).

Before discussing these potential functions, we should note that, while our analysis does not assume citizens would know all the details about the inner workings of different types of minipublics, we do assume that citizens would have become sufficiently familiar with them so as to be aware of the higher quality of political deliberation that they enable in terms of representativeness (inclusion and diversity), access to reliable and balanced information, independence, impartiality, orientation toward the public interest, and so on. If the use of minipublics keeps spreading at its current pace, then this is not an unrealistic assumption.[10]

8.2 Minipublics' Potential Contribution to Improving Public Debates

Amid growing discontent with democracy, there are plenty of reasons to be worried about the increasing deterioration of the public sphere in democratic societies.[11] In addition to long-standing threats such as the excessive influence of money on political discourse, the potential for manipulation by powerful social groups, and the exclusion of marginalized voices, nowadays technological innovations such as social media platforms and big data collection are generating new types of threats. These threats are being generated more quickly than society's ability to regulate them. The business model of social media platforms is based on maximizing user engagement through algorithmic personalization and mass data harvesting. The preselection of content for users based on data about their past preferences facilitates the creation of filter bubbles and echo chambers with the consequence that those who mainly rely on social media almost never receive information, news, or opinions that they do not already agree with. These features of social media not only increase group isolation, fragmentation, and polarization but also facilitate the dissemination of misinformation, fake news, conspiracy theories, and the microtargeted manipulation of voters. Amid these threatening developments, we are seeing a decline

---

[10] According to the 2020 OECD report, *Innovative Citizen Participation and New Democratic Institutions: Catching the Deliberative Wave* (Paris: OECD Publishing, 2020), between 1986 and 2019, 289 minipublics were organized across the world.

[11] In this section, we draw from Cristina Lafont, "A Democracy, If We Can Keep It: Remarks on J. Habermas' *The New Structural Transformation of the Public Sphere*," special issue, *Constellations* 30, no. 1 (2023): 77–83.

in traditional media outlets that operate under journalistic norms of impartiality, accuracy, accountability, and so on. Consequently, it is unclear how citizens can stay sufficiently politically informed to engage in meaningful debate with their fellow citizens, even with respect to the most fundamental political problems that they face. At this historical juncture, there is an alarmingly real danger that a shared sense of community simply disappears from the polity. Yet, democratic self-government is only possible if citizens can forge a collective political will by changing one another's hearts and minds on important political decisions in public debate. Democracy is impossible without an inclusive public sphere.

In that context, it is not surprising that deliberative democrats are enthusiastic about the quality of the political deliberation that minipublics enable participants to engage in.[12] Moreover, the inclusiveness and diversity that are characteristics of these deliberative fora provide participants with an experience that is diametrically opposed to an echo chamber or a polarized political debate. This is certainly an important part of the appeal of minipublics, not only among advocates but also among citizens who have had a chance to participate in them. However, there is a tendency to evaluate the potential benefits of these institutional innovations exclusively in terms of either the *positive experience* they provide to participating citizens or the *valuable input* they provide to the political institutions that organize them. Without denying those benefits, we would like to focus on the benefits that properly institutionalized deliberative minipublics could provide not just to the citizens that participate in them but also to *the citizenry as a whole*. In particular, we would like to highlight some *distinctive* contributions that they could make toward *maintaining an inclusive public sphere*.

Political debates in the public sphere tend to be dominated by powerful political actors whose interests often deviate from those of the general public. As mentioned earlier, this has only gotten worse with the spread of social media that facilitates the formation of filter bubbles and echo chambers. In stark contrast, minipublics facilitate well-informed, high-quality deliberation on important political decisions among a randomly selected sample of citizens that reflects the diversity of the specific population that will be subject to the decisions in question. Indeed, as we analyzed in Chapter 2, across all relevant dimensions—inclusion, diversity, access to reliable and balanced information, independence, impartiality, orientation toward the public interest, and so on—the deliberative conditions available to minipublic participants are the exact opposite of those that prevail in most social forums currently

---

[12] This may eventually be also the case for online deliberation. New communication technologies are enabling experimentation for scaling online deliberation so as to allow an unlimited number of participants to deliberate in small groups together simultaneously. These technological developments are still in their infancy. Yet, if they were to succeed, it could be an extraordinary "effect multiplier" with respect to the benefits that the information generated in these fora could have for political debates, both online and offline. See, e.g., the Stanford Online Deliberation Platform, at https://cdd.stanford.edu/online-deliberation-platform/; John Gastil, "A Theoretical Model of How Digital Platforms for Public Consultation Can Leverage Deliberation to Boost Democratic Legitimacy," *Journal of Deliberative Democracy* 17, no. 1 (2021): 78–89. https://doi.org/10.16997/10.16997/jdd.963; Hélène Landemore, "Can AI Bring Deliberation to the Masses?," in *Conversations in Philosophy, Law and Politics*, ed. R. Chang and A. Srinivasan (Oxford University Press, forthcoming).

240 The Lottocratic Mentality

accessible to citizens. Thus, it does not seem far-fetched to imagine that as more and more citizens become familiar with the workings of minipublics they would become increasingly enthusiastic about them. Indeed, if deliberative minipublics were institutionalized for a variety of purposes at the local, national, and even transnational level, they could become an extremely valuable *resource* to *the entire citizenry* at precisely the time when reliable sources of inclusive, well-informed, impartial political deliberation are getting harder and harder to come by. How could minipublics help improve the inclusiveness and deliberative quality of public debates?

To begin with, minipublics could serve some important functions that are not all that different from those that traditional media outlets (used to) fulfill. As is the case with traditional media outlets, their contribution would not consist in doing the thinking or deciding *for* the citizenry.[13] Rather, their distinctive contribution would be to articulate the most relevant arguments for and against policies from a variety of political perspectives readily available to all citizens. Minipublics can do this by filtering out irrelevant or patently manipulative considerations that cannot survive public scrutiny while highlighting the key information, potential trade-offs, and long-term consequences of the available alternatives as evaluated from the diverse political perspectives that resonate with the citizenry of a specific political community at a given time.

Minipublics are particularly well suited to serve this function. Precisely to the extent that their randomly selected participants reflect the diversity of perspectives from within the specific population in question, the reasons and considerations that lead them to form their considered judgments are likely to be those that resonate with the rest of the citizenry.[14] Moreover, by highlighting the considerations that are most relevant to reaching a considered judgment on the political issue in question, minipublics would not simply reduce the costs of acquiring that type of information for members of the public at large.[15] Minipublics would also serve the crucial function of sorting out the "wheat from the chaff," i.e., the information that reflects the considered views of citizens as opposed to the many misleading claims that are strategically deployed to subvert rather than inform and that are simply unable to survive deliberative scrutiny.[16] By testing the available arguments and providing their considered judgments to their fellow citizens, minipublics could play a constructive role

---

[13] In fact, if minipublics were institutionalized so that they had binding authority to make decisions while bypassing public debates by the citizenry, they would undermine rather than support the maintenance of a democratic public sphere. For a detailed discussion of this question, see Lafont, *Democracy without Shortcuts*. For some empirical evidence in support of the concern that empowered minipublics could be an illegitimate shortcut to the broader public, see L. G. Giraudet et al., "'Co-construction' in Deliberative Democracy: Lessons from the French Citizens' Convention for Climate," *Humanities and Social Sciences Communications* 9, no. 1 (2022): 1–16, esp. 12–3.

[14] See Fishkin, *Democracy When the People Are Thinking*, 72.

[15] On the importance of citizens' use of informational shortcuts in our complex modern societies, see Arthur Lupia, "Shortcuts versus Encyclopedias," *American Political Science Review* 88, no. 1 (1994): 63–76; Lupia, *Uninformed: Why People Know So Little about Politics and What We Can Do about It* (New York: Oxford University Press, 2016). See also Kevin J. Elliott, *Democracy for Busy People* (Chicago: University of Chicago Press, 2023).

[16] See Simon Niemeyer, "Scaling Up Deliberation to Mass Publics: Harnessing Mini-publics in a Deliberative System," in *Deliberative Mini-publics: Involving Citizens in the Democratic Process*, ed. Kimmo Grönlund, André Bächtiger, and Maija Setälä, 177–201. (Colchester: ECPR Press, 2014), 14.

in *structuring public discourses*. On important political decisions, minipublics could act as a regulator of information in the public sphere by doing the hard work of sorting through arguments and then providing reasons for the resulting positions to the rest of the public. Moreover, due to their inclusiveness, minipublics could not only identify acceptable public arguments, but they could also help publicize the concerns of marginalized groups that, at present, hardly ever find a voice among the influential political actors that dominate public debates.

Here it is important to highlight that the participants in minipublics are as diverse as the citizenry itself, and they are therefore just as likely to disagree in their considered opinions on contested political issues as the rest of the citizenry is. However, this does not make minipublics useless. To the contrary, if their reasoning and recommendations are made widely available, they can provide *crucial* information to the rest of the citizenry. Precisely in cases where we disagree, it is essential to know the interests, values, and lines of reasoning that resonate with our fellow citizens with respect to contentious political issues. Knowing the genuine sources of contention and disagreement on specific political issues—as opposed to the manipulative claims and pseudoarguments that constantly circulate in the public sphere—would enable citizens to figure out the kind of information, evidence, arguments, or counterarguments that they would need to provide to their fellow citizens in order to advance the public debate on these issues. This is precisely what citizens have a difficult time doing in an increasingly fragmented and polarized public sphere.

So far, we have only highlighted the democratic significance of the distinctive information that minipublics' can provide to the rest of the citizenry for important political decisions. They can provide (1) recommendations for or against the decisions in question and, even more importantly, (2) the main reasons for and against them. In contrast to similar information provided by other actors (e.g., experts, politicians, activists, etc.), the information provided by minipublics has a *distinctive democratic significance* precisely because it reflects the diversity of interests, values, and perspectives that are present in the citizenry. However, it is important to keep in mind that this is the case regarding the recommendations, reasons, and perspectives endorsed by *all the participants in a minipublic* and not just those endorsed by the majority. After all, participants who find themselves in the minority of a minipublic have reviewed the same information and deliberated as much as the other participants, even if they have reached different conclusions. Participants in a minipublic disagree in their considered opinions on political decisions just as much as the rest of the citizenry does. This is particularly clear in the case of Deliberative Polls. Since participants are under no pressure to come to an agreement on some collective opinion or recommendation, deliberative polling always reflects the percentage of those in favor (or against) a decision on a certain political issue. But this is why nonparticipating citizens have no reason to assume that the recommendations endorsed either by the majority or the minority of the sample are the ones that reflect their own concerns, interests, and policy objectives. If this is so, then what possible use could the information provided by minipublics have for the rest of the citizenry?

242 The Lottocratic Mentality

Citizens would have very good reasons to take the opinions and recommendations of minipublics *seriously* to the extent that they are indicative of the considered political views that are likely to resonate with their fellow citizens. To be used in this way, minipublics would need to publicize not just a recommendation but also the background information that they took to be essential for a proper understanding of what is at stake as well as the most important reasons and arguments for and against the recommendation that achieved majority support. Nonparticipants could use this information to make up their minds about the issues under debate. But, for any particular political issue, since nonparticipating citizens have no reason to assume a higher congruence between their interests or values and those of the minipublic's majority rather than its minority, they have no good reason to simply *trust* and blindly follow the majority's recommendation (e.g., when voting on referenda, initiatives, etc.). As we argued in Chapter 6, if it is true that the random sample reflects the plurality of views, interests, and values of the citizenry, then it cannot be true that all nonparticipating citizens are *like* the sample's majority and unlike its minority. This is why the populist conception of representation as embodiment is *inadequate* for understanding the relationship between minipublics participants and the rest of the citizenry. But, how should this relationship be properly understood? This fundamental question needs to be addressed before we can evaluate specific proposals for institutionalizing minipublics.

8.3 An Alternative to Usurpation: From Being *Like Us* to Speaking *to Us*

In order to get a better grasp on the relationship between the participants in a minipublic and the citizenry as a whole, it is important to keep in mind that this is a many-to-many relationship. At its best, the *random sample as a whole* reflects (the interests, values, and perspectives of) the *citizenry as a whole*. This is why the former can provide interesting information about the latter to nonparticipating citizens. However, this is the case only for the information that is *collectively* selected by all members of the sample and is therefore *representative of the whole sample*. By contrast, since nonparticipating citizens have not chosen any specific members of the sample to represent their concerns, interests, and values, there is no relationship of individual representation involved between them and any particular member or specific subset of the sample (there is neither a one-to-one nor a one-to-many relationship of representation). This also explains why nonparticipants have no reason to expect greater congruence between their interests, values, and objectives and those of some particular subset of the sample as opposed to any other, and thus why they have no good reason to blindly trust a recommendation that has been arrived at by *merely a subset of the sample* (e.g., the majority) regardless of how big or small each subset might be. Citizens can trust the minipublics' *collective* selection of relevant information for understanding the issue in question. They can also trust that the *collectively* selected reasons for and against the majority's recommendation accurately reflect those considerations that will most likely resonate with the citizenry. But to determine whether or not they want to endorse the *majority*'s recommendation citizens need to figure out for themselves *which* of these opposing reasons are most congruent with their own interests, values, and policy objectives.

This is what the populist conception of representation as embodiment gets wrong. Minipublic participants cannot speak *for us* because we have not elected them to do so. Moreover, they cannot speak *like us* because we, the people, are not a politically homogeneous group. Instead, they should speak *to us*, their fellow citizens, so that we can collectively improve the deliberative and democratic quality of our political decisions. Instead of usurping our decision-making power, they can provide us with crucial information about the reasons for and against particular policy decisions that are likely to resonate with our fellow citizens so that we can make up our own minds and better understand the concerns, interests, and values of our fellow citizens, especially those with whom we disagree. Since participants in minipublics are not empowered to act as our political representatives and make decisions for us, there are no legitimacy concerns that stem from the fact that, over the course of deliberation, they often end up changing their minds and thereby come to disagree with the majority of their fellow citizens. While it would be a clear case of usurpation to claim that the voice of the minipublic after deliberation is the voice of "the people," especially in cases when they are on record *dissenting from the actual people* on the issue in question, this ceases to be a problem if their role is not to be a proxy of the people but rather to inform the people about the most important reasons for and against certain political decisions that will likely resonate with the public at large. This is all the more important if minipublics are expected to close representational "gaps" that afflict current democratic institutions and which have fueled the recent rise in populism. In order to do so, deliberative minipublics need to be designed with participatory rather than populist aims in mind.[17] They must highlight the diversity of interests, values, and policy objectives among participants instead of conveying a misleading impression of political homogeneity. For instance, minipublics such as Deliberative Polls that do not require participants to unanimously agree on a single recommendation offer a clearly preferable model in this regard. In addition, instead of simply issuing a recommendation, minipublics should also provide the citizenry with information about the most important reasons for and against a decision that were singled out by their participants. This would assist the citizenry in making up their own minds about the decisions in question while also making them aware of the need to take the reasonable views of dissenting fellow citizens seriously.[18] By contrast, designing minipublics with a lottocratic expectation that citizens blindly follow their

---

[17] For a discussion of the implications of a participatory reorientation in the design and implementation of deliberative minipublics, see Nicole Curato, Julien Vrydagh, and André Bächtiger, "Democracy without Shortcuts: Introduction to the Special Issue," *Journal of Deliberative Democracy* 16, no. 2 (2020): 4–5. https://doi.org/10.16997/jdd/413.

[18] For a detailed defense of the democratic advantages of designing minipublics in this way, see Simon Niemeyer, "The Emancipatory Effect of Deliberation: Empirical Lessons from Mini-publics," *Politics & Society* 39, no. 1 (2011): 128.

244 The Lottocratic Mentality

recommendations because their participants are "like them" would reinforce rather than undermine populist assumptions.

So far, we have only highlighted why citizens have good reasons to pay attention to what deliberative minipublics have to say with respect to any political decisions under consideration. But we have not yet addressed the question of what specific functions minipublics could fulfill if they were properly institutionalized. This is a very broad question, and it would be nearly impossible to give an exhaustive survey of all the proposals currently under discussion.[19] We will therefore simply highlight a few proposals to illustrate some of various ways that minipublics could empower the citizenry to make the political system more responsive to their interests, values, and policy objectives and thereby bolster democratization. The point of discussing these proposals is simply to show that, if they are designed with participatory instead of lottocratic aims in mind, lottery-based institutions could fulfill very ambitious democratic functions.

8.4 Minipublics' Contribution to Empowering the Citizenry: A Few Examples

Before discussing proposals that have not yet been put into practice, we would like to mention a couple of actual examples that exemplify the participatory approach we favor while fostering different levels of empowerment in the citizenry.[20] On the weakest end of this empowerment spectrum, some minipublics are organized independently of formal institutions and with the exclusive aim of activating public debate on contested issues. Fishkin's Deliberative Polls such as "America in One Room" (A1R) fit into this category. A1R gathered 500 American voters for a nonpartisan discussion of the major issues in the 2020 presidential election.[21] While it was organized in the run-up to a presidential election, it was not institutionally connected to a formal decision-making process. The potential to induce broader debate entirely depended upon uptake by the media. By contrast, an actual example of a minipublic located on the stronger end of the citizen empowerment spectrum is the Citizens' Initiative Review in Oregon.[22] After having the opportunity to become informed and deliberate about an active ballot measure, participants in the citizens' jury are asked

---

[19] For a useful typology of current proposals, see Dimitri Courant, "Institutionalizing Deliberative Mini-publics? Issues of Legitimacy and Power for Randomly Selected Assemblies in Political Systems," *Critical Policy Studies* 16, no. 2 (2022): 175. doi:10.1080/19460171.2021.2000453. For an overview of existing models of deliberative minipublics and potential routes to institutionalization, see the OECD's report *Innovative Citizen Participation and New Democratic Institutions*, chaps. 2 and 6.

[20] For a more detailed discussion of these proposals, see Cristina Lafont, "Which Decision-Making Authority for Citizens' Assemblies," in *De Gruyter Handbook of Citizen's Assemblies*, ed. Reuchamps, Vrydagh, and Welp, 47–58.

[21] See James Fishkin, Alice Siu, Larry Diamond, and Norman Bradburn, "Is Deliberation an Antidote to Extreme Partisan Polarization? Reflections on 'America in One Room,'" *American Political Science Review* 115, no. 4 (2021): 1464–81. doi:10.1017/S0003055421000642.

[22] For an in-depth analysis, see John Gastil et al., "Assessing the Electoral Impact of the 2010 Oregon Citizens' Initiative Review," *American Politics Research* 46, no. 3 (2018): 534–63. https://doi.org/10.1177/1532673X17715620.

to produce a statement that contains key facts as well as the best reasons to vote both for and against the measure in question. This statement is then sent to every registered voter in the state as part of the official Voters' Pamphlet. This information helps citizens exercise their voting power more thoughtfully and democratically by lowering the cost of becoming informed about both the political decision in question and the main concerns of their fellow citizens.

Apart from these actual examples, there are many proposals that envision minipublics being used as tools for even *stronger* forms of citizen empowerment. We would like to mention two proposals that exemplify different degrees of stronger empowerment. Although these examples by no means exhaust the range of possible institutional designs of minipublics, they exemplify the participatory approach that we favor. The citizen-initiated citizens' assemblies recently discussed by the Flemish parliament in Belgium is an interesting proposal. According to a Green Party proposed bill, after gathering 80,000 signatures, citizens could demand a citizens' assembly on any topic within the competencies of Flanders. The citizens' assembly would scrutinize the proposal in question and have the power to amend it accordingly. Although the bill was defeated in parliament, it nevertheless offered an ambitious model for how citizens' assemblies could be institutionalized with strong participatory aims in mind.[23] Still, this proposal would only give citizens the power to petition parliament to consider certain policies. This would certainly enhance citizens' ability to set the political agenda, but it would not give them the final say. To that extent, this proposal falls on the weaker side of the citizen empowerment spectrum.

On the strongest side of the spectrum is a proposal that would enable deliberative agenda setting for ballot propositions. Fishkin has articulated this proposal based on his experience with a deliberative poll he organized in California in 2011 (*What's Next California*). This proposal would give citizens the power of both agenda setting and ratification.[24] The idea is to periodically convene minipublics to assess proposals for initiatives submitted by civic groups that satisfy some low threshold of signatures and then to determine which should go on the ballot. Participants would receive relevant, balanced information about the proposed initiatives. After deliberating about the "pros and cons," they would then have the power to select the best initiatives to be included on the ballot and to even amend those initiatives in light of their deliberations. This proposal would give some decision-making authority to citizens' assemblies (e.g., selecting among initiatives and amending them), but the citizenry would retain the power to both propose initiatives and ratify them. Institutionalizing minipublics to regularly serve in this role would significantly enhance citizens' capacity to shape the political agenda and to make the political process more responsive to

---

[23] Ronald Van Crombrugge, "The Derailed Promise of a Participatory Minipublic: The Citizens' Assembly Bill in Flanders," *Journal of Deliberative Democracy* 16, no. 2 (2020): 63–72. https://doi.org/10.16997/jdd.402.

[24] James Fishkin, Thad Kousser, Robert C. Luskin, and Alice Siu, "Deliberative Agenda Setting: Piloting Reform of Direct Democracy in California," *Perspectives on Politics* 13, no. 4 (2015): 1030–42; James Fishkin, "Random Assemblies for Lawmaking: Prospects and Limits," in *Legislature by Lot*, ed. Gastil and Wright, 79–103.

their concerns, interests, and policy objectives. Indeed, lowering the number of signatures needed for initiatives to be eligible for review by minipublics would enable citizens from marginalized groups to put issues on the political agenda that have thus far been ignored in public debates. While it is true that sharp disagreements among citizens on contested political issues may impede the adoption of many initiatives and this may mean that the review process carried out by the minipublic may not make a big difference, it would nevertheless make a big difference for all cases wherein an overwhelming majority of citizens endorse policies that elected politicians see as either intractable or not worth confronting.[25] Precisely in cases of political "gridlock" or the "capture" of political institutions by special interests, it becomes particularly clear that a bottom-up approach to institutionalizing minipublics has enormous democratic potential. Giving minipublics the power to review citizens' initiatives and decide which ones to include in the ballot would severely constrain elected officials' discretion to keep ignoring concerns and priorities that enjoy wide support among the citizenry. It would also energize the citizenry to actively participate in the process of proposing and publicly discussing initiatives, as they will now know that there is an effective institutional mechanism to get them reviewed and that it will be ultimately up to citizens whether or not to approve them. Strengthening citizen participation in this way would provide a very much needed democratic boost precisely at a time of increasing citizen dissatisfaction with democracy. But, it would not be its only democratic impact.

Giving minipublics the power to review initiatives based on all the relevant information and processes of inclusive deliberation would also enhance the inclusiveness and deliberative quality of direct democracy mechanisms such as voting. Under our currently dismal conditions of political deliberation in the public sphere, voting can at best make the political process responsive to citizens' raw and uniformed preferences. However, institutionalizing minipublics in a mediating role would help enhance not just any form of responsiveness but also *deliberative responsiveness*, i.e., responsiveness to considered public opinion.[26] As Fishkin notes, if the entire electorate is provided with not only the initiatives but also the best arguments both for and against them, then this use of minipublics "would add a truly deliberative element to mass direct democracy and fulfill many of the initial aspirations of the initiative to empower the people to engage in thoughtful self-government."[27]

In sum, lottery-based institutions offer numerous possibilities for enhancing the democratic quality of our electoral-representative institutions. But, they can only do

---

[25] To mention just a few US examples where a large majority of the citizenry supports policies that nevertheless have trouble advancing through the legislature: raising the tax rate on the very wealthy (76%), enacting limits on campaign contributions (77%), requiring criminal and mental background checks for all gun sales (77%), preventing people with a history of mental illness from owning guns (78%), providing a path to citizenship for currently undocumented immigrants in the United States (81%), raising the federal minimum wage from $7.25 to $10 per hour (71%), and providing free lunch to low-income students in public schools (86%).

[26] We borrow the term "deliberative responsiveness" from Claudia Landwehr and Armin Schäfer, "The Promise of Representative Democracy: Deliberative Responsiveness," *Research Publica* (2023). https://doi.org/10.1007/s11158-023-09640-0.

[27] Fishkin, *Democracy When the People Are Thinking*, 101.

so if they are designed to play an intermediary role between the political system and the wider public rather than being directly coupled with formal political institutions while also *bypassing the citizenry*. Undoubtedly, minipublics are not a panacea for overcoming the grave democratic deficits in our contemporary democracies. But precisely in light of the current crisis in democracy, citizens cannot afford to squander any potential assistance that institutional innovations may provide in their struggles for democratization. It would be a shame to waste whatever democratic contribution lottery-based institutions could make to civic empowerment by letting these institutions become yet another shortcut that bypasses the citizenry and further cements the rule of the few.

As we have shown earlier, the lottocratic mentality explains why this latter option has been so alluring to so many scholars. Unfortunately, the dangers of that mentality go well beyond the fate of lottery-based institutions. They are deeply problematic for sustaining democratic ideals in general. But given that proposals for institutionalizing lottery-based institutions are at the center of the development of the lottocratic mentality, they are the perfect pivot point to combat and counteract its nefarious effects. If those involved in designing and organizing minipublics explicitly distance themselves from the lottocratic mentality, then there is a chance that the institutionalization of minipublics might follow the democratic path of empowering the many, instead of the few. For the sake of democracy, we very much hope that the lottocratic alternative remains the path not taken.

Conclusion

Constitutional democracy is a complex and highly institutionalized legal and political order. It cannot be understood within the simple binary logic of the relations between the state and the individual. The legal system and the bureaucracy, the local and national administrative bodies, and the civil and military sectors are the structural pillars of the state on which constitutional democracy rests. If we shift our attention to the political activity that inspires and animates the institutions where lawmaking actually takes place, then we encounter another system of public agencies. "Representative democracy" is the broad label for this further set of integrated activities that bubbles up from civil society and that utilizes institutions and norms to lend coherence and articulation to forms of life and social relations. Unlike in ancient democracies, in modern democracies *kratos* has become complex and mediated such that power is, on the one hand, less raw and direct in terms of its impact on political subjects and, on the other, less clear in terms of where it should be used and who should use it. Lefort famously wrote that in representative democracies power is dispersed—it is not contained in any particular place or institution but rather is constructed by the citizens through direct and indirect forms of individual and collective public agency. Thus, both opinion formation and decision-making institutions are part of *kratos*, even if they belong to it under the color of different authorities. Both, however, are indispensable and intertwined. This is why, for instance, even a minor change in the constitution immediately impacts the political and social life of citizens and their institutions more generally. Conversely, even if the formal constitution does not change, shifts in the political climate or the tenor of public discourse can impact the constitutional order and ethos—for example, through the rise of polarizing identities or populist leaders. This circulation of opinions and energies is what characterizes representative democracy. Representative democracy consists of a system of institutions and practices that are either directly authorized with power or which hold power in an auxiliary, "semisovereign," or informal fashion, but which are vital insofar as the authorizing power of institutions could hardly be democratically conceived and activated in their absence.

We understand auxiliary bodies and practices in contemporary democracies to include the plethora of organized agencies and activities that interact with formal institutions to train personnel, set political agendas, and disseminate the information and opinions that then shape the formation of legislative proposals and decisions. Paradigmatic examples of these sorts of auxiliary bodies and practices would include political parties, interest groups, civic associations, traditional and digital media, schools and universities, religions (with dedicated places of worship, advocacy

The Lottocratic Mentality. Cristina Lafont and Nadia Urbinati, Oxford University Press. © Cristina Lafont and Nadia Urbinati (2024). DOI: 10.1093/9780191982903.003.0010

associations, and educational institutions), labor unions, social movements, and mutual associations of various kinds. All of these groups and the various practices and activities that they structure count as auxiliary bodies within a democracy (indeed, depending on a country's cultural and political traditions there will likely be even more or more important bodies than these). In many contemporary democracies, innovations such as minipublics, citizens' assemblies, and citizens' juries—that is, forms of aggregation that select by lot—present additional new forms of auxiliary institutions that have gained prominence and are demonstrating democratic promise. Lottery can function to integrate and lend coherence to the amorphous and complex nature of these various auxiliary democratic entities.

However, lottery-based institutional innovations are not just one more auxiliary body. As we noted, in the domain of public opinion and institutions even a modest change may turn out to have a large impact upon the entire system. For example, an auxiliary use of minipublics can have a direct impact on the structures of political parties and their activities. Today, political parties in several countries are experimenting with and adopting new forms of consultation and guidance to reflect citizens' concerns and proposals more effectively. Their traditional antennas are no longer a unique channel of communication and information; they are seeking new ways of relating to citizens outside the tight circle formed by their most ardent devotees and those they assume will follow them. In the past, traditional mass-based political parties were able to do this work. However, mass-based political parties have declined—with the consequence that discerning citizens' preferences, emotions, and ideas is now a more fluid and uncertain endeavor. Amid these circumstances, political parties and democracy more generally can benefit from innovative lottery-based auxiliary bodies. Lottery has changed and is changing not only the nature of parties but also the nature of political ideas themselves and the relation between partisan views and critical approaches to concrete problems.

We observed that concern with corruption, particularly within an elected political class, is the backbone of the lottocratic mentality. The fight over corruption is controversial since citizens, politicians, and scholars disagree about its precise definition and meaning. This generates different views about the effects of corruption and the various ways to combat it. Here too lotteries can play a valuable role. One argument that lottocrats deploy to criticize electoral accountability and emphasize the "corrupting logic" of elections is that legislators are often effectively in charge of judging their own cases and causes (e.g., drawing electoral district lines, determining congressional salaries, (not) passing anticorruption laws, etc.). In this respect, lottocrats are right; such blatant conflicts of interest plague the entire system. We agree that it is a serious problem when a political authority is put in charge of judging and legislating about itself. Certainly, in order to avoid what scholars call "mediated corruption," it would be worth "considering the establishment of an external body to judge cases of ethical violations."[1] Selection by lot, with criteria specified by the legislature, could

---

[1] Dennis F. Thompson, *Restoring Responsibility: Ethics in Government, Business, and Healthcare* (Cambridge: Cambridge University Press, 2005), 164–5; as mentioned in Chapter 3, a similar proposal recently came from Hein and Buchstein in relation to the EU parliament.

greatly help in this regard, as it would create an independent institution that, while not taking away the legislature's final say, could nonetheless place a burden on the legislature to publicly justify any opposition.

So, calling such bodies "auxiliary" does not imply that they have a secondary or unimportant function. On the contrary, precisely in a complex system like constitutional representative democracy, auxiliary bodies such as this can be decisive. The terms "auxilium" and "subsidium" come from a military vernacular. The former began to be used in the Roman Republic and the latter was used more systematically in the Roman Empire to denote assistance coming from "non-official" troops, troops that only served in some circumstances or as supplementary forces. When used in wartime, these troops worked as "reinforcements" and very often determined the success of a military operation; in peacetime, they were used as "reserves." In both cases, their actions were not fully authoritative but instead complementary and supplementary. In this way, they were both useful and necessary. Today, the public itself can fulfill auxiliary and subsidiary functions when it is convened in the role of an "auxiliary troupe" that is largely associational and nonofficial, but which is indispensable insofar as it supports "regular forces."

Lottery-based institutions that are structured as auxiliary institutions are more elastic and adaptable to a multitude of functions precisely because they are *not* structured as agencies of the state. In addition to the functions that we analyzed in Chapter 8, they can be adapted to help the work of state functions: in administration and justice (as mentioned above), as oversight agencies (e.g., for the use and control of money in electoral campaigns and to ameliorate gerrymandering), as consultative bodies with respect to changes in the electoral system, and as collaborative bodies when it comes to constitutional amendments. In addition, as noted above, political parties can also make fruitful use of lottery-based bodies deployed in an auxiliary fashion: just like parties, they can monitor, guide, and exert some sense of order and "control" over citizens' concerns and agendas in ways that the law by itself cannot. Lottery-based institutions that were used as intermediary bodies would be able to help form and shape the multifarious channels of political communication that ultimately lead to decision-making. Even in legislative bodies like Congress or parliament, they could be important tools that are used to preside over the formation of parliamentary committees and to distribute responsibilities among representatives so as to prevent the majority (or high-profile members within various political parties) from dominating the entire agenda.

As Dahl, Elster, and Dowlin (among others) have repeatedly emphasized, we must understand the quality and nature of any lottery-based body before we can understand precisely where it can be most usefully and functionally deployed. If a lottery-based institutional innovation is beneficial because it provides impartiality and treats individuals as "indifferent" to one another (as "equals" in a particular sense), then it may be extremely relevant in those areas where information and fairness are important. But if, as lottocrats propose, we were to use lotteries to create laws or choose lawmakers who have a final say over decisions that authorize coercion, then lotteries would function to empowering the few to rule over the many. This would only reinforce the undemocratic flaws of current electoral institutions that lottocrats denounce—namely, the dualism between the few who rule and the many who submit to their decisions. This dynamic would persist irrespective of whether the few were selected or elected (indeed, if they were selected then this would aggravate matters insofar as accountability disappears altogether). As we have argued throughout the book, by giving the sovereign *kratos* to lotteries we would need to enhance the power of bureaucrats and create and strengthen new legal sanctions. Moreover, we would not avoid the risk that the state could be "captured" by an elite group—we would instead transform the expert bureaucrats into the capturers, i.e., professionals and technicians who are unlikely to be accountable to ordinary citizens and who can seize the state instead.

References

Abizadeh, Arash. "In Defense of Imperfection: An Election-Sortition Compromise." In *Legislature by Lot: Transformative Designs for Deliberative Governance*, edited by John Gastil and Erik Olin Wright, 249–255. London: Verso, 2019.

Abizadeh, Arash. "Representation, Bicameralism, Political Equality and Sortition: Reconstituting the Second Chamber as a Randomly Selected Assembly." *Perspectives on Politics* 19, no. 3 (2021): 791–806.

Achen, Christopher H., and Larry M. Bartels. *Democracy for Realists*. Princeton, NJ: Princeton University Press, 2016.

Ackerman, Bruce. *Social Justice in the Liberal States*. New Haven, CT: Yale University Press, 1980.

Ackerman, Bruce. *We the People*. Vol. 1, *Foundations*. Cambridge: Cambridge University Press, 1991.

Adams, John. "Letter to John Penn." In *The Works of John Adams*. A 10 volumes collections of Adams' most important writings, letters, and state papers edited by his Grandson, Charles Francis Adams. Vol. 4, 209–213. Boston: Little and Brown, 1851.

Amar, Akhil Reed. "Choosing Representatives by Lottery Voting." *Yale Law Journal* 6, no. 7 (1984): 1283–1308.

Anderson, Greg. *The Athenian Experiment: Building an Imagined Political Community in Ancient Attica, 508–490 B.C.* Ann Arbor: University of Michigan Press, 2003.

Arendt, Hannah. *On Revolution*. London: Penguin Books, 1990.

Atchison, Thomas C. "Distrusting Climate Science: A Problem in Practical Epistemology for Citizens." In *Between Scientists and Citizens*, edited by Jean Goodwin, 61–73. Iowa City: Great Plains Society for the Study of Argumentation, 2012.

Bächtiger, André, John S. Dryzek, Jane Mansbridge, and Mark E. Warren, eds. *The Oxford Handbook of Deliberative Democracy*. Oxford: Oxford University Press, 2018.

Barber, Benjamin. *Strong Democracy: Participatory Politics for a New Age*. Berkeley: University of California Press, 1984.

Barnett, Anthony, and Peter Carty. *The Athenian Option: Radical Reform of the House of Lords*. Exeter: Imprint Academic, 1998.

Beauvais, Edana, and Mark E. Warren. "What Can Deliberative Mini-publics Contribute to Democratic Systems?" *European Journal of Political Research* 58, no. 3 (2019): 893–914.

Beitz, Charles. *Political Equality*. Princeton, NJ: Princeton University Press, 1989.

Bellamy, Richard. *Political Constitutionalism*. Cambridge: Cambridge University Press, 2007.

Benhabib, Seyla, ed. *Democracy and Difference: Contesting the Boundaries of the Political*. Princeton, NJ: Princeton University Press, 1996.

Besson, Samantha, and José Luis Martí, eds. *Deliberative Democracy and Its Discontents*. Aldershot, UK: Ashgate, 2006.

Bettermann, K. A. "Die Aufgabe: Fachgericht für Verfassungsrecht." *Frankfurter Allgemeine Zeitung*, (20 December 1996).

Bikerton, Christopher, and Carlo Invernizzi. *Technopopulism: The New Logic of Democratic Politics*. Oxford: Oxford University Press, 2021.

Blum, Christian, and Christina Isabel Zuber. "Liquid Democracy: Potentials, Problems, and Perspectives." *Journal of Political Philosophy* 24, no. 2 (2016): 162–182.

References 253

Bluntschli, Johan Caspar. "What Is a Political Party?" In *Perspectives on Political Parties: Classic Readings*, edited by Susan E. Scarrow, 75–81. New York: Palgrave Macmillan, 2002.

Bobbio, Norberto. *The Future of Democracy: A Defence of the Rules of the Game*. Translated by Roger Griffin. Minneapolis: University of Minnesota Press, 1987.

Bohman, James. "Survey Article: The Coming of Age of Deliberative Democracy." *Journal of Political Philosophy* 6, no. 4 (1998): 400–425.

Bohman, James, and William Rehg, eds. *Deliberative Democracy*. Cambridge, MA: MIT Press, 1999.

Bonotti, Matteo. *Partisanship and Political Liberalism in Diverse Societies*. Oxford: Oxford University Press, 2017.

Bonotti, Matteo and Zim Nwokora (forthcoming). *Money, Parties and Democracy: Political Finance Between Fat Cats and Big Government*. Oxford: Oxford University Press.

Bontempi, Milena. "Il misto della 'politeia' in Platone." *Filosofia politica* 19, no. 1 (2005): 9–24.

Bouricius, Terrill. "Democracy through Multi-body Sortition: Athenian Lessons for the Modern Day." *Journal of Public Deliberation* 9, no. 1 (2013): 1–19.

Bouricius, Terrill. "Why Hybrid Bicameralism Is Not Right for Sortition." *Politics & Society* 46, no. 3 (2018): 435–451.

Boyle, Connan. "Organizations Selecting People: How the Process Could Be Made Fairer by the Appropriate Use of Lotteries." *Journal of the Royal Statistical Society*, ser. D, 47, no. 2 (1998): 291–321.

Brady, David W., John Ferejohn, and Laurel Harbridge. "Polarization and Public Policy: A General Assessment." In *Red and Blue Nation?*, vol. 1, *Characteristics and Causes of America's Polarized Politics*, edited by Pietro S. Nivola and David W. Brady, 185–216. Washington, DC: Brookings Institution, 2008.

Brennan, Jason, and Lisa Hill. *Compulsory Voting: For and Against*. Cambridge: Cambridge University Press, 2014.

Brennan, Jason, and Hélène Landemore. *Debating Democracy: Do We Need More or Less?* Oxford: Oxford University Press, 2022.

Brizzi, Giovanni. *Imperium. Il potere a Roma*. Roma-Bari: Laterza, 2024.

Brown, Mark B. "Survey Article: Citizen Panels and the Concept of Representation." *Journal of Political Philosophy* 14, no. 2 (2006): 203–225.

Bruni, Leonardo. *History of the Florentine People*. Vol. 2, *Books 5–8*. Translated by James Hankins. Cambridge, MA: Harvard University Press, 2004.

Buchstein, Hubertus. "Countering the 'Democracy Thesis'—Sortition in Ancient Greek Political Theory." *Redescriptions* 18, no. 2 (2015): 126–157.

Buchstein, Hubertus. "Democracy and Lottery: Revisited." *Constellations* 26, no. 3 (2019): 361–377.

Buchstein, Hubertus, and Michael Hein. "Randomizing Europe: The Lottery as a Political Instrument for a Reformed European Union." In *Sortition: Theory and Practice*, edited by Gil Delannoi and Oliver Dowlen, 119–156. Exeter: Imprint Academic, 2010.

Burnheim, John. *Is Democracy Possible? The Alternative to Electoral Politics*. Sydney: Sydney University Press, 1985; new ed., 2006.

Bussu, Sonia, and Dannica Fleuß. "Citizens' Assemblies: Top-Down or Bottom-Up?—Both, Please!" In *De Gruyter Handbook of Citizens' Assemblies. Citizens' Assemblies and Mini-Publics*, vol. 1, edited by M Reuchamps, J Vrydagh & Y Welp, 141–154. Berlin: De Gruyter, 2023.

Calise, Mauro. "The Personal Party: An Analytical Framework." *Italian Political Science Review* 45, no. 3 (2015): 301–315.

Callenbach, Ernest, and Michael Phillips. *A Citizen Legislature*. Berkeley, CA: Banyan Tree Books, 1985.

254 References

Cammack, Daniela. "The Democratic Significance of the Classical Athenian Courts" (September 21, 2016). In *Decline: Decadence, Decay and Decline in History and Society*, edited by William O'Reilly. (Central European University Press, originally expected 2017). Available at SSRN: https://ssrn.com/abstract=2110824

Canevaro, Mirko. "Institutions and Variations in Greek Democracy" (2023). In *The Cambridge History of Democracy*, vol. 1, edited by Valentina Arena and Eric Robinson. Cambridge: Cambridge University. (Accepted/In press).

Canevaro, Mirko. "Majority Rule versus Consensus: The Practice of Democratic Deliberation in the Greek *Poleis*." In *Ancient Greek History and Contemporary Social Science*, edited by Mirko Canevaro, Andrew Erskine, Benjamin Gray, and Josiah Ober, 101–156. Edinburgh: Edinburgh University Press, 2018.

Canevaro, Mirko. "Politica, diritto e giustizia tra oralità e scrittura." In *Atene, vivere in una città antica*, edited by Marco Bettalli and Maurizio Giangiulio, 263–282. Rome: Carocci, 2023.

Canevaro, Mirko, and Alberto Esu. "Extreme Democracy and Mixed Constitution in Theory and Practice: *Nomophylakia* and Fourth-Century *Nomothesia* in the Aristotelian *Athenaion Politeia*." In *Athenaion Politeiai tra storia, politica e sociologia: Aristotele e Pseudo-Senofonte*, edited by C. Bearzot, M. Canevaro, T. Gargiulo, and E. Poddighe, 105–145. Milan: LED, 2018.

Canovan, Margaret. *Populism*. New York: Harcourt Brace Jovanovich, 1981.

Canovan, Margaret. "'Trust the People!' Populism and the Two Faces of Democracy." *Political Studies* 47, no. 1 (1999): 2–16.

Carpenter, Daniel. *Democracy by Petition: Popular Politics in Transformations, 1790–1870*. Cambridge, MA: Harvard University Press, 2021.

Carson, Lyn. "How to Ensure Deliberation within a Sortition Chamber." In *Legislature by Lot: Transformative Designs for Deliberative Governance*, edited by John Gastil and Erik Olin Wright, 205–228. London: Verso, 2019.

Cartledge, Paul. "Comparatively Equal." In *Dēmokratia: A Conversation on Democracies, Ancient and Modern*, edited by Josiah Ober and Charles Hedrick, 75–86. Princeton, NJ: Princeton University Press, 1996.

Casaleggio, Gianroberto. *Web ergo sum*. Milan: Sperling & Kupfer, 2004.

Castoriadis, Cornelius. "The Greek Polis and the Creation of Democracy." In Id., *Philosophy, Politics, Autonomy: Essays in Political Philosophy*, 81–123. New York: Oxford University Press, 1991.

Cerovac, Ivan. "The Epistemic Value of Partisanship." *Croatian Journal of Philosophy* 18, no. 55 (2019): 99–117.

Ceva, Emanuela, and Valeria Ottonelli. "Second-Personal Authority and the Practice of Democracy." *Constellations* 29, no. 4 (2021): 460–474.

Chambers, Simone. *Contemporary Democratic Theory*. Cambridge: Polity, 2024.

Chambers, Simone. "Deliberative Democratic Theory." *Annual Review of Political Science*, vol. 6 (2003): 307–326.

Chambers, Simone. "Rhetoric and the Public Sphere: Has Deliberative Democracy Abandoned Mass Democracy?" *Political Theory* 37, no. 3 (2009): 323–350.

Chapman, Emilee Booth. *Election Day: How We Vote and What It Means for Democracy*. Princeton, NJ: Princeton University Press, 2022.

Chollet, Antoine, and Aurèle Dupuis. "Kübellos in the Canton of Glarus: A Unique Experience of Sortition in Politics." In *Sortition and Democracy: History, Tools, Theories*, edited by Liliane Lopez-Rabatel and Yves Sintomer, 264–280. Exeter: Imprint Academic, 2020.

Christiano, Thomas. *The Constitution of Equality: Democratic Authority and Its Limits*. Oxford: Oxford University Press, 2008.

Christiano, Thomas. *The Rule of the Many: Fundamental Issues in Democratic Theory.* Boulder, CO: Westview, 1996.

Cohen, Joshua. "Procedure and Substance in Deliberative Democracy." In *Democracy and Difference: Contesting the Boundaries of the Political*, edited by Seyla Benhabib, 407–437. Princeton, NJ: Princeton University Press, 1996.

Cohen, Joshua. "Reflections on Deliberative Democracy." In Id., *Philosophy, Politics, Democracy: Selected Essays*, 326–347. Cambridge, MA: Harvard University Press, 2009.

Constant, Benjamin. "Principles of Politics Applicable to All Representative Governments." In Id., *Political Writings*, edited by Biancamaria Fontana, 170–305. Cambridge: Cambridge University Press, 1988.

Conti, Gregory. *Parliament the Mirror of the Nation: Representation, Deliberation, and Democracy in Victorian Britain.* Cambridge: Cambridge University Press, 2019.

Cottrell, Allin, and Paul Cockshott. *Toward a New Socialism.* Nottingham: Spokesman, 1993.

Courant, Dimitri. "From Kleroterion to Cryptology: The Act of Sortition in the 21st Century." In *Sortition and Democracy: History, Tools, Theories*, edited by Liliane Lopez-Rabatel and Yves Sintomer, 343–371. Exeter: Imprint Academic, 2020.

Courant, Dimitri. "Institutionalizing Deliberative Mini-publics? Issues of Legitimacy and Power for Randomly Selected Assemblies in Political Systems." *Critical Policy Studies* vol. 16, no. 2 (2022): 162–180. doi:10.1080/19460171.2021.2000453.

Courant, Dimitri. "Sortition and Democratic Principles: A Comparative Analysis." In *Legislature by Lot: Transformative Designs for Deliberative Governance*, edited by John Gastil and Erik Olin Wright, 229–247. London: Verso, 2019.

Crosby, Ned. "Citizens Juries: One Solution for Difficult Environmental Questions." In *Fairness and Competence in Citizen Participation.* Technology, Risk, and Society 10, edited by Jeryl Mumpower, Ortwin Renn, and Peter Wiedemann, 157–174. Springer: Dordrecht, 1995.

Crosby, Ned. *In Search of the Competent Citizen.* Plymouth: Center for New Democratic Processes, 1975.

Crosby, Ned, and Doug Nethercut. "Citizen Juries: Creating a Trustworthy Voice of the People." In *Deliberative Democracy Handbook*, edited by John Gastil and Peter Levine, 111–119. San Francisco: Jossey-Bass, 2005.

Curato, Nicole, Julien Vrydagh, and André Bächtiger. "Democracy without Shortcuts: Introduction to the Special Issue." *Journal of Deliberative Democracy* vol. 16, no. 2 (2020): 1–9. https://doi.org/10.16997/jdd/413.

Dahl, Robert A. *After the Revolution? Authority in a Good Society.* New Haven, CT: Yale University Press, 1970.

Dahl, Robert A. *Controlling Nuclear Weapons: Democracy versus Guardianship.* Syracuse, NY: Syracuse University Press, 1985.

Dahl, Robert A. *Democracy and Its Critics.* New Haven, CT: Yale University Press, 1989.

Dahl, Robert A. *A Preface to Democratic Theory.* Chicago: University of Chicago Press, 1956.

Dahl, Robert A. "Procedural Democracy." In *Contemporary Political Philosophy: An Anthology*, edited by Robert Goodin and Philip Pettit, 107–125. Oxford: Blackwell, 1996.

Dahl, Robert A. "Sketches for a Democratic Utopia." *Scandinavian Political Studies* 10, no. 3 (1987): 195–206.

De Sanctis, Gaetano. *Studi di storia della storiografia greca.* Florence: La Nuova Italia, 1951.

Deaton, Angus. *The Great Escape: Health, Wealth, and the Origins of Inequality.* Princeton, NJ: Princeton University Press, 2013.

Delannoi, Gil. *Le retour du tirage au sort en politique.* Paris: Fondapol, 2010.

256 References

Delannoi, Gil, and Oliver Dowlen, eds. *Sortition: Theory and Practice*. Exeter: Imprint Academic, 2010.

Destri, Chiara, and Annabelle Lever. "Égalité démocratique et tirage au sort." *Raison publique*, 26 no. 1 (2023): 63–79.

Dienel, Peter C., and Ortwin Renn. "Planning Cells: A Gate to 'Fractal' Mediation." In *Fairness and Competence in Citizen Participation: Evaluating Models for Environmental Discourse*, edited by Ortwin Renn, Thomas Webler, and Peter Wiedemann, 117–140. Dordrecht: Kluwer Academic, 1995.

Disch, Lisa. "The Constructivist Turn in Democratic Representation: A Normative Dead-End?" *Constellations* 22, no. 4 (2015): 487–499.

Disch, Lisa. *Making Constituencies: Representation as Mobilization in Mass Democracy*. Chicago: University of Chicago Press, 2021.

Dovi, Susan. *The Good Representative*. Oxford: Blackwell, 2007.

Dovi, Susan. "Preferable Descriptive Representatives: Or Will Just Any Woman, Black, or Latino Do?" *American Political Science Review* 96, no. 4 (2002): 745–754.

Dowlen, Oliver. *The Political Potential of Sortition: A Study of the Random Selection of Citizens for Public Policy*. Exeter: Imprint Academic, 2008.

Dowlen, Oliver. "Random Recruitment as an Element in Constitutional and Institutional Design: A Dialogue between Means and Desired Outcomes." In *Sortition and Democracy: History, Tools, Theories*, edited by Liliane Lopez-Rabatel and Yves Sintomer, 499–525. Exeter: Imprint Academic, 2020.

Dowlen, Oliver. "Sortition and Liberal Democracy: Finding a Way Forward." In *Sortition: Theory and Practice*, edited by Gil Delannoi and Oliver Dowlen, 53–69. Exeter: Imprint Academic, 2010.

Dryzek, John. "The Deliberative Turn in Democratic Theory." In Id., *Deliberative Democracy and Beyond: Liberals, Critics, and Contestation*, 1–7. Oxford: Oxford University Press, 2002.

Dryzek, John, and Simon Niemeyer. "Deliberative Turns." In *Foundations and Frontiers of Deliberative Governance*, edited by John Dryzek, 3–18. Oxford: Oxford University Press, 2010.

Dunn, John. "Situating Democratic Political Accountability." In *Democracy, Accountability, and Representation*, edited by Adam Przeworski, Susan C. Stokes, and Bernard Manin, 329–344. Cambridge: Cambridge University Press, 1999.

Durant, John. "An Experiment in Democracy." In *Public Participation in Science: The Role of Consensus Conferences in Europe*, edited by Simon Joss and John Durant, 75–80. London: Science Museum, 1995.

Elliott, Kevin J. *Democracy for Busy People*. Chicago: University of Chicago Press, 2023.

Elster, Jon, ed. *Deliberative Democracy*. Cambridge: Cambridge University Press, 1998.

Elster, Jon. *Solomonic Judgments: Studies in the Limitations of Rationality*. Cambridge: Cambridge University Press, 1989.

Elstub, Stephen, and Zohreh Khoban. "Citizens' Assemblies: A Critical Perspective." In *De Gruyter Handbook of Citizens' Assemblies. Citizens' Assemblies and Mini-Publics*, vol. 1, edited by M Reuchamps, J Vrydagh & Y Welp, 113–126. Berlin: De Gruyter, 2023.

Errejón, Inigo, and Chantal Mouffe. *Podemos: In the Name of the People*. With a preface by Owen Jones. London: Lawrence and Wishart, 2016.

Esterling, K. M., A. Fung, and T. Lee. "When Deliberation Produces Persuasion Rather than Polarization: Measuring and Modeling Small Group Dynamics in a Field Experiment." *British Journal of Political Science* 51, no. 2 (2021): 666–684.

Estlund, David. *Democratic Authority: A Philosophical Framework*. Princeton, NJ: Princeton University Press, 2008.

Estlund, David, and Hélène Landemore. "The Epistemic Value of Democratic Deliberation." In Bächtiger, André, John S. Dryzek, Jane Mansbridge, and Mark E. Warren, 113–131. Oxford: Oxford University Press, 2018.

Farrar, Cynthia. "Taking our Chances with the Ancient Athenians." In *Démocratie Athénienne, Démocratie Moderne: Tradition et influences: neuf exposés suivis de discussions*, edited by Pasquino, Pasquale, Hansen, Mogens Herman, Hernández, Alain-Christian, 167–217. Vandoevres: Fondation Hardt; Entretiens sur l'Antiquité Classique, 2009.

Felicetti, Andrea, and Donatella Della Porta. "Joining Forces: The Sortition Chamber from a Social Movement Perspective." In *Legislature by Lot: Transformative Designs for Deliberative Governance*, edited by John Gastil and Erik Olin Wright, 145–165. London: Verso, 2019.

Ferejohn, John, and Francis McCall Rosenbluth. "Electoral Representation and the Aristocratic Thesis." In *Political Representation*, edited by Ian Shapiro, Susan C. Stokes, Elisabeth Jean Wood, and Alexander S. Kirshner, 271–303. Cambridge: Cambridge University Press, 2009.

Finley, M. I. *Democracy Ancient and Modernn*. Rev. ed. New Brunswick, NJ: Rutgers University Press, 1988.

Fisher Nick and Hans Van Wees, eds. 'Aristocracy' in *Antiquity: Redefining Greek and Roman Elites*. Swansea: Classical Press of Wales, 2015.

Fishkin, James S. "Deliberation by the People Themselves: Entry Points for the Public Voice." *Election Law Journal* 12, no. 4 (2013): 490–507.

Fishkin, James S. *Democracy and Deliberation*. New Haven, CT: Yale University Press, 1991.

Fishkin, James S. *Democracy When the People Are Thinking*. Oxford: Oxford University Press, 2018.

Fishkin, James S. "Random Assemblies for Lawmaking: Prospects and Limits." In *Legislature by Lot: Transformative Designs for Deliberative Governance*. edited by John Gastil and Erik Olin Wrigh. London: Verso, 2019.

Fishkin, James S. *The Voice of the People: Public Opinion and Democracy*. New Haven, CT: Yale University Press, 1997.

Fishkin, James S. *When the People Speak: Deliberative Democracy and Public Consultation*. Oxford: Oxford University Press, 2009.

Fishkin, James, Thad Kousser, Robert C. Luskin, and Alice Siu. "Deliberative Agenda Setting: Piloting Reform of Direct Democracy in California." *Perspectives on Politics* 13, no. 4 (2015): 1030–1042.

Fishkin, James S., and Peter Laslett, eds. *Debating Deliberative Democracy*. Oxford: Blackwell, 2003.

Fishkin, James, Alice Siu, Larry Diamond, and Norman Bradburn. "Is Deliberation an Antidote to Extreme Partisan Polarization? Reflections on 'America in One Room.'" *American Political Science Review* 115, no. 4 (2021): 1464–1481. doi:10.1017/S0003055421000642.

Floridia, Antonio. *From Participation to Deliberation: A Critical Genealogy of Deliberative Democracy*. Colchester: ECPR Press, 2017.

Floridia, Antonio. "The Origins of the Deliberative Turn." In *Oxford Handbook of Deliberative Democracy*, edited by Bächtiger, Dryzek, Mansbridge, and Warren, 35–54. Oxford: Oxford University Press, 2018.

Fraser, Nancy. "Identity, Exclusion, and Critique: A Response to Four Critics." *European Journal of Political Theory* 6, no. 3 (2007): 313–314.

Fung, Archon. "Minipublics: Deliberative Designs and Their Consequences." In *Deliberation, Participation and Democracy: Can the People Govern?*, edited by Shawn W. Rosenberg, 159–183. New York: Palgrave Macmillan, 2007.

Fung, Archon. "Varieties of Participation in Complex Governance." In "Collaborative Public Management," special issue. *Public Administration Review* 66, (2006): 66–75.

258 References

Fustel de Coulanges, Numa Denis. *The Ancient City: A Study on the Religion, Laws, and Institutions of Greece and Rome*. Garden City, NY: Doubleday Anchor Books, 1956.

Gagarin, Michael, and Paul Woodruff, eds. *Early Greek Political Thought from Homer to the Sophists*. Cambridge: Cambridge University Press, 1995.

Galgano, Francesco. *La forza del numero e la legge della ragione. Storia del principio di maggioranza*. Bologna: Il Mulino, 2007.

Gastil, John. "A Theoretical Model of How Digital Platforms for Public Consultation Can Leverage Deliberation to Boost Democratic Legitimacy." *Journal of Deliberative Democracy* 17, no. 1 (2021): 78–89. https://doi.org/10.16997/10.16997/jdd.963.

Gastil, John, and Katherine R. Knobloch. *Hope For Democracy: How Citizens Can Bring Reason Back into Politics*. New York: Oxford University Press, 2020.

Gastil, John, Katherine R. Knobloch, Justin Reedy, Mark Henkels, and Katherine Cramer. "Assessing the Electoral Impact of the 2010 Oregon Citizens' Initiative Review." *American Politics Research* 46, no. 3 (2018): 534–563. https://doi.org/10.1177/1532673X17715620.

Gastil, John, and Peter Levine, eds. *The Deliberative Democracy Handbook*. San Francisco: Jossey-Bass, 2005.

Gastil, John, and Erik Olin Wright. "Legislature by Lot: Envisioning Sortition within a Bicameral System." In *Legislature by Lot: Transformative Designs for Deliberative Governance*. edited by John Gastil and Erik Olin Wright, 3–38. London: Verso, 2019.

Gastil, John, and Erik Olin Wright, eds. *Legislature by Lot: Transformative Designs for Deliberative Governance*. London: Verso, 2019.

Gauchet, Marcel. *La révolution des pouvoirs: La souveraineté, le peuple, et la représentation, 1789–1799*. Paris: Gallimard, 1995.

Geiselberger, Heinrich, Arjun Appadurai, and Zygmunt Bauman. *The Great Regression*. Cambridge: Polity, 2017.

Gerber, M., A. Bächtiger, S. Shikano, S. Reber, and S. Rohr. "Deliberative Abilities and Deliberative Influence in a Transnational Deliberative Poll (EuroPolis)." *British Journal of Political Science* 48, no. 4 (2018): 1093–1118.

Giannini, Guglielmo. *La Folla. Seimila anni di lotta contro la tirannide*. Abridged, with a debate between G. Orsina and V. Zanone and afterword by S. Sette. Soveria Mannelli: Rubettino, 2002.

Giraudet, L. G., B. Apouey, H. Arab, S. Baeckelandt, P. Begout, N. Berghmans, N., Blanc, J. Y. Boulin, E. Buge, D. Courant, and A. Dahan. "'Co-construction' in Deliberative Democracy: Lessons from the French Citizens' Convention for Climate." *Humanities and Social Sciences Communications* 9, no. 1 (2022): 1–16.

Goodin, Robert. *Innovating Democracy: Democratic Theory and Practice after the Deliberative Turn*. Oxford: Oxford University Press, 2008.

Greely, Horace. "The Equality of Allocation by Lot." *Harvard Civil Rights-Civil Liberties Law Review* 12 (1977): 122–123.

Green, Jeffrey Edward. *The Eyes of the People: Democracy in the Age of Spectatorship*. Oxford: Oxford University Press, 2010.

Griffiths, A. Phillips, and Richard Wollheim. "How Can One Person Represent Another?" *Proceedings of the Aristotelian Society*, suppl. vols., no. 34 (1960): 187–224.

Guerrero, Alexander. "Against Elections: The Lottocratic Alternative." *Philosophy & Public Affairs* 42, no. 2 (2014): 135–178.

Guerrero, Alexander. "The Epistemic Pathologies of Elections and the Epistemic Promises of Lottocracy." In *Political Epistemology*, edited by Elizabeth Edenberg and Michael Hannon, 156–169. Oxford: Oxford University Press, 2021.

Guerrero, Alexander. *Lottocracy: Democracy Without Elections*. Oxford: Oxford University Press, 2024.

Guicciardini, Francesco. *Dialogo del reggimento di Firenze*. Edited by Gian Mario Anselmi and Carlo Varotti. Turin: Bollati Boringhieri, 1994.

Guinier, Lani. *The Tyranny of the Majority*. New York: Free Press, 1994.

Gutmann, Amy. "Democracy, Philosophy, and Justification." In *Democracy and Difference: Contesting the Boundaries of the Political*, edited by Seyla Benhabib, 340–347. Princeton, NJ: Princeton University Press, 1996.

Gutmann, Amy, and Dennis F. Thompson. *The Spirit of Compromise: Why Governing Demands It and Campaigning Undermines It*. Princeton, NJ: Princeton University Press, 2012.

Habermas, Jürgen. *Between Facts and Norms: Contribution to a Discourse Theory of Law and Democracy*. Translated by William Rehg. Cambridge, MA: MIT Press, 1996.

Habermas, Jürgen. "Political Communication in Media Society." In Id., *Europe: The Faltering Project*, 138–183. Cambridge: Polity, 2009.

Hamburger, Philip. *Is Administrative Law Unlawful?* Chicago: University of Chicago Press, 2014.

Hansen, Mogens H. *The Athenian Democracy in the Age of Demosthenes*. London: Bristol Classical, 1991.

Hansen, Mogens H. "The Autheticity of the Law about *Nomothesia* Inserted in Demosthenes *Against Timokrates 33*." *Greek, Roman and Byzantine Studies* 56, no. 4 (2016): 594–610.

Hansen, Mogens H., ed. *Démocratie athénienne—démocratie moderne: Tradition et influences*. Geneva: Édition Fondation Hardt, 2009.

Hardin, Russell. "Public Choice versus Democracy." In *The Idea of Democracy*, edited by David Copp, Jean Hampton, and John E. Roemer, 157–172. Cambridge: Cambridge University Press, 1993.

Hayat, Samuel. "Incarner le peuple souverain: Les usages de la représentation-incarnation sous la Seconde République." *Raisons politiques*, 72 no. 4 (2018): 137–164.

Hayat, Samuel. "La carrière militante de la référence à Bernard Manin dans les mouvements français pour le tirage au sort." *Participations*, hors série (2019): 437–451. https://www.cairn.info/revue-participations-2019-HS-page-437.html.

Hayek, Friedrich A. *Law, Legislation and Liberty*. Vol. 1, *Rules and Order*, and vol. 3, *The Political Order of a Free People*. Chicago: University of Chicago Press, 1978 and 1981.

Hayek, Friedrich A. "The Use of Knowledge in Society." *American Economic Review* 35, no. 4 (1945): 519–530.

He, Boagang. "Deliberative Citizenship and Deliberative Governance: A Case Study of One Deliberative Experiment in China." *Citizenship Studies* 22, no. 3 (2018): 294–311.

Headlam, James Wycliffe. *Election by Lot at Athens*. Cambridge: Cambridge University Press, 1891.

Hennig, Brett. "Who Needs Elections? Accountability, Equality, and Legitimacy under Sortition." In *Legislature by Lot: Transformative Designs for Deliberative Governance*, edited by John Gastil and Erik Olin Wright, 301–312. London: Verso, 2019.

Herodotus. *The Histories*. Translated by Aubrey de Sélincourt. London: Penguin Books, 1972.

Hirschman, Albert O. *The Passions and the Interests: Political Arguments for Capitalism before Its Triumph*. Princeton, NJ: Princeton University Press, 1997.

Hirst, Paul. *Representative Democracy and Its Limits*. Cambridge: Polity, 1990.

Hofstadter, Richard. *The Idea of a Party System: The Rise of Legitimate Opposition in the United States, 1780–1840*. Berkeley: University of California Press, 1972.

Ignazi, Piero. *Party and Democracy: The Uneven Road to Party Legitimacy*. Oxford: Oxford University Press, 2017.

Jacobson, Gary C. "2008 Presidential and Congressional Elections: Anti-Bush Referendum and Prospect for the Democratic Majority." In *Perspectives on Presidential Elections,*

1991–2020, edited by Robert Y. Shapiro, 195–225. New York: Academy of Political Science, 2021.

Jacoby, Stanford M. *Labor in the Age of Finance.* Princeton NJ: Princeton University Press, 2021.

Katz, Richard S., and Peter Mair. "Changing Models of Party Organization and Party Democracy: The Emergence of the Cartel Party." *Party Politics* 1, no. 1 (1995): 5–28.

Kelsen, Hans. *The Essence and Value of Democracy.* Edited by Nadia Urbinati and Carlo Invernizzi Accetti. Translated by Brian Graf. Lanham, MD: Rowman and Littlefield, 2013.

Kelsen, Hans. *General Theory of Law and State.* Translated by Anders Wedberg. Clark, NJ: Lawbook Exchange, 2007.

Kirchheimer, Otto. "The Transformation of the Western European Party Systems." In *Political Parties and Political Development*, edited by Joseph La Palombara and Myron Weiner, 177–200. Princeton, NJ: Princeton University Press, 1966.

Kishlansky, Mark A. *Parliamentary Selection: Social and Political Choice in Early Modern England.* Cambridge: Cambridge University Press, 1986.

Kymlicka, Will. *Multicultural Citizenship.* Oxford: Clarendon, 1995.

Laclau, Ernesto. *On Populist Reason.* London: Verso, 2005.

Laclau, Ernesto. *Politics and Ideology in Marxist Theory: Capitalism, Fascism, Populism.* London: Verso, 2011.

Laclau, Ernesto. "Populism: What's in a Name." In *Populism and the Mirror of Democracy*, edited by Francisco Panizza, 32–49. London: Verso, 2005.

Lafont, Cristina. "Against Anti-democratic Shortcuts: A Few Replies to Critics." *Journal of Deliberative Democracy* 16, no. 2 (2020): 96–109.

Lafont, Cristina. "Deliberation, Participation and Democratic Legitimacy: Should Deliberative Minipublics Shape Public Policy?" *Journal of Political Philosophy* 23, no. 1 (2015): 40–63.

Lafont, Cristina. "A Democracy, If We Can Keep It: Remarks on J. Habermas' *The New Structural Transformation of the Public Sphere*." Special issue, *Constellations* 30, no. 1 (2023): 77–83.

Lafont, Cristina. *Democracy without Shortcuts: A Participatory Conception of Deliberative Democracy.* Oxford: Oxford University Press, 2020.

Lafont, Cristina. "Which Decision-Making Authority for Citizens' Assemblies." In *De Gruyter Handbook of Citizens' Assemblies*, edited by Min Reuchamps, Julien Vrydagh, and Yanina Welp, 47–58. Berlin: De Gruyter, 2023.

Landa, Dimitri, and Ryan Pevnick, "Is Random Selection a Cure for the Ills of Electoral Representation?" *Journal of Political Philosophy* 29, no. 1 (2021): 46–72.

Landemore, Hélène. "Beyond the Fact of Disagreement? The Epistemic Turn in Deliberative Democracy." *Social Epistemology* 31, no. 3 (2017): 277–295.

Landemore, Hélène. "Can AI Bring Deliberation to the Masses?" In *Conversations in Philosophy, Law and Politics*, edited by R. Chang and A. Srinivasan. Oxford University Press, forthcoming.

Landemore, Hélène. *Democratic Reason: Politics, Collective Intelligence, and the Rule of the Many.* Princeton, NJ: Princeton University Press, 2013.

Landemore, Hélène. "La democrazia funziona meglio col sorteggio." *Domani*, (11 December 2022).

Landemore, Hélène. *Open Democracy: Reinventing Popular Rule for the Twenty-First Century.* Princeton, NJ: Princeton University Press, 2020.

Landemore, Hélène, and Scott E. Page. "Deliberation and Disagreement: Problem Solving, Prediction, and Positive Dissensus." *Politics, Philosophy and Economics* 14, no. 3 (2015): 229–254.

Landwehr, Claudia, and Armin Schäfer. "The Promise of Representative Democracy: Deliberative Responsiveness." *Res Publica*, (2023). https://doi.org/10.1007/s11158-023-09640-0.

Lane, Melissa. *The Birth of Politics: Eight Greek and Roman Political Ideas and Why They Matter*. Princeton, NJ: Princeton University Press, 2014.

Laski, Harold J. *Democracy in Crisis*. Chapel Hill: University of North Carolina Press, 1933.

Layman, Geoffrey C., Thomas M. Carsey, and Juliana Menasce Horowitz. "Party Polarization in American Politics: Characteristics, Causes, and Consequences." *Annual Review of Political Science*, vol. 9 (2006): 83–110.

Lefort, Claude. *Complications: Communism and the Dilemmas of Democracy*. Translated by Julian Bourg. New York: Columbia University Press, 2007.

Leib, Ethan. *Deliberative Democracy in America: A Proposal for a Popular Branch of Government*. University Park, PA: Penn State University Press, 2004.

Levitski, Steven, and Daniel Ziblatt. *How Democracies Die*. New York: Crown, 2018.

Lijphart, Arend. *Patterns of Democracy: Government Forms and Performance in Thirty-Six Countries*. New Haven, CT: Yale University Press, 1999.

Lintott, Andrew. *The Constitution of the Roman Republic*. Oxford: Oxford University Press, 2004.

Lopez Maya, Margarita, and Alexandra Panzarelli. "Populism, Rentierism, and Socialism in the Twenty-First Century: The Case of Venezuela." In *Latin American Populism in the Twenty-First Century*, edited by Carlos de la Torre and Cynthia J. Arnson, 239–268. Baltimore, MD: Johns Hopkins University Press, 2013.

López-Guerra, Claudio. "The Enfranchisement Lottery." *Politics, Philosophy and Economics* 10, no. 2 (2011): 211–233.

Loraux, Nicole. "L'autochtonie: Une topique athénienne. Le mythe dans l'espace civique." *Annales: Économies, Sociétés, Civilisations* 34, no. 1 (1979): 1–26.

Loraux, Nicole. *La cité divisé: L'oubli dans la mémoire d'Athènes*. Paris: Éditions Payot & Rivages, 2005.

Lupia, Arthur. "Shortcuts versus Encyclopedias." *American Political Science Review* 88, no. 1 (1994): 63–76.

Lupia, Arthur. *Uninformed: Why People Know So Little about Politics and What We Can Do about It*. New York: Oxford University Press, 2016.

Macedo, Stephen, ed. *Deliberative Politics*. Oxford: Oxford University Press, 1999.

Mackie, Gerry. "All Men Are Liars: Is Democracy Meaningless?" In *Deliberative Democracy*, edited by Elster, 69–96. Cambridge: Cambridge University Press, 1998.

Mair, Peter. "Populist Democracy vs. Party Democracy." In *Democracies and the Populist Challenge*, edited by Yves Mény and Yves Surel, 81–98. New York: Palgrave Macmillan, 2002.

Malkin, Irad and Josine Blok. *Drawing Lots: From Egalitarianism to Democracy in Ancient Greece*. Oxford University Press, 2024.

Malkopoulou, Anthoula. "The Paradox of Democratic Selection: Is Sortition Better than Voting?" In *Parliamentarism and Democratic Theory: Historical and Contemporary Perspectives*, edited by Kari Palonen and José María Rosales, 229–254. Opladen: Verlag Barbara Budrich, 2015.

Malleson, Tom. "Should Democracy Work through Elections or Sortition?" In *Legislature by Lot: Transformative Designs for Deliberative Governance*, edited by John Gastil and Erik Olin Wright, 169–188. London: Verso, 2019.

Manin, Bernard. *Kritik der repräsentativen Demokratie*. Berlin: Matthes & Seitz, 2007.

Manin, Bernard. *The Principles of Representative Government*. Cambridge: Cambridge University Press, 1997.

262   References

Mansbridge, Jane. "Accountability in the Constituent-Representative Relationship." *Legislature by Lot:Transformative Designs for Deliberative Governance*, edited by John Gastil and Erik Olin Wright, 189–204.London: Verso, 2019.

Mansbridge, Jane. *Beyond Adversary Democracy*. With a revised preface. Chicago: University of Chicago Press, 1980.

Mansbridge, Jane. "Deliberative Polling as the Gold Standard." *The Good Society* 19, no. 1 (2010): 55–62.

Mansbridge, Jane. "Rethinking Representation." *American Political Science Review* 97, no. 4 (2003): 515–528.

Mansbridge, Jane. "A 'Selection Model' of Political Representation." *Journal of Political Philosophy* 17, no. 4 (2009): 369–398.

Mansbridge, Jane. "Should Blacks Represent Blacks and Women Represent Women? A Contingent 'Yes.'" *Journal of Politics* 61, (1999): 629–657.

Martí, José Luis. "The Epistemic Conception of Deliberative Democracy Defended." In *Deliberative Democracy and Its Discontents*, edited by Samantha Besson and José Luis Martí, 27–56. Aldershot, UK: Ashgate, 2006.

McCormick, John P. *Machiavellian Democracy*. Cambridge: Cambridge University Press, 2011.

Mill, John Stuart. *Considerations on Representative Government*. In *Collected Works*, edited by John M. Robson, vol. 19, 371–578. Toronto: University of Toronto Press; London: Routledge and Kegan Paul, 1977.

Mill, John Stuart. *The Subjection of Women*. In *On Liberty and Other Essays*, edited by Nadia Urbinati, 158–248. New York: Norton, 2023.

Montesquieu. *The Spirit of the Laws*. Translated by Anne M. Cohler, Basia Carolyn Miller, and Harold Samuel Stone. Cambridge: Cambridge University Press, 1989.

Morris, Ian. "The Strong Principle of Equality and the Archaic Origins of Greek Democracy." In *Dēmokratia: A Conversation on Democracies, Ancient and Modern*, edited by Josiah Ober and Charles Hedrick, 19–48. Princeton, NJ: Princeton University Press, 1996.

Mudde, Cas. *The Far-Right Today*. Cambridge: Polity, 2019.

Mudde, Cas, and Cristobal Rovira Kaltwasser, eds. *Populism in Europe and the Americas: Threat or Corrective for Democracy?* Cambridge: Cambridge University Press, 2013.

Muirhead, Russell. *The Promise of Party in a Polarized Age*. Cambridge, MA: Harvard University Press, 2014.

Muirhead, Russell, and Nancy L. Rosenblum. "The Political Theory of Parties and Partisanship: Catching Up." *Annual Review of Political Science*, vol. 23 (2020): 95–110.

Müller, Jan-Werner. *What Is Populism?* Philadelphia: University of Pennsylvania Press, 2016.

Nacos, Brigitte, Yaeli Block-Elkon, and Robert Y. Shapiro. *Hate Speech and Political Violence: Far-Right Rhetoric from the Tea Party to the Insurrection*. New York: Columbia University Press, 2024.

Neblo, Michael A. *Deliberative Democracy between Theory and Practice*. Cambridge: Cambridge University Press, 2015.

Newton, Ken. "Curing the Democratic Malaise with Democratic Innovations." In *Evaluating Democratic Innovations: Curing the Democratic Malaise?*, edited by Brigitte Geissel and Kenneth Newton, 3–20. London: Routledge, 2012.

Niemeyer, Simon. "The Emancipatory Effect of Deliberation: Empirical Lessons from Minipublics." *Politics & Society* 39, no. 1 (2011): 103–140.

Niemeyer, Simon. "Scaling Up Deliberation to Mass Publics: Harnessing Mini-publics in a Deliberative System." In *Deliberative Mini-publics: Involving Citizens in the Democratic Process*, edited by Kimmo Grönlund, André Bächtiger, and Maija Setälä, 177–201. Colchester: ECPR Press, 2014.

Nino, Carlos. *The Constitution of Deliberative Democracy*. New Haven, CT: Yale University Press, 1998.

Ober, Josiah. *Mass and Elite in Democratic Athens: Rhetoric, Ideology, and the Power of the People*. Princeton, NJ: Princeton University Press, 1989.

Ober, Josiah, and Charles Hedrick, eds. *Dēmokratia: A Conversation on Democracies, Ancient and Modern*. Princeton, NJ: Princeton University Press, 1996.

OECD. *Innovative Citizen Participation and New Democratic Institutions: Catching the Deliberative Wave*. Paris: OECD Publishing, 2020.

Owen, David, and Graham Smith, "Sortition, Rotation, and Mandate: Conditions for Political Equality and Deliberative Reasoning." In *Legislature by Lot: Transformative Designs for Deliberative Governance*, edited by John Gastil and Erik Olin Wright, 278–300. London: Verso, 2019.

Parkinson, John. *Deliberating in the Real World: Problems of Legitimacy in Deliberative Democracy*. Oxford: Oxford University Press, 2006.

Parkinson, John, and Jane Mansbridge, eds., *Deliberative Systems: Deliberative Democracy at the Large Scale*. New York: Cambridge University Press, 2012.

Pasquino, Pasquale. "Democracy Ancient and Modern: Divided Power." In *Démocratie Athénienne, Démocratie Moderne: Tradition et influences: neuf exposés suivis de discussions*, edited by Pasquale Pasquino, Mogens Herman Hansen, Alain-ChristianHernández, 1–49. Vandoevres: Fondation Hardt; Entretiens sur l'Antiquité Classique, 2009.

Pazé Valentina, *I non rappresentati. Esclusi, arrabbiati, disillusi*. Turin: Gruppo Abele, 2024.

Peonidis, Filimon. "On Two Anti-democratic Uses of Sortition." *Democratic Theory* 3, no. 2 (2016): 26–45.

Pettit, Philip. "Meritocratic Representation." In *The East Asian Challenge for Democracy: Political Meritocracy in Comparative Perspective*, edited by D. A. Bell and C. Li., 138–160. Cambridge: Cambridge University Press, 2013.

Pettit, Philip. "Representation, Responsive and Indicative." *Constellations* 17, no. 3 (2010): 426–434.

Pew Research Center. "Global Public Opinion in an Era of Democratic Anxiety." International survey. https://www.pewresearch.org/global/2021/12/07/global-public-opinion-in-an-era-of-democratic-anxiety/.

Phillips, Anne. *The Politics of Presence*. Oxford: Clarendon, 1995.

Piepenbrink, Karen. "Zur Relation von politischen und sozialen Ordnungsmustern und Handlungsfeldern in der attischen Demokratie des vierten Jahrhunderts v. Chr." *Göttinger Forum für Altertumswissenschaft*, no. 22 (2019): 117–139. https://journals.ub.uni-heidelberg.de/index.php/gfa/issue/view/5184.

Piérart, M. "Qui étaient les nomothètes à Athènes à l'époque de Démosthène?" In *La codificationdes lois dans l'antiquité*, edited by E. Lévy, 229–256. Paris: Diffusion de Boccard, 2000.

Piketty, Thomas. *Capital in the Twenty-First Century*. Cambridge, MA: Harvard University Press, 2017.

Pitkin, Hanna Fenichel. *The Concept of Representation*. Berkeley: University of California Press, 1967.

Plato. *The Dialogues of Plato*. 4 vols. Translated by B. Jowett. Boston: Jefferson Press, circa 1900.

Plotke, David "Representation Is Democracy," *Constellations* 4, no. 1 (1997): 19–34.

Pope, Maurice. *The Keys to Democracy: Sortition as a New Model for Citizen Power*. With a foreword by Hélène Landemore and a preface by Paul Cartledge. Exeter: Imprint Academic, 2023.

264   References

Pow, James, Lisa van Dijk, and Sofie Marien. "It's Not Just the Taking Part That Counts: 'Like Me' Perceptions Connect the Wider Public to Minipublics." *Journal of Deliberative Democracy* 16, no. 2 (2020): 43–55.

Powell, G. Bingham Jr. *Elections as Instruments of Democracy: Majoritarian and Proportional Visions.* New Haven, CT: Yale University Press, 2000.

Przeworski, Adam, Michael Alvarez, Jose Antonio Cheibub, and Fernando Limongi. *Democracy and Development: Political Institutions and Well-Being in the World, 1950–1990.* Cambridge: Cambridge University Press, 2000.

Queiroz, Regina. "Jeopardizing Liberal Democracy: The Trouble with Demarchy." *Critical Political Studies,* published online 16 Oct 2023. https://www.tandfonline.com/doi/full/10.1080/19460171.2023.2267631?src=.

Raaflaub, Kurt A. "Equalities and Inequalities in Athenian Democracy." In *Dēmokratia: A Conversation on Democracies, Ancient and Modern,* edited by Josiah Ober and Charles Hedrick, 139–174. Princeton, NJ: Princeton University Press, 1996.

Raaflaub, Kurt A., and Robert W. Wallace. "'People's Power' and Egalitarian Trends in Ancient Greece." In *Origins of Democracy in Ancient Greece,* edited by Kurt A. Raaflaub, Josiah Ober, Robert W. Wallace. Berkeley: University of California Press, 2007.

Rawls, John. "The Idea of Public Reason Revisited." In *Collected Papers,* edited by Samuel Freeman, 573–61. Cambridge, MA: Harvard University Press, 1999.

Rawls, John. *Political Liberalism.* Cambridge, MA: Harvard University Press, 1993.

Rawls, John. *A Theory of Justice.* Cambridge, MA: Harvard University Press, 1999.

Rehfeld, Andrew. *The Concept of Constituency: Political Representation, Democratic Legitimacy, and Institutional Design.* Cambridge: Cambridge University Press, 2005.

Reuchamps, Min, Didier Caluwaerts, Jérémy Dodeigne, Vincent Jacquet, Jonathan Moskovic, and Sophie Devillers. "Le G1000: Une expérience citoyenne de démocratie délibérative." *Courrier Hebdomadaire du CRISP,* nos. 2344–45 (2017): 5–104.

Reuchamps, Min, Julien Vrydagh, and Yanina Welp. *De Gruyter Handbook of Citizens' Assemblies.* Berlin: De Gruyter, 2023.

Rhodes, P. J. "Sessions of *Nomothetai* in Fourth-Century Athens." *Classical Quarterly* 53, no. 1 (2003): 124–129.

Roberts, Kenneth M. "Populism and Democracy in Venezuela under Hugo Chávez." In *Populism in Europe and the Americas,* edited by Mudde and Rovira Kaltwasser, 136–159. Cambridge: Cambridge University Press, 2012.

Rosanvallon, Pierre. *La contre-démocratie: La politique à l'âge de la défiance.* Paris: Seuil, 2006.

Rosanvallon, Pierre. *The Populist Century.* Translated by Catherine Porter. Cambridge: Polity, 2020.

Rosenblum, Nancy L. *On the Side of the Angels: An Appreciation of Parties and Partisanship.* Princeton, NJ: Princeton University Press, 2008.

Rosenbluth, Frances McCall, and Ian Shapiro. *Responsible Parties: Saving Democracy from Itself.* New Haven, CT: Yale University Press, 2018.

Rosivach, Vincent J. "Autochthony and the Athenians." *Classical Quarterly* 37, no. 2 (1987): 294–306.

Rousseau, Jean-Jacques. *The Basic Political Writings.* Translated by Donald A. Cress. Indianapolis, IN: Hackett, 1987.

Rubinstein, Nicolai. "Politics and Constitution in Florence at the End of the Fifteenth Century." In *Italian Renaissance Studies,* edited by Ernest F. Jacob, 148–183. London: Faber & Faber, 1960.

Runciman, David. *Political Hypocrisy: The Mask of Power, from Hobbes to Orwell and Beyond.* Princeton, NJ: Princeton University Press, 2008.

Sabine, George. *History of Political Theory.* New York: Holt, 1959.

References 265

Saffon, Maria Paula, and Nadia Urbinati. "Procedural Democracy, the Bulwark of Equal Liberty." *Political Theory* 41, no. 3 (2013): 441–481.

Samons, Loren J., II. *What's Wrong with Democracy? From Athenian Practice to American Worship*. Berkeley: University of California Press, 2004.

Sartori, Giovanni. *Democratic Theory*. Detroit: Wayne State University Press, 1962.

Sartori, Giovanni. *Parties and Party Systems: A Framework for Analysis*. Cambridge: Cambridge University Press, 1976.

Saunders, Ben. "Democracy, Political Equality, and Majority Rule." *Ethics* 121, (October 2010): 148–177.

Saward, Michael. *The Representative Claim*. Oxford: Oxford University Press, 2010.

Scarrow, Susan E. "Party Subsidies and the Freezing of Party Competition: Do Cartel Mechanisms Work?" *West European Politics* 29, no. 4 (2006): 619–639.

Schattschneider, E. E. *Party Government*. New York: Farrar & Rinehart, 1942.

Schattschneider, E. E. *The Semisovereign People: A Realist's View of Democracy in America*. Chicago: Holt, Rinehart and Winston, 1960.

Schmitt, Carl. *Constitutional Theory*. Translated and edited by Jeffrey Seitzer. Foreword by Ellen Kennedy. Durham, NC: Duke University Press, 2008.

Schumpeter, Joseph A. *Capitalism, Socialism, and Democracy*. London: Allen & Unwin, 1943.

Schwartzberg, Melissa. *Counting the Many: The Origins of Supermajority Rule*. Cambridge: Cambridge University Press, 2014.

Selinger, William. *Parliamentarism: From Burke to Weber*. Cambridge: Cambridge University Press, 2019.

Setälä, Maija. "Advisory, Collaborative and Scrutinizing Roles of Deliberative Mini-publics." *Frontiers in Political Science*, no. 2 (Jan. 2021): 1–10. doi:10.3389/fpos.2020.591844.

Shapiro, Ian. *Uncommon Sense*. New Haven, CT: Yale University Press, 2024.

Simonton, Matthew. "'Ambition for Office' and the Nature of Election in Ancient Greek Democracies." Forthcoming (2025) in *Journal of Sortition*.

Simonton, Matthew. *Classical Greek Oligarchy: A Political History*. Princeton, NJ: Princeton University Press, 2017.

Sinclair, R. K. *Democracy and Participation in Athens*. Cambridge: Cambridge University Press, 1988.

Sintomer, Yves. *The Government of Chance: Sortition and Democracy from Athens to the Present*. Cambridge: Cambridge University Press, 2023.

Sintomer, Yves. "The Meanings of Political Representation: Uses and Misuses of a Notion." *Raisons politiques* 50, no. 2 (2013): 13–34.

Sintomer, Yves. "Random Selection and Deliberative Democracy: Note for an Historical Comparison." In *Sortition: Theory and Practice*, edited by Gil Delannoi and Oliver Dowlen, 31–50. Exeter: Imprint Academic, 2010.

Sintomer, Yves. "La représentation-incarnation: Idéaltype et configurations historiques." *Raisons politiques*, 72, no. 4 (2018): 21–52.

Sintomer, Yves. "Sortition and Politics: From Radical to Deliberative Democracy—and Back?" In *Brill's Companion to the Reception of Athenian Democracy*, edited by Dino Piovan and Giovanni Giorgini, 490–521. Leiden: Brill, 2021.

Sintomer, Yves, and Liliane Lopez-Rabatel. *Sortition and Democracy: History, Tools, Theories*. Exeter: Imprint Academic, 2020.

Smith, Graham, and Corinne Wales. "The Theory and Practice of Citizen Juries." *Policy and Politics* 27, (1999): 295–308.

Smith, Graham, and Maija Setälä. "Mini-publics and Deliberative Democracy." In *The Oxford Handbook of Deliberative Democracy*, edited by Bächtiger, André, John S. Dryzek, Jane Mansbridge, and Mark E. Warren, 300–314. Oxford: Oxford University Press, 2018.

References

Spinoza, Baruch. *Political Treatise*. Translated by Samuel Shirley. With introduction and notes by Steven Barbone and Lee Rice. Indianapolis, IN: Hackett, 2000.

Staveley, E. S. *Greek and Roman Voting and Elections*. London: Thames and Hudson, 1972.

Stone, Peter A. *The Luck of the Draw: The Role of Lotteries in Decision-Making*. New York: Oxford University Press, 2011.

Storing, Herbert, ed. *The Complete Anti-Federalist*. Chicago: University of Chicago Press, 1981.

Streeck, Wolfgang, and Armin Shäfer, *Politics in the Age of Austerity*. New York: Polity, 2013.

Swabey, Marie Collins. *Theory of the Democratic State*. Cambridge, MA: Harvard University Press, 1937.

Tanzini, Lorenzo. "Représentation et décision politique dans les assemblées communales italiennes du 13ᵉ siècle." *Raisons politiques*, 72, no. 4 (2018): 53–70.

Tanzini, Lorenzo. "The Practices and Rhetoric of Sortition in Medieval Public Life (13th–14th Centuries)." In *Sortition and Democracy: History, Tools, Theories*, edited by Liliane Lopez-Rabatel and Yves Sintomer, 201–218. Exeter: Imprint Academic, 2020.

Thompson, Dennis. "Deliberative Democratic Theory and Empirical Political Science." *Annual Review of Political Science*, vol. 11 (2008): 497–520.

Thompson, Dennis F. *Just Elections: Creating a Fair Electoral Process in The United States*. Chicago: University of Chicago Press, 2002.

Thompson, Dennis F. *Political Ethics and Public Office*. Cambridge, MA: Harvard University Press, 1987.

Thompson, Dennis F. *Restoring Responsibility: Ethics in Government, Business, and Healthcare*. Cambridge: Cambridge University Press, 2005.

Tocqueville, Alexis de. *Democracy in America*. Translated by J. P. Mayer. New York: Harper Perennial, 1969.

Tridimas, George. "Constitutional Choice in Ancient Athens: The Rationality of Selection to Office by Lot." *Constitutional Political Economy* 23, no. 1 (2012): 1–21.

Umbers, Lachlan Montgomery. "Against Lottocracy." *European Journal of Political Theory* 20, no. 2 (2021): 312–334.

Urbinati, Nadia. "Anti-Party-ism within Party Democracy." In *Multiple Populisms: Italy as Democracy's Mirror*, edited by Paul Blokker and Manuel Anselmi, 67–85. Oxford: Routledge, 2020.

Urbinati, Nadia. "Continuity and Rupture: The Power of Judgment in Democratic Representation." *Constellations* 12, no. 2 (2005): 194–222.

Urbinati, Nadia. "Liquid Parties, Dense Populism." *Philosophy and Social Criticism* 45, nos. 9–10 (2019): 1069–1083

Urbinati, Nadia. *Me the People: How Populism Transforms Democracy*. Cambridge, MA: Harvard University Press, 2019.

Urbinati, Nadia. *Representative Democracy: Principles and Genealogy*. Chicago: University of Chicago Press, 2006.

Urbinati, Nadia. "A Revolt against Intermediary Bodies." *Constellations* 22, no. 4 (2015): 477–486.

Urbinati, Nadia, and Mark Warren. "The Concept of Representation in Contemporary Democratic Theory." *Annual Review of Political Science*, vol. 11 (2008): 387–412.

Vallier, Kevin. "Public Justification." In *Stanford Encyclopedia of Philosophy*, edited by Edward N. Zalta and Uri Nodelman. Winter 2022 ed. https://plato.stanford.edu/archives/win2022/entries/justification-public/. First published Tue Feb 27, 1996; substantive revision Fri Dec 2, 2022.

Van Crombrugge, Ronald. "The Derailed Promise of a Participatory Minipublic: The Citizens' Assembly Bill in Flanders." *Journal of Deliberative Democracy* 16, no. 2 (2020): 63–72. https://doi.org/10.16997/jdd.402.

Van Reybrouck, David. *Against Elections: The Case for Democracy*. Translated by Liz Waters. London: Bodley Head, 2016.

Vermeule, Adrian. "'No.' Review of Philip Hamburger, *Is Administrative Law Unlawful?*" *Texas Law Review* 93, (2015): 1547. https://ssrn.com/abstract=2488724.

Wachtel, Ted. *True Representation: How Citizens' Assemblies and Sortition Will Save Democracy*. Pipersville, PA: Piper's, 2020.

Waldron, Jeremy. *Law and Disagreement*. Oxford: Oxford University Press, 1999.

Waldron, Jeremy. *Political Political Theory*. Cambridge, MA: Harvard University Press, 2016.

Waley, Daniel. *The Italian City-Republics*. New York: McGraw-Hill, 1978.

Walzer, Michael. *On Toleration*. New Haven, CT: Yale University Press, 1997.

Walzer, Michael. "Political Action: The Problem of Dirty Hands." *Philosophy & Public Affairs* 2, no. 2 (1973): 160–182.

Warren, Mark. "Citizen Representatives." In *Representation: Elections and Beyond*, edited by Jack H. Nagel and Rogers M. Smith, chap. 12. Philadelphia: University of Pennsylvania Press, 2013.

Weil, Simone. "On the Abolition of Political Parties." https://theanarchistlibrary.org/library/simone-weil-on-the-abolition-of-all-political-parties.

West, M. L., ed. and trans. *Greek Lyric Poetry*. Oxford: Oxford University Press, 1993.

White, Jonathan, and Lea Ypi. *The Meaning of Partisanship*. Oxford: Oxford University Press, 2016.

White, Stuart. "Citizens' Assemblies and Republican Democracy." In *Radical Republicanism*, edited by Bruno Leipold, Karma Nabulsi, and Stuart White, 81–100. Oxford: Oxford University Press, 2020.

Williams, Melissa S. *Voice, Trust, and Memory: Marginalized Groups and the Failings of Liberal Representation*. Princeton, NJ: Princeton University Press, 1998.

Wolff, Robert Paul. *In Defense of Anarchism*. Berkeley: University of California Press, 1970.

Wolkenstein, Fabio. "Party Reforms and Electoral Systems: Proportional Representation Is More Hospitable to Internal Democratization." *Journal of Representative Democracy* 57, no. 3 (2021): 313–328.

Wolterstorff, Nicholas. *Understanding Liberal Democracy: Essays in Political Philosophy*. Edited by Terence Cuneo. Oxford: Oxford University Press, 2012.

Young, Iris Marion. "Deferring Group Representation." In *Ethnicity and Group Rights*, edited by Ian Shapiro and Will Kymlicka, 349–376. Nomos 39. New York: New York University Press, 1997.

Zakaras, Alex. "Lot and Democratic Representation: A Modest Proposal." *Constellations* 17, no. 3 (2010): 456–457.

Index

For the benefit of digital users, indexed terms that span two pages (e.g., 52–53) may, on occasion, appear on only one of those pages.

Abizadeh, A. 103–104, 185–187, 208
accountability 7–8, 38–39, 49, 249–250
    electoral 120, 125, 144, 147–148
    equalizing asymmetric power relations 182
    formal 143–144
    functional 121–122
    horizontal 113, 124–125, 149
    inequalities 189–190
    informal 120–121, 142–144
    lack of 37
    leader as embodiment of the people 204–206
    lottocratic 120
    parties and partisan divisions among citizens 160–161, 165, 167–168
    stricto sensu 143
    voting power and elections 124–125, 126–127
    see also mandate representation and accountability
Achen, C.H. 154–155 n.113, 185–186 n.25
Ackerman, B. 36
Adams, J. 45, 194–195 n.5
advisory assemblies, diffuse 22–25
advisory councils 24
advocacy 7–8, 140, 150, 196–198
agency 161–162, 167–168, 226–227 n.18, 230, 248
agenda setting 245–246
aggregative conceptions of democracy 83–84
algorithmic personalization 238–239
Amar, A.R. 32, 36, 103–104
ambiguity of election 76–77
'America in One Room' (AIR) 244–245
American Civil Liberties Union 95
Anderson, G. 54–55 n.110
anti-Federalists 45–46, 194–195
anticorruption 30–36, 72
antidemocratic effects 230
antiestablishment 201–203
antifactionalism (equality before the law and stability) 49
antipartisanship 168–169
antiparty-ism (old and new) 156–162
Antipater 43 n.80
arbitrariness 112–113, 121–122
Arendt, H. 165

Argentina 173 n.1
Aristophanes 63
Aristotle 5–6, 17, 21, 72, 74–76, 107–108, 136–137 n.59
    oligarchs, democrats and the polis 54–57, 59–60, 63–66, 67–68 n.163, 68–69
    parties and partisan divisions among citizens 151–152, 157
    voluntary decision and equality of probability 47–48, 50–52
asymmetric power relations *see under* disempowerment reinterpretation of political equality
Athens 17–18, 54, 80–81
    Dahl 26
    democracy 21, 45–46, 54–56
    elections 72–75
    electoral democracy 95
    Elster 30, 33–34, 35 n.52
    equality 57–58, 59–60
    goal of democrats 61–62, 63–64
    implementation of lottery 64–67
    mandate representation and accountability 143
    Manin 40–41, 43–46, 47–51, 53–54
    oligarchy 40, 54–56
    parties and partisan divisions among citizens 158–160, 166
    religious justification (let the Gods decide) 60–61
Athens Assembly 29, 34, 43–44, 47, 52, 54–57, 58–60, 62
    elections 74–75
    implementation of lottery 64–67
    nomothetai 66–69
Athens Council 43–44, 54–55, 59–60, 62
    implementation of lottery 64–65
    nomothetai 67–69
Augustus 61 n.138
authoritarian regimes 121–122, 183–185, 187, 198, 217–218
autochthony 58
auxiliary bodies 248–250
    minipublics as 233–238
auxiliary proposals 2–4, 96, 115–121
auxiliary role of lottery 24

ballooning bureaucracy paradox 27
ballot propositions 12, 245
Barber, B. 21
Barnett, A. 102–103
Bartels, L.M. 154–155 n.113, 185–186 n.25
Belgium
  citizens' assemblies 245
  G1000 Citizens' Summits 116–117
Berlusconi, S. 202 n.26
bicameral parliamentary system 102
big data collection 238–239
Bikerton, C. 227–228
Blair, T. 102–103
blind deference 26–27, 212–215
Bodin, J. 43 n.79
Boétie, É. de la 134
Bolivia 173 n.1
Bouricius, T. 108
Boyle, C. 102–103 n.22
Brazil 173 n.1
British Columbia Citizens' Assembly 88–89 n.16, 104, 116–117
Brown, M. 215
Bruni, L. 29, 30–31, 52–53, 69–70, 71–72, 76
Buchstein, H. 18, 55–56 n.113, 116
'Building a New Reality' initiative 95
Burke, E. 139–140
Burnheim, J. 21, 208

Callenbach, E. 102–103
Campanella, T. 63 n.146
Canada
  British Columbia Citizens' Assembly 88–89 n.16, 104, 116–117
  Ontario Citizens' Assembly 88–89 n.16, 104, 116–117
  Senate 103–104
Canevaro, M. 67–68
Canovan, M. 204, 226
capture 110–111, 192, 245–246
party cartelization 154–155
Cartledge, P. 59
Carty, P. 102–103
Casaleggio, G. 102–103 n.20
Castoriadis, C. 74–75 n.184
catch-all parties 153–154
Chapman, E.B. 131–132
Chávez, H. 203
Chile 173 n.1
China 137–138, 185
choice by lot 123
Cicero 157 n.119
citizens' assemblies 12, 88–89 n.16, 206–215, 248–249
  auxiliary proposals 115–117
  Belgium 245

blind deference 212–215
  British Columbia 88–89 n.16, 104, 116–117
  citizens-representatives 207–212
  complementarity proposals 103–104
  electoral democracy 96
  Ontario 88–89 n.16, 104, 116–117
citizens' committees 21
Citizens Convention for Climate (France) 88–89 n.16, 116–117
citizen's juries 19, 21, 87 n.12, 115–116, 235, 249
citizens-representatives 207–212
civil associations 108
Cleisthenes 54–55, 56–57, 59–60, 65–66 n.157, 109
Cockshott, P. 21
cognitive advantage 78–79
cognitive diversity 139–140, 164, 222–223
Cohen, J. 84–86 n.9, 90
collective moments and impacts 108
Collor de Mello, F. 202 n.26
Colombia 173 n.1
'common good' 226, 228
competence 25–26, 34, 46, 49
  criterion of 27
  epistemic 225
  technical 221–222
competitive view 130
complementarity proposals 2–3, 6–7, 11, 99–100, 120–121, 233
compromise 7, 163–164
Condorcet, Marquis de 134–135
congressional committees 115–116
congruence 209–210
consensus conferences 115–116
consent 46, 53, 127–128, 133–134, 138, 148
  legitimation by 137–138
  voluntary 128
conspiracy theories 238–239
Constant, B. 27–28, 43, 48–49
Constitutional Courts 115–116
constitutional redesign 116–117
constitutional reform 116–117
Constitutional Treaty of Europe 39–40 n.64
constitutionalism 17
Conti, G. 195–196
continuity, lack of 37
Convention on the Constitution in Ireland 116–117
corruption 7, 27–28, 33–34
  complementarity proposals 106, 111–112
  epistocracy 227
  leader as embodiment of the people 199, 201

270 Index

corruption (*Continued*)
  mediated 249–250
  parties and partisan divisions among citizens
    153–154, 159
  systemic 159–160
Cottrell, A. 21
Coulanges, F. de 60
counterdemocracy 117–118
'crisis of democracy' 19, 97–98, 106, 135–136, 153,
    164–165, 246–247
Crosby, N. 87 n.12, 115–116 n.43
Czech Republic 129 n.28

Dahl, R.A. 5, 19–28, 39, 46, 51–52, 96, 138–139
    n.64, 192, 250–251
  auxiliary role of lottery 24, 119–120
  contrasting conclusion 25–27
  definition (as first argument) 24
  diffuse advisory assemblies or participation by
    lot 22–25
  elections 75
  limitations on functions 24
  minipublics 87
  oligarchs, democrats and the polis 68–69
  partisanship 115
  polyarchy, ameliorative character of 24–25
  voluntary participation 25
De Sanctis, G. 40
De Witt, J. 194–195 n.5
de-accountability 203
deference 182
  see also blind deference
Delannoi, G. 106
deliberation 6–7, 90–91, 164–165, 222–223
  in tension with mass participation 90–2
deliberative democracy 6, 46–47, 82–94
  microdeliberative turn 87–89
  minipublics 234, 239
  parties and partisan divisions among citizens
    164
  technopopulism 229–230 n.22
deliberative filter 88, 229, 229–230 n.22
deliberative input principle 108
Deliberative Polls 12, 87, 91, 93–94, 96, 115–116,
    241, 243–246
deliberative responsiveness 246
demarchy 20–21
democracy thesis of the lottery 40–41
democratic effects 12
democratization after regime change 116–117
Demosthenes 43–44
Dienel, P. 87 n.12, 115–116 n.43
direct democracy 40–44, 46, 132–133
  elections 72–73
  epistocracy 221 n.6

equalizing asymmetric power relations
    176–177, 183 n.21
mandate representation and accountability
    138–139, 150–151
Manin 39–47, 49, 51–52
minipublics 246
parties and partisan divisions among citizens
    168–169
substitution proposals 100
voting power and elections 124
disempowerment reinterpretation of political
    equality 3–4, 8–9, 173–193
  asymmetric power relations, equalizing
    176–188
    equality requirements 179–180
    exclusion of citizenry from decision-making
      181–188
    rotation 177–179
  inequalities 189–193
  levelling down for equality 174–175
dishonesty 28–29
  see also corruption
distinction principle 77–79
diversity 88, 105, 238–239
Diversity Trumps Ability Theorem 222–223
division 226–227
double draw 65
Dowlen, O. 65–66 n.156, 250–251
Draco 54–55
Dunn, J. 124–125 n.8
dysfunctionality 226–227

echo chambers 238–240
efficiency 128
egalitarianism 175 n.5
elections 7–8, 108
  as irreducibly a choice of persons 78
  see also voting power and elections
electoral democracy 11, 95–122
  auxiliary proposals 96, 115–121
  complementarity proposals 99–100, 102–115
    arbitrariness 112–113
    capture 110–111
    censorial power 113–114
    leaderism 112
    partisanship in disguise 114–115
    plurality without pluralism 111–112
    veto power 109–110
  epistocracy 226–227
  equalizing asymmetric power relations
    181–182, 183 n.21, 185–186, 187–188
  inequalities 189, 192–193
  issues with lottocratic representation 217–218
  Manin 43
  substitution proposals 96–101
  technocracy 221

voting power and elections 124
elite democrats 185–186 n.25
Elster, J. 5, 17, 27–41, 53–54, 250–251
  advantages 31–35
  auxiliary proposals 115–116 n.41
  bureaucracy 37
  complementarity 102–103
  direct democracy 46
  disadvantages and problems 35–37
  equioptimality 60
  fairness towards the candidates 31–35
  freedom 166
  see also political freedom
  individualism 37
  inequality 189–190, 192
  lottery voting: anticorruption and fair
    representation 31–36
  minorities, justice toward 36
  professional politicians, elimination of 36
  voluntary decision and equality of probability
    50
  voters to candidates, from 27–31
  wasted votes, reduction of 35–36
embodied representation 9–10, 194–198, 215–217
  issues with lottocratic representation 216–217
  see also citizens' assemblies
empowerment 167, 234, 244–247
epistemic conceptions of democracy 84–86, 219
epistocracy: technical problem-solving vs.
    political freedom 221–228
equal political freedom (*isonomia* and *eleutheria*)
    63
equal say 174, 176, 182–4
equality 8–9, 32–33, 50–51, 54
  aggregative 131–132
  aristocratic (proportional) 59–60
  arithmetical and geometrical 50–51, 59–60
  complementarity proposals 103–104, 106
  deliberative democracy 90–91
  elections 76
  epistocracy 221–222
  historical paradigm 57–60
  horizontal 18
  levelling down for 174–175
  mandate representation and accountability 141
  mixed 50–51
  political
  radical 30–31
  substantive 48–50
  voting power and elections 126–128, 134
  see also disempowerment reinterpretation of
    political equality
  see also political equality
equality of opportunity 48–51, 53, 57–58,
    106–107, 168–169
equality of probability 41, 47–52, 57–58

auxiliary proposals 119–120
complementarity proposals 106–108, 110
elections 72–73
goal of democrats 63–64
oligarchs and democrats 57
equality under the law (*isonomia*) 57–58, 59–60
Esu, A. 67–68
ethics 150
European Commission 115–116
European Union/Europe 116, 137–138, 198
exclusion of citizenry from decision-making
    181–188

factionalism 25
fairness 31–35, 65–66, 127, 250–251
fake news 238–239
far-right movements 154–155
fascism 159–160, 198
Federalists 45, 71
filter bubbles 238–240
Finley, M.I. 157 n.119
first-past-the-post 35, 98, 127, 163
Fishkin, J. 21–23, 87, 88–89 n.18, 90–92, 93–94,
    212 n.56, 229–230 n.22, 244–246
Five Star Movement (M5S) 104–105, 111
Florence/Florentine Republic 17, 29–31, 52–54
  factions 70–2, 74–5
  elections 73–76
  instability 29–30, 71
  stability 69–72
fluidity of parties 153–155, 159
former Yugoslavia 116–117
Founding Fathers (USA) 17, 188 n.29
fragmentation 238–239
France 39–40 n.64, 52–53, 102–103, 148–149
  Citizens Convention for Climate 88–89 n.16,
    116–117
  National Assembly 195–196
  Revolution 216–217
freedom 7–8, 11, 51, 220–221, 226–227 n.18, 230
  negative and positive 48–49
  political 165–9, 221–8
  political parties and partisan divisions among
    citizens 165–169
  voting power and elections 138
Fujimori, A. 202 n.26
functionalism 38, 161–162 n.135
Fung, A. 88–89 n.16

G1000 Citizens' Summits (Belgium and
    Netherlands) 116–117
Gastil, J. 103–104, 112–113
Germany 19, 87 n.12, 115–116 n.41, 166–167
Giannini, G. 97–98
goal of democrats 61–64
Goodin, R. 151, 159

272 Index

Greece 157
  see also Athens
Greely, H. 37
gridlock 245–246
Grillo, B. 102–103
group isolation 238–239
group representation 127
Guerrero, A. 121–122, 216–217, 226–227
  asymmetric power relations 176–177, 181 n.16,
    182–183, 208
  complementarity proposals 105, 109, 114–115
  inequalities, balancing out of 209–210, 211–212
  lottocratic system defense vs electoral system
    177
  mandate representation and accountability 142,
    144
  parties and partisan divisions among citizens
    154–155 n.113, 161–162 n.135
  substitution proposals 96–98, 99–101
Guicciardini, F. 41–43, 46, 52–53, 71
Gutmann, A. 83

Habermas, J. 86, 132–133
Haider, J. 202 n.26
Hansen, M.H. 44, 47–49, 57–58 n.123, 60, 62
  n.140, 64–65, 67–68
Harrington, J. 109–110
Headlam, J.W. 40, 56
Hegel, G.W.F. 194–195
Hein, M. 116
Herodotus 59, 69
Hesiod 58
Hirschman, A.O. 135–136 n.55
historical or interpretive argument 52–53
historical paradigm 54–80
  elections past and present 72–80
  oligarchs, democrats and the polis 54–69
    ancient Athens and lottery implementation
      64–67
    democratic and oligarchic 54–57
    equality 57–60
    goal of democrats 61–64
    nomothetai, contested role of 65–69
    stability 69–72
ho boulomenos (whoever wishes) 44, 56–57
Hobbes, T. 169
Hofstadter, R. 162
homogeneity 10–11, 216–218, 226–229
honesty 27, 34
Hong, L. 222–223

Iceland 116–117
impartiality 65–66, 88, 250–251
  complementarity proposals 103–104, 106–107
  electoral democracy 122
  mandate representation and accountability 141

stability 54, 72
  substitution proposals 98–100
  voting power and elections 126–127
impersonality 200–201
impolitical principle 61 n.138
incarnation 204
inclusiveness 88, 163–164, 238–240
independence 88
indirect democracy 39–43, 52, 102, 132–133
individualism 53, 130
  anomic 37
  dissociative 110
inequality 77, 96–97, 179, 182, 189–193
  political
information 53, 84–87, 122, 164, 189, 192, 213,
  250–251
  access to 84–86
  assemblies 25–26
  background 211, 242
  balanced 86, 238, 239–240, 245–246
  collection 23
  collective selection 242–243
  crucial 241, 243–244
  dissemination 78–79, 248–249
  distinctive 241
  flow 152
  gathering 135–136
  goals of 109
  independent 106–107
  key 240
  processing 97
  provision of 88
  quality 208–209, 222–223
  raw 249
  regulator of 240–241
  relevant 246
  sociological 105
  type of 240–241
instability 29, 52–53, 69–71
  radical 69–70
  social 28–29
interchangeability of decision-makers
  222–223
interests, values and objectives 243–244
Invernizzi Accetti, C. 227–228
Ireland 88–89 n.16, 116–117
  Citizens' Assembly 116–117
  Convention on the Constitution 116–117
Isegoria 161–162
Isocrates 54–55
Italy 115 n.41, 154 n.10, 167
Italian Republics 5–6, 28–29, 46
  auxiliary proposals 115–116 n.41
  complementarity proposals 102–104
  Constituent Assembly 97

parties and partisan divisions among citizens
157, 166–167
substitution proposals 96–97
voting power and elections 129 n.28
see also Florence/Florentine Republic; Rome;
Venice

judgments 122
considered 88
juridical representation 194–195
juries, popular 22–23
jurors' councils 43–44
jury selection 119–120
justice 127–128, 149–150
electoral 136–137
as impartiality 107–108, 125–126
numerical 134
proportional 134
as prudence and utility 107–108
related to (in)exclusion 126–127

kallipolis 63
Kateb, G. 42
Kelsen, H. 132–133 n.43
Kirkheimer, O. 153–154
Kishlansky, M.A. 52–53 n.104, 72
kratos 248, 250–251

Laclau, E. 202
Lafont, C. 26–27
Landa, D. 189–190, 192
Landemore, H. 100–101, 114–115, 146–147, 156
n.117
asymmetric power relations 176–177 n.9,
177–178, 181 n.17, 183 n.21, 185–186, 187
n.28, 188 n.29
lottocracy defense vs electoral democracy
mandate representation and accountability
146–147
post-party democracy 156 n.117
technocracy 219–220, 222–225, 229–230 n.22
Laski, H.J. 19
Latin America 198
leader as embodiment of the people 199–206
leadership 25, 112
Lefort, C. 200–201, 248
legal coercion (imperative mandate) 166–167
legal or formal equality *see* equality of opportunity
legal mandate
legitimacy 9, 53
deliberative democracy 83–84, 86
microdeliberative turn within deliberative
democracy 84–86, 88–89
minipublics 234–235
moral 168–169

parties and partisan divisions among citizens
166
public justification criterion of 84
substitution proposals 97
voting power and elections 126
Leib, E. 103–104
leveling down objection to egalitarianism 175
Levellers 134–135
Lindblom, C. 19–20
Locke, J. 128, 134–135
lottery 5–6, 198, 217, 249
electoral democracy and lottocracy, clash
between 98, 100, 102–3, 106, 109–11,
113–20, 122
lottocratic reinterpretation of political equality
173, 175–7, 189–90
targets of lottocracy revisited 123, 126–7,
141–5, 160, 163–4
see also lottery revival
religious justification (let the Gods decide)
60–61
lottery-based institutions 2–3, 6–8, 11–13, 102,
116, 174, 229–30, 249–50
deliberative democracy's turn to 82–94
minipublics 238, 244, 246–7
lottery beyond democracy 52–54
lottery revival 17–81
Dahl, R.A. 19–20, 21–28, 39, 46
Elster, J. 27–41, 46
Manin, B. 39–54
see also historical paradigm
lottocracy 2–4, 7, 9, 41, 72
clash between electoral democracy and 95–122
Fishkin on 22
lottocratic reintepretation of political equality
173–9, 180, 182, 185, 187–9, 193
Manin on 39
new populist conception of representation
198–9, 203, 206, 214, 216, 218
technocratic conception of politics 220–1,
227–9
see also targets of lottocracy revisited
lottocratic representation 123, 143–4, 146–7, 178,
215–18
Löwenstein, K. 19
loyalty 29

McCormick, J.P. 108–109
Machiavelli, N. 17
Mackie, G. 134
macrodeliberation 92
Madison, J. 159–160, 188 n.29
Mair, P. 154–155
majoritarianism, exclusionary 10

274   Index

majority rule 32, 83–84

mandate representation 7–9, 194–195, 198, 204–205

mandate representation and accountability 138–151
  accountability 140–142, 144–146, 148, 151
  data speaks for itself 144–148
  political work of representing 148–151
  two peoples 138–144

Manin, B. 5, 17, 21, 27 n.45, 28–30, 39–54, 80–81, 183 n.21, 185–186
  direct democracy 40–47
  elections 72–74, 76–80
  equality 57–58
  intuition of Athenians 63–64
  lottery beyond democracy 52–54
  probabilistic logic 60
  voluntary decision and equality of probability 47–52

Mansbridge, J. 39, 112, 120, 121–122, 133–134, 204 n.50

marginalized groups 88, 109, 149, 217, 240–241, 245–246

Marx, K. 144–145

mass data harvesting 238–239

mass democracy 6

mass participation 90–92

mechanical device (*klērōtērion*) 61, 65

Mélenchon, J.-L. 102–103

Michels, R. 21 n.15, 153

microdeliberative turn in deliberative democracy 87–89

Mill, J.S. 5–6 n.5, 194–196

minipublics 21–23, 87, 100–101, 233–249
  as auxiliary institutions 233–238
  auxiliary proposals 117–119
  bottom-up approach 245–246
  conferring decision-making authority to 220
  deliberative 21–22
  deliberative democracy 82–83, 86, 90–94
  deliberative, institutionalizing 12–13
  empowerment of citizenry 244–247
  horizontal/bottom-up approach 237
  lottocratic approach 236
  microdeliberative turn within deliberative democracy 88–89
  participatory approach 236
  parties and partisan divisions among citizens 155–156, 164–165
  public debates, improving 238–242
  technopopulism 229–230
  usurpation, alternative to 242–244
  vertical/top-down approach 237

minorities, justice toward 36

Mirabeau, H.G. 45 n.83

mirroring representation 9, 45–46

blind deference 213–215

citizens' assemblies as embodiment of the people 206–207

citizens' representatives 208–210

complementarity proposals 113

issues with lottocratic representation 215–217

mandate representation and accountability 139–140

microdeliberative turn within deliberative democracy 88

populism 194–198

sociological representation 113

technopopulism 228–230

misinformation 164–165, 237 n.7, 238–239

mixed system 72–73, 102, 105–106, 109–110, 114–115

moderate lottocrats 113

monarchy 69
  absolutism 136

Montesquieu 41–43, 47–48, 51–52, 73–74, 76, 112–113, 202

Morales, E. 202 n.26

Mouffe, C. 153 n.106

multiparty democracy 79–80

Napoleon III 198

national referendum 100–101

natural rights 53

neoliberals 19–20

Netherlands 88–89 n.16
  citizens' assembly 116–117
  G1000 Citizens' Summits 116–117

neutrality 107

nomothesia 59–60

nomothetai 17–18, 43–44, 47, 64–69

nondomination 161–162

Ober, J. 65–66 n.157

Occupy Wall Street 198

ochlocracy 136

oligarchy 5–6, 17–18, 21, 54, 80–81
  democrats and the polis *see under* historical paradigm
    see under aristocracy
  religious justification (let the Gods decide) 60
  disempowerment 173
  electoral democracy 95–96
  Elster 30–31
  equality 57–59
  goal of democrats 62–64
  Manin 39–40, 42–43, 50, 53–54
  parties and partisan divisions among citizens 155, 159–160, 163
  pure 50
  stability 70–71
  substitution proposals 96–97

voting power and elections 127–128, 138
one-party rule systems 184–185, 187
 see also authoritarian regimes
one-person-one-vote 8–9, 26–27, 127–128, 133 n.45, 134–135 n.50
 disempowerment 174
 equalizing asymmetric power relations 183–185, 188
 issues with lottocratic representation 216–218
 mandate representation and accountability 149
online deliberation 239 n.12
Ontario Citizens' Assembly 88–89 n.16, 104, 116–117
order and concord 29
Oregon Citizens' Initiative Review 244–245
Othanes 69
Owen, D. 190–191

Page, S.E. 222–223
Paine, T. 134–135
Paraguay 173 n.1
Parkinson, J. 235
parliamentarization 116
parliamentary commissions 5–6 n.5
parliamentary committees 115–116
parliamentary debate 108
parliamentary system 93, 102, 134
participation by lot 22–25
participatory democracy 12, 19–20, 46–47, 49, 51
partisan dealignment 154–155
partisan divisions *see* political parties and partisan divisions among citizens
partisanship 114–115, 141
partitocracy 153–154
Party List systems 78
Pasquino, P. 66–68
patronage politics 159
People's Tribunal 108–109
Pericles 55–56, 58 n.124
Perón, J.D. 200–201, 203
personal choice 25–27
Pettit, P. 142
Pevnick, R. 189–190, 192
Philip of Macedonia 43
Phillips, M. 102–103
Piérart, M. 67 n.161, 67–68
Pisistratus 54–55
Pitkin, H.F. 19, 123, 146–147, 194–195, 197–198
Plato 34, 50, 136–137 n.59
 oligarchs, democrats and the polis 55–57, 58–61, 63, 65–66
plebiscite 129, 200–201, 202–204
 versus party pluralism 204
Plotke, D. 42
pluralism

complementarity proposals 104–105, 106–107, 111–112
epistocracy 222–223
parties and partisan divisions among citizens 163–164, 168–169
voting power and elections 132–133, 137–138
plurality without pluralism 111–112
polarization 153, 154–155, 226–227, 238–239, 248
political agendas 186–187
political equality 2, 3, 4, 7, 196, 221
 lottery revival 22–3, 25, 32, 59, 64, 70, 75
 lottery-based institutions 91, 103, 106, 109
 targets of lottocracy revisited 134, 141, 149, 153, 168
 see also disempowerment reinterpretation of political equality
political freedom 3–4, 6–8, 10–11, 180, 216–17, 228
 electoral democracy and lottocracy, clash between 106, 107, 108, 115
 lottery revival 26, 28, 38, 41, 48, 59, 63
 targets of lottocracy revisited 125–6, 128–32, 134, 136, 138, 141, 149, 151–3, 157–62, 165–9
 technical problem solving versus 221–7
political mandate 9, 37, 45, 134, 138–51, 167, 184, 187, 194, 198–9, 201, 204–5
political representation 3, 8–9, 28, 193, 194, 199, 217, 228, 230
 electoral democracy and lottocracy, clash between 95, 97, 103, 115, 121
 targets of lottocracy revisited 139–44, 148–51, 160–1, 167–8
political opinion formation 220
political parties 7–8
political parties and partisan divisions among citizens 7, 151–169
 antiparty-ism (old and new) 156–162
 defence of parties 162–165
 parties, problems with 153–156
 political freedom 165–169
 political representation
political values, priorities and goals/objectives 224–225, 227
political will 217, 220–221
polyarchy 22–23, 24–27
Polybius 17
Pope, M. 40
Popular Assembly 26
populism 9–10, 194–218, 248
 auxiliary proposals 117–118
 contemporary 159
 epistocracy 226–227
 inequalities 192
 issues of lottocratic representation 215–218
 leader as embodiment of the people 199–206

276 Index

populism (*Continued*)
minipublics 243–244
parties and partisan divisions among citizens
154–155
see also citizens' assemblies; technopopulism
post-party democracy 154–155
power 8–9
censorial 113–114
unilateral 181
presidentialization 116
pressure politics 157–158
primary democracy 22–23, 25–26
principal-agent model 148–150
probabilistic logic 60
probability 33
problem-solving contexts, pure 223–224
professional politicians, elimination of 36
propaganda 202–203
proportional representation 19, 32–33, 35–36, 79,
127, 195–197
proximity 163–164
Pseudo-Xenophon 55–56
public consultation 235
public debates, minipublics improving 238–242
public deliberation 83–84
public interest 88
public opinion 84–86
actual versus considered
public sphere 1, 12, 35, 86, 88–9, 101, 121, 130,
137, 238–9, 240, 246
pure democracy 50

quotas 36, 79, 127

radical democracy 37, 49, 50–52, 63–64, 174
radical lottocracy 11, 113
Rancière, J. 119–120
random sample/selection 32–33, 37, 79, 119–120
blind deference 212–215
citizens' representatives 211
issues with lottocratic representation 215–217
minipublics 242–243
pure 208–209
stratified 87–88, 206–207, 208–209, 217–218
ratification 245–246
rationality, individual and collective 28–29
Rawls, J. 84–86 n.9, 157–158, 179 n.12
reasonable 180, 214
reciprocity 132–133
referenda 92, 101, 103, 109, 126, 127, 173, 175,
180, 182, 185, 229, 242
religious justification (let the Gods decide) 60–61
replacing electoral institutions 6–7, 234
representation 7–8, 10
as a form of participation
by lottery 126–127

conceptions 9
Dahl 19
descriptive 194–195
electoral democracy 121–122
as embodiment 11–12, 229–230, 242–244
indicative 142
lottocratic 123, 143–4, 146–7, 178, 215–18
see also political representation
Manin on 39, 41–2, 45–7
microdeliberative turn within deliberative
democracy 88
populism 196–197
mandate theory of
reinterpretation 3–4
representational gaps, closing 243–244
representative democracy 4–7, 54, 80–81, 248
auxiliary proposals 120–122
complementarity proposals 105–106
Dahl 21–23
elections 75
electoral democracy 96, 101
equalizing asymmetric power relations
176–177, 183 n.21, 184–186, 188 n.29
leader as embodiment of the people 199,
200–201, 205–206
mandate representation and accountability
138–139, 141–142
parties and partisan divisions among citizens
163, 167–168
populism 194–195, 197–198
stability 72
voting power and elections 134–135
representative government
elections 72–73, 76
Manin 39–41, 51–53
voting power and elections 124
respect for others 132–133, 164
responsibility 7–8, 139–140
responsiveness 77–79, 103–104
rhetorical speech 107–108, 202–203
Rome 61–62, 112–113, 157, 250
Rosanvallon, P. 117–118
rotation 29, 62, 64–66, 72, 177–181
Rousseau, J.-J. 43, 47–48, 121–122, 141, 145–146,
151, 158, 226 n.15
Rubinstein, N. 71–72 n.179
rule by the few 175

Sabine, G. 40
safety and surveillance trade-off 224
sanction model 208–210
Saunders, B. 32
Schattsschneider, E.E. 130–131 n.56, 157–158, 159
n.127, 166–167
Schmitt, C. 41–43, 45 n.84, 47 n.89, 98–99,
136–137, 141, 158, 204

Schumpeter, J.A. 28–29, 130, 158
selection, method of 51–52
selection model of representation 208–212
self-control 163–164
self-selection 119–120
Sieyes, E.J. 45
Simonton, M. 56
Sinclair, R.K. 63–64
single-issue lottery-selected legislature (SILLs) 209–210, 216–217
single-member plurality voting 32–33
Sintomer, Y. 19, 28–29, 52–53, 71 n.176, 119
Slovakia 129 n.28
Smith, G. 190–191
social media platforms 238–239
socialist democracy 21
Solon 54–55, 58
sortition 61–62
    citizens' representatives 208
    complementarity proposals 103–104, 109–110
    electoral democracy 96
    equalizing asymmetric power relations 177–178, 179–180
    inequalities 191
    issues with lottocratic representation 215
    mandate representation and accountability 138–139, 141, 143
    stability 69–71
    substitution proposals 97, 101
    voting power and elections 133
sovereignty 6–7, 43, 106–107
    auxiliary proposals 117–118
    centralized collective 100
    denaturalization and depersonification 199–200
    electoral democracy 121–122
    leader as embodiment of the people 200–201
    parties and partisan divisions among citizens 157–158
    popular 122, 201
    substitution proposals 3, 96–101
Sparta 58–59
special seats in parliament 127
Spinoza, B. 60
stability 29, 49, 63 n.146, 69–72, 126–128, 157–159, 192
    social 29, 52–54
Staveley, E.S. 29, 56, 62
stratified random sampling 87–88, 206–207, 208–209, 217–218
substitution model 96–101, 233–234
suffrage 126–127, 134–135 n.50, 144, 198
    equal 32–33
    see also universal suffrage and democratic sovereignty
superiority 79

supplementing electoral institutions 6–7
Swabey, M.C. 19–20, 102–103, 123
systemic turn 88–89 n.19

targets of lottocracy revisited 123–169
    political mandate representation and accountability 138–151
        data speaks for itself 144–148
        political work of representing 148–151
        two peoples 138–144
    political parties and partisan divisions among citizens 151–169
        antiparty-ism (old and new) 156–162
        defence of parties 162–165
        parties, problems with 153–156
        political freedom 165–169
    voting power and elections 123–138
        argument (authors) 127–134
        elections, problem with 123–127
        history rethought 134–138
Tea Party 155
technocracy 3–4, 11–12, 144, 146, 219–230
    epistocracy: technical problem-solving vs. political freedom 221–228
    technopopulism 228–230
technopopulism 3–4, 11, 227–230
Thompson, D. 90–91
Thucydides 58 n.124
Tocqueville, A. de 37
tolerance 132–133
transparency 27, 29–31
tribunes 112–113
Trump, D. 202 n.26, 203
trust 71, 217
    citizens' representatives 210–211
    mandate representation and accountability 148, 150
    minipublics 242–243
    technopopulism 228–229
    through faith 205–206
Tuck, R. 138–139
Tudor, C.V. 202 n.26
two-party systems 163

United Kingdom 60, 75–76, 195–196
    English Revolution 47, 52–53
    House of Lords 102–103
United Nations 95
United States 19, 39, 137–138
    auxiliary proposals 115–116
    complementarity proposals 103–104
    Congress 123
    Constitution 136 n.56
    Democratic Party 173 n.1
    epistocracy 226–227
    House of Representatives 23, 102–103

278 Index

United States (*Continued*)
jury selection 119–120
minipublics 245–246 n.25
parties and partisan divisions among citizens 162
representative government 52–53
Republicans 173 n.1
Senate 23
stability 72
universal participation, standard of 136–137
universal suffrage 9, 101, 123–124, 126–128, 134–135 n.50, 138, 196–197, 217–218
usurpation 243–244

Van Reybrouck, D. 97–98, 176 n.6
vanguard parties 152
Venice 17, 30–31, 52–54
veto power 109–110, 112–113
Villam, G. 69–70
virtual representation 139–140
voluntariness 24–25, 47–52, 119–120
von Gierke, O. 19
von Hayek, F.A. 20–21
Voters' Pamphlet 244–245

voters to candidates, from 27–31
voting 7–8, 126–127, 246
anticorruption and fair representation 31–36
manipulation 238–239
voting power and elections 123–138
argument (authors) 127–134
elections, problem with 123–127
history rethought 134–138

Wachtel, T. 95
Waldron, J. 133 n.45
wasted votes, reduction of 35–36
weakness of parties 155–156, 159
Weil, S. 164–165
What's Next California deliberative poll 245–246
White, J. 163–164 n.142
Wilders, G. 202 n.26
'will of the people' 167
Wolff, R.P. 36
Wright, E.O. 103–104, 112–113

Ypi, L. 163–164 n.142

Zakaras, A. 103–104